Agency-Based Social Work

Agency-Based Social Work

Neglected Aspects of Clinical Practice

Harold Weissman, Irwin Epstein,
and Andrea Savage

Temple University Press
Philadelphia

Temple University Press, Philadelphia 19122
© 1983 by Temple University. All rights reserved
Published 1983
Printed in the United States of America

Library of Congress Cataloging in Publication Data

Weissman, Harold H.
  Agency-based social work.

  Includes bibliographies and index.
  1. Social work administration—Addresses, essays,
lectures.   I. Epstein, Irwin.   II. Savage, Andrea.
III. Title.
HV40.W435   1983   361'.0068   83-9314
ISBN 0-87722-322-X
ISBN 0-87722-330-0 (pbk.)

To Henry Street Settlement,
its clients, and workers,
from 1893 onwards

CONTENTS

PREFACE

The importance of dealing with the administrative aspects of the direct service work of clinical social workers was first suggested to us by Bertram Beck in 1977. At that time he was the executive director of the Henry Street Settlement.

He and other prominent social workers in New York City were then involved in forming a new organization called the Center for the Study of Social Administration, whose mission was to improve the management of social agencies through a program of research, training, demonstration projects, and publication. In carrying out these programs, the center was to be guided by the operating perspective that social administration is practiced at three organizational levels—the institutional, managerial, and technical—each requiring a somewhat different set of knowledge and skills, yet representing a continuum of activities that link top administration and direct service workers in a coherent effort to deliver services.

Given this rationale, the first programmatic effort of the center was the development of a proposal to the National Institute of Mental Health for a curriculum development project whose intent was to specify the administrative skills, values, and knowledge that clinical social workers need to carry out their direct service work. The project was to be carried out at the Henry Street Settlement and the Hunter College School of Social Work.

The National Institute of Mental Health funded the project for four years, beginning on July 1, 1978, under grant number TO1 MH 15377-01 to 04. The overall goals of the project were: (1) the identification of administrative skills and knowledge involved in clinical social work practice; (2) the development of a model curriculum and training materials for training clinical social workers in administrative aspects of their work; (3) the training of two cycles of approximately ten second-year MSW students selected from the clinical social work sequence at the Hunter College School of Social Work; (4) the monitoring and evaluation of the training cycles so that both training techniques and curriculum content could be modified as needed; and (5) the dissemination of knowledge and materials developed in this project.*

Harold Weissman was project director, Irwin Epstein was research director, and Andrea Savage was the curriculum developer. This book is the direct outcome of our efforts to achieve the above goals. Based on concepts, training techniques, and curriculum materials developed within the project, it represents the project's major effort to disseminate its central ideas.

A number of people gave significant support to achieving the project's goals. Aaron Rosenblatt, Milton Wittman, and Neilson Smith as staff and members of the site-visit team of NIMH encouraged our efforts. We hope the results merit their support.

Harold Lewis, dean of the Hunter College School of Social Work, provided the administrative support required to carry out many of the innovative aspects of the project. Our colleagues at Hunter, Phyllis Caroff, Florence Vigilante, and Mildred Mailick, served on the advisory committee to the project, which also included these other distinguished clinicians: Sydney Pinsky, Joseph Wagman, Carel Germain, and Patricia Goodman.

Special thanks are due to the staff of the Henry Street Settlement and to Lorraine Ahto, who was director of the Community Consultation Center of the Settlement during the four years of the project. Without their help, this project could not have been carried out. Special note should also be made of Donna Rich of the Settlement's development staff, who assisted in formulating the original proposal to NIMH. We also owe special thanks to the two cohorts of students who participated in the project and provided much valuable feedback.

We are indebted to Carel Germain, Elaine Marshack, and Brett Seabury for reading the first draft and making extensive comments and suggestions. Much of the book's hoped-for clarity and focus is directly related to their efforts.

A. E. Dreyfuss served as administrative assistant on the project, and never was flustered. We appreciate her efforts.

Some of the articles are reprinted in their entirety in the book. Where excerpts are reprinted, this in no way reflects a judgement on the quality of the article. In such situations we used only those portions of the article that directly related to the points under discussion in that chapter.

We conceive of this work as a guide to practice and not simply as a collection of articles. As such, the articles were selected to illustrate points that we wished to amplify rather than to make the points, as is the case in most readers or collections.

---

*For a discussion of how the project was operationalized, see Irwin Epstein, Andrea Savage-Abramovitz, and Harold Weissman, "Training Clinician-Managers in Community Mental Health Settings: A Progress Report," *Social Work Education Reporter* 30 (Jan. 1982): 10–15.

In writing this book, we have attempted to chart some new territory. Our purpose is to define and describe a set of roles and sets of skills that we believe must be part of every clinician's repertoire. As a result, at times we have had to invent labels for these roles, such as "the expediter," when no such labels existed. Other labels, such as "diagnostician," may coincide with those used in more conventional conceptions of clinical practice. Ultimately, others may develop better labels. What is most relevant, however, is that readers achieve an understanding of how the concepts, knowledge, and skills discussed in each chapter can improve their practice of clinical social work. We hope that our efforts have made this possible and on this basis accept whatever praise and criticism they merit.

Harold Weissman
Irwin Epstein
Andrea Savage

FOREWORD

For almost one hundred years, some have criticized social work clinicians for allegedly overlooking environmental factors in the etiology of personal problems. Others have contended that social reform and clinical practice are incompatible activities because they require very different knowledge and skills. No experienced practitioner would argue that there are no differences. Yet in today's world it is difficult to see how most clients who come to social agencies can be helped unless attention is paid both to their personal and social concerns.

What was missed by many participants in the "either-or" argument is that most efforts to help clients take place in an agency context. The agency is the locus of both psychological and environmental help and will have a crucial effect on either of these endeavors. The real issue is how the agency can be utilized to carry out these functions.

I believe that this blind spot about agencies can be partly understood as resulting from a lack of specific practice-oriented concepts and principles for integrating environmental and psychological efforts on behalf of clients in an agency context. What has been needed is a framework of knowledge and skills that can be readily learned and applied by social work clinicians from their agency base, regardless of their preferred practice modalities and methods. And this, precisely, is the contribution to clinical social work that the authors have now made.

Agency-Based Social Work: Neglected Aspects of Clinical Practice will be read profitably by the most experienced clinician, and it will serve as an exciting text for the student-practitioner. The practice of both will be enhanced, and the services of the agency will surely be made more congruent with client needs by those who incorporate its message into their practice.

The authors have conceptualized a set of organizational roles for the clinician. They have set forth the theoretical and value concepts, the tasks, and the skills required for each of the roles. Throughout, they both draw parallels and show the differences between traditional practice concepts and principles and those required to fulfill the roles under discussion. Practice analogues at the end of each chapter bring these parallels and differences to light through case examples that relate not only to practice techniques but also to values and attitudes.

At last some of the old tensions can be laid to rest. Yes, there are constraints, but clinical practice focused on the person and the environment is possible to the degree agencies can handle the strains a dual focus may create for them and clinicians can assume the roles described in the text. This knowledge can be taught in an integrated way to students in methods courses and to seasoned practitioners in staff development seminars and continuing education programs.

But there is still more in this singular contribution to clinical social work. The authors have for the first time articulated the importance of such roles—significant, but taken for granted—as expediter, practice researcher, program developer, and employee, connecting each to the imperatives of clinical practice in an organizational context. Their realistic appraisal of organizational structures and processes—both strengths and weaknesses—helps dispel negative stereotypes of how organizations function by articulating the reciprocal ways in which practice and the agency influence each other.

Given the economic and political realities of the 1980s, it is essential that clinical social workers adopt these organizational roles, drawing on the knowledge and skills they represent. In doing so, practitioners will help their agencies to be more responsive to the rights, needs, and goals of those they serve. This can only enhance the effectiveness of their practice.

Carel Germain

Agency-Based Social Work

INTRODUCTION

In prior decades it was thought by many that the major function of social work was to provide a type of assistance that rested heavily on forming a helping relationship with the client and, through the use of this relationship, enabling the client to gain self-insight and thereby help himself or herself. The focus of help lay in the psyche of the individual. There is now general agreement in the field, however, that help is more than simply providing counseling or emotional assistance.

There are a number of tasks that social workers perform in the act of helping that go beyond psychological assistance. These include providing access and information to clients about services; securing services for clients; activating social networks to support clients; working to change clients' physical and social environments; and coordinating the work of other organizations and staff whose services the clients need.

A great deal of this change in focus can be related to changes in the field itself. Policies, programs, and such societal concerns as the deinstitutionalization of mental hospitals, client and consumer rights movements, cost containment, and accountability have all combined to change the relationships among the helping professions, the demand for certain types of workers possessing certain sets of skills, the priorities among agency goals, and ultimately the nature of clinical practice.

We start with the assumption that the everyday activities of most clinical social workers involve the performance of a variety of helping roles that in varying degrees require both administrative and therapeutic knowledge and skill. The underpinning of this assumption lies not only in the change in social conditions but also in a fundamental element of social work practice, its context. The vast majority of social work practice takes place in social agencies. The agency is the hidden reality of social work. Agency decisions determine, among other things, which clients will be served, how they will be served, by whom, for how long, and at what cost. These decisions have a profound effect on what transpires between workers and clients. Limited resources, disagreement among large segments of the public about the value of certain programs, vested organizational and professional interests, and rapidly changing social, economic, and political environments are factors external to the agency that affect what workers do with clients. Internally, there is the need of the organization to survive, workers to ensure their tenure, conflicts among equally valid program goals, disputes over treatment ideology, and the formation of an informal organization—all of which can divert energy from accomplishing service goals.*

Our intent is to help workers understand and deal with such contextual pressures. What we attempt to do is to go beyond organizational analyses and to suggest how a variety of helping roles can be practiced in ways that take into account the strain between organizational needs and client needs.

Our stance is that strain between what is good for the client and what is good for the agency is inevitable in some degree. What is not inevitable, is the way the tension is handled. Too often the strain is treated as a nasty secret not to be talked about in public or in a "we-they" stance on the part of clinicians or administrators, with the other party being the "they," unconcerned about clients. In such a context it is unlikely the strain will be handled in ways that aid the delivery of service.

With similar effort, in their desire to avoid tension, many clinical social workers assume, to paraphrase the maxim about government, that the agency is best which does least. These professionals conceive of the agency as simply providing them with an office and a client with whom to do "therapy." Their working model is a private practice with a regular paycheck, retirement benefits, and so on. For them it is the individual professional, guided by his or her code of ethics, who should determine what is best for the client.

This point of view ignores the fact that society itself determines what shall be done for those in need, and therefore society demands accountability: agencies must have an organized and reliable procedure for allocating scarce resources for help; standardized procedures for determining who shall be eligible and for what; and some control over the cost of these services. In no way does society sanction an agency to be merely a repository of private practitioners.

Reality demands that most social workers operate through agencies and understand how they function. Yet many observers have documented the problems that traditionally trained clinicians have in perceiving social agencies as organizations and recognizing how organizational dynamics affect their ability to deliver services.† The agency view of these clinicians seldom transcends the level of individual clients or the

*Ruth Middleman and Gale Goldberg, *Social Service Delivery: A Structural Approach* (New York: Columbia University Press, 1974), pp. 172–174.

†Rino Patti and Michael Austin, "Socializing the District Service Practitioner in the Ways of Supervisory Management," *Administration in Social Work* 1 (1977): 273–280.

individual social workers who serve them. For them, organizational interventions are for administrators only and are to be avoided whenever possible.

Some schools of social work attempt to deal with this problem by offering courses in administration or complex organizations to prepare students better for the transition to supervisory or administrative roles. In our view, however, these efforts are deficient in that they too tend to ignore the organizational aspects of direct service to clients. Many of the obstacles to effective service are related to the functioning and dysfunctioning of organizational structures and those who work within them. For example:

- A clinical social worker in a medical health center is furious when she is told that the intricate arrangements she has made to see a family member before regular clinic hours must be canceled because the agency just can't be opened that early, according to the head of maintenance and security.
- A worker in a pediatrics ward is taken aback when the mother of a very ill neonate asks her why she and the nurse keep asking her the same dumb questions: "Don't y'all know what each other is doing?"
- The return from maternity leave of a receptionist at a day treatment program coincides with a remarkable improvement in the behavior of the chronically disturbed patients.

All of these incidents reflect structural conditions that affect client service. Some are related to gaps in communication and poor administrative arrangements, and others to direct worker-client interaction.

In this book we explore a number of roles that workers must assume in helping clients in social agencies. In reality, the roles are not necessarily discrete. At any one time, with any client, a clinical worker may assume several of the roles—for example, advocate, expediter, and colleague in addition to his therapeutic or counseling role. Some of the roles, such as advocate, colleague, and expediter, are almost completely intertwined with the counseling role. Others, such as case manager and supervisor, represent a different form of practice requiring a new set of skills. They are a response to the changing nature and personnel needs of certain types of practice. Other roles, such as program developer, organizational reformer, and practice researcher, are indirectly but crucially related to the interaction between workers and clients. And, finally, the diagnostician and employee roles illuminate the context in which clinical social workers practice.

Our view of these roles, regardless of the occupant, is that in an agency "there is a set of expectations concerning how the position-holder should behave, think, and feel. These expectations are called *role demands*. The term 'demands' implies that other members of the system exert influence upon position-holders to meet these expectations, and will reward when role demands are met and punish when they are not.''*

Role demands are external pressures on role encumbents. There are also internal pressures in that each person occupying a position brings to it attitudes, feelings and beliefs about how they feel they should perform the role. These personal *role conceptions* influence the behavior of role encumbents. Each of the chapters attempts first to describe the requisites to fill the demands of particular roles and second to note the differences where they exist between role demands and role conceptions, and to suggest how role encumbents can deal with these discrepancies in their *role performance†* Without the ability to handle demands and discrepancies clinical workers will not know when and where to use their skills.

We have drawn on many different theories other than role theory, from ego psychology to systems theory to behavioral psychology, because we feel that the test of a theory is its operability and utility. In our view some theories are simply more useful than others in dealing with certain problems.

Various chapters in the text discuss the way in which influence is developed through exchanges. Influence is one of the major concepts infusing our discussions of roles. The other conceptual motif is the idea of an organization as an open system. The actions one takes as an expediter will have an effect on the actions one can take as an organizational reformer, and so on.

The parts of an organization are interconnected. The agency is a product of the interaction of formal and informal, planned and unplanned, internal and external, rational and nonrational, elements. Thus, although we do not subscribe to a systems approach that treats organizational equilibrium as a superordinate goal, we do not view all change as necessarily beneficial to clients. The sources of the organizational status quo must be understood lest one weak program or supervisor be replaced by an even weaker one.

Clinical social workers should apply the same rationale to currently fashionable administrative ideas, even those with a strong humanistic base. While it is beyond the scope of this text to explore such ideas in depth, such as participative management, fewer levels of hierarchy, matrix management, and the like, they must be seen in the context of an agency as a system. They are to be tried and evaluated in terms of experience, rather than believed in as a matter of faith.‡ If there is any

---

*Sheila Feld and Norma Radin, *Social Psychology for Social Work and the Mental Health Professions* (New York: Columbia University Press, 1982), p. 62.

†Ibid, p.62.

‡For example, extensive research on leadership shows that the task-oriented leader is superior to the person-oriented leader in chaotic organizational situations where conflict, confusion, and hostility are endemic. Sheila Feld and Norma Radin, *Social Psychology for Social Work and the Mental Health Professions*, (New York: Columbia University Press, 1982) pp. 322–326.

bias in the text, it is an administrative bias—what counts in the long run is the quality of the service provided.

Each of the chapters that follows begins with an overview of the knowledge and skills required to carry out a particular role. Interspersed in the discussion are already published articles or excerpts of articles that provide case examples of workers acting out the role. This section is followed by one entitled "Practice Analogues," which attempts to show to what extent the traditional counseling skills of clinical social workers overlap with those required to fulfill the role under discussion, and to what extent and degree new skills and techniques are required. The third section attempts to deal with these similarities and differences in terms of attitudes and values: which contribute to the fulfillment of the role, and which detract from it? Each chapter ends with a list of additional readings.

The purpose of this book is to prepare clinical social workers to do agency-based practice. We use the term "clinical social work" to refer to all the efforts of caseworkers, group workers, and generically trained workers to help individuals, families, and groups to resolve their personal and social problems. In prior decades "clinical" was used to refer to the "therapeutic" aspects of direct service and to downplay the more social and environmental aspects of helping people. This is not our purpose in using the term. But while we assume that many variables other than a worker's counseling skill have a crucial impact on what happens to clients, our intention is not to suggest that the traditional therapeutic skills are in some way obsolete or unnecessary. All that we contend is that there are other skills that are equally important in helping people in an agency context. What is perhaps unique in our approach is the emphasis given to the organizational aspects of client-worker interaction.

We also suggest that many traditional skills are readily adaptable to this organizational perspective. For example, "sometimes miscommunication stems from the parties' being afraid to hurt others, or to be hurt by others; sometimes from being unsure themselves of what they mean to convey; and sometimes from the problems of the differences in meaning drawn from words. . . . Common communication problems stem from too much or too little information, arriving too early or too late, with irrelevant effect, in an 'improper' place."* The traditional clinical training needed to correct many of these problems is important not only to worker-client interaction but also to the myriad other relationships and roles that workers assume in helping clients in agencies.

The ability to handle an expanded role repertoire framed by an organizational perspective provides the clinical social worker with access to the array of problem-solving resources agencies provide. Harnessing these

---

*Ruth Middleman and Gale Goldberg, *Social Service Delivery: A Structural Approach to Social Work Practice* (New York: Columbia University Press, 1974), p. 126.

resources and putting them to work for clients means more effective service and a more gratifying work experience. Not using them means poorer service and feelings of powerlessness on the part of the worker.

Learning how to harness an agency's resources takes time, effort, and experience. It is not something to be mastered in one class or one year. Nor is it something that should be overwhelming.

Most books suffer from suggesting that the authors have *the* answers. No doubt this work in some measure has this fault. Yet it is intended to urge others to offer their thoughts on the issues addressed as well as to suggest the pleasure and excitement that go along with mastering a new tool.

CHAPTER 1

DIAGNOSTICIAN

Social work is an organizational profession, and most clinical practice takes place in an organizational context. This has become increasingly true as society has become bureaucratized. For clients, this means that help can only be received when the social agency, as an organization, is responsive to their needs. Responsiveness entails offering the kind of service clients want, when it is needed, and in sufficient amounts. For social workers, not only is the organization an important tool for providing help, but it also serves to support and develop the skills and job satisfaction of the staff. Often, however, the organizational structure, policies, and procedures are viewed as obstacles to good service and breeders of "burnout."

The most effective clinical social workers are those who are as adept at diagnosing organizational obstacles to good service as they are at diagnosing client problems. Moreover, just as skillful clinical diagnosis involves identifying client strengths and potential for positive change, organizational diagnosis involves seeing the positive features of the organization and building on these.

The following example illustrates some of the organizational factors that interfere with meeting a client's needs:

A young man of seventeen appears at the intake of a mental health center reporting that he is under a lot of stress and needs help. His mother is hospitalized, and he is worried he will get sick "just like her." The worker also discovers at intake that the youth has been supervising his three younger brothers and has dropped out of school. He hopes to find a job but has been unsuccessful.

The worker promises that he will be assigned a worker in a week or so, after she presents his case at intake review. The agency director, however, uses the intake review time to discuss budgetary restraint measures that need to be instituted. In addition, the intake summary has not been typed because the secretary has been too busy logging cases. The intake review is postponed.

The worker, however, attempts to refer the youth to a job training program that the agency operates. In order to enter, he must undergo a psychiatric evaluation. Funding and licensing requirements for the agency forbid the use of psychiatric consultation time for nonclients. In order to be a client, the youth must be assigned a permanent worker authorized by the director.

The director's secretary says that the director's schedule is quite tight, with little free time until the following week. The job training program will be closed out in two days.

What the above vignette suggests is that the nature of practice has changed. It no longer consists of the worker, the client, and their relationship. There are now many relationships and, to a certain extent, many clients.*

To deal effectively with such problems, this chapter suggests that the clinician must conduct a study and diagnosis of the agency as well as of the client. Thus, helping does not require psychological skills alone. The clinician must have a set of organizational skills as well, based on organizational theories, concepts, and strategies—which are what this book is about.

In this chapter we present some key concepts for understanding one's own social agency and discuss some of the values, attitudes, and assumptions that traditionally have inhibited clinical social workers from making the most effective use of their agencies. Three papers that illustrate these issues and concerns are included.

Overview

Formal Structure: The formal structure of an organization rests on some degree of specialization of labor. Once we have people who specialize—some do intake, some do brief treatment, some relate to funding sources, some clean rooms, some type—we need some way to coordinate the specialists. Once there is the need to coordinate, an authority system is required whereby one person is given the right to tell another person what to do and when. To support the legitimacy of the authority, there will have to be a system of rewards—for example, salary increments, the opportunity to develop professional skills, and the like. In addition, there will also have to be procedures for deciding who can make what decisions and for applying sanctions against those who won't accept them.

These are the basic features of formal organization. They do not occur because people love organizations, or because bureaucracies have to get bigger according to some sort of natural law, or because some people desire to control others as an outgrowth of their authoritarian personali-

*For case examples, see Allison D. Murdach, "A Political Perspective in Problem Solving," *Social Work* 27 (1982): 417–421.

ties. They occur because of the need to coordinate the work of a variety of organizational specialists.

Probably every social agency has some of the following structural characteristics:

- a set of stated goals that the agency is trying to achieve;
- a set of stated policies and procedures for achieving these goals;
- a formally stated division of labor that indicates who is supposed to do what; and
- an authority structure that states who is responsible to whom and who can dispense rewards and punishments.

Goals are generally stated in such documents as the organization's charter, its bylaws, and its annual reports. Policies and procedures may be codified in staff manuals and guides. The division of labor and authority structure are detailed in the agency's organizational chart and in job descriptions for particular positions. All of these together make up the formal or bureaucratic structure of the organization.

Some organizations place greater stock in their formal structure than do others. For example, a large public welfare agency located in an urban environment is likely to have a highly refined division of labor. By contrast, a three-person family service agency in a rural area may give relatively little attention to who does what.

It is important to make it clear that we are not using the word "bureaucratic" in its common, negative sense. Our view is that formal structures contain within them both positive and negative elements. We are all aware of the negative aspects of bureaucracy. These are captured in the common complaints about the rigidity of workers who place conformity with procedures above helping clients, the lack of organizational responsiveness and openness to change, and the like. But formal structure can also have the effect of promoting organizational rationality and the most efficient use of scarce resources. Some have suggested that a properly running bureaucracy can be the most democratic form of organization, in that all clients with a common problem will be treated alike, without regard to personal influence, political preference, and so on. Finally, formal structure creates a context in which workers can experience job stability and continuity.

Whatever one's view of bureaucracy, the fact is that most, if not all, social work settings have formal structures. Some have organizational charts that follow the classic pyramidal shape, which entails a high level of *centralization*; that is, most decisions are left to higher-level administrators. Other charts look more like flattened pyramids. These structures are more *decentralized* and give more decision-making authority to lower-level staff. In general, more centralized organizations emphasize control and efficiency, whereas decentralized organizations often aim at adaptability and responsiveness but may present problems of coordination and duplication of services.

Informal Structures: There are aspects of organizational reality that do not appear in the organizational chart or the rules and procedures, yet are equally important. For example, an organization may pursue certain goals that are never explicitly stated. These unstated or *informal goals* may be positive (for example, furthering career opportunities for oppressed minorities) or negative (for example, practicing institutional racism or sexism). In addition, some organizations fall prey to *goal displacement*. In this informal pattern, the means of achieving the formal goals become goals or ends in themselves. Thus, a treatment organization may prescribe the same treatment for everyone who enters the agency whether he or she needs it or not, because of the staff's career investment in that particular treatment. The treatment comes to be viewed as beneficial without regard to specific client needs or objectives to be reached.

Similarly, the agency's formal division of labor may be at odds with the way things are actually done: the work of highly competent secretaries is credited to their administrative superiors; competent workers pick up the slack from their less competent peer. The departure from formal structure has real consequences for staff and clients.

The organization chart would lead one to assume that the closer a person is to the top of the pyramid, the more power and influence he or she has. Yet in every organization there are people with relatively low rank who enjoy a high level of influence, and vice versa. Thus, to get administrative approval for some action, it might be extremely important to win over the administrator's secretary. On the other hand, some high-ranking staff may be so incompetent as to have relatively little influence over their subordinates.

The informal structure can either support or undermine the formal structure. It comprises staff and client sentiments and exchanges that develop over time and that translate organizational events into personal terms. It can influence the interpretation of a particular administrative initiative. Thus, the same policy may be perceived as an effort to "just make us work harder" or as a "terrific idea, and we should have been doing that for years, so let's get on with it."

The informal organization develops over time because of the needs of workers at various levels. First, to maintain a sense that they can do their job and be respected at the same time, workers develop mutual assistance networks. Rather than frequently go to superiors for assistance, which would require revealing an incapacity, it is easier to go to one's peers. And if one cannot give assistance in return, one can at least give back respect and appreciation for the help. Once patterns of exchanges are developed and respect becomes part of the exchange, a system of social ranking develops. Some people are thought to have higher status or to be more valuable than others, and from these valuations comes informal leadership.

At the same time, workers need and want to be treated fairly, to have some control over their work environment, and not to be merely the puppets of the administration. Thus, norms of fairness are developed. How much work can legitimately be demanded of one for what one is getting in return from the organization? And if the organization's demands are illegitimate, what can one do about them?

There is, in fact, a great deal that can be done. Collectively the staff can resist passively or actively. They can constantly point out that if *this* is done, something else *will not* be done. They can punish colleagues who violate the norms of fairness by social ostracism: not including them at lunch, not offering them assistance, accusing them of personal desires for gain or glory, making it unpleasant for them to remain at the worksite. The informal organization can support or hinder effective service in this way.

The informal organization is thus a system of mutual assistance, having definite norms, standards of practice, and a system of social ranking. It has, moreover, a communication network. Workers do not wish to be dependent on the information flowing out of the formal system when their job security and personal lives are at stake. They will strive to get timely and accurate information through informal contacts and other means. From this need, an informal communication system or grapevine derives.

It is probably more accurate to say that there are informal organizations rather than an informal organization: one for clericals, one for supervisors, and so on. The informal organizations are neither as stable nor as chartable as the formal organization. Given that there are informal organizations in every organization, however, it is vital to know how to use them to get what one wants because formality, as noted, has severe limitations. If precedents are going to be set, chances are that decisions will not be made quickly; in such cases the informal organization will have to be utilized. How?

It is not difficult to learn about the informal organizations in one's agency. Who eats together? Who has coffee together? Who speaks up at staff meetings and puts everybody to sleep, and who speaks up and captures everybody's attention? Whom do people go to with their problems? Who has pipelines into the administration? And why are certain standards and norms accepted, and on what basis?

Organizational Theories: To help us understand how organizations work and how they can be made to work better, various organizational theories have been proposed. Some place greater emphasis on formal structure; others emphasize informal structure.

In America, perhaps the earliest theory of administration was called _scientific management_. Frederick Taylor developed this idea, suggesting that there was "one best way" to do any organizational task. If one could figure out the best way to carry out a task and train workers to carry it out in that precise way, and then pay them according to their ability to do the work correctly and with speed, one would have a very efficient organization.

Another early approach was called _administrative management._ Mary Follett, a social worker, became interested in organizations through her experience in working with groups. She argued that just as one might discover laws of nature, such as gravity, one might discover laws of organizational life. She and her followers were interested in such issues as centralization versus decentralization, span of control, communication gaps, and overlapping responsibilities.

In this view, men and women are basically rational, and so is the organization. Everything can be planned beforehand because the organization, no matter whether it is concerned with business or social work, is an entity unto itself, governed by its own laws. If one can understand these laws, one can run an efficient organization. To run counter to these laws is about as productive as running counter to the law of gravity.

The third prominent approach to administration, a more current one, is called _human relations theory_. Social workers find it very congenial. Its emphasis is on informal structure, and its core is the observation that there are unplanned-for stresses and emotions in day-to-day organizational life that hinder the efficient functioning of the organization. Unless these stresses and feelings are addressed and tended to, the organization will be blocked from the efficient and effective delivery of its service.

The human relations theorists developed such techniques as T-groups and sensitivity training. They were concerned about morale and its connection to productivity, about leadership, and about relationships among members of working groups and their effects on productivity.

If scientific management was criticized as too mechanistic and administrative management as too rationalistic, human relations theory has come under fire for focusing too much on workers' feelings and making job satisfaction an end in itself. Another theory rests on the _open system_ concept and to an extent incorporates elements of the other theories. This view says simply that all parts of an organization are interconnected. Change in one part affects the others: a change in a reward system, for example, will have an effect on goals, and vice versa.

It also draws attention to the fact that an organization is embedded in an environment: political, economic, cultural, geographic, and regulatory. Often a great deal of administrative effort (not always known or apparent to staff) goes into maintaining productive exchanges with these environmental components.

Systems theory, like the other theories, has been extensively criticized, and the arguments still rage. Are the human relationists "soft on power" and overly optimistic about resolving the strains between worker and organization? Are the systems analysts so concerned about the interconnection of variables that they lose sight of the practical needs of managers?

We take the view in subsequent chapters that certain theories are more useful than others in dealing with certain types of problems: human relations theories with personnel issues, administrative management with structural issues, and so on. For social workers, the test of a theory is its usefulness.

Perhaps more important than the differences in perspective among the various theories is the basic assumption that underlies them all: that organizations and social agencies are purposive structures planned to achieve a specific end. Yet experience indicates that different groups have quite different views of the purposes and ends of any one organization. Charles Perrow has suggested that groups use organizations for different and often contradictory purposes—clients for service, staff for employment, and society for expressing compassion and control, political parties for patronage and votes, and professions for prestige and turf. These different uses give the lie to the idea that organizations are simply focused on achieving some specific end. In Perrow's view, Lockheed is a pension plan that incidentally produces airplanes.*

In a similar view, Middleman and Goldberg quote Heraud, who suggests "that organizational theory predicated on such assumptions as common goals, shared values, and unity of purpose is not useful for understanding social agencies and should be replaced by a theory which pre-supposes no central value system, multiple, vague goals, and goal conflict that arises from forces outside the organization as much as within it."†

Kenneth Westhues's article on a "drop-in center," which follows, similarly illustrates the difference between client, staff, and board points of view. Helping a client in such an agency is more complex than most management theories might suggest.

---

*Charles Perrow, "Demystifying Organizations," in R. Sarri and J. Hasenfeld, eds., *The Management of Human Services* (New York: Columbia University Press, 1978), pp. 105–120.

†Ruth Middleman and Gale Goldberg, *Social Service Delivery: A Structural Approach to Social Work Practice* (New York: Columbia University Press, 1974), p. 173.

The Drop-In Center: A Study
in Conflicting Realities*

KENNETH WESTHUES

During the last decade drop-in centers have appeared across North America in greater numbers than ever before. The institution itself is not new; there were drop-in centers near military bases for the benefit of servicemen during both world wars, and similar establishments have long existed in New York's Bowery and in counterpart districts in other large cities. With the rise of hippiedom in the early 1960s, drop-in centers multiplied across the continent; in church basements, in storefronts, and in old houses, these centers became regular stops for drug-using, penniless, long-haired youths willing to accept almost anything the center had to offer, so long as it was not linked with the American middle class. Many drop-in centers are still operating, and they are likely to remain one of the more novel of contemporary social welfare institutions.

More than other social welfare institutions, the drop-in center is usually quite volatile; it is constantly beset with crises and often forced to close because of internal dissension or the intervention of police authority. This article is intended to provide an explanation for the instability of drop-in centers and to suggest some of the conditions under which stability may be achieved. It is based on a nine-month participant observation study of one such center, on interview and survey data from a second center, and on more casual observations made on visits to other drop-in centers in the northeastern United States and southern Ontario. This article will report first the conclusions of the case study, supplemented by the survey data, and then suggest a more general model of conflict processes in drop-in centers.

The Domino Drop-In Center

The Domino Drop-In Center was founded early in 1969 in a medium-sized city under the general sponsorship of one of the churches in the downtown area. Its founding coincided with the initial appearance of significant numbers of young drug users in the city and was a response to their appearance. Early in its history, however, the center passed from the control of the church to that of an independent and secular community organization. As a corporation, the Domino board is composed of eleven members, all respectable community figures, including a physi-

*Reprinted with permission of the Family Service Association of America from *Social Casework* 5 (1972): 361–368.

cian, a lawyer, representatives of the founding church, and professionals from the social welfare field.

The Dominio board entrusts the affairs of the center to the Domino council, which meets monthly and is composed of the board members and others involved in the drop-in center. These monthly meetings provide the arena for policy formation and program initiation; they typically attract staff members, users of the center facilities, and other community figures. About twenty-five people usually attend, and decisions are made on a one-man, one-vote basis.

Conflict among involved groups

This drop-in center's two-year history has been a tempestuous one. The center has been the scene of explosive brawls every two or three months, and the police have been called to quell about half of them. The center has been closed for varying periods five times. Monthly council meetings have repeatedly been the scene of heated exchanges concerning purposes and procedures. The central thesis of this article is that this tempestuous history is best understood as resulting from the interplay of three conflicting groups—the board members, who have provided money and public legitimacy; the staff personnel, who have operated the center; and the adolescent youths, who have made use of it. Each of these groups carries its own definition of a drop-in center, and specifically of the Domino Drop-In Center. The material below describes each of these realities.*

Board of directors

Members of the board of directors perceive the goal of the drop-in center as the rehabilitation of psychologically, occupationally, educationally, or socially maladjusted young people in a subtle and low-key manner. Board members speak of wanting to help youths who "do not have a good home or a good social environment in which to mature," "to help these young people find themselves," and "to help downtown kids cope with their environment."

In the perception of board members, the Domino Drop-In Center exists because many young people in need of reintegration into the

*For a framework for the study of such competing realities, see Robert A. Stebbins, "Studying the Definition of the Situation: Theory and Field Research Strategies," *Canadian Review of Sociology and Anthropology* 6 (Nov. 1969): 193–211. More specifically, for a discussion of conflicting goals in the social welfare field, see Mayer Zald, "Comparative Analysis and Measurement of Organizational Goals: Correctional Institutions for Delinquents," *Sociological Quarterly* 4 (1963): 206–230.

community are so alienated that they will not seek integration through the normal channels of school, church, Young Men's Christian Association (YMCA), and similar community organizations. The unkempt appearance of the center, the bizarre posters on its walls, the high-volume rock music that fills the rooms, the casual atmosphere, and the freedom to come and go are all means of attracting otherwise unreachable youths. The board members emphasize the development of trust between users of the center and the establishment, but they know from experience that this purpose must not be too obvious. Board members sometimes discuss their desire to encourage the users of the center to lead more Christian lives, but they realize that, given the kind of young people being served, it is inappropriate to broach such topics as attendance at church.

The members of the board consider themselves part of a society that has been too inattentive to the problems of young people who are growing up. Their role, as they perceive it, is to help those young people who have such severe problems that they have turned their backs on society. They realize that this role is a difficult one. They are willing to disregard the long hair and dirty clothes and the drugs and obscenities and to accept the demand for participatory democracy at council meetings, if they receive assurance that young people are not turning away from this last link with the dominant society. This assurance is made possible by the center's existence and patronage by local youths, as well as by the appearance of users of the center at council meetings.

This orientation of the board members appears quite clearly in the explanations they give for their unwillingness to visit the center. Most board members never appear; one lady, a church worker, stops in only to leave the cookies she bakes regularly, and then she quickly leaves. The reiterated explanation is that the purpose of the center might be subverted by the presence of men and women in conventional clothes and with conventional attitudes. One board member commented, "I think the best way for me to contribute to solving the problems of youth is just to raise money." For this reason, a closing of the center because of disruptive or destructive behavior causes profound concern among the board members; even if the center is "only keeping them off the streets and out of trouble," this procedure is better than the severing of this last tenuous link to the mainstream of society.

Staff personnel

The second important constituency of the Domino Drop-In Center is the staff, comprising a group of volunteers, ranging in number from eight to twenty-five. Staff members take turns supervising the center's activities, maintain a degree of order, refer medical or psychiatric cases to other agencies, soothe drug users experiencing bad reactions, and otherwise handle the day-to-day operation of the center. The board of directors has usually found it possible to pay a part-time general director of the drop-in center to coordinate efforts and schedule the staff volunteers. Members of the staff are, for the most part, university students who are more or less alienated from contemporary society; most of them have used drugs at some time and remain sympathetic to the drug culture. Although a few of the volunteers have accepted the purposes and orientation of the board of directors, the staff has repeatedly articulated its own views regarding the Domino Drop-In Center.

One group of volunteers phrased the purpose of the drop-in center as a way "to provide a place to go where activities can take place without hassles from landlords or whatever, providing both physical and 'rapping' (unstructured) activities which are mutually rewarding to both staff and kids." Another staff report called the center "a place where teen-agers can meet and be themselves in an atmosphere of their own design."

The goal of the drop-in center, as perceived by staff volunteers, is the encouragement of innovative ideas and projects which will further the kind of alternative culture they themselves are seeking. Staff volunteers have been most interested in projects such as producing an underground newspaper, organizing high school students to protect their interests, pressuring hospitals to provide better facilities for treatment of drug cases, and arranging coffeehouse discussions with stimulating university professors.

Staff members usually agree with board members that the young people who use the center are not integrated into the community, but they differ with the board regarding what should be done. In the staff's view, some kind of social change is the only answer. If schools and other institutions cannot be changed to meet the demands of alienated youth—a category into which they put both themselves and the users of the center—then some place must be maintained as an island where dissidents can survive. In their perception the drop-in center is such an island at the present time. It is a refuge from the pressures of the corrupt world. With the distinctive appearance both of itself and the people who use it, the center is a symbol of the alternative culture to which they want to belong.

Young participants in center

The third constituency is composed of the young people who use the center. At the Domino Drop-In Center, the number of regular users has hovered around seventy-five, with a constant turnover. The young people at this center have not been formally interviewed. On the basis of informal interviews, they do not seem to differ in important respects from the users of another drop-in center who were the subject of more systematic research. Therefore, this article reports results of analysis of the available questionnaire data, along with informal observations.*

The drop-in center users were predominantly male and white. They were fairly evenly distributed between the ages of sixteen and twenty-five. Most of them visited the center once every day or two, and about 60 percent spent more than two hours at each visit. More than 75 percent had an arrest history. 44 percent panhandled, almost 33 percent used "speed," and less than 25 percent used no drugs at all. Other results of the survey data showed that most users of the drop-in center had dropped out of school and were unemployed; the majority were living away from home. The data suggest that drop-in center users constitute a marginally deviant population, not integrated into the dominant society and having a great deal of time at their disposal.

The purpose of the drop-in center, as perceived by the users, is reflected in the survey results in Table 1. The only concrete services that elicited a positive response from more than 60 percent of the users were food and medical aid. Users approached the center mainly in an instrumental relationship for the sake of the basic necessities of life; they did not approach it with much interest in group activities which might involve an admission of deviant identity and imply a willingness to reintegrate themselves into the mainstream of society. Table 2 shows that interest in the kind of activities that imply acceptance of the goal of reintegration progressively declined with age; the further progressed was the deviant career, the less interest there was in terminating it.

Comments of Domino Drop-In Center users support this appraisal by users of another facility. They react with little more enthusiasm to the goals of the staff volunteers than they do to the goals of board members. Failing or having already failed in the educational system and with little prospect of succeeding occupationally, they display a notable boredom with life itself and little confidence in proposals for attempts at social change. Asked why they frequent the drop-in center, the usual reply is that there is nowhere else to go. The scene, evening after evening, is one of drifting in and out, sitting on a bench listening to the music and talking to no one, petting in a dark corner, waiting for a visit from drug dealers who cannot be kept completely away from the center, and otherwise frustrating the purposes of ardent staff members who wait in vain to talk about the revolution.

Such retreatism is common to almost all users of the Domino Drop-In Center, even though there have been distinct subgroups among them. For example, leather-jacketed motorcycle enthusiasts—the "greasers"—have had little to do with "speed freaks," who tend to remain apart from

*Grateful acknowledgment is made by the writer to the Educational Alliance, New York, New York, for permission to analyze survey data collected for one center.

Table 1. Percentage of drop-in center users expressing need for or interest in services[a]

Service	% of respondents
Food	89
Medical aid (clinic)	67
Clothing	56
Shelter	53
Work referral	52
Counseling	52
Group therapy	41
Psychiatric services	33

[a]The "no response" category has been omitted.

Table 2. Percentage of drop-in center users expressing need for or interest in services, by age category[a]

Service	% of respondents by age		
	Under 17	17–20	Over 20
Group therapy	80	43	31
	(n = 10)	(n = 21)	(n = 29)
Work referral	90	55	40
	(n = 10)	(n = 22)	(n = 30)
Counseling	88	71	54
	(n = 8)	(n = 17)	(n = 26)

[a]The "no response" category has been omitted.

all other users and also, for the most part, from one another. The differences between groups of users, however, have been far less than those between the users as a whole and the staff. It is the important difference, in Kenneth Keniston's words, "between those who *cannot* meet the demands of their society, and those who *choose not* to do so."*

Interrelationships of three factions

These three conflicting definitions of the reality of a drop-in center confront one another at the monthly council meeting, to which each group brings its own distinctive interests. The board of directors usually controls these meetings and uses them to discuss finances, to plan fund-raising campaigns, and to receive assurance that the Domino Drop-In Center is still functioning. Representatives of the staff at these meetings

*Kenneth Keniston, *The Uncommitted* (New York: Dell, 1965), p. 386.

repeatedly complain that the board is interested only in money and that discussion of goals and projects should take precedence; when such discussion does take place, however, the conflicting orientations become apparent, and little agreement is reached. Drop-in center users, who appear at the meetings only when induced by the staff to come as their allies, remain uninterested; except for occasional hostile reactions to the board members, they say little. Their usual complaint is that somebody is trying to "lay his trip" on them: that is, to influence them. Their expressed preference is freedom to "do their own thing."

Although they hold disparate orientations, the three groups are dependent upon one another. The board of directors holds financial control, but either staff or users can simply refuse to visit the center; if visits decreased, the center would have to close, depriving the board of the satisfaction of doing something to help youth. Staff members can organize activities as they wish, but the users of the center will not cooperate with anything demanding structure or long-term commitment. The most powerful group of the three is the users themselves, whose cooperation is needed by each of the two other groups as a source of confirmation of the worth of its reality-definition.

Because the groups are both disparate in orientation and dependent in practice, the Domino Drop-In Center has operated at a minimal level of activity throughout the two-year period from 1969 to 1971. It has become simply a place to sit, to talk, to neck, to listen to music, and to wait for excitement that seldom comes. There has been a high turnover of staff members. When a group of staff became discouraged and resigned, the board panicked at the thought of closing the center and sought other volunteers, whose enthusiasm gradually lessened in the course of working with the young people who use the center. On several occasions the nervous void of activity has been shattered by physical violence between staff and users or between groups of users. Every time the center has been closed, it has soon reopened on the same basis as before.

General model of a drop-in center

This analysis of the Domino Drop-In Center seems to represent processes that occur in the operation of virtually all such centers and that give rise to many of the same problems. Every youth-oriented drop-in center with which the writer is familiar must contend with three distinct constituencies. First is the establishment, which owns or rents the building and provides the funds necessary for whatever services are available. Structurally, this constituency may take the form of a federal, state, provincial, or municipal agency, a church, or an independent community organization. Its orientation is toward the reintegration of problem youth. The advocates of social change, the second faction, are usually found on staff

positions. They are typically university students, members of such organizations as Volunteers in Service to America (VISTA) or the Company
of Young Canadians, or reformed drug addicts. Their orientation is
toward innovative projects that might result in reform of the dominant
society. The third constituency is the young people who use the center,
who have opted out of society or work. They remain unwilling to commit
themselves to any organized plan of action.* Some mixing of orientations
across the three groups is possible. These groups approximate, however,
three conflicting forces with which drop-in centers must contend.

Imbalances in the power equilibrium among these three groups result
in failure to achieve the goals of any one of them. If, for example, the
establishment is removed from the situation as a distant government
agency, the staff may assume more power and by emphasizing intellectual
activities, give the center the atmosphere of a campus coffeehouse. This
atmosphere discourages retreatist drug users from patronizing the center;
they no longer feel free to drop in, and the center no longer lives up to its
name. The same result can occur when an establishment group assumes
sole authority; its inclination will be to give the center an exceedingly
wholesome image by locating it in a church hall, a "good" section of the
city, or the local YMCA. In this situation, both drug users and advocates
of social change are likely to avoid the place.

The same failure results, however, when the balance of power favors
retreatist drug users. In one such instance the center became the domain
of a strong-man guru, who demanded unquestioning personal allegiance
of all those who came through the door. This kind of imbalance of power
destroys the openness and the atmosphere of acceptance necessary in a
drop-in center just as much as an imbalance that favors either of the other
two constituencies. Most drug-using populations, left to control a drop-in
center by themselves, tend to let it become the meeting place of one or
another subgroup, often "greasers," to the exclusion of other subgroups,
like speed users, that a drop-in center should serve.

Ways to achieve stability

This research suggests the maintenance of a power equilibrium among
the three groups as a first means of ensuring relative stability in a drop-in
center. Because a drop-in center is a point of convergence for three
disparate realities, each reality by itself is its own worst enemy. Only by
permitting constant tension among the three groups and by preventing
one group from dominating can the goals of all three groups be achieved
to some minimal extent. Even when it has the chance to assume greater

*These three constituencies are examples of the conformity, rebellion, and retreatism
types in Robert Merton's classic typology. See Robert Merton, "Social Structure and
Anomie," *American Sociological Review* 3 (1938): 672–682.

power, none of the three constituencies should seize it. Such an act would prevent the accomplishment of even its own definition of the center's goals.

A second means of ensuring a degree of stability and goal achievement is to emphasize those programs that require a minimum of organized activity. Must users of drop-in centers reject a high degree of organization. Activities in which individuals can engage singly or in groups of two or three are preferred. A table for tennis, card tables and cards (tarot or otherwise), and craft tools such as potters' wheels or sewing machines are better investments than facilities for team sports, planned lectures, or classes of any kind. Similarly, because most drug users think in short-range terms of immediate gratification of needs, excessive scheduling of activities will not prove successful. Even the idea of making appointments to talk to staff personnel is impractical. What the drop-in center offers should be available as much as possible at any time the center is open, to as many or as few people who come in. A high degree of organization of time, of facilities of staff personnel, or of users of the center leads to failure.

A third way of ensuring stability is through activities or offerings that require only an instrumental orientation on the part of users of the center. These activities are preferable to those that require acceptance of establishment values. Food is an example. Most drug-using teenagers will patronize a center that offers food, whether pastries, soda, potato chips, or soup, as long as they do not receive a sermon while they eat or pressure to conform to conventional norms. Both physicians and lawyers can provide needed and important services in drop-in centers. However, if they let their young patients or clients know that they expect them to rehabilitate themselves as part of the payment for these services, the services will be without takers.

Many centers serve as information networks in which parents of runaway children can post letters on bulletin boards and young people get directions to welfare offices, abortion clinics, and similar facilities. The provision of information is an important and workable project and succeeds as long as users of the center are sure that the center will not report them to their parents or, if they are using illegal drugs, to the police. Drop-in center programs that require an investment of self—group therapy programs, for example—can succeed on a small scale when it is made clear that participation is wholly voluntary and that nonparticipants will not be pressured, however subtly, to join.

A fourth consideration is the avoidance of activities or programs that give rise to value conflict by dramatizing the conflicting realities. These activities can range from religious programs advocated by a church board, to nude sensitivity sessions advocated by users of the center, to programs of civil disobedience suggested by advocates of social change. If any such activity is proposed, the three groups that must necessarily cooperate for the drop-in center's survival are pitted against one another, and the center's existence is threatened.

It is not necesary that all the groups see the same value in the center's activities, but each activity should be structured so that each group can find some value in it. Legal aid, for example, may be viewed by establishment figures as present for the sake of justice and by those who use it for the sake of evading penalties for law breaking; nevertheless, it typically wins the support of both groups. Each constituency must know that the drop-in center is not the place to do everything it thinks needs to be done; it can be the place to implement projects that appear equally desirable to constituencies with varied views of the world.

A fifth and very important condition for relative stability is that the director of the center be able to mediate conflicts among the three constituencies, fulfill to some minimal extent the expectations of each, and win from each sufficient support so that the center can continue operation. Observation of eight directors suggests that the most effective are lowkey, reluctant to state opinions, and difficult to fluster. The effective director is one whose appearance approaches that of users of the center, whose age and physical strength are greater than theirs, and whose academic background wins respect from members of the establishment. The effective director in the typical drop-in center is an anti-leader—relaxed, unexcitable, and phlegmatic.

In summary, the continued operation of a youth-oriented drop-in center requires that each constituency not seek to maximize achievement of the goals dictated by its own definition of the reality of the situation. If establishment members attempt a vigorous program for rehabilitation of youth, or if advocates of social change on the staff attempt to launch a revolution through the center, or if the users themselves are absolute in their rejection of the establishment, the drop-in center ceases to be the only kind of institution it can be—a relaxed and accepting setting in which conflicting realities live uncomfortably with one another. The volatility that results from the interplay of the three constituencies is, in fact, the drop-in center's strength. By serving as a least common denominator among conflicting realities, the drop-in center serves its unique yet modest role in mediating some of the problems in the world of contemporary alienated youth.

The preceding article and the others reprinted in this chapter were chosen to emphasize certain issues, not to direct the reader, step by step, in diagnosing organizational problems. The analysis of the drop-in center clearly demonstrates the importance of understanding the role of boards of directors in the delivery of services. It also demonstrates that organizational tension is not something to be gotten rid of like a headache.

It is necessary to maintain a balance between the interests of different constituencies. A balance must also be maintained between an organization's need to survive and its need to be effective; the need to control the delivery of services and the need to gain the consent and commitment of its workers; the need to have open communications and the need to make decisions in a timely fashion; the need for a routine that provides stability and the need for initiative; and the need to nourish creative and dynamic parts and the need to maintain the integrity of the whole.

The appropriate balance in particular situations will often be a subject of disagreement. If the line workers fall back upon superficial analysis and rhetoric, then they will without question fail to serve their clients, for they will not be able to distinguish between problems that are solvable and the strains inherent in any organized structure, which can only be managed, as the Westhue's article illustrates.

To make this distinction, line workers need to understand the difference between the words "administer" and "manage." "Administer" conveys the idea of achieving goals, telling people what to do, and getting things done. "Manage" conveys the idea that there are conflicting needs and inevitable strains and dilemmas in organizational life that can only be balanced, as they cannot be completely solved.

Managers deal with dilemmas, with situations that have within them a set of constraints. One operative factor in management is *precedent*. Obviously a constraint against giving a worker a vacation in mid-winter is that other workers might make the same request. If one client receives a service, how can one refuse the same service to other clients? And what if there are insufficient resources to provide the service to all clients? Moreover, if one provides a client with all the services he or she may need, what happens to all the other services and all the other clients, since we live with limited resources? These are the managers' dilemmas, and they call for managerial skill in setting up systems of triage, of routing, of specialization, to handle them.

To give help to clients, it is necessary to understand not only the dilemmas of formal organizations, but also how an organization contrives to overcome them. The same is true of understanding clients: one focuses not simply on their limitations, but also on their strengths as they struggle to overcome their problems because from these struggles one can develop insights on how best to be of help.

Most agencies have more than one goal. A teaching hospital wants to train doctors and social workers; it wants to add to the knowledge, the techniques, and the methodology of various disciplines; and, obviously, it wants to serve patients. Perhaps one of the key organizational secrets of social agencies is the considerable conflict between and among equally good goals. These goal conflicts are one of the major causes of conflict within the organization.

If social workers and doctors in teaching hospitals are promoted mainly on the basis of their ability to do research and add to knowledge, doctors and social workers will have less energy for, and be less committed to, patient services. Similarly, if resources, or a major proportion of them, are allocated to new research projects, there will be less for routine patient service.

The existence of goal conflicts is not in itself a sign of trouble in the agency. The real issue is how the agency handles the inevitable conflicts among its goals. Does it talk out of all sides of its mouth at one time? Does it give lip service and nothing else to some of its goals? Or does it consciously adjust its priorities and rewards, recognizing the limitations on its ability to achieve any or all of its goals?

Most important, if one wants to secure a service for a client from one's own organization or from an outside one, one must be aware of the goal conflicts of these organizations and of the organizational dilemmas that they face. Unfortunately, the fact that the client needs a particular service is not always enough to ensure that he or she gets it. A request based solely on the worker's desire or recommendation may be turned down. Instead, one must couch service requests with the agency's constraints and dilemmas in mind. Success often depends on one's skill in finding some common ground between administrative needs and pressures, staff interests and concerns, and client needs. (See the article by Julie Abramson in Chapter 2.)

What are the major dilemmas that you can count on facing in helping clients through organizations? First, there is what is called the *functional autonomy* of the parts. Every organization wants its various departments to show initiative and creativity. If departments do this, however, they come into conflict with other departments because resources are scarce.

Each department, if it is to realize its initiatives and creative ideas, must try to garner a larger share of the resources than others have. To outsiders, it may seem that one hand does not know what the other is doing. It looks as if people do not want to cooperate with a legitimate request for service; yet they may in fact be trying to do what they think is best in the long run for clients. The dilemma of functional autonomy of the parts is a real one.

The second major dilemma results from the need of every organization to survive if it is to do any good—to help people. And yet it may have to do certain things to survive that make it less effective in reaching its goals. If an agency's budget is based on the number of people it serves, it either may be forced to increase that number, even if it means lowering the quality of the service, or get the funders to change the basis on which they fund, which is no easy task. In this day and age, organizational survival is not something to be scoffed at.

How to deal with the strain between survival and goal attainment is the province of managers. And how this dilemma is handled distinguishes the good manager from the bad manager, for there are innumerable ways to survive. Should one, in one's desire to help clients, discount the need for organizational survival, one will probably overlook a whole set of options for getting the clients what they need.

Perhaps the main dilemma that one feels in working through organizations is the one between the need for routine, order, and stability, and the need for creativity, change, and adjustment. If the organization has to decide its procedures anew every day, there will be very little time left to do anything. On the other hand, if procedures must be followed no matter what—"This is the way we've always done it, and this is the way we're always going to do it"—then human service organizations will not be able to help most of their clients. How to strike a balance is the dilemma.

Workers should not demand flexibility before the positive as well as the negative consequences of following specific procedures and regulations are understood. Their task is to make it possible for the organization to fulfill its legitimate need for order and stability and still adjust to clients' needs. Organizations need help with this just as much as clients need help with their problems and dilemmas. Attacking the client or attacking the agency is seldom a good initial strategy.

The last dilemma that workers often feel strongly is the strain between the need to coordinate and the need to have free-flowing communication of ideas and sentiments. If one insists that communications be shared with everyone, the process of communication will take longer and quick coordination will be impossible. Who is to say at what point communication should stop and decisions should be made? Because of the strain between hierarchy and communication, one should count on a certain amount of slowness in response to one's initiatives. In helping clients one learns that while slowness can be frustrating, impulsive actions may be destructive. Likewise, from an organizational point of view, rashness can be costly. Is speed with which the client takes action the most important factor in all situations? We think not, for clients or for organizations.

Once one begins to conceptualize the difficulty organizations have in dealing with such structural dilemmas, one understands the complexity of working with organizations. If a client was facing a serious breakdown in functioning, this possibility would engage the theoretical understanding and dedicated practice of workers. We contend that if the organization is to better serve clients, that same kind of understanding and skill must be applied to the organization and its problems.

The article that follows not only presents the dilemmas of child welfare work but also discusses some current practice "myths." In this context a myth is a part truth that makes us feel ennobled by what we are doing for clients and comfortable about what we are not doing. There are different myths in different fields of practice and different agencies. At the core, myths are cherished beliefs. To challenge someone's cherished beliefs may at times be necessary, though it will seldom be easy for either party.

Myths and Dilemmas
in Child Welfare*

ALFRED KADUSHIN

Every profession, over time, develops its own mythology and persistently wrestles with the dilemmas inherent in its operation. This paper is an effort to make explicit some of the more significant myths and dilemmas currently encountered in child welfare.

Definition of a Myth

A myth is a partial truth that has achieved validation by virtue of repetition. The more people proclaim an idea, the more it sounds incontrovertible. A myth gains currency because it has the appearance of truth. It is selected for repetition because in some way it expresses collective wishes, justifies cherished beliefs, supports a general point of view. Because it expresses the feelings of the group, a myth makes us feel more comfortable about what we are doing or want to do.

The Myth of Failure

The first myth is a popular target because countering it is flattering; the wonder is that it was ever accepted in the first place. It is, however, persistently repeated in the literature. The myth is that the child welfare agencies, including child care institutions, have failed to do the job required of them.

A conservative estimate is that, over the last ten years, as a consequence of the work of the agencies, about 500,000 children were placed for adoption with parents who nurtured them and cared for them as their own. These were children who had lost, or never had, a home of their own. Many studies yield the same conclusions—that the failure rate during the first year of placement, as measured by the number of children returned to the agency, is extremely low, 2 percent to 4 percent, and that 75 percent to 80 percent of the adopted children grew to healthy, satisfactory maturity in such homes. This is a rate of success rarely equaled for a large-scale, complex enterprise.†

During each year of the last decade, agencies have placed about 200,000 children in foster family homes for temporary or long-term care. For the most part the care these children received was at a level of

---

*Excerpted by special permission of the Child Welfare League of America from *Child Welfare* 56 (1977): 141–153.

†Alfred Kadushin, *Child Welfare Services*, 2d ed. (New York: Macmillan, 1974), pp. 565–578.

adequacy beyond that available in their own home at the time. The few available follow-up studies of adult functioning of former foster children show a high success rate.

About 350,000 children have been cared for during the last decade in institutions for dependent, neglected and/or emotionally disturbed children. If the children have not always been "cured," a benign, salutary environment has been provided for them for a period during which whatever potentials they had for healthy growth had a fighting chance for actualization.*

These are notable victories. That the whole enterprise has its problems, its shortcomings, and its deficits is admittedly true—and this is what supports the myth. The charge of failure is, in part, accurate. But in measuring the gain for society, one has to estimate the incontrovertible damage that would have been sustained if we were not in the picture. Abolish the institutions, the foster family and group homes, the adoption agencies, tomorrow, and we return to the horrors of irresponsible, unregulated, unsystematic, haphazard care. Child welfare agencies provide a clearly defined, responsible, socially oriented apparatus to deal with a widespread problem.

These results have been achieved with relatively little scandal regarding misuse or misappropriation of the sizable sums of money involved in carrying out our charge. Few, if any, other professional groups in the country have had equally large appropriations of public funds and managed them so responsibly.

The Myth of Community Support of Manifest Functions

A second myth is that child care facilities and agencies are sanctioned and supported by the community primarily out of concern for children and what is best for the child. Once again, the myth has force because it is partly true. This is the manifest justification for the support of this enterprise. The latent reasons are, however, more potent and more fundamental. Society supports child care facilities and workers because it is in the interest of the maintenance and preservation of social stability and of some of the essential values basic to our way of life. Child welfare agencies remove embarrassing debris from visibility; they act as agents of social control; they salve the conscience of the community.

There is some comfort for us in recognizing this because it implies that society is not so concerned about our effectiveness as we might think. We need to be supported, and probably will continue to be supported (although not, perhaps, in the style we would like), even if we are not particularly effective. Our very existence, rather than our effectiveness, meets the latent needs of society. Does anyone rate the effectiveness of religious organizations, the efficacy of prayer?

*Kadushin, *Child Welfare Services*.

The Myth of the Superiority of Community Care

A myth that is somewhat more specific is that community care for almost all children who need substitute care is the desirable choice. Once again, this myth, like all myths, acquires its force because it has an element of truth in it and because it expresses prevailing ideological prejudices. Heightened concern with the "dehumanizing" aspect of "deindividualized" settings and with rights, liberties and entitlements currently feeds the ever-present latent bias against the institution. A rich literature documents the shortcomings of the institutions, but where is the research literature that, as yet, establishes, by contrast, the effectiveness of community care? If institutional care is not so good, does that establish the fact that community care is better, cheaper, more humane?

Even with regard to the dependent and neglected child in an institution, the most likely candidate for deinstitutionalization, a recent review of knowledge in the child welfare field concludes that the empirical evidence is incomplete in support of the presumption that the "living environment provided by a foster family home or a group home is better than that provided by a residential institution. It is nonexistent where one is interested only in comparing the effects on children of a series of foster family homes with those of a given institution."*

One considerable advantage community care has is its relatively recent development. Relatively recent developments have not yet had a chance to be critically examined. It takes time for "horrible examples" and "exceptional cases" to become evident; it takes time for deficiences to make themselves felt. And new developments have the advantage of the enthusiasm, the commitment, the surge of hope, that accompany them. The placebo effect of optimism is a potent factor in their favor.

However, the experience is not so new and not so recent that we lack some beginnings of a critical re-evaluation. In addition to recognizing that even adequate preparation does not permit obtaining a sufficient number of acceptable community-based substitute care facilities to replace institutional placements, we are beginning to suspect that community programs may not, in fact, be more economical or more humane than institutions. Costs are rapidly escalating. A recent study of a New York state legislature committee concerned with child welfare estimated annual cost per child at $15,400 in a group home, $16,500 in a group residence, and $16,900 in an institution.† One need not be unduly cynical to express concern about what costs will be when proprietary group homes become the only game in town. Dismantled institutions are not

---

*J. Koshel, *Deinstitutionalization: Dependent and Neglected Children* (Washington, D.C.: Urban Institute, 1973), p. v.

†B. S. Bernstein, D. S. Snider, and W. Meezan, *Foster Care Needs and Alternatives to Placement: A Projection for 1975–1985* (Albany: New York State Board of Social Welfare, 1975), p. 44.

easily reconstituted. What may appear more economical in the short run may be more expensive over time.

Lerman's recent restudy of the California Community Treatment Project indicated that from the point of view of deprivation of individual freedom and exercise of control, the community program for youthful delinquents was no more humane than the institution program.* At the very least, the same question should be asked of the community-oriented approach that is asked of institutional child care: where is the evidence for the claims made?

The Myth of Client Noncontribution

The final myth to be considered here—this one perhaps the most controversial—is that the difficulties presented by client families and children are primarily, if not exclusively the consequences of failures in society generally and often, more immediately, of the organization and delivery of child care services. Once again there is an element of truth in this. Social arrangements are disordered and pathogenic; clients are disadvantaged and deprived; child care organizations and service delivery can impose their own additional difficulties. And once again the myth is in line with the ideological Zeitgeist. Any suggestion that we are "blaming the victim" is currently taboo.

And yet clinical experience repeatedly indicates that people bring different capacities and potentialities to the same external situation, that one child's trauma is another child's inconvenience. This not "blaming the victim." It is an effort to understand, as objectively as possible and without reference to ideological preferences, the nature of the situation in which child welfare agencies are required to intervene. To deny what we would rather not believe is no great service to the client. To "excuse" is as disrespectful of the client's humanity as it is to "blame," where either contravenes reality. The client is often both victim of and contributor to the psychosocial difficulty being experienced.

In many child care situations, the child and the family bring their own way of dealing with the problem situation, which makes successful coping difficult. One clear trend over the last two decades is that we are now more frequently asked to help parents and children with limited strength, limited capacity, limited potentialities for change—parents and children whose contribution to the problem situation needs to be compassionately but objectively understood.

In essence the myth suggests that solving all social problems would solve all personal problems. There is a version of this myth with which directors of child care agencies are particularly affected: that is, if agen-

*P. Lerman, *Community Treatment and Social Control* (Chicago: University of Chicago Press, 1975).

cies had enough money, enough fully trained personnel, the problems of the agencies would be solved. This ignores the factors inherent in the human failings that contribute to the problems faced by child care.

The myth is important to recognize because it is associated to a related submyth, namely, that if we could radically reorganize the environment, correct all of the deficiencies of institutions, provide the best possible foster group homes, etc., this would result in effectively changing the client's behavior, in the resolution of the problem situation. We are constantly disappointed that suggested changes of this nature, once enacted, seem to have a limited impact on the problems. The novel *The Caseworker*, by a Hungarian child care worker who turned writer, may be of interest here.* Writing of his experiences as child welfare worker in Budapest twenty-five years after the revolution, he describes a host of intractable child care problems that mirror those encountered in Boston or Cincinnati or Atlanta or Dallas.

Definition of a Dilemma

A dilemma is presented by a situation that requires choosing between two relatively equally balanced, equally attractive, or equally unattractive alternatives. To choose one precludes choosing the other. To satisfy one alternative involves rejection of the other. Nor do we have the luxury of not making a choice; we must decide and act on one alternative or the other.

General Dilemma

A general dilemma emerges from the fact that, most often, we are unable to do only one thing. In doing the thing we think is desirable, we also find that we have, inevitably, done other things we did not mean to do or want to do. Many damaging, unanticipated consequences of the things done come as part of an inseparable package deal. To do the good requires accepting the bad as a calculated social risk. For instance, if the administration gives the children in the institution a greater measure of real autonomy and control, this may threaten the child care staff, make their jobs more difficult, as they see it, and incur the possibility of greater staff turnover. If the autonomy of the child care staff is increased, so is the possibility that they will use this additional discretionary power and freedom from administrative control to make their jobs easier, more satisfying, to the detriment of the needs of the children. The bad must be taken with the good.

*G. Konrad, *The Caseworker* (New York: Harcourt Brace Jovanovich, 1974).

The Dilemma of the Rights of Parents versus the Rights of Children

The clear dilemma between equitably meeting the rights of parents and the rights of children is becoming increasingly insistent. Recently the rights of the biological father were established in a decision relating to the adoption of children born out of wedlock. The Supreme Court, in protecting the father's rights, requires some delay in the adoption placement until the father can be contacted and his wishes in the matter determined. As a consequence, the child's right to the earliest possible permanent placement is violated.

We recently discovered the right of the child to continuity of care in a situation in which psychological parenthood has been established. For example, a child is placed in a foster family home because of a mother's prolonged physical illness. After a five-year struggle, the mother is now well and fully capable, physically and emotionally, of caring for her child. During the five years in care, however, the child has established strong emotional ties with the foster parents, who are eager and willing to care for her. Firm bonds of psychological parenthood have been established. To return the child to the biological mother violates the rights of the child to continuity of care; to refuse to return the child violates the right of the biological mother to her own child, for whom she is ready, willing, and able to care.

Similar dilemmas plague use currently between the right of adoptive children to information about the identity of their biological parents and the right of the biological parents to be protected from intrusion into their lives of children they once surrendered for adoption; between the right of a group—racial, ethnic, or religious—to protect their heritage by advocating placement of a child only with members of his own group and the right of the child to the best and earliest permanent substitute care. . . .

The Dilemma of Stability versus Innovation

Staff and children need some stability in their environment. One needs to have some assurance that things tomorrow will be somewhat like things today. We are made anxious by the uncertainty of change, by a lack of structure in whose predictability we can have some confidence. It takes time to learn the lay of the land, the institutional procedures, and the people to whom we have to relate.

Yet stability leads to rigidity and, in turn, to ossification. Procedures may no longer be applicable to a changed situation. So although stability is necessary, so is change or instability. Deliberate, planned change is needed, despite the unhappy recognition that children in all child care facilities face the trauma of frequent unintended, unplanned change—in caretaking personnel, for instance. The dilemma throughout the child care system is how to provide a stable environment for children in the context of conditions in which deliberate, planned change is added to unplanned change. We respond to this dilemma by prescriptions on how to introduce change so that it is least traumatic. The prescriptions are general, but the children are individuals; some need a greater measure of stability than others and respond to change with greater anxiety. The need for stability and the need for change present antithetical choices difficult to make without incurring some unhappy consequences for some children. . . .

The Dilemma of Operating Efficiently versus Operating Selectively

This dilemma is related to size. Optimum selectivity implies that the child care facility takes only those children with characteristics that meet the institutional design and program rationale. Such selectivity may result in empty beds and reduce income in the face of continuing fixed costs. Inefficient operation risks criticism from the donor constituency. To take into a facility children who are not the kinds for which it was established violates the criterion of selectivity, while meeting the criterion of efficiency. Ergo, a dilemma.

The Dilemma of Efficiency versus Equity

We are and always have been faced with limited resources. Recently we have begun to accept the depressing likelihood that this will always be true. This creates a dilemma between operating efficiently and operating equitably. There is the choice between providing service to all who need it without regard to their ability to make best use of it, as against selecting for service those whose attributes give some assurance that intervention will have some effect. To accept all may mean that in the end little of sufficient consequence is done for anybody. Selective intake may inequitably deny service to some to ensure effective help to a limited number of others.

The Dilemma of Quality versus Quantity

If too high a standard is set for staff, if qualifications for licensing of institutions or day care facilities are too demanding, there is difficulty in obtaining the people the facilities need to meet the demands for service. Rigorous application of high standards for foster homes may result in too few homes available. The kind of intensive study of cases that good professional service requires may lead to processing too few cases in the time available. Offering a more intensive service to one client may mean denying service to another client. . . .

The Dilemma of Meeting the Needs of Consumer Subgroups versus the Need for a Well-Integrated Child Care System

It is a justifiable complaint that the child welfare system is a maze of small, autonomous units—that it is frustratingly fractionated. At the same time there is the complaint that various identifiable constituencies are not adequately served because there are few or no agencies to meet their specific needs. Agencies exist for Catholic, Protestant, and Jewish constituents, but there is a demand that special agencies be organized to serve the needs of blacks and Hispanics and American Indians and that all of these agencies be permitted to operate under standards and procedures that meet the unique needs of their particular constituency. Both complaints—of fractionation and of inadequate service to ethnic, racial groups—may be justified. But it is difficult to see how moving in one direction would fail to compound the difficulty in the other direction.

The Dilemma of the Right of Access versus the Promise of Confidentiality

More than ever before there is consensus that the client has the right of access to his records. Schools and social agencies and child care institutions, if challenged, may be required to permit the family and the child to read his record. On the other hand, we solicit all sorts of communications from professionals about their perceptions and assessments of our clients—communications previously assured confidentiality. The promise of confidentiality freed the professional to share not only his valid findings but his hunches, intuitions, and professionally educated guesses, often useful in alerting us to what we need to know to help the client. Abrogating the promise of confidentiality permits satisfying the client's rightful claim to access; it also makes the less useful, less helpful communications as the professional becomes more circumspect in what he says.

Conclusion

The foregoing list of myths and dilemmas is far from complete. It calls attention, however, to the fact that we frequently operate on partial truths in contexts in which our very successes in certain aspects doom us to failure in others. This is, however, the human condition as expressed in the professional situation.

The trained clinician sees a dilemma as a professional challenge, not as an excuse for inaction or expediency. The untrained eye, seeing no constraints, often takes up the wrong challenge at the wrong time.

Client Needs: The starting point in assessing how to handle dilemmas in child welfare and similar programs is understanding what the client wants or needs. It is not enough to understand the client, moreover; he or she must be understood in the context of the agency. Most programs operate with an implicit assumption about how clients should behave; they should not be disruptive; they should attend their therapy sessions; they should value the help given them; they should not be dependent; and so on. Problems arise when programs require that clients act and behave in a certain manner, and clients do not. Some adolescents would rather hang out at the corner than come into the settlement house. Clients do not keep their appointments and often drop out of services.

Probably clients do their own cost-benefit analyses of service. We ask the adolescent to come into the settlement house, where he will have a gymnasium and a club group and an opportunity to go to camp and get remedial education and work training, all of which seem valuable and important. But what we often miss is that we are asking him to give up the excitement of the gang, the possibility of gaining status by fighting, the thrill of not knowing what is going to happen next, and the emotional satisfaction of acting out rebelliousness.

Our services are not unalloyed rewards. Clients always pay a price. The issue is whether the programs and the services are more rewarding to them than the costs that the programs impose. Anthony Maluccio's article describes this issue in some detail.

The Influence of the Agency Environment on Clinical Practice*

ANTHONY N. MALUCCIO

It has long been recognized that an agency's physical and social environment influences the nature and quality of services provided by its staff. Social work theorists with diverse orientations to practice have stressed that the agency setting should be viewed as an important part of the therapeutic process.† However, the specific nature and extent of these

*Excerpted from Chapter 10 of Anthony N. Maluccio, *Learning from Clients: Interpersonal Helping as Viewed by Clients and Social Workers*. Copyright 1979 by The Free Press, A Division of Macmillan Publishing Company, Inc. By permission of the publisher.

†F. Hollis, *Casework: A Psychosocial Therapy*, 2d ed. (New York: Random House, 1972); H. H. Perlman, *Social Casework: A Problem-Solving Model* (Chicago: University of Chicago Press, 1957); R. Smalley, *Theory for Social Work Practice* (New York: Columbia University Press, 1967).

influences have not been clearly understood or considered fully. In particular, there has been limited exploration of clients' views regarding the impact of the agency environment on the service.

As we are increasingly realizing, feedback from clients can be useful in suggesting practice implications and issues for further investigation. In this paper I therefore discuss the views of clients and workers regarding the role of the agency environment in clinical practice. In so doing, I draw upon selected findings from an in-depth study of client and worker perception of treatment in a family service agency.* . . .

Social Environment

Over two-thirds of the clients offered positive comments about the agency's social environment, that is, the agency's staff, social climate, or atmosphere. Representative remarks were:

Everyone was friendly. . . .

   Mrs. Donnelly: The waiting room when you first go in—I thought that was excellent. . . . They have things to do which is good—you know, it calmed people down a little bit before they went upstairs. . . .
   They were very, very nice, especially the girl at the desk when you first go in. . . . She is a very, very likable person, and she's just the receptionist. You see, right there, it's like they have an open door. . . . If I had gotten a cold feeling, I probably wouldn't have gone upstairs or never finished.

Even people who were dissatisfied with the service or its outcome had positive impressions of the agency as a whole. For example, one of the clients who dropped out said:

   Mrs. Norton: They were very nice, not like other places I've been to. In my life I've been to a lot of welfare places and hospitals where you feel like they don't want to talk to you nohow. . . . Here they treat you like a real person . . . like someone who has feelings. . . . They don't act like you're there just because it's free.

As seen in the above excerpts, clients expressed a variety of favorable comments about agency's staff and climate. A recurring theme was comparison of the agency with other community systems, such as hospitals and welfare agencies; clients contrasted the agency's warm climate with the impersonal or dehumanizing quality of larger bureaucratic organizations. Other key themes pertained to the friendliness of staff members, their readiness to be of help, and the feeling that clients were regarded as individuals.

   *A. N. Maluccio, *Learning from Clients: Interpersonal Helping as Viewed by Clients and Social Workers* (New York: Free Press, 1979).

Workers, on the other hand, had little to say about the agency's social environment, frequently indicating that they had not considered its meaning for clients or discussed it with them. The only exception was in relation to the receptionist: most workers brought out that she played a significant role with clients and that clients often commented positively about her.

Role of the Receptionist

As suggested . . . in the preceding section, most clients singled out the receptionist as a prominent member of the agency's staff. They pointed in particular to their pleasure in knowing her and their feeling comfortable with her. At the time of the study, the receptionist was a warm and caring person who related easily and spontaneously to people and who was very effective in meeting clients and making them feel at home. Her work area was located directly across from the waiting room, thus facilitating interaction between her and the clients while they were waiting for their appointments. Many clients reported that she was very interested in them and that they could talk easily with her about such matters as current events or, in some instances, about some of the changes and experiences in their lives from week to week. Several clients indicated that as a result of the receptionist's encouragement, they decided to continue in treatment despite their ambivalence.

As these findings imply, the role played by the receptionist in the helping process demands further attention. It is obvious that, in entering a new system such as a social agency, an applicant or client forms initial impressions that can influence his or her attitudes toward the service. Yet as various authors have suggested, receptionists at times are set up in such a way as to be barriers to service.* Others have observed that the receptionist or secretary in a mental health setting is an essential part of the success or failure of the program:

> secretaries are forced by necessity to function as part of the therapeutic team in community health centers. They talk first with prospective patients, family, and interested members of the community on the phone . . . The secretaries usually make and change appointments, handle fee dispositions, and transact with the patients and family in the waiting room.†

Despite the significance accorded to the functions of the receptionist or secretary, very little research has been carried out in this area. In one of the few available studies, Hall analyzed the reception process in several

---

*E. Cumming, *Systems of Social Regulation* (New York: Atherton Press, 1968), p. 115.
†G. W. Nyman, D. Watson, and S. E. James, "The Role of the Secretary in Community Mental Health: A Training Model for Integrating Secretaries into the Therapeutic Team in Community Mental Health," *Community Mental Health Journal* 9 (1973): 368–377.

British social agencies. He concluded that receptionists have a marked impact on the delivery of services, since they perform a variety of functions, including: (1) being the first point of contact with the agency at the time of the initial interview; (2) offering support and encouragement through their informal relationship with the client; and (3) acting as the client's advocate or controlling the client's access to the social work staff.*

The roles of the receptionist and other staff members, such as secretaries, should therefore be examined and developed more systematically. For example, an agency may consider how to enrich the reception process and maximize its potentially positive impact. Training programs may be introduced to facilitate the integration of receptionists or secretaries into the therapeutic team.† Ways may be found to enhance the roles of the cadre of clerical and maintenance staff, which is often an underused resource in various agencies.‡ . . .

Physical Environment

As practitioners and theorists have noted, the agency's physical environment is another feature that may affect client-worker interaction.§

In giving their impression of the agency as a whole, at least two-thirds of the clients in fact offered remarks about the physical setting. Most of these were negative comments about the location and physical appearance of the agency, the size and condition of the waiting room and offices, and the lack of parking. These comments came from satisfied as well as dissatisfied respondents. It may be that some persons found it easier to criticize the physical environment rather than the workers or other staff members with whom they had developed a personal relationship.

Some typical remarks about the physical setting were:

Location
I was leery about going there.
Parking very bad.
Didn't like going to that area.
Hard to get there.
Location very poor.

*A. S. Hall, *The Point of Entry: A Study of Client Reception in the Social Services* (London: Allen and Unwin, 1974), pp. 124–218.

†R. Benitez, "Psychiatric Consultation with Clerical Staff: A Systems Approach," *Social Casework* 60 (1979): 75–81; Nyman, Watson, and James, "Role of the Secretary."

‡Benitez, "Psychiatric Consultation," describes an interesting training program for clerical staff that has helped to enhance the therapeutic environment in a family service agency.

§C. B. Germain, "Space: An Ecological Variable in Social Work Practice," *Social Casework* 59 (1978): 515–522; B. A. Seabury, "Arrangements of Physical Space in Social Work Settings," *Social Work* 16 (1971):43–49; F. J. Turner, *Psychosocial Therapy* (New York: Free Press, 1978).

Appearance

An old building.
Looks like it needs a coat of paint.
Physical surroundings bad.
Looked rundown.

Office

Tiny offices. . . . I felt closed in.
Office looked cold; no rug or pictures.
Office too small.
Office seemed empty. . . .

While declaring their dissatisfaction with the quality of the physical environment, over one-third of the clients also proceeded to explain it as something that they had expected in view of the agency's nonprofit status and its identity as a charitable organization.

Some representative remarks follow:

Mrs. Mosca: It was poorly kept, an old building . . . but that's what you can expect for this type of agency. . . . You know, a charitable agency. They can't have a fancy place or location.

Mrs. Gates: As a subsidized agency, it's always working on a minimal budget. They can't afford really adequate facilities.

Mrs. Crompton: The building isn't too appealing. . . . It's very plain. . . . Well, you know, they can't do much about that, since the fact of the matter is that most people who go there are poor, elderly, or on welfare. . . . They couldn't afford to pay for anything more elaborate.

One wonders how the helping process was influenced by the client's negative views about the physical environment of the agency or perception of it as an organization for the poor or those on welfare. The clients in the three excerpts above were middle-class persons who indicated that they had selected this agency at least partly because they could not afford more expensive treatment from other sources such as private practitioners. In general, they reported that they were satisfied with the service and its outcome. While these clients were concerned about inadequacies in the agency's physical environment, in the long run this factor did not seem to matter to them enough to affect the outcome. For one thing, as with most other middle-class respondents, they tended to disassociate themselves from the charity cases which they perceived as constituting the bulk of the clientele. Mrs. Lodano, for instance, was one of the suburban residents who questioned whether she belonged in this particular agency, even though she and her husband had found the service to be very helpful:

Well, oh. . . . Someone from the suburbs usually wouldn't go there. . . . We couldn't afford anything else at the time. . . . Oh, I felt a little odd whenever we met someone who was obviously poor in the waiting room. . . . My husband felt like me. . . . We didn't really belong there. Those people had more serious problems. . . . They were really poor.

I asked Mrs. Lodano and other clients why they continued with the service and why they found it effective despite their strong negative feelings regarding the physical setting. In response, they generally referred to their strong attachment to their worker and conviction that he or she was helpful. It appeared thus that other variables, such as the worker's competence and the strength of the client-worker relationship, counteracted the potentially negative influence of the agency's physical environment. . . .

Over one-fourth of the clients were especially critical of the size or appearance of the worker's office:

Mrs. Donnelly: It feels good when you first meet her [the worker]. . . . She shakes your hand or she shows some sign of affection. . . . Then you go to her office and the room is completely different from what she's showing you. You know, it's cold and it looks empty. . . . It was kind of hard, but I felt, well, they didn't have the money because it was an *association*. . . . It was connected with the church. . . . That's why I overlooked it. . . .

Miss Moore: The room was very small—just a desk and some chairs. The social worker put in some plants and tried to make it homey . . . but it was still an office. . . . The room looked empty like I felt for quite a while. . . . Sometimes, well, it made it hard to get going. . . .

. . . The issue of the impact of the physical environment on the helping process and its outcome should not be glossed over. Most clients remarked about it, although their responses reflected a variety of views. Moreover, it is noteworthy that for many clients the poor quality of the physical environment accentuated the stigma of going to this particular agency, which they already perceived as a setting for poor or lower-class clients. This evidence supports the assertion that "space, design and decoration in our agency settings communicate messages about their status and worth to users of service and affect self-esteem and psychic comfort."* . . .

In one of the few pertinent studies conducted by social workers, Seabury analyzed the physical setting in six different social work agencies, ranging from a private practitioner's office to a large public welfare center.† He found that there were different space arrangements in such areas as waiting rooms and interviewing offices. The various physical

*Germain, "Space," p. 20.
†Seabury, "Arrangements of Physical Space."

patterns conveyed different messages to clients. For example, while both the family service agency and the public welfare center were large, bureaucratic organizations, the latter had a distant and dehumanizing atmosphere, while the former conveyed a sense of cheerfulness, comfort, and warmth. Similarly, the hospital social service department presented a most unpleasant appearance, while private offices and private agencies seemed most comfortable.

Seabury concluded that the optimal arrangements of the physical setting in any agency should be based on its functions and the needs of its clients. At the present time, however, there are few guidelines to assist agencies in this effort. Consequently, it has been proposed that social workers collaborate with other professionals, such as architects, as a means of improving service delivery.* In addition, further research in this area is essential, to clarify the specific role that the environment of an agency may play in treatment and to devise ways of maximizing the positive impact of the physical setting.

Conclusion

. . . An essential task in clinical practice is to evaluate the quality of an agency's environment as a salient force in the life spaces of clients and workers and as a critical component of the helping system. This means, first of all, that a practitioner needs to evaluate the quality and meaning of the environment for each client. Secondly, and perhaps more important, numerous questions should be asked at a broader level, such as the following:

> Does the setting give a first appearance of concern, competence, comfort, of a place where an individual, family or group will find the kind of understanding and wise help that is sought? Or does the setting give the message of incompetence, lack of respect, lack of privacy, lack of comfort that could well deter persons?†

On the basis of the answers to such questions, an agency's staff and administration should be better able to effect necessary changes making the environment more attractive and supportive to both clients and practitioners.

---

*F. D. Wittman and M. Wittman, "Architecture and Social Work: Some Impressions about Educational Issues Facing Both Professions," *Journal of Education for Social Work* 12 (1976):51–58.

†Turner, *Psychosocial Theory*, p. 191.

Practice Analogues

The assessment of organizational problems is similar to the assessment of client problems and to a certain extent requires the same skills and techniques. Organizational structures often have as much influence on the outcome of service as does the client's state of mind. A worker's ability to diagnosis why he or she is unable to deliver effective service may make it possible eventually to deliver that service. To what extent is the effectiveness of service related to the personality of the client, the skill of the worker, the adequacy of the interventive theory, or the effect of organizational variables? The same diagnostic process, embodying logical deductions on the basis of facts, values, assumptions, and theories, can be used to determine which variables are the source of a particular problem.

The assessment processes for client and organizational problems are also similar in that both are affected by theories of causality: which ones will we focus on, and which one will we ignore? If one makes the assumption that all organizations are rigid and unresponsive, then one will automatically define the cause of problems as lack of flexibility in organizational procedures, whether that is in fact the cause or not. Similarly, one may assume that clients do not keep their appointments because they are resistant to or threatened by therapy, whether that is the case or not. Such assumptions preclude a search for alternative explanations.

A family therapist will assess the problem of an acting-out adolescent differently than will a therapist who sees patients individually. An analytically oriented caseworker will diagnose problems differently than will a behaviorist. Each has his or her own theories of causality; each has a system of value preferences that support those theories; each has a certain set of assumptions about human nature. These assumptions do not always arise from formal training and education, as was dramatically illustrated by a paraprofessional who had taken several in-training courses on the diagnosis of depressed patients. Asked to make a presentation to the board of directors on her work, she gave an excellent, clear, and precise description of a client's depression and its sources. In the discussion that followed, she was asked by a board member what she thought would help this woman and responded, "Oh, all she needs to do is get married." One's theories are not always resistant to one's basic assumptions about human nature.

The key point is that good diagnosticians are aware of the theories that they use and the assumptions that they brings to them. This holds whether one is assessing a problem in a client, a problem in an agency, or an intersection of the two.

This text utilizes a variety of theoretical ideas and assumptions about organizations derived from sociology, psychology, and social psychology.

No one theory is exclusively relied upon. As noted, tension is an enduring part of organizational life. Conflict theory is thus obviously important:* an agency that has poorly developed mechanisms for handling conflict is in as much trouble as a client with the same difficulty. We also, as noted in the Introduction, lean heavily on George Homans's conception that social behavior can be understood as a form of exchange.† In this frame of reference, individuals, groups, and organizations make contributions to social agencies in the hope of gaining certain rewards. In so doing they also incur costs. These costs and rewards may be such tangible items as money or such intangibles as prestige, status, and friendship.

Exchange theory can be applied retrospectively in analyzing what has occurred or prospectively in planning a set of rewards to induce certain types of responses. It holds that organizational actors try to maximize their rewards and minimize their costs in all of their transactions. Thus, if workers or clients seem to be giving more than they are getting from the agency, they can be expected to take actions to rectify the balance through lowering their costs or raising their rewards. This viewpoint is implied in much of the discussion of the nine roles that follow. We use it as an orienting concept, however, rather than as a precise, operational theory.‡

Attitudes, Values and Skills

A number of unspoken assumptions impede workers' efforts to work effectively in organizations. Perhaps the major assumption is the one already mentioned: that informal organization is somehow illegitimate, and all work should be done in a manner consistent with formal rules. For example, one should send memos up through channels; one should never talk to people outside formal meetings unless they are at one's own level. Such an assumption rests on the idea that organizations are really best represented by the organizational chart, where everyone has a slot and every slot is clearly responsible to someone who is in authority over it. This approach obviously places a great deal of emphasis on organizational rationality and disregards the impact of the personal characteristics of the members—the people who structure and perform the organization's roles.

A second and related assumption about structure is that it is basically

*Marvin Weisbord, ed., *Organizational Diagnosis* (Reading, Mass.: Addison-Wesley, 1978), p. 35.

†George Homans, "Social Behavior as Exchange," *American Journal of Sociology* 63 (1958): 597–606.

‡ For a brief critique of exchange theory, see Harold H. Weissman, *Community Councils and Community Control* (Pittsburgh: University of Pittsburgh Press, 1970), pp. 19–26. For an extensive critique, see S. N. Eisenstadt, "Review of Exchange and Power in Social Life," *American Journal of Sociology* 71 (1965): 333–334.

an impediment. Now, from the point of view of a hypothetical individual worker with complete access to resources, clearly any organizational structure *is* an impediment; there is no need for structure since one has control over all the resources. But since one in fact needs to coordinate one's own efforts with those of others, to get sanction for carrying out one's tasks, and to get resources, structure is an absolute necessity.

Perhaps many workers have a secret idea that they do not really need the agency ("I am really striving to be an autonomous professional"). "Autonomy" here means operating on one's own, without any organizational constraint: the model is private practice. The question that needs to be asked is whether the traditional social work clients who cannot afford to pay can be offered service through private practice. The answer, if private practice is conceptualized as an individual working in his or her private office, is no. Their real material and service needs require resources that only social agencies can provide.

Another attitude that negatively affects the ability of workers to help clients is a misguided view of professionalism. Some workers have a mistaken view that professionalism is measured by rigid adherence to bureaucratic rules and professional standards. Instead, professionalism is, at the core, concern for clients, and it is broad enough to encompass a variety of ways of achieving help for them. The essence of professionalism is the ability to deliver effective service. At times this will require workers to use the informal system to introduce program innovations; at other times it may involve them in attempts to change the structure of agency through both formal and informal means; in extreme cases, it may even require them to resign if they feel the agency is doing the clients more harm than good.

Perhaps the most disabling attitude for workers stems from a secret desire to have the organization be like a family: workers want to be loved and supported unconditionally, to be cared about, to be allowed to relax the rules and blur roles, and to have their needs come first or almost first. This attitude is a particularly easy one for social workers to fall into because of their familiarity with the family as a unit of attention. It is important to keep in mind both the similarities and the differences between the family and the social work agency.

The primary difference lies in their goals. Family goals are basically *expressive* and nurturing. Organizational goals are *instrumental*. It is more important that the agency deliver effective service to clients than that workers feel nurtured, self-actualized, or even appreciated. Human relations theory suggests that one cannot achieve the instrumental goals without meeting the expressive needs of workers. Staff members undeniably need opportunities to develop competence, experience pride in their work, and gain a sense of autonomy and self-directedness; yet while there is no doubt a connection between agency and worker needs, the connection is not direct, and to disregard the strain between what the workers want and what the clients need is to underestimate the complexity of human relationships.

The second major difference is that families are relatively small and organizations are often quite large. The possibilities of face-to-face communication, of sharing all information, the of being available for all members, exist in a family. In an organization, especially a large organization, they do not.

Perhaps most significantly, an individual's position in an organization is assured by his or her performance in specific job functions. Nonperformance or poor results will cause expulsion and replacement by a new worker. Obviously, such a pattern is not considered appropriate for a family.

Finally, one is chosen for an organization because of one's specific set of skills, and one may elect to leave it or even be asked to leave. This certainly is not the case with the family, and one's allegiance to it is not limited by one's other interests.

Nevertheless, there are similarities between organizations and families. Certain problems of organizational life are amenable to solution through techniques akin to those used in family therapy: seeing the organization as a system of interdependent roles; opening up and clarifying communication; recognizing the need to maintain a balance in the system; understanding that the system is not closed and has boundary links to a complex environment. In dealing with organizational problems that impede one's ability to provide services to clients, however, one must take care not to limit one's efforts to these techniques when others are more appropriate.

Whatever technique is chosen, the agency context will affect its utilization for better or worse. In deciding how to deal with these organizational effects, it is important not to see oneself as simply a detached organizational analyst. Self-awareness is also required in that all organizational actors go through developmental stages in their organizational lives.

Tuckman, for example, suggests one progression of organizational learning and development which moves from 1) testing and dependency; 2) conflict and struggle for power; 3) growth of commitment and stable norms; and 4) functional role-relatedness.* This is by no means an inevitable progression. Some may never develop any commitment to the organization and its norms.

Nevertheless, the important factor is to recognize how one can best cope with these developmental transitions, one's own and those of other organizational actors. It is possible to respond to the normal confusion

*Quoted by Sheila Feld and Norma Radin, *Social Psychology For Social Work and the Mental Health Professions* (New York: Columbia Univ. Press, 1982) pp. 407–408.

and anxiety of a new job by overworking and denying any problems or to try consciously to understand the norms, patterns, and personalities involved in the informal organization.

As one worker noted, her transition involved both a dynamic and analytic process. "What are the norms, can I accept them? What does it mean if I don't? How do I respond to others while I'm deciding? The decision on how to fit in to the informal organization can follow one throughout one's stay at an agency. As a result of interaction, one may be labelled as a "follower," a "troublemaker," an "apple-polisher," and such labels are of course difficult to shake off."*

The ability to factor out one's relationship to an agency is important in gauging not only what to do in certain situations but how to do it. One can get too comfortable with the existing norms, Tuckman's Stage 3, to really acknowledge the discomfort of others.

Additional Readings

Blau, Peter, and Richard Scott. *Formal Organizations*, pp. 242–253. San Francisco: Chandler, 1962.

Clapps, Neil. "Diagnosing an Informal System." In Marvin Weisbord, ed., *Organizational Diagnosis*, pp. 86–89. Reading, Mass.: Addison-Wesley, 1978.

Feldman, Saul. "Budgeting and Behavior." In Saul Feldman, ed., *The Administrator in Mental Health Services*, pp. 29–56. Springfield, Mass., Charles Thomas, 1973.

Merton, Robert. "Bureaucratic Structure and Personality." In Amitai Etzioni, ed., *A Sociological Reader in Complex Organizations*, pp. 47–58. New York: Holt, Rinehart, and Winston, 1961.

Perrow, Charles. "The Analysis of Goals in Complex Organizations." *American Sociological Review* 26 (1961): 856–865.

Weisbord, Marvin, ed. *Organizational Diagnosis*. Reading, Mass.: Addison-Wesley, 1978.

Weissman, Harold H. *Overcoming Mismanagement in Human Service Professions*, pp. 9–22. San Francisco: Jossey-Bass, 1973.

*Lynne Spevack, Unpublished log. Hunter College School of Social Work, May 1983.

CHAPTER 2

EXPEDITER

Lyndon Johnson was fond of asking potential presidential appointees whether they were "can-do people." Could they get things done? He could, and he wanted to be sure that his support staff could do the same. Least of all did he want staff who would tell him why things could not be done.

Working effectively in any organization—political or otherwise—involves expediting. This is true whether one is an administrator seeking support for a new program unit or a line caseworker trying to get an individual client into a job-training program. Both have to get things done. Both are operating in an organizational context.

Overview

Expediting in an agency setting is no simple task. If it were, the old adage "if you want it done well, do it yourself" would apply. Unfortunately, it does not. Doing it oneself in an organization requires one to have sufficient information, authority, resources, and skills to achieve one's goal. In many situations clinical social workers will not possess all of these requisites. Even when they do, however, expediting may require overcoming everything from passive lack of cooperation to downright resistance from others, including agency superiors, subordinates, peers, clients, clients' family members, and staff in other agencies.

Hence, no matter what the task, expediting can be conceptualized as a three-part process: (1) securing the cooperation of significant others; (2) carrying out the task; and (3) following up to ensure that the task was done, and done well. So, for example, a school social worker might want to refer a youngster to a child guidance clinic for treatment. Effective expediting of that referral might involve negotiating with the clinic to bypass the clinic's waiting list, contacting other professionals working with the child to pressure the clinic, providing necessary referral information, and follow-up to ensure that the child's parents have gone ahead with the referral and that the clinic has indeed accepted the child for treatment.

Context and Task: From our point of view, all social work involves expediting. In this section, we describe the key requisites of this role, although the reader will also find concepts and skills related to effective expediting in other sections. We begin with an article by Carole Soskis that clearly illustrates the need for expediters in an hospital emergency room.

Emergency Room on Weekends: The Only Game in Town*

CAROLE W. SOSKIS

In problem-ridden urban areas, where the social and economic needs can barely be met by the available social, welfare, and governmental agencies, the hospital emergency room is a widely used but little-appreciated resource. Since 1954, the number of hospitals in the United States has increased by about 14 percent, while the number of visits to emergency rooms has grown more than 380 percent.† In certain areas, particularly ghettos, emergency rooms are providing up to 80 percent of the health care for the surrounding population.‡ The relative accessibility of hospitals and the difficulty of finding private medical care in poor neighborhoods are two of the factors responsible for this heavy use. In addition, like the police department—another heavily used and misunderstood resource—the emergency room is always open. Transportation is generally available through police and fire rescue services, and once there, the patient will usually be seen by some medical person. Furthermore, there will not be too much pressure for payment, since hospitals are anxious about potential liability and are becoming less and less likely to turn people away. Unfortunately, however, "the increased attention being paid to specialized techniques (defensive and otherwise) of emergency care has not been matched by an increasing emphasis on the psychosocial aspects of this care."§

*Reprinted with permission from *Health and Social Work* 5 (Aug. 1980): 37–43. Copyright 1980, National Association of Social Workers, Inc.
†John Collins Harvey, "The Emergency Medical Service Systems Act of 1973," *New England Journal of Medicine* 292 (1975): 529–530.
‡"The Potentials and Limitations of Emergency Services," editorial notes, *Hospitals* 47 (May 16, 1973): 57–66.
§Dorothy S. Lane and David Evans, "Study Measures Impact of Emergency Department Ombudsman,"*Hospitals* 52 (Feb. 1, 1978): 99.

During the work week, the emergency room may be one of several sources of assistance, depending on an individual's particular problem: on the weekend, however, as well as at night and on holidays, the choices are limited. It has been said that "when people experience problems that have built to crisis proportions or that involve antisocial behavior, they most often think of the local police department . . . as the first source of aid."* Yet for those whose problems have some kind of physical component, an even more likely source of help is the emergency room. On the weekends, when many people have nowhere else to turn, the emergency room is forced to be all things to all people, in other words, to function as a multipurpose social agency.

The thesis of this article, then, is that some emergency rooms, no matter how their functions are defined by medical and administrative staff, are seen by the community they serve as the only social agency available on weekends and during other off-hours. Consequently, a revised assessment is in order of the nonmedical services that patients expect and those the emergency room provides, and personnel with social work training, experience, and perspective are best equipped to do this. The emergency room offers both a unique challenge and an opportunity to apply social work's perspective and practice.

The source of the material in this article was the emergency room at Temple University Hospital, a large teaching hospital in a black ghetto of Philadelphia. It serves one of the poorest sections of the city, including the poorest ward. The area has poor housing and high rates of unemployment and crime. The catchment area includes several lower-class white neighborhoods and serves many elderly people, both black and white, who have been unable to leave the area. The emergency room logs over 46,000 visits a year and has consistently been the second busiest in Philadelphia. With the recent closing of the city hospital, it now often ranks first.†

The author was a social worker at this emergency room during the daytime hours on Saturday and Sunday from 1971 to 1973. The original function of the position was to avoid frequent emergency calls from the staff to the director and assistant director of the social work department during the weekend, particularly about disposition problems. This goal was met, but in addition the author defined and developed a number of other tasks for social workers, which will be discussed in the following sections. An understanding of these tasks may prove useful to those who practice in emergency rooms or who are responsibile for planning or administration in this area.

*Donald A. Woolf and Marvin Rudman, "A Police–Social Service Cooperative Program," *Social Work* 22 (1977): 62–63.
†Joseph Williamson, president, Delaware Valley Hospital Council, Philadelphia, Pa., personal communication, January 24, 1978.

Special Weekend Problems

The hospital's role as a community agency rather than a purely medical facility is most apparent on weekends. Other facilities are closed, and they make no provisions for crises that may occur during off-hours. Consequently, emergency rooms have a twofold problem: first, people arrive whose primary problems are not medical; and second, when the staff have seen and perhaps treated these people, they often have nowhere else to send them. In the winter, for instance, staff experience considerable discomfort about having to send patients without homes or heat back into the bitter cold.

In addition, the emergency room can barely function at times because of crowding, and it is often intolerable for both staff and patients. Sunday afternoon brings the working people who may not be able to or cannot seek care at any other time. The closing of their usual sources of support brings lonely people, often the elderly, who know that the way to get attention is to couch their complaints in medical terms. The reduced number of staff on weekends and the difficulty in obtaining consultants, who may be on call but not immediately available, make waiting times even longer and aggravate the crowding and people's frayed tempers.

The emergency room staff, besieged by a hord of minimally or moderately ill patients, who cannot or will not be seen during the work week, and burdened by the weekend load of fight and accident victims, have little time or tolerance for patients whose conditions cannot be readily defined as medical emergencies. "Crisis intervention," to the staff, means always being ready for the next stabbing victim or critically injured motorist. Other patients are expected to require a minimum of staff time and to present clear medical problems. These are considered legitimate demands on emergency room resources, as opposed to the vague, guilt-evoking, frustrating needs of the helpless and, in the eyes of the staff, the unattractive.* Since the techniques and expertise staff have available are of little use in the latter cases, they feel thwarted and angry. They project their anger onto these patients, who are seen as a threat to the routine order of the emergency room and are ejected as soon as possible.

The expectations and training of the emergency room staff are not well suited to patients who are alcoholic, drug-dependent, overdosed, emotionally disturbed, victimized, neglected, or abandoned. Thus, it is crucial that a social worker, who can recognize, evaluate, and cope with the multiplicity of social problems presented on weekends, be part of the staff of the emergency room. Although some large hospitals provide

*See James M. Mannon, "Defining and Treating 'Problem Patients' in a Hospital Emergency Room," *Medical Care* 14 (1976): 1004–1013. For a discussion of the physician's need to translate all problems into medical categories, see David G. Satin and Frederick J. Duhl, "Help?: The Hospital Emergency Unit as Community Physician," *Medical Care* 10 (1972): 248–260.

social services during the week, only a few have coverage on week
when the need is greatest. The social worker can be of greatest value
the hospital during this period, by saving the time of nurses and physicians, preventing unnecessary repeat visits, and diverting difficult and
morale-destroying patients. The latter function is particularly important
because by helping to see that morale does not sink below tolerable
levels, the worker is contributing to that particular team spirit that
develops in many setting during off-hours. The staff feel that they are a
small group helping to keep the world going while everyone else rests.
Such an attitude promotes cooperation and goodwill among the staff.

Problem Patients

As already indicated, particular kinds of patients tend to sap the energy
and morale of staff. Users of the emergency room generally tend to be
underprivileged, have many needs, and make much use of community
and social service resources.* Among these patients are disproportionate
numbers of nonwhites and new immigrants. These people tend to have
poor educations, minimal social ties, and a great many recent life stresses, especially psychosocial stresses. They often have large reservoirs of
background needs and problems that antedate the presenting illness.
These affect patients' ability to cope and their illness behavior (behavioral responses to symptoms and illness).† These difficult patients are just
the population with which social workers are most familiar, and social
workers are best equipped to help them. Following are the major categories of difficult patients who are heavily represented in the emergency
room on weekends.

Regulars are people with chronic and complex problems who appear
frequently in emergency rooms. They are often demanding and hostile,
and treating them is seen as frustrating and futile by the emergency room
staff. Some have only minor physical problems and suffer mostly from
depression and isolation. Mannon has pointed out that

> the ER [emergency room], in some respects, is similar to many public
> settings such as bars and restaurants, where a number of clientele frequent
> the setting on a regular basis. In commercial establishments a "regular
> clientele" is usually highly valued and sought out. However, in the ER the
> regular patients are neither valued nor welcomed.‡

Those with chronic physical problems that are not emergencies are seen
as unwelcome intruders. Thus, at the very time they are seeking relief,

*Satin and Duhl, "Help?"
†David G. Satin, "'Help': The Hospital Emergency Unit Patient and His Presenting
Picture," *Medical Care* 11 (1973): 328–337.
‡Mannon, "Problem Patients," p. 1011.

they find themselves having to justify their presence to their potential helpers.*

Disrupters are generally the emotionally disturbed and those with drug and alcohol problems, whose lack of response to treatment and disruptive behavior become threatening to the medical staff. Sometimes they are brought in by police, often after fights or accidents. At times they may be in a state of advanced physical and mental deterioration and are then looked upon resentfully as "dumps." Others come in as a result of suicidal or homicidal attempts, physical abuse, and violent reactions to recent life stresses, such as unemployment and marital problems.† They are evaluated, in some cases treated, and sent out as soon as possible, sometimes only to return within a few hours.

The elderly present special problems, even though many fall into one or both of the first two categories. They are never welcome in the emergency room. While some have true medical emergencies, others are merely frightened and confused by symptoms of the aging process, such as sleeplessness, loss of mobility and memory, aches and pains in bones and joints, malnutrition from low funds and lack of energy to plan meals, and vague, disturbing feelings of being unable to cope. Their problems in self-management are reflected in feelings of depression, anxiety, and loneliness.‡ The author has seen several elderly patients walk into the emergency room on a Sunday afternoon, carrying a suitcase, and announce they could not take care of themselves any longer and were ready to be placed. Concerned family or neighbors will sometimes insist that a patient in need of chronic care be admitted to the hospital, often at a point when exhaustion of emotional resources makes the family desperate for immediate action.

Social Work Tasks

As Bergman has noted:

To the social worker, the emergency room presents a tremendous variety of problems calling for many social work skills. Traditional social work roles, such as crisis intervention, discharge planning, and family counseling, assume greater importance in the context of an emergency room. The immediacy of the problem, the pressure in the emergency room to act

*Lane and Evans, "Emergency Department Ombudsman"; and Paul Errera and Mary C. Dye, "Emotional Steam Clouds Emergency Care," *Modern Hospital* 104 (Feb. 1965): 87–92.

†William Getz et al., "Paraprofessional Crisis Counseling in the Emergency Room," *Health and Social Work* 2 (May 1977): 57–73.

‡Ibid.

quickly to alleviate stress and to empty beds for more acutely ill patients, a
the need to move patients on to more appropriate settings require rapid an
innovative response on the part of the social worker.*

Flexibility is also called for, since the worker may be required to do
everything from quick family therapy to hunting for shoes to holding the
end of a stretcher. The following are the major social work functions
needed in the emergency room.

Monitoring the waiting room. This is not merely a public relations job,
although often it is the worker who apologizes for the wait and explains
the causes of delay. Such public relations activities are useful to the
hospital, comforting to some patients, and a relief to the medical staff.
More important, however, the worker must be visible and accessible, and
this can best be accomplished in the waiting room, where he or she can
keep an eye and ear open for problems and familiar faces. Monitoring
treatment rooms is also helpful. Case-finding is far more effectively done
in this way than by medical referral.

*Dealing with psychosocial issues that affect or interfere with medical
treatment.* Social workers also must teach the medical team the contribution of these issues to illness behavior, the relevance of community
resources, and the possible detrimental effects of environment on the
prescribed treatment.†

Promoting communication. Tasks in this area include helping patients
articulate their real problems when the general medical complaint is too
vague to be acceptable to screening personnel; translating medical terms,
instructions, and prognoses; communicating with families at home to
obtain more history, inform them of patients' whereabouts, and assess
the nature and extent of their interest and cooperation; obtaining translation services when necessary; and beginning a social work record for later
use.‡ The following case example illustrates the importance of promoting
communication with patients.

Ms. A, a young mother in the neighborhood, came in complaining of wrist
pain. Examination revealed gonococcal arthritis, with a need for immediate
admission and intensive treatment to save the use of the hand. She refused
admission and was referred to the social worker. The worker realized that
the woman had no idea she was in danger of losing the use of her hand. In
addition, Ms. A was resisting hospitalization because of worries about child

---

*Anne S. Bergman, "Emergency Room: A Role for Social Workers," *Health and Social
Work* 1 (Feb. 1976): 35. See also Margaret Jane Bennett, "Emergency Services: The Social
Worker's Role,"*Hospitals* 47 (May 16, 1973): 111, 114, and 118.

†Bergman, "Emergency Room."

‡Jules V. Coleman, "Psychiatric Studies of Patient Needs in Emergency Services of
General Hospitals," *Medical Care* 5 (1967): 255–259.

care and her new job. After explaining her condition to her, the worker discussed child care arrangements and ways of dealing with the employer and asked the staff to arrange for admission two days hence. Telephone support during the next two days helped Ms. A mobilize her resources and admit herself to the hospital.

Dealing with disposition problems and patients who need further non-medical or nonemergency medical services. The emergency room contact may be the patient's only chance for referral to another agency. The worker must recognize and make use of the opportunity to connect the patient with a more appropriate helping system, such as a visiting nurse service, family service agency, or welfare organization. Disposition problems may be solved by referral to a shelter or by an arrangement with family, but for some elderly or chronically ill patients, they may simply be insoluble. In any case, the worker must evaluate the patient's needs and try to find an appropriate referral, placement, or other source of help.

Providing concrete services. These include finding shelter, clothing, food, funds, and transportation and arranging for medication when nearby stores are closed on Sunday or will not accept Medicaid or other forms of medical assistance in payment. The following are examples of cases in which such services were provided:

> Mr. Z set himself on fire while smoking in bed, and lost everything he owned. Since his burns were not severe, he was discharged quickly from the emergency room, but he had no resources. The worker was able not only to provide food, clothes, and temporary shelter, but also to do supportive counseling that helped Mr. Z assess his financial and social resources and plan for the immediate future.

> Miss Q, an elderly woman living alone, had been looking for new housing. In the meantime her landlord turned off the electricity. After falling in the dark, she was brought to the emergency room and treated for minor injuries. The worker found sufficient food and candles for the weekend and provided telephone support. Early Monday morning, the worker began a successful effort to get the electricity turned back on.

Providing brief counseling and dealing with family problems and psychiatric issues. This area includes the important functions of alleviating the anxiety of patients and family and counseling them about emotional problems related to illness. In addition, the worker can assist with psychiatric screening and evaluation of patients whose emotional problems appear to be paramount.

At the same time, the worker must avoid—and help others to avoid—the stereotypical assumption that those who are emotionally ill or alcoholic cannot have simple medical problems. This problem arose in the following case:

Mr. X, an alcoholic known to the emergency room staff, was brought in by police because of loud, obstreperous, agitated behavior. He refused to be examined and broke several thermometers. When his blood pressure was finally obtained, it was dangerously high. The social worker sat with him for some time and managed to elicit some family and medical history. She then challenged the medical staff's conclusion that the man was drunk, pointing out his clean, neat appearance and his own assurances and those of his family (by telephone) that he had not had a drink for six months. The worker pleaded for a further evaluation, which revealed that Mr. X was suffering a hypertensive crisis. He was admitted briefly and did well.

Providing and promoting patient advocacy. Only the social worker of all the emergency room staff examines the hospital and its services somewhat objectively to see what may not be beneficial to the patient and looks outside the system for needed resources. Ombudsmen are used in busy emergency rooms to ensure patient satisfaction and education and to provide some relief for medical staff.* However, they cannot assess and support patients' needs in the same way as a social worker.

The advocacy function, however, is hardly free of conflict, as the following example illustrates:

On a Sunday afternoon in a hectic emergency room, an elderly woman is cleared medically and ordered sent home. In the physician's opinion, the patient does not need acute medical care. The hospital's policy is not to admit patients who do not need such care, because they use valuable beds and physicians' time, lower morale among nurses, and create disposition problems. After some investigation, the social worker believes that the woman is being returned to a dangerous and inadequate environment, when she is in need of a clean, safe, supportive setting where she can be cared for. The worker believes she would be far better off in the hospital than at home.

This is clearly a case in which the interests of the hospital and those of the patient are at odds. What is the worker to do? The Ad Hoc Committee of Advocacy of the National Association of Social Workers has stated that "It is . . . clear [in the Code of Ethics] . . . that the obligation to the client takes primacy over the obligation to the employer when the two interests compete with each other.† The new Code of Ethics, passed by the 1979 Delegate Assembly and implemented July 1, 1980, states, "The social worker's primary responsibility is to clients."‡

How far can social workers go in this situation? They can hunt frantically for resources, including friends and family; they can send the patient home, maintain telephone contact, and try to arrange for appropriate

*Lane and Evans, "Emergency Department Ombudsman."
†The Ad Hoc Committee on Advocacy, "The Social Worker as Advocate: Champion of Social Victims," *Social Work* 14 (April 1969): 18.
‡"The NASW Code of Ethics," *NASW News* 25 (Jan. 1980): 24–25.

services; they can attempt to persuade the physician to admit the patient; they can refuse to help get the patient home, so that admission may be the inevitable result. Whatever course is chosen—and it is likely to be all of them at various times—social workers are agents of conflict. They are also agents of help, since in even the worst situations they can usually manage some small intervention that may bring comfort to the patient and attention from other agencies during the week.

The patients that the emergency room staff do not want cannot be shunted off to clinics and agencies on the weekend, and they have only the social worker to advocate for them. Other staff may not pick up the nonmedical cues that tell of the patient's anger or desperation; for instance, they see the elderly person who walks in with a suitcase as comical instead of as someone trying to deal with failure and incapacity with as much dignity as possible.

Conclusion

Anyone who comes into an emergency room has, in his or her own eyes, a need for immediate attention and assistance. On Saturday and Sunday and other off-hours, the situation is exacerbated by the lack of other resources. Although the hospital may be the wrong place, or not the best place, it is usually the only place to get such help. Consequently, since emergency room visits are unlikely to decrease, hospitals with large emergency rooms should make provision for the needs that are expressed through weekend visits. To say that this is not the hospital's function is missing the point; although the emergency room cannot provide all the services desired, the visits will continue, may be frequently repeated, and may use physicians' valuable time. As one study of emergency room visitors concluded, the emergency room should

> be prepared to act as a major crisis intervention and screening agency for the broad range of problems brought to it. . . . [It] must be seen as part of the broad range of health and helping resources in the welfare community.*

The social worker is an indispensable member of the emergency room team as a result of his or her ability to recognize and screen both medically related and other problems; to separate acute from chronic problems; to supply support, information, and resources; and to arrange continued attention for those in need of it through knowledge of community services. Only the social worker is constantly thinking about what resources might be needed and where they might be available. It rarely occurs to medical staff to look beyond the presenting complaint or to

*Satin, "'Help': The Hospital Emergency Unit Patient," p. 258.

question the availability of resources; and when they must do so, they react to the patient by feeling negative and frustrated. By taking the pressure off physicians and nurses to deal with certain difficult patients, the social worker encourages a needed increase in tolerance, since medical staff can afford to be more pleasant to those whom they will soon refer elsewhere. The improvements in staff attitudes, morale, and efficiency that result from the social worker's contribution mean a higher quality of service for all patients in the emergency room.

———————

Authority: The preceding article graphically illustrates the need for expediting—for knowing how to get things done. Specifically, the author points to such tasks as case-finding, education of the medical team, the promotion of communication with patients and their families, and referral. Although substantive knowledge is required to carry out each of these tasks—for example, one needs to know how the medical team operates—a general knowledge of expediting is also needed. To carry out the above-mentioned tasks, clinicians must develop and exercise authority with patients, with medical and nonmedical staff, and with the staffs of outside agencies.

In an organizational context, *authority* is the legal right to tell someone what to do and to expect compliance with that order or request. By contrast, *power* is the ability to force someone to do something even against his or her will. Although the distinction is not always so clear in real-life agencies, most organizational expediting rests on the authority of the person initiating a request, suggestion, or command and on the acceptance of that authority by the recipient. In some agency situations, social workers clearly have the authority to expedite. In many, however, they do not. For example, a medical social worker would seldom be able to tell a public health nurse from another agency to coordinate her visits to a frail, elderly homebound client with her own visits, even if this coordination was important for the patient's well-being.

Basically, there are two types of organizational authority. *Formal authority* is derived from the position or status one occupies in the organization. The public health nurse's supervisor has formal authority over her. A supervisor has the right to request that workers coordinate their efforts with other workers. This right is supported by a structure of organizational rules and regulations and a system of sanctions and punishments for noncompliance. In fact, however, we generally assume that the authority of the supervisor is so well established that sanctions will not need to be applied. Thus, the supervisee is expected to accept the legitimacy of the supervisor's request and, ultimately, of his or her authority.

Functional authority derives from the competence or expertise demonstrated by a person occupying a particular agency position. It does not come with the position: it must be earned. If you do not have the formal authority to get something done, you must either get someone who has the right to delegate authority to delegate it to you, or you must develop the functional authority to get it done. Demonstrated competence in job performance is the best way to enhance your functional authority. If other staff members see that you are a competent practitioner who can be counted on in a crisis, who shows sound judgment, and so on, they are more likely to grant you functional authority. As a result, your ability to exercise influence in areas where you lack formal authority will increase.

In the example noted above, the social worker was unable to get her agency and the public health agency to formally coordinate their efforts. What she did, therefore, was schedule her monthly home visits to coincide with one of the nurse's visits. As her relationship with the public health nurse developed, and as the nurse began to appreciate what she was doing for the client, the nurse began calling every week to report on the client's condition. The functional authority of the clinician had affected the nurse's actions.

The reason functional authority is so very important is that it is often difficult to get formal authority delegated. Those who have it may guard it jealously. In addition, not all areas of decision making are or can be clearly defined and allocated to specific positions. In some instances lines of authority may overlap. Who is responsible for unruly clients—the guard or the social worker? In cases of vague or overlapping authority, clarifying the lines of authority makes expediting easier. If policy cannot be clarified, functional authority becomes crucial. Moreover, functional authority increases the influence of those who have formal authority. The demonstrably competent supervisor has more influence over his or her workers than the supervisor whose authority rests only on agency status.

Another important aspect of expediting is the relationship between responsibility and authority. They do not always go together. If one is given the responsibility to do something—to make all agency contacts with the welfare system, for example—then it is absolutely vital that one be delegated the authority to carry out the responsibility as well. Not to have the authority to speak for the agency and to ask others to do what is needed, when it is needed, is a situation guaranteed to produce failure.

For example, a worker at a family agency was asked by his director to develop an in-service training program on teenage suicide for the agency's whole staff and to invite the psychiatric staff of the nearby city hospital to attend. Although the dates were cleared with the director and a memo announcing the sessions was sent, on the first day no one from the agency's satellite office came: the satellite supervisors, assuming that the program was optional because the memo carried the worker's signature, would not permit anyone to attend. The second session was held several weeks later, and this time no one from the hospital attended. The secretary whom the social worker had asked to send out the invitation said, "I really wanted to help you out, but we were backlogged on dictation so I just didn't have time."

Responsibility and authority both can be delegated to some degree. That is, one can delegate responsibilities, but one cannot completely get rid of one's responsibility. If people are given the responsibility to do something and fail to carry it out, the person who gave them the authority or responsibility is not absolved. Because of this, and because many people verbally accept responsibility but do not follow through, effective expediting involves some system of follow-up. An expediter depends not on what people say, but on what they do.

Information: Another crucial element of effective expediting is organizational information. Although certain types of substantive information will be important in specific situations, in general the various facets of organizational functioning discussed in Chapter 1 will help the expediter determine what should be done in any particular situation. What is the relationship of the formal organization to the informal organization? What are the organization's goals? What priorities has the organization assigned to these goals? What are the strains in the formal organization? Where do they occur, and how do they play themselves out?

For example, a worker in a community mental health center raised with her supervisor the problem that two of her clients were having with the local day care center: whenever the children acted up at the center, its director called the mothers at work to come and take the children home or to stay with them at the center. This disrupted the working mothers' days, endangered their jobs, and made them extremely agitated.

This situation could be solved by a simple phone call, or by a meeting of the staffs of both agencies to share problems and concerns, or by organizing the parents at the day care center to mount a protest to the center's board. Information about the center's operation, however—its stresses and strains—was required before anything could be done or planned.

Bargaining for Resources: In expediting some task, one often needs some resource over which one does not have control—an emergency allotment from the welfare department, or assistance from a staff person from another department. If one cannot get the authority to command these resources delegated to one and one doesn't have functional authority, then to expedite one must in essence *bargain* for the resources.

George Homans conceptualized all social behavior as a form of exchange.* In this view, every interaction can be expressed as an equation in which somebody gives something in order to get something. These exchanges may occur between individuals, groups, or entire organizations.

If one must bargain to get needed resources, the question is what the partner in the bargain needs or wants. The dimensions of the bargain are often not stated explicitly before the process begins, but the rewards that others seek may be such tangible things as money and information or such intangible things as prestige, social standing, and approval. Sometimes what is exchanged is not so much a reward as a lessening of costs—for example, making someone's job easier or covering up someone's mistakes. Sometimes all that is exchanged is respect. When one lets other people know that one is aware of their hard work, for example, they may assist one with the necessary resources even when they do not have to. Whatever the terms, a good expediter is an expert bargainer.

In the case of the day care center described the social worker wanted to call the center and complain. Her supervisor, however, advised calling the director and requesting a case conference so that the day care center staff could share their knowledge and perspective. The supervisor suggested that instead of complaining, the worker might engage them in exchanging perspectives and exploring the effects of the current policy on the families and the children. The worker would at least learn more about the effects of the disruptive children on the day care center, and at best a solution satisfactory to both parties might be found on the basis of shared values—in essence, a good bargain.

Techniques: There are a variety of other techniques an expediter needs in addition to bargaining. As indicated earlier, one needs to know about the organization and its functioning, and one has to be skilled in getting the authority required to carry out one's responsibilities. Yet perhaps the basic skill for an expediter is the ability to plan how to get things done. Some things can be done by picking up a telephone; some will require a committee meeting; and some require months of steady and patient work based on clear strategy and effective tactics.

In thinking about something that needs to be done, one must ask several questions. Who can do it best? What must be the sequence of actions taken? What must be done to ensure that they actually do it? Involved in all these concerns are the issues of timing and resources: what should be done first, second, third, and how does one get the resources one needs, whether they are tangible or intangible.

Whether they decide to proceed through informal contacts or to go formally to the board of directors, expediters must learn to pyramid their

*George Homans, "Social Behavior as Exchange," *American Journal of Sociology* 63 (1958): 597–606.

resources. *Pyramiding* is the art of starting with very little and ending up with a great deal of influence. A medical social worker who became an excellent pyramider started by positioning herself at the coffee urn where the doctors gathered every morning for a coffee break. Gradually she was included in their conversations. She discovered what their work complaints were and tried to assist them in dealing with these problems, many of which were in fact of no direct concern to a social worker. The more helpful she was, the more she had to exchange and the more functional authority she enjoyed. Ultimately, she was the most powerful social worker, or at least the most influential one, with the medical staff. She could achieve things that it was even difficult for the head of her department to achieve.

The virtue of pyramiding is that it enables the expediter to see beyond any one particular problem—to see the interconnection of activities in one sphere with those in another one. What is done in March in one context can bear fruit in December in another.

Another important skill for the organizational expediter is the ability to work in and through *committees*. In many organizations a great many decisions are made in committees. The effective expediter must know if and when to bring an issue to a committee, when to set up a new committee, whom to ask to join one, how it should be structured, who should lead it, and so on. These issues will be dealt with at length in Chapter 4, our discussion of the role of colleague. Suffice it to say here that the effective expediter is an effective committee participant.

Resistance or Lack of Cooperation: The ultimate test of the expediter is the ability to get something done when other people are not interested in cooperating. This problem separates those who know how to expedite from those who do not. The ineffective expediter often makes appeals to certain vague and general values, such as the client's well-being, in an effort to get things done—"I need this done because it's obviously going to help the client." Unfortunately, this appeal seldom works. It does not work because other workers have conflicting priorities or other clients in need of the same scarce resources. Although we call these appeals attempts at coordination, they are best understood as efforts to control others or their resources. And people resist being controlled.

Alvin Zander describes resistance as behavior intended to protect an individual from the effects of real or imagined change. He points out that when a therapist works with a client, resistance is to be expected. Likewise, one should expect resistance when one expedites. It should be viewed as the rule rather than the exception.*

Resistance takes many forms. The expediter might face open or

*Alvin Zander, "Resistance to Change," in Harry Schatz, ed., *Social Work Administration: A Resource Book* (New York: Council on Social Work Education, 1970), pp. 253–257.

oblique hostility. Or, despite verbal agreement, resistance may take a more passive-aggressive form, such as sloppiness or forgetfulness. For example, the psychiatric consultant for a group home is asked to medicate a child who the staff feels is hyperactive and cannot be retained in the residence unless he calms down. The consultant says that, indeed, they *could* medicate the child, but he keeps forgetting to bring a prescription pad on his monthly visits.

The first step in dealing with resistance is understanding the reasons for it. Probably one of the major causes of resistance to an expediter's efforts lies in the area of values. Values and attitudes have a great effect on what workers believe is right, ethical, and important; they provide the standards and norms by which staff members guide their day-to-day behavior. They exert a powerful influence on their willingness to work with different kinds of people, and they largely determine which ideas, principles, and concepts staff people can accept, assimilate, remember, and transmit without distortion.*

Other causes might also inhibit one's ability to expedite: "The same resistant behavior, for example, may indicate that one person feels he has lost prestige by the change, to another it may mean that he has lost power over an area of influence which he formerly controlled; and to still another it may mean that he fears that his friends will think less well of him."†

The following vignette illustrates resistance based on both a clash of values and a perceived loss of influence over a professional area of concern. A school social worker decides that the best way to handle a particularly difficult learning-disabled child is to employ a behaviorist approach implementing a token economy. She discusses this with the child and begins the process of giving him scented stickers for restrained behavior in her activity group. The child's classroom teacher says that she will let the social worker know each afternoon and morning whether the child is acting more appropriately in class so that he can be rewarded. After two weeks the child asks the worker why he gets stickers no matter what he does. After exploration it becomes clear that the teacher has not been giving accurate reports of the child's behavior. When asked about this, she says, "You never asked me what I thought—these token things are just a way to manipulate kids, not help them."

Expediting in the face of resistance always requires a strategy. Strategies can be classified as rational, collaborative (or bargaining), or adversarial. A *rational strategy* depends on both parties' agreeing that the goal is important but that the means are open to question. If there is that kind of agreement, pointing out the facts and showing specifically how a

---

*Robert McMurry, "Conflicts in Human Values," in Schatz, *Social Work Administration: A Resource Book*, p. 266.
†Zander, "Resistance to Change," p. 256.

certain course of action will help a client may facilitate matters. Initial resistance may be simply the result of a misunderstanding or a confusion in communication.

When there is disagreement over specific goals but a shared commitment to overall objectives, a *collaborative strategy* may be employed. This usually involves bargaining for what is desired. The essential elements of bargaining were discussed earlier. When bargaining does not work and there is real disagreement about how overall objectives will be affected by any specific action, an *adversarial strategy* may have to be used. Whereas bargaining is characterized by a trade-off, an adversarial strategy is characterized by conflict and threats. Typical threats might involve invoking a higher authority, public exposure, loss of employment, and the like. These will be discussed in greater detail in our section on advocacy, Chapter 5. Whatever strategy is chosen, however, one must be sure that one has the resources and determination to carry it through. Failure to do so diminishes functional authority and the possibilities of future expediting.

In the following article Julie Abramson describes how an effective expediter goes about making referrals.

Six Steps to Effective Referrals

JULIE ABRAMSON

A majority of social work clients require services beyond those provided by the initial agency contact, usually from a governmental bureaucracy or community resource. Unfortunately, social workers have often had an ambivalent attitude toward this aspect of the job, with a resulting tendency to create a dichotomy between "concrete" and "counseling" services and accord higher status to the latter.*

This tendency has effectively brought about a devaluation of the skills involved in the provision of services. In addition, such dichotomizing fragments one's understanding of the client, making it more difficult for clinical social workers to assess and work with individuals in their social context.

The skills needed to make more effective agency referrals are enumerated in this paper, along with the steps involved in becoming an effective expediter, facilitator, or advocate on behalf of the individual client. The role of the individual worker in this process is the focus, but certain steps that agencies should take will also be identified.

*Kay Davidson, "Evolving Social Work Roles in Health Care: The Case of Discharge Planning," *Social Work in Health Care* 4 (1978): 46.

Step One: Data Gathering and Assessment

Good clinical social work skills are essential in making referrals. One cannot persuade another agency to provide a service unless the request is based on a sound process of data collection and assessment.

All relevant facts documenting the need for a service must be obtained and framed by the social worker's assessment of the client's unique character, situation, capacity, and limitations as they apply to the problem being addressed.

Agency and worker credibility can suffer severely if the assessment process has been inadequate. If another agency or department is already overburdened,* it tends to find reasons to avoid further overextension. What better excuse for assigning a case low priority than the absence of key data from the referring social worker? Future referrals are likely to be obstructed as well if the referral agency perceives the information and assessment provided by a referring worker as unreliable. The social worker who identifies making referrals as a routine mechanical process is particularly vulnerable to this hazard.

For example, a referral for "meals on wheels" that does not explore adequately the degree of neighbor involvement or the food habits of the client can end in disappointment for both client and agency. The client may not get the necessary attention, and the referral agency is going to be skeptical of future requests because the referral was not framed in terms of the client's situation.

Step Two: Developing Knowledge of the Referral Agency

In order to expedite a request for service effectively, the social worker must understand the system from which the service is being requested.† This crucial step is often overlooked, as any given staff member is usually interacting with a large number of social agencies, and the very notion of comprehending their different systems and priorities can be overwhelming. There are usually a few core agencies, however, and learning their procedures can enormously enhance a worker's effectiveness in obtaining client services. The practitioner must decide which agencies are most relevant for his or her work. Mastering the procedures and regulations of these agencies can be facilitated by visits to them or by asking key agency personnel for an orientation to the processing of a referral.

*For practical techniques for studying organizations, see Marvin Weisbord, ed., *Organizational Diagnosis* (Reading, Mass.: Addison-Wesley, 1980).

†For a discussion of interagency stances, "domain consensus," and boundary control, see James Greenley and Stuart Kirk, "Organizational Characteristics," in Herman Resnick and Rino Patti, Eds., *Change from Within* (Philadelphia: Temple University Press, 1980), pp. 57–72.

In the case of certain central and frequently overburdened agencies, such as Medicaid or welfare offices, copies of the agencies' own regulations and procedures should be obtained and consulted when making referrals. Many local welfare rights groups and community legal services programs have developed their own summaries of these regulations in order to facilitate advocacy. These can be extremely useful to social work staff members.

The referring worker must often know the referral agency's regulations better than its own staff, especially in certain key areas where significant client abuse may take place or where there is room for worker discretion in granting a service request. Take, for example, the following scenario, which takes place frequently in New York State:

> Mrs. D, a thirty-five-year-old woman with two children, loses her garment center job and makes application for public assistance at the local Department of Welfare office. In the initial interview with the welfare worker, she is asked if she sees a doctor for any condition. She notes that she goes to the local hospital's out-patient clinic, where she is treated for hypertension. It should seem obvious that she is able to work and is not disabled by this condition, given that she has been working up to the point of application. However, the welfare worker tells her to go to the hospital to get a letter from the doctor about her condition.
>
> Mrs. D assumes from the tone of the discussion that she will not get help unless the doctor says that she cannot work. She therefore goes to see her doctor to request a letter stating that she is disabled. The doctor is annoyed and frustrated by the request, as he feels that Mrs. D's hypertension is well controlled and therefore not disabling. He does want to help Mrs D, however, so he refers her to the clinic social worker. Ms. M, the clinician, has handled similar situations before and is well acquainted with welfare department regulations. She explains to the physician and to the patient that in fact the regulations state that eligibility for public assistance rests on the ability to prove need, not disability. In the presence of the patient, she calls the welfare worker and reviews this regulation with him.
>
> He still requests the letter because "after all, Mrs. D is seeing the doctor." Ms. M notes that the doctor will be glad to write a letter saying that the patient is not disabled, but that such a document seems beside the point. She then indicates that she would like to speak with his supervisor.
>
> The supervisor and Ms. M have had similar discussions in the past, and she comments on this as she opens the conversation, noting the help received with these matters previously. She describes the situation and asks the supervisor to waive the letter in this case. She also promises that she will help Mrs. D obtain the necessary documents to prove her need for assistance. The supervisor agrees, and the social worker and the patient then direct their efforts toward gathering the necessary financial data.

Because of her knowledge of the welfare regulations, the social worker in this case is on firm ground when she questions the welfare worker's request. As a result, she is able to redirect her energy and that of her client into activity that will facilitate the application, rather than assisting in the dubious process of persuading a reluctant doctor to document a nonexistent disability.

The other point highlighted in this case history is that the worker must understand the implications of her request for the referral system—that is, the parameters within which the system operates and within which there is room for discretion.* For example, she understands that the medical letter was discretionary but that more rigid standards would apply to financial data, so that Mrs. D will not be accepted without showing past pay stubs. Therefore, she could "push the system" in one area but not the other. Directors may want to assign social workers who have developed a depth of knowledge and skills at dealing with specific agency systems to function as consultants to other staff members when problems arise with them.

Step Three: Identification of Mutual Concerns and Goals

The referring social worker must communicate to the referral agency worker the assumption that the referral agency will want to cooperate and be responsive to the request for help. Effort must be made to *enlist* the other worker on behalf of the client—to encourage him or her to become identified with the referring worker in a common effort to help the client. This is a conscious process that can be facilitated by (1) calling on past positive experiences (as did Ms. M in the case cited above); (2) presenting the problem as a challenge, but one that rational, committed people can resolve; or (3) through evoking pride and compassion according to the personality of the particular worker—"Aren't you the Mr. Smith who was so helpful to me last year on the Michaels case? Yes, I'm sure it was you. Well, this time it's an even tougher problem, but you did get me through that one, so how about giving this one the same kind of try?"

Whatever technique is used, the referring worker is trying to set up an alliance with the agency worker that pits the two of them against the strictures and red tape of the bureaucracy. The goal is to make the worker more flexible and more willing to bend the rules in the client's interest. There is usually much more latitude in regulations than is presented initially, especially by front line staff.

Step Four: Going Up the Ladder

In most agencies, especially public ones, the complexity of regulations is such that many line staff people have not adequately mastered them. If

---

*For a discussion of line worker discretionary power, see Michael Lipsky, *Street Level Bureaucracy* (New York: Russell Sage Foundation, 1980).

the referring worker receives a response to a request for service that does not seem logical, although the line worker in the referral agency insists that it is correct, it is important to verify this procedure with someone at the next level of responsibility. The responses often tend to be less arbitrary in the higher echelons of an agency.

It is important to know at what point to move to the next level.* Many workers go too many rounds with the same person when the effort is clearly stalled. A general rule of thumb is: do not call on the same person more than twice without getting results, especially if his or her recalcitrance is value-centered—for example, "Those loafers don't deserve this."

Depending on the complexity of the problem, the next move should be a call to the supervisor of the person with whom one is dealing, or the director's office, or even a local politician. One's goal now is to be referred from the top down. When the problem warrants it, working from the top down carries much more weight. To illustrate this point, we can draw on another example:

A social worker in a neighborhood antipoverty program was told by several community residents about a local "bag lady," whose circumstances were reported to be deteriorating with the onset of cold weather and who was requesting help in getting public assistance and housing. After interviewing the woman, Mrs. G, the worker determined that the usual documentation required by the welfare department proving identity and "past financial management" would be extremely difficult to come by in this case. The worker anticipated enormous obstacles in getting this client's application accepted for public assistance if the usual rules were enforced.

Mrs. G had worked many years before as a nurse, so the worker accompanied her to the local Social Security office to attempt to obtain her Social Security number. She also wrote away for a copy of Mrs. G's birth certificate. Only after these efforts were made did she send Mrs. G to the local welfare office to begin the process of applying for assistance.

As expected, Mrs. G was asked to produce a variety of documents proving past management. As she had had no "formal" relationship with any government agency, bank, or even landlord for several years, it seemed impossible for her to meet the welfare requirements.

The social worker called the welfare worker and attempted to communicate the seriousness of Mrs. G's situation but was met with a repetition of the same request for unobtainable documents. The worker expressed sympathy with agency procedures and noted her own efforts to faciliate these by writing for the Social Security number and birth certificate. The welfare worker said to call back when those arrived.

The social worker felt that Mrs. G's condition made a wait of several weeks intolerable. She called the director of the welfare center and put the problem before her, indicating that this case called for unusual measures and

*For a discussion of how to achieve goals without ruining relationships, see Gene Hooyman, "Team Building in the Human Services," in Beulah Roberts Compton and Burt Galloway, eds., *Social Work Processes* (Homewood, Ill.: Dorsey Press, 1973), pp. 465–478.

flexibility, as the client could not meet the usual criteria for eligibility and yet was clearly in need.

The social worker offered to obtain written statements from community residents regarding Mrs. G's tenure on the local streets as a substitute form of documentation. She also communicated to the director her awareness of a special emergency procedure through which temporary assistance could be granted while investigation of eligibility was continuing. She also reminded the director of the recent highly publicized death of another bag lady who was awaiting assistance.

The director expressed her sympathy for the client and acknowledged the difficulty of fitting such individuals into a bureaucratic system. She agreed to speak with the worker and suggest the use of the emergency procedure. The social worker and the client were encouraged, and the client agreed to return to the center again.

However, the social worker felt that some additional pressure was needed to ensure collaboration from the welfare department. She called a special assistant to the mayor whom she knew of from newspaper articles about the incident mentioned above. She also requested that two of the local residents who had been most concerned about Mrs. G do the same. The mayor's assistant agreed to call the center director about the case as well. Mrs. G did get temporary assistance on her next visit to the center.

Step Five: Location of Key Resource People

After several experiences with a particular agency, it is crucial to identify one or more key staff people to whom one can turn for troubleshooting intervention or simply for information when the need arises. Their identification can be based either on the positive nature of past interactions or on their positions in the referral agency hierarchy.

The referring social worker should explicitly ask to be allowed to call on these people for expert knowledge when he or she comes up against obstacles. There should be a real attempt to establish a significant bond by face-to-face contact, feedback regarding common cases—the successful ones as well as the problems—status acknowledgment and appreciation, and, most important, an expressed willingness on the part of the referring social worker to function reciprocally as a liaison and troubleshooter for the referral agency.

The offer of reciprocity is crucial in that it acknowledges that the referral agency is not the only one with problems and puts the relationship on a more equal footing. To preserve credibility, of course, the social worker must respond helpfully if called on.

Step Six: Development of Formal and Informal Accountability Mechanisms

The index of a successful referral is that the client gets the service he or she needs. In addition to their own follow-up efforts, clinicians can encourage a variety of forms of interagency contact to promote accountability.

The interagency case conference often serves as a significant source of interagency bonding and identification of common interests. Joint staff meetings can be set up around issues of common concern, either for administrative resolution or for staff development. A newsletter or another system of information sharing can be developed. Last but not least, semisocial occasions can be set up to achieve the same purpose: interagency lunches, teas, or receptions or, less formally, occasional lunches with a few staff people from a key agency.

An imaginative staff member can think of many other possibilities. The essential purpose of all such activities is to create a climate in which the staff and administration of the referral agency feel psychologically allied with the staff and the mission of the referring agency and therefore facilitate a referring worker's interest in ensuring that clients get the service that they need.*

Practice Analogues

Earlier in this section we emphasized the contribution that organizational expediting makes to clinical social work practice. Clinical skills can also contribute to effective expediting. If one is going to determine the reasons for resistance, for example, observation skills and the ability to hear the hidden content of messages are extremely important. If one is going to expedite through informal contacts, the ability to form and maintain relationships becomes crucial. These are certainly part of the skill repertoire of any clinician.

There are differences, though, between a work relationship and a therapeutic relationship. Although the element of mutual trust is common to both, the therapeutic relationship requires a deeper exchange of feelings and concerns. The work relationship functions on a more instrumental basis: its purpose is to get certain things done, and emotional exchanges are secondary. In a therapeutic relationship, by contrast, the emphasis is on the expressive or emotional exchange. Even when a therapist uses the relationship to direct a client, the ultimate aim is to get the client to do things for himself or herself, rather than to attain a specific instrumental task.

Expediters often use skills similar to those used in crisis intervention. In crisis intervention the goal is to help clients overcome the trauma of dealing with their needs relative to the precipitating crisis. Such programs as victim services and bereavement counseling utilize crisis theory. In

*For a discussion of a problem-solving model of accountability, see Harold H. Weissman, "Accountability and Pseudo-Accountability: A Non-Linear Approach," *Social Service Review* 57 (1983): 323–336.

these situations, the treatment is generally short-term, the therapist works from a fairly clear view of the progression of traumatic events—the stages of feeling that a person who has suffered a loss goes through, or the emotional statements and needs that most people have who have suffered a certain kind of trauma express. The therapist tries to build immediately on the client's strengths rather than concerning himself or herself with issues of transference and long-term relationships.

There is also a progression in expediting interactions, and the expediter can anticipate typical problems. The expediter has to know first of all if his or her request has been understood and, second, if the person to whom the request has been made has the resources, authority, and skill, to comply with it. Third, motives for compliance or resistance have to be understood and dealt with. And, last, a means of follow-up or account-ability has to be instituted.

All of this takes time. If one's model for expediting is "I call you on the phone and tell you what the client needs, and you do it because you're concerned about clients," more often than not, in nonroutine situations, failure will be the result. People who are asked to do something have to be given an opportunity to express their feelings and questions about the request. They have to explain, for example, what additional help they may need and what conflicts fulfilling the request might cause with their superiors.

Managing the feelings aroused by the request is also important. The clinical skills of support, respect, concern, and collaborative problem solving all come into play here. It is important that worker self-esteem not be lowered, that self-directedness or autonomy not be threatened, and that competence be supported—all clinical notions equally applicable to expediting.

Finally, if one gets a service for a client with assistance from people in other departments or agencies, these people need to be told that they have in fact achieved something. Workers need recognition of what they have done, as clients do when they have worked through a problem.

Attitudes, Values, and Skills

What values and attitudes contribute to success in organizational expediting? An expediter is a take-charge person. A "can-do" attitude is required—the feeling that one can achieve what one wants to achieve. This feeling involves much more than simply self-exhortation or positive thinking.

Few people are willing or able to pay close attention to a problem over a long period of time, and there are great vacuums in organizational life that expediters can manipulate. These vacuums develop as people turn their attention from one case or issue to other things. An expediter who is willing to stick with an issue can garner fantastic amounts of influence.

Another can-do requisite is, as we have observed, the knowledge that there is a system—that events are connected. On a very simple level, the more people see one as someone who can do things, the more one is able to do things. The expediter consciously allows others to see that he or she can expedite. This is not "blowing one's own horn" or self-aggrandizing. It is merely a way of developing the influence one needs to get something done. If, in the course of this process, people come to view you as someone who should be promoted, so be it.

Perhaps the major attitudinal obstacle to effective expediting is an exclusive reliance on clear communication and explanation of client need, when differing values and priorities may in fact be at the core of the problem. Just because an organization's stated goal is client service does not mean that it always will or can function in the best interests of any particular client. Assuming that it can or will do so is naive. Railing about its not doing so is ineffective. Ignoring it produces burnout. In such circumstances, expediting skills are likely to be most effective.

A final attitudinal issue relates to a fact of life in many jobs. Clinicians may find that their planned activities are constantly being interrupted by a series of unexpected but usually predictable client crises. Some workers tend to resent this aspect of their work, feeling that they are being cheated out of a sense of task completion. This is an understandable feeling but a dysfunctional one.

These crises should not be seen as interruptions to the job at hand, but as an essential part of the primary professional task. Keeping a log of exactly how time is spent for a typical week or two can clarify the extent of the problem. Analyzing the actions noted in the log according to whether they are responsive to the demands of others or under the control of the worker, or whether they are routine and repetitive or exceptional, can at least prevent some stress by providing the data upon which to base a consideration of ways to handle these issues.*

Additional Readings

Edson, Gene. "How to Survive on a Committee," *Social Work* 22 (1977): 224–226.

Jay, Antony. "How To Run A Meeting," in Fred M. Cox et al., eds., *Tactics and Techniques of Community Practice*, pp. 255–269. Itasca, Ill.: Peacock, 1977.

McMurry, Robert N. "Conflicts in Human Values," in Harry Schatz, ed., *Social Work Administration: A Resource Book*, pp. 264–278. New York: Council on Social Work Education, 1970.

Zander, Alvin. "Resistance to Change," in Harry Schatz, ed., *Social Work Administration: A Resource Book*, pp. 253–257. New York: Council on Social Work Education, 1970.

*Julie Abramson, personal communication.

CHAPTER 3

CASE MANAGER

What social workers are called upon to do in working with clients has slowly evolved over the decades. This evolution has not been marked by sharp divisions or abrupt reversals. Rather, as the field has responded to changing societal conditions, techniques have been altered, added onto, and re-emphasized. The case manager role is one such response to the complex service system that now exists in many fields of practice.

The following case summary illustrates how practice today can differ from the one-client/one-worker model that predominated in the past.

A custodian of a neighborhood tenement reported that one of the tenants spent nearly all her days crying, locked in her apartment. Upon investigation it was realized that . . . a Vietnam refugee with four children, aged 6 to 14, was the person reported about. This woman had lost her husband and youngest son in Vietnam. She had no relative or friend in this country and did not speak English. Her small apartment was completely bare except for two beds. The allotment she received from public assistance was not sufficient to buy furniture or clothing and no special allowance had been provided for these purposes. The situation was potentially dangerous— all the family possessed was warm weather clothing and winter was approaching.

The children, because of their home situation and inability to communicate, had problems in school. The fact that the family had been affluent in Vietnam compounded the difficulties that they were experiencing. The mother felt that she might be on the verge of a breakdown. Five major problem areas were isolated:

1. Financial—more money required for family's basic needs
2. Socialization—human contact needed particularly by the mother
3. Language—need by all family members to learn English
4. Health—children's teeth particularly in need of work
5. Housing—need for a larger apartment.

A staff worker monitored the provision of services and participation of the client. The following services have been provided to the family as of this date:

1. International Rescue Committee supplied $600 for furniture, $275 for winter clothing and $80 for a sewing machine.

2. A neighbor agreed to help the mother shop and along with the worker provided some of the human contact that was needed.
3. The mother and children were enrolled in special English classes provided by the Board of Education and Immigration services.
4. Governeur Hospital gave all members of the family physical checkups and provided the dental work required by the children.
5. A local agency contracted to work with the family in finding more appropriate housing.*

It is obvious that this woman could not be helped by merely providing emotional insight. Five or six organizations, besides the focal agency that took on her case, had to provide services. Some person had to see to it that all the needed services were arranged for, that they were actually provided, and that they were sufficient to help this woman provide for herself and her family. The role this type of worker plays is the case manager role.

Overview

As is true of any relatively new role, this one is performed in a number of different ways. Some case managers function as generalist social workers, rather as the old family doctor did. The generalist is responsible for providing psychological counseling and any other services available in his or her own agency and, in addition, for securing specialized services from other agencies and other sources and coordinating them in the best interest of the client. The generalist focuses on coordination and meeting client needs. He or she carries diagnostic, service delivery, and coordinating responsibilities.

Robert Ryan and others have suggested a different model of case management that splits the diagnostic and service roles from the managerial one.† This model deviates from the traditional one-worker, one-supervisor concept. Accountability is managerial; that is, the case manager is responsible for ensuring that service is provided to a client by others. The existing lines of professional accountability and supervision remain with the unit to which the program specialist is permanently assigned. In other contexts this is called "matrix management." The matrix permits various types of programs—for example, homemaker services, legal services, child welfare, mental health—to maintain their functional autonomy, leaving intact the usual lines of responsibility while permitting individual workers from these programs to come together on an ad hoc basis with respect to a given client whenever the case manager

*Lower East Side Family Union, case record, 1977.

†Robert Ryan, "Case Manager Function in the Delivery of Social Services," in Bernard Ross and S. K. Khinduka, eds., Social Work Practice (Washington, D.C.: National Association of Social Workers, 1976), pp. 229–239.

calls them together. This conception focuses on the managerial aspects of the case manager's role, rather than the diagnostic and therapeutic ones.

Tasks: Whatever the theoretical merits of these different analyses of the case manager's role, it is unlikely that it can be performed satisfactorily unless the case manager has both managerial and therapeutic skills. In the article that follows, Anne Vandeberg Bertsche and Charles Horejsi describe in considerable detail the skills and abilities required by case managers.

Coordination of Client Services*

ANNE VANDEBERG BERTSCHE AND CHARLES R. HOREJSI

• • •

Underpinnings

Certain concepts drawn from social systems theory and general systems theory are useful in teaching the case coordination process. Essentially, case coordination is what Hearn describes as "boundary work," or intervention at the interface of systems.† The social worker must understand system boundaries, know the formal and informal channels that permit access to those systems, and understand the many variables of ideology, procedure, policy, and protocol that affect how one system interacts with another.

The conceptualization of client system, target system, action system, and change agent system developed by Pincus and Minahan can be used to explain certain aspects of case coordination, especially the establishment of a working group. For example, the action system consists of "several people who may not at any one time be engaged in direct interaction with one another but whom the worker will coordinate and work with to change a target on behalf of a client."‡ In the process of forming an action system to develop and implement an individual program plan, each party becomes a subsystem. Then, like a symphony conductor, the case coordinator orchestrates and attempts to influence the behavior of each subsystem so that it performs as expected by all other subsystems and especially by the client.

*Excerpted with permission from *Social Work* 25 (1980): 94–98. Copyright 1980, National Association of Social Workers, Inc.

†Gordon Hearn, "Progress toward an Holistic Conception of Social Work," in Gordon Hearn, ed., *The General Systems Approach: Contributions toward an Holistic Conception of Social Work* (New York: Council on Social Work Education, 1969).

‡Allen Pincus and Anne Minahan, *Social Work Practice: Model and Method* (Itasca, Ill.: Peacock, 1973), p. 62.

In general systems theory, the concept of entropy is used to describe the natural tendency of a system to run down or become disorganized. Entropy exists within all human groups and organizations, including the action system designed to facilitate service delivery to a client. Unless the case coordinator works to counter the natural tendency toward disorganization, the service delivery will break down, and individual professionals and agencies will digress from the original plan and intentions. Basically, the case coordinator uses information to counteract entropy. The flow of information is managed in a way that everyone is kept up to date on the actions of others, all activities are goal-oriented, and digressions are redirected toward the overall intervention plan. It is clear that the written plan is a tool that keeps everyone on the same track.

An understanding of basic behavioral theory is essential to case coordination. It provides, in particular, the orientation needed to develop precise and measurable statements of goals.* In addition, the creative case coordinator applies concepts of reinforcement to the complexities of keeping everyone on task and maintaining the motivation of participants to coordinate their activities. Because there are many barriers to coordination, the case coordinator must find ways of rewarding cooperative behavior.

The factors that make coordination difficult are almost too numerous to mention. The identification of a few, however, will provide added insight into the knowledge and skills needed by a successful case coordinator. Differences among professional ideologies are the source of many interagency and interprofessional conflicts. Thus, the coordinator must be able to work cooperatively with diverse professional groups with conflicting ideas and ideals.

The case coordinator must have a grasp of the human service dynamics in the community. The fallout of previous conflicts and skirmishes among agencies and professional groups and between individual service providers must be anticipated and counteracted with diplomacy. Personality conflicts must be managed or mediated so that they do not distort or disrupt service delivery.

Effective coordination is time consuming, and ways must be found to conserve valuable time. The coordinator must be creative in finding methods of reinforcing the cooperative behaviors of others. For example, the coordinator must demonstrate that the time invested is well spent and necessary, or professionals and agencies will gradually lose interest. This requires documentation that the level of client progress and service delivery achieved through coordination would be impossible without the planned interprofessional and interagency action. Praise, individual rec-

---

*See, for example, Julie Vargas, *Writing Worthwhile Behavioral Objectives* (New York: Harper & Row, 1972); Peter Pipe, *Objectives: Tools for Change* (Belmont, Cal.: Fearon, 1975); Robert Mager and Peter Pipe, *Analyzing Performance Problems* (Belmont, Cal.: Fearon, 1973); and Robert Mager, *Goal Analysis* (Belmont, Cal.: Fearon, 1972).

ognition before members of the action system, and letters of appreciation sent to an agency director are just a few of the ways a case coordinator can reward people for their participation in the otherwise thankless and time-consuming job of case coordination.

Closely related to the issue of time is the question of funding. In staff time alone, case coordination is an expensive activity. Because case coordination is not a clearly defined or recognized service, it may be difficult to justify the staff time spent in group discussion, preparing a written plan, and other such activities. There is also an obvious problem associated with requesting private practitioners to participate in a time-consuming activity. Medicaid, for example, does not adequately cover this activity. The coordinator must look for ways to provide nonfinancial incentives for those who cannot be paid for time spent in coordination activities.

Basic Tasks

As a result of an intensive group discussion with several successful case coordinators, the authors identified thirteen basic tasks of the case coordinator:

1. complete the initial interviews with the client and his or her family to assess the client's eligibility for services;

2. gather relevant and useful data from the client, family, other agencies, and so on to formulate a psychosocial assessment of the client and his or her family;

3. assemble and guide group discussions and decision-making sessions among relevant professionals and program representatives, the client and his or her family, and significant others to formulate goals and design an integrated intervention plan;

4. monitor adherence to the plan and manage the flow of accurate information within the action system to maintain a goal orientation and coordination momentum;

5. provide "follow-along" to the client and his or her family to speed identification of unexpected problems in service delivery and to serve as a general troubleshooter on behalf of the client;

6. provide counseling and information to help the client and his or her family in situations of crisis and conflict with service providers;

7. provide ongoing emotional support to the client and his or her family so they can cope better with problems and utilize professionals and complex services;

8. complete the necessary paperwork to maintain documentation of client progress and adherence to the plan by all concerned;

9. act as a liaison between the client and his or her family and all relevant professionals, programs, and informal resources involved in the overall intervention plan to help the client make his or her preferences known and secure the services needed;

10. act as a liaison between programs, providing services to the client to ensure the smooth flow of information and minimize conflict between the subsystems;

11. establish and maintain credibility and good public relations with significant formal and informal resource systems to mobilize resources for current and future clients;

12. perform effectively and as a "good bureaucrat" within the organization to be in a position to develop and modify policies and procedures affecting clients and the effectiveness of the service delivery system;* and

13. secure and maintain the respect and support of those in positions of authority so their influence can be enlisted on behalf of the client and used, when necessary, to encourage other individuals and agencies to participate in the coordination effort.

Skills

Since case coordination is highly compatible with the basic principles and conceptualizations of social work practice, much of what is taught in programs of social work education is applicable to case coordination. Kane has described educational objectives that should be emphasized in preparing social workers for interprofessional teamwork.† Many of these apply to case coordination. They include a knowledge of group process and the problem-solving process and of the principles of evaluation and the characteristics of professional groups, of organizational structure, and of teamwork dynamics. Skills in group process and communication, both verbal and written, are also central to effective teamwork. Kane identified certain attitudes or styles of worker behavior related to teamwork. These include self-confidence and self-respect, respect for and confidence in others, willingness to share and to trust, tolerance of disagreement, personal flexibility, research-mindedness, and a favorable attitude toward the procedures of intake and referral.

The authors' survey of case coordination has identified additional areas of knowledge and skill that should be emphasized in the training and supervision of case coordinators: advocacy principles, the broker role, the mediation model, crisis intervention, systems of record keeping, state and federal regulations regarding the handling of client data, the consultation process, informal resource systems in the community, prevailing community attitudes toward various client groups, the normalization principle, public relations, principles of organizational behavior and change, and approaches to organizational management. Skills of special importance include helping the client to communicate with professionals and assert wants and needs, writing behavioral objectives, preparing

*Robert Pruger, "The Good Bureaucrat," *Social Work* 18 (1973): 26–32.

†Rosalie Kane, *Training for Teamwork*, Manpower Monograph no. 9 (Syracuse, N.Y.: Syracuse University School of Social Work, 1975), pp. 16–26.

written reports for professionals and lay persons, abstracting and summarizing data drawn from diverse sources, verbal transmission of information, public speaking and dealing with the media, and using supervision and consultation effectively. An additional skill is maintaining a degree of autonomy within one's own organization.

Summary

Case coordination, a form of intervention at the interface of systems, is an area of practice that should be of central concern to the social work profession. The article has presented an overview of the conceptual underpinnings of case coordination . . . and described the knowledge, skills, and activities essential to the successful application of this characteristic service.

The skills that a case manager must possess are embodied in all the chapters of this book, and they exist to some extent in the repertoire of skills of any trained clinician. Nevertheless, there are certain crucial concepts that require elaboration.

One of the first and saddest lessons the case manager learns is that no matter how skillful he or she may be, if the services are not present, case management skills are of little use. A large part of the case manager's role is to deal with a variety of gaps in services. For this reason a chapter on advocacy has been included in this book. In this chapter we will not emphasize this aspect of the case manager's role, but only reiterate its importance.

After being assigned a case, a case manager engages in three basic functions besides resources development: assessment and planning, coordinating the delivery of basic services, and monitoring and reviewing the progress of particular clients.

Assessment and Planning: Planning always takes place in a context. For case managers this context is the service system. They must therefore understand what systems are, and specifically the service delivery system and the system of friends, relatives, groups, and organizations with which the client is involved.

A simple way of describing a system is to say that its parts are interconnected: a change in one part will produce a change in another. Often, for example, various parts of a system are in conflict. Agencies and departments compete for resources, for clients, for prestige, and, ultimately, for organizational survival. Whenever vital interests come into play, it is highly unlikely that organizations or even other parts of one organization will cooperate with case managers. The case manager has to understand what is going on, not only between organizations, but between departments in organizations, between professions, and so on.

Another way of looking at a system is to conceptualize it as having three basic parts: the *input*, which for social agencies would be primarily money, staff, and facilities, and the *throughput*, or service delivery system, the technology that transforms the inputs through a system of procedures and activities into an *output*; in social agencies the output is what happens to the client or the environment.

System concepts are useful for a case manager because they alert him or her to think about how the agency's output is transformed into additional inputs for the agency. How does the output of the agency—that is, what happens to clients—affect its financing? Treatment success may result in funding loss, as a discharged patient leaves an empty bed, or funding gain, as the patient's departure cuts the organization's costs or helps it to garner more funds based on its successes. In assessment and planning, awareness of where the agency gets its input or "energy" is crucial.

In every agency there is a strain between the need to survive within its environment and the need to attain its goals (the delivery of treatment or services). If residential treatment centers are funded on a per capita basis, they will be constrained to keep their beds filled. The case manager operates in the context of this contraint. For example, an agency may admit clients who might benefit more from some other mix of services in order to fill empty beds. The pressure to account for a large number of individual sessions may encourage mental health centers to provide individual treatment and discourage family meetings that do not "count." A community agency may be reluctant to provide an unusual service to a case manager's client if it requires unusual energy expenditures. This agency may be husbanding its resources.

Likewise, the completion of all of the paperwork needed to secure an agency's financial resources may leave the staff with limited time to provide services. Case managers have to be aware of such demands. It is impossible for an agency to ignore its survival needs, for if it does so it will be unable to attain its goals. There is therefore an ongoing tension between the organization's survival needs and the clients' service needs.

Some ways of handling this tension are more functional than others, "functional" being defined as promoting effective service to clients. Triage, for example, allows agencies to maximize their ability to service clients and yet maintain their capacity to survive; instead of providing everyone with the same service, agencies structure themselves to provide different levels of service to different types of clients, thereby maximizing the use of scarce resources.

In seeking a service for a client, a case manager must recognize that the system he or she is asking to provide the service is concerned not only with providing that service, but with the costs in staff, money, and time of doing so and with effects of those costs on its ability to maintain itself. The strategies, tactics, and plans of the case manager must always take this into consideration.

Organizations incur costs in cooperating. By cooperating they may gain needed services for clients, legitimacy or respect, increased knowledge and access to referral agencies, and in some cases a greater willingness on the part of other agencies to cooperate in the future. Yet they pay a price. The autonomy of the coordinated agency is limited. Decisions about who, how, and when to provide service become a matter for interagency negotiation and are no longer totally in each individual agency's control. Success is out of the agency's control, and, more important, so is failure. The coordinated agency may have to use time and energy that might otherwise be applied directly to services to other clients or to organizational self-maintenance. Among the more sensitive costs is the fact that its staff's practice becomes visible to other agencies, increasing the organization's vulnerability to outside scrutiny and evaluation.

For these reasons an agency may not relish coordination. The effective case manager has to be skilled at analyzing such costs. The guiding principle that systems theory suggests is that one must identify and minimize the costs to an agency of coordination and maximize the benefits. Strategies for doing this can be drawn from a comprehensive analysis of the interagency system. It is possible to create benefits for coordination if one has a complete picture of the interagency network and how it operates.*

The article that follows, by Carol Austin, examines in considerable detail the factors in organizations and interorganizational networks that affect the assessment of client needs and the ability of case managers to deliver needed services.

---

*For a discussion of a variety of issues related to teamwork and case management, see Thomas Briggs, "Obstacles to Implementing Social-Work Teams in the United States of America," in Susan Lonsdale, Adrian Webb, and Thomas L. Briggs, eds., *Teamwork in the Personal Social Services and Healthcare* (Syracuse: Syracuse University School of Social Work, 1980), pp. 75–89.

Client Assessment in Context*

Carol D. Austin

In the narrowest sense, assessment of clients for social services represents a measurement problem requiring the development of valid and reliable instruments, protocols, and procedures for evaluating clients' circumstances and capabilities. From this perspective, assessment is essentially seen as a technological problem that can be solved by the refinement of instrumentation.

It would be naive, however, to assume that assessment of clients is merely a measurement problem. The most elegant, standardized, and reliable assessment tool can be rendered useless by the manner and context in which it is administered. Client assessment is not an isolated or technically pure activity. It occurs in a complex context—a broader reality comprising a mulitiplicity of organizations. This article explores the inter- and intraorganizational context in which assessment activities occur.

Client assessment is part of a larger organizational process by which agencies determine the kinds and quantities of services clients will receive. From an organizational perspective, the outcome of the process by which agencies allocate services to clients is most important. Assessment is only one of several significant sources of information used in this allocation process. . . .

Acquisition of Resources

Preconditions for specifying the variables and generating the hypotheses in a model of service allocation are provided by a perspective on organizational behavior that focuses on the need to acquire adequate resources. Today's social service agencies are presented with harsh realities. As government funds dry up, agencies must come up with ways to cut costs and find new resources. Agencies are turning to foundations and volunteer staff and switching to program models based on self-help approaches. Stability and predictability are becoming major goals as agencies try to deal with uncertain and unpredictable circumstances. Activities that are centered on protecting agencies' current resources, defending against potential cutbacks, and exploiting opportunities to expand resources are also crucial to this effort. This situation affects the way agencies relate to other organizations and how they set internal policies and procedures.

*Excerpted with permission from *Social Work Research and Abstracts* 17 (Spring 1981): 4–12. Copyright 1981, National Association of Social Workers, Inc.

Several analysts suggest that agency decision-makers and administrators are typically oriented toward the acquisition and defense of an adequate supply of resources.* For decision-makers, the focus is the operational definition of the organization's purpose and of their mandate as managers. Agency executives must develop and maintain vital and supportive links between the agency and its environment. They must also organize internal work structures to achieve organizational goals. Executives' success is measured by their ability to exploit opportunities and to manage constraints and contingencies both within and outside of the agency. Administrators' central concern becomes the development of a stable, predictable, and potentially expanding resource base.

Resources available to agencies include funding, labor, information, equipment, and clients. Clients bring agencies several kinds of resources. Clients provide funds by virtue of their eligibility for entitlement programs or their ability to pay for the services they receive. Specific kinds of clients enhance agencies' capacity to acquire resources. For example, the medical assistance program (Medicaid, Title XIX of the Social Security Act) is a relatively open-ended entitlement, making eligible clients an attractive target population for an agency. Clients also provide agencies with status and reputation. Cloward and Epstein illustrate ways in which family adjustment agencies sought to improve their image and attract a more prestigious clientele.† A major strategy was withdrawal of services from poor clients—individuals and families who did not confer the desired kinds of status and reputation on the agencies. According to Levine and White, state rehabilitation agencies selected clients who were likely to be effectively rehabilitated, not necessarily those most in need of help.‡

The effort made by agencies to serve clients (as represented by their caseload) and their inability to meet demands for service (as shown by their waiting lists) are often used to demonstrate the need for additional resources.§ Pressures to maintain the stability of resources may influence

*James D. Thompson, *Organizations in Action* (New York: McGraw-Hill, 1967); Ephraim Yuchtman and Stanley Seashore, "A System Resource Approach to Organizational Effectiveness," *American Sociological Review* 32 (1967): 891–903; and Jeffrey Pfeffer and Gerald R. Salancik, *The External Control of Organizations: A Resource Dependence Perspective* (New York: Harper & Row, 1978).

†Richard Cloward and Irwin Epstein, "Private Social Welfare's Disengagement from the Poor: The Case of the Family Adjustment Agencies," in Mayer Zald, ed., *Social Welfare Institutions* (New York: John Wiley & Sons, 1965), pp. 623–644.

‡Sol Levine and Paul E. White, "Exchange as a Conceptual Framework for the Study of Interorganizational Relationships," *Administrative Science Quarterly* 5 (1961): 583–601.

§Suchman identifies presentation of statistical evidence of effort, such as caseloads, as a method agencies use to deal with demands for accountability when other data, such as on performance, adequacy, or efficiency, are not available. Effort represents evidence of agencies' activity rather than outcomes. See Edward Suchman, *Evaluative Research* (New York: Russell Sage Foundation, 1967), pp. 60–66.

the way agencies select and assess clients and allocate services to them.* Agencies' success in acquiring resources is also significantly shaped by their interorganizational relationships.

Interorganizational Networks

The central concept in the interorganizational literature is interdependence.† Agencies are said to be interdependent if they must take each other into account to accomplish their individual goals. Basically, social welfare agencies are dependent on each other for resources. Given the environment of scarce resources in which these agencies operate, it is reasonable to expect that they will be acutely aware of this interdependence. Agencies actively negotiate with other members of the local service delivery network, identifying resources to be exchanged and establishing consensus regarding domains in the network.

Domain Consensus

Establishing domain consensus is the process through which turf is negotiated, and it can be conceptualized as a way to divide up resources that are available in the local network.‡ Resources associated with the negotiated territory can be legitimately claimed by the organization performing functions in the agreed-on area (the domain). The process of achieving domain consensus constitutes much of the interaction among organizations.§ As a result of the diverse functions characteristic of social welfare agencies, the process of achieving domain consensus is characterized by readjustment and compromise and is accomplished through

*For discussions of the issue of client selection, see, for example, James Greenley and Stuart Kirk, "Organization Characteristics of Agencies and the Distribution of Services to Clients," *Journal of Health and Social Behavior* 14 (Mar. 1963): 70–79; Kirk and Greenley, "Denying or Delivering Services," *Social Work* 19 (1974): 439–447; Robert Scott, "The Selection of Clients by Social Welfare Agencies: The Case of the Blind," *Social Problems* 14 (1967): 218–257; Edward Teele and Sol Levine, "The Acceptance of Emotionally Retarded Children by Psychiatric Agencies," in Stanton Wheeler, ed., *Controlling Delinquents* (New York: John Wiley & Sons, 1968), pp. 103–126; and Elliot G. Mishler and Nancy E. Waxler, "Decision Process in Psychiatric Hospitalization: Patients Referred, Accepted and Admitted to a Psychiatric Hospital," *American Sociological Review* 28 (1963): 576–587.

†Eugene Litwak and Lydia Hylton, "Interorganizational Analysis: A Hypothesis on Coordinating Agencies,"*Administrative Science Quarterly* 6 (1962): 395–426.

‡Levine and White, "Exchange as a Conceptual Framework."

§For an attempt to conceptualize some of the determinants of domain consensus, see C. David Hollister and Joe Hudson, "Interorganizational Conflict: The Case of Police Youth Bureaus and the Juvenile Court," *Journal of Sociology and Social Welfare* 1 (1974): 206–216. For a discussion of the concepts of core and marginal domain, see Uri Aviram, "Mental Health Reform and the Aftercare State Service Agency" (Ph.D. dissertation, School of Social Welfare, University of California, Berkeley, 1972).

negotiation and bargaining. Negotiating domains is one of the primary ways in which organizational resources are acquired, defended, and potentially expanded.

The presence of a common service ideology among agency staff is the basis on which workers develop a consensus regarding the effectiveness of their interventions and services for appropriate clients. Consensus among workers produces a stereotype of the most attractive client. Applicants who are assessed as inappropriate, in light of the workers' commonly held ideologies and stereotypes, are often referred to other agencies. Appropriate clients can also be stereotyped, resulting in more routine service allocation decisions and more systematic routing of clients to agency service.

A domain represents a legitimated claim on specified resources. Consequently, agencies can be expected to perceive alterations in the established consensus as threats to the stability of their flow of resources. Assessment procedures, then, can be used as a strategy to protect agencies' domains.

An illustration is provided by recent experience in the development of a continuum of care for the elderly and others in need of long-term care services. The virtual monopoly enjoyed by nursing homes as the major providers of long-term care services constitutes an extreme case of domain consensus. Clients are often assessed as needing those services that are available, and nursing home care is the most frequently available long-term care service. Efforts to develop so-called alternatives to nursing home care suggest the potential for a fundamental redistribution of resources in long-term care, upsetting the existing domain consensus. Claims that clients have been institutionalized inappropriately have put nursing homes on the defensive. A viable continuum of care for long-term care clients remains an elusive goal, primarily because no funding is available for programs to develop a fuller range of long-term care services. In anticipation of the eventual availability of such funding, nursing homes and other long-term care providers are actively negotiating their domains so that they will be able to make legitimate claims on those resources, if and when they become available. . . .

Targeting

. . . Thus far it has been argued that agencies pursue a stable, legitimated flow of resources through domain negotiations. Since agency administrators want to maximize their organization's vitality and institutionalize its purpose, they actively monitor environmental conditions. Their major concern becomes mediating environmental influences that affect the agency's operations and initiating internal changes in the face of environmental opportunities, constraints, and contingencies.

This discussion of targeting and domain consensus suggests three important independent variables that may affect the kinds and amounts of services clients receive: the adequacy of funding available for services, the stability of the emphases of federal and state policies and programs, and the stability of domain consensus in the local delivery network. It can be hypothesized that the availability of funding will directly affect the kinds and amounts of services clients receive. Relatively unchanging state and federal programs and policies contribute to the stability of domain consensus among provider agencies in local delivery systems. Each variable can be expected to produce systematic patterns in the services that agencies allocate to clients.

Intraorganizational Conflict

Another set of variables that influences service allocation decisions in agencies is related to the amount of internal conflict that is present. A top-down perspective on organizations views them as unitary, monolithic structures shaped solely by the positions of top-level administrators. This conception suggests a high degree of consensus with little disagreement among individuals and groups at various levels in an agency. This view is misleading and does not further understanding of the intraorganizational variables that influence assessment of clients and service allocation decisions. An interest group perspective offers greater explanatory power.*

Interest Groups

Interest groups can form around a wide range of issues of common concern, including differing positions on the agency's goals, technology, working conditions, allocation decisions, and philosophy of service. An individual's location in the agency's hierarchy is frequently a powerful determinant of his or her position on various issues.† Social workers in the front line of service delivery can be expected to see issues in the agency from a different perspective than middle-management supervisors or agency administrators. Location in the hierarchy is only one of many possible common experiences or concerns around which interest groups form. Philosophy of service and ideology of intervention are also possible bases for coalition. Interest groups that form around specific issues may cut across professions and hierarchical levels in the organization. For example, a fundamental shift in an agency's orientation from

*See Richard M. Cyert and James G. March, *A Behavioral Theory of the Firm* (Englewood Cliffs, N.J.: Prentice-Hall, 1963), pp. 26–43.
†See, for example, David Mechanic, "Sources of Power of Lower Level Participants in Complex Organizations," *Administrative Science Quarterly* 7 (1962): 349–364.

providing direct services rooted in an ego-psychological approach to delivering services based on sociobehavioral principles can be expected to generate considerable activity among interest groups.

Professionalization

The number of professionals and the presence of different professional groups in an agency further complicate assessment procedures, producing numerous potential conflicts for practitioners and challenging them to maintain an autonomous stance vis-à-vis their employers. Although agencies vary in levels of formalization, specialization, and amount of discretion permitted, autonomous professionals can be expected to resist bureaucratic rules and supervision, reject bureaucratic standards, and manifest conditional loyalty to the organization.

Their orientation to provision of service often brings professionals into conflict with administrative demands for documentation, particularly when those demands take the form of increased paperwork. Time spent filling out forms is taken away from time more appropriately spent delivering services to clients. Administrators who need to monitor professionals' activities encounter resistance from practitioners who would rather spend their time serving clients than attending seemingly unending case conferences and supervisory sessions. Front line workers may resist shifts in the agency's domain if they see the changes moving the agency away from serving the clients they view as most in need. Practitioners may resist administrative directives to increase standardization in screening and assessment, viewing such moves as threatening their ability to individualize service. Increased conflict can be expected if such standardized tasks are performed by workers with less training to improve the efficient use of agency staff. Professionals may see such personnel as inadequately equipped to perform a set of tasks they believe require considerable experience and expertise.

Middle-management and supervisory staff are caught in the gap between agency administration and direct service workers. They translate, interpret, and implement administrative directives to workers on the one hand and absorb and communicate workers' concerns on the other. Middle management is the level within the agency where the agency's partially conflicting formal goals are translated into its day-to-day operational goals, procedures, and policies. Administrators are concerned with the survival of the agency and accountability to funders. Workers are focused on the delivery of services to clients. Middle managers and supervisors monitor the work flow and attempt to stabilize the agency's day-to-day operations.

At the intraorganizational level of analysis, two independent variables have been discussed: the level of conflict among interest groups in the agency and the agency's level of professionalization. It can be hypothesized that the higher the level of conflict within the agency, the greater the variation in the types and amounts of services clients will receive. The potential effects of professionalization are less clear. The extent to which assessment and allocation of services are interdisciplinary and the models of intervention that professionals use are also important variables, and they should be carefully considered in building a model of service allocation.

Indeterminate Technology

Perrow specifies three dimensions along which organizations' technologies vary: the extent to which desired outcomes are tangible and well defined, the degree of stability and invariability in the organization's "raw material," and the completeness of knowledge concerning cause-and-effect relationships when intervening with the "raw material."† On all three counts, social work's technology is indeterminate. There is little consensus regarding desired outcomes, and in many cases outcomes remain intangible, lacking clear operation definitions. Social work's "raw material" (that is, clients) varies widely as individuals, as groups, and as communities, and it changes over time. Thus, social workers' knowledge of causal relationships is primitive. Given high levels of uncertainty on all three dimensions, social welfare organizations engage in service delivery that is characteristically nonroutine. What are the organizational consequences of this nonroutine, indeterminate technology?

Routinizing Technology

Defining each client's situation as completely unique and idiosyncratic would make the flow of the agency's activities chaotic. Nonroutine tasks create high levels of administrative costs and difficulty in structuring work flow and procedures.* In the absence of valid and reliable measurement procedures for assessing clients' attributes, an organization, through its staff, develops a series of working assumptions about its clients.‡ These assumptions may become reified as the agency's technology, although the

*Charles Perrow, "A Framework for the Comparative Analysis of Organizations," *American Sociological Review* 32 (1967): 194–208.

†For a discussion of the effects of technology on organizational structure, see Eugene Litwak, "Models of Bureaucracy Which Permit Conflict," *American Journal of Sociology* 67 (1961): 177–185; and Andrew H. Van de Ven and Andre L. Delbecq, "A Task Contingent Model of Work Unit Structure," *Administrative Science Quarterly* 19 (1974): 183–197.

‡See, for example; August B. Hollingshead and Fredrick C. Redlich, *Social Class and Mental Illness* (New York: John Wiley & Sons, 1958); Thomas J. Scheff, "The Societal Reactions to Deviance: Ascriptive Elements in the Psychiatric Screening of Mental Patients in a Midwestern State," *Social Problems* 11 (1964): 401–413; and Irving Piliavin and Scott Briar, "Police Encounters with Juveniles," *American Journal of Sociology* 70 (1964): 206–214.

factual validity of the assumptions may vary widely. The value of such assumptions, which collectively provide the agency with an ideology of intervention, is to increase the routineness of the agency's tasks. A basic function of organizational ideologies is to support stereotypes of clients and thereby reduce the range of variation in the flow of work.

A more highly routinized technology enhances standardization of tasks and reinforces the formalization and centralization of the agency's structure. Interdependence among internal units and coordination of work flow among them reflect the level of technological routinization.* Increased routinization facilitates efficiency and emphasizes the quantity of clients served. Stereotyping of clients, a form of standardization, facilitates screening and referral to other service providers.

Domain negotiations among agencies in any local delivery system do not occur in a vacuum. Shifts in programs emphasized by state and federal policies can directly alter domain consensus. The availability of new or expanded funding provides a powerful incentive to agencies to alter the range of services they provide. These incentives are particularly strong if changes in state and/or federal policies result in more adequate levels of funding for scarce services, enabling agencies to serve their target populations more effectively. An illustration of these shifts can be seen in the movement among some nursing homes into the provision of home health services, home-delivered meals, and adult day care services. These services have traditionally been provided by community health and social service agencies. Only recently have some nursing homes become more interested in delivering a broader range of services, thus altering the existing domain consensus. . . .

Professional Judgment

Agencies hire professionals to bring their expertise to bear on areas of agency operations about which knowledge is incomplete.† Decision making under such conditions requires practitioners to draw on their knowledge, skill, experience, and values to deal with situations that are often complex and ambiguous and whose outcomes are difficult to predict. The use of professional judgment represents a way to solve a difficult problem—having to make day-to-day decisions with incomplete knowledge. . . .

It is critical that assessment provide an answer to the following question: given the client's situation, level of functioning, capacity for self-care, and access to informal supports, how much and what kinds or combinations of services should or can be provided? Once this question is

---

*See Thompson, *Organizations in Action*, pp. 51–65.

†Harold Wilensky, "The Professionalization of Everyone?" *American Journal of Sociology* 70 (1964): 137–158.

answered, some person or group must make decisions about how to allocate services. Resources committed and spent on the provision of services to one client cannot be spent on others. The economists remind us that there is no such thing as a free lunch. Assessment is one part of a broader process, a process designed to rationalize as much as possible decisions about allocation of services.

Allocation of Services

Allocation of services, the process by which agencies commit resources to clients in the form of services provided, can be conceptualized as involving three distinct phases: screening, assessment, and care planning.* Each of these phases will be discussed in turn.

Screening

Screening of applicants potentially enhances a program's ability to reach the client population that is the most at risk. Screening often consists of two stages: first, determining whether clients are eligible for the program (program eligibility) and, second, determining whether they are among the at-risk population (target eligibility). Determining whether a client is eligible for the program is often based on a means test. After a formal investigation of eligibility, the applicant may be accepted or rejected on the basis of well-defined criteria. Determining whether a client is a member of the at-risk population is usually based on available assessment data and professional judgment.

Operationally, agencies try to distinguish between those merely in need and those who are at risk. The criteria for both forms of screening can shift over time, reflecting the agency's needs to defend its domain and maintain caseload levels, the influence of professional judgment, and difficulties in gaining access to clients at risk.

An example of difficulties in accurately targeting services to at-risk clients is provided by the experience of several home care demonstration projects.† Their problem was not simply one of classifying clients into risk categories but also one of negotiating access to the target population. Hospitals, nursing homes, and social service agencies viewed the demonstration projects as competitors in the local long-term care marketplace. Thus, the context of the system in which agencies exist, with the prevailing relationships of power, turf, and domain, frequently means that agencies may not be able to reach their intended target populations.

*For an in-depth discussion of this process, see Jay N. Greenberg et al., *A Comparative Study of Long Term Care Demonstrations: Lessons for Future Inquiry* (Washington, D.C.: Project Share, in press).
†Ibid.

Assessment

Assessment is the second phase of allocating services. In addition to problems of gathering valid and reliable assessment data, assessment subsumes two other significant variables: who performs the assessment and when it occurs. The length of the interval between intake and assessment has significant consequences for changes in a client's status over time. Numerous client indicators can change with the passage of time—for example, income, health, family situation, and functional capacities. If a high-risk client survives an extended wait for services, the entire notion of being at risk is thrown into question.

Determining responsibility for the assessment process involves locating accountability in an agency and assigning the task to an assessor. There is little empirical guidance for evaluating the differences among assessment strategies, so it is difficult to recommend an optimal location for assessment. There appear to be three general strategies, however: (1) the agency itself does the assessing, (2) the agency contracts out for the assessment to another agency in the local delivery system, or (3) an independent party does the assessment. Two other important variables come into play here: is assessment an individual or team responsibility? what kind of professional training should the assessor or assessors have? There is little evidence that one assessment strategy is preferable, gives more accurate results, or even is easier than another. The point is that there are a number of possible locations and methods for discharging the responsibility of assessments, and the location may influence how decisions are made.

Care Planning

Care planning is the process that translates the data about clients collected during the assessment phase into a service plan. Care planning is one of the most important functions an agency performs. Basically, this is the process in which services are allocated to the agency's clients. Invariably, the translation of assessment data into care plans is based on professional judgment or practice experience. Three aspects of care planning merit further attention: the development of the plan itself, the relationship between the assessor and the care planner, and the nature of the rules for deciding on care plans.

Care planning encompasses estimating needs for service, contacting service providers, arranging for services, and explaining the plan to the client. Like the assessment process, care planning can be either an individual or a team responsibility. Considerable variation can be introduced through the professional training of the individual care planner or the interdisciplinary character of a care-planning team. There is little empirical guidance on the preferable strategy, but one might speculate that the individual approach might foster a closer relationship with more continuity between care planner and client. On the other hand, an interdisciplinary team might develop a plan based on a more comprehensive understanding of the client's situation. In the absence of hard evidence, however, the question remains undecided.

There appear to be three possible relationships between the processes of care planning and assessment. They may be completely separate; the assessor may be partially involved in the care-planning team; or the care planner and the assessor may be the same person. It is important to be aware of these differences across agencies, which may influence decisions made about care plans. For example, placing responsibility for assessment and care planning with the same person and locating that person in a provider agency could introduce substantial bias into these decisions. These workers could come under distinct pressure from their employers to translate assessment data into care plans that include services the employing agency provides. Without documentation of the existence and degree of bias from this potential source, the issue of how assessment and care planning could interrelate in an ongoing system is itself a subject for systematic investigation.

How are care plans decided on? In response to this critical question, the notion of rules for making decisions on care plans is important. These rules concern the manner in which resources are allocated and clients' service needs are determined. If agencies are to provide services with high levels of accountability, the nature, specificity, and uniformity of these rules must be specified. In essence the question is, what are the rules by which a care planner selects the mix and intensity of services to be authorized in behalf of a client? It is important to recognize that some form of professional judgment lies behind most decisions about allocating services. To the extent that there is a choice among available services, the care planner will identify to the best of his or her professional judgment services that are appropriate for the client

With this principle in mind, three strategies for decision making in care planning will be considered. Use of unrestrained clinical or professional judgment is one familiar strategy. The practitioner develops a service plan based on professional knowledge of existing community resources and expertise in assessing clients' needs. This model assumes unlimited resources and a ready supply of the services selected, but it can be criticized for not reflecting the reality that availability of services and cost considerations severely constrain professional judgment. If an agency decides to use this strategy, it should require detailed documentation to support and justify the decisions practitioners reach.

The second strategy is using professional judgment within well-defined constraints, usually strict cost ceilings. Clients can receive a combination of services if the package does not cost more than a previously established maximum. Another variation of this approach entails limiting the amount of any one service a client can receive. This approach is used by agencies that are trying to spread limited resources around and provide some equity in service delivery. Both variations suggest the development of practice norms.

The situation regarding care planning is reminiscent of circumstances surrounding the beginning of hospital care utilization review committees several years ago. Initially, physicians insisted that professional judgment was involved in every case, arguing that general rules could not be specified since every case is unique. As experience accrued, however, the notion of professional judgment gave way to "best practice," a consensus among professionals regarding state-of-the-art practice in specific situations. As a result, general rules of practice became apparent, as did exceptions to those rules. Social workers' understanding of the process of planning services for clients could also lead in the direction of identifying norms of practice and developing fixed criteria for services.

The third approach to decision making in care planning rests on the development of uniform standards and criteria. This strategy seems most consistent in the context of a fixed budget or a cost-containment effort. Allocation decisions would be standardized, and a score on a set of weighted criteria would indicate the maximum amount of service a client would receive. A recent experiment with this type of rule for making decisions on allocations indicated that the approach did not have any negative impact on clients in the short run.*

These three strategies represent a scale of increasing agency and intraorganizational control of decisions regarding care planning and allocation of services and provide possible directions for planned testing and manipulation of important variables. Discovering norms of practice and specifying the nature of organizational influence on care planning are important areas for investigation.

This discussion has suggested that considerable variability can exist in the processes agencies use to allocate services. A summary of these independent variables by phase of the allocation process, as well as a recapitulation of the organizational and technological variables discussed earlier, is provided in Table 1.

Areas for Future Inquiry

The purpose of this article has been to identify major categories of independent variables that affect agencies' allocation of services to clients. It has been argued that the view of client assessment as a purely

*Michael A. Garrick and William L. Moore, "The Application of Uniform Assessment and Standards on Aged and Disabled Recipients of Social and Health Care Support Systems," in Robert A. Solen et al., eds., *Community-Based Care Systems for the Functionally Disabled: A Project in Independent Living* (Olympia: State of Washington, Department of Social and Health Services, 1979), pp. 311–325.

Table 1. Independent Variables Affecting Agencies' Allocation of Services

Inter- and Intraorganizational Variables	Structure of the Process of Allocating Services
Interorganizational network	*Screening*
Stability of emphases of federal and state policies and programs	Stability and standardization of screening (both program and target eligibility)
Stability of domain consensus	Accessibility of target populations
Adequacy of funding	*Assessment*
Interorganizational conflict	Validity and reliability of assessment instruments
Amount of conflict among interest groups	Responsibility for assessment (individual or team) and extent of professional training required
Level of professionalization	Organizational location (separation from screening)
Indeterminate technology	Extent of lag between intake and assessment
Degree of stereotyping of clients	*Care planning*
Degree to which staff have common ideology of intervention	Responsibility for care planning (individual or team) and extent of professional training required
Extent to which professional judgment is the primary approach for planning treatment	Organizational separation from assessment
	Rules for decision making (specificity, uniformity, and organizational constraints) and degree of professional judgment exercised

technical problem does not address the complex context within which assessment activities occur. The extent to which assessment data are reliable and valid is one variable in a complex set of relationships that determine the kinds and quantities of services clients receive. Considerable effort has been focused recently on the refinement of assessment instruments, attempting to improve the reliability and validity of assessment data. Relatively little attention has been given to the contextual issues addressed here. Perhaps by now the reader has some idea of why this is the case. Given the extremely complex context and the unspecified character of important contextual relationships, improving the quality of assessment instruments may be a far more tractable problem. Even the most highly developed assessment tool can be rendered useless by the context and manner in which it is administered. It is clear that highly related and parallel lines of inquiry are in order, one focusing on instrumentation and the other dealing with contextual issues. . . .

Client Systems: Carol Austin presents a complex picture of interlocking systems and subsystems. Many of the problems she enumerates are clearly administrative issues of great magnitude and importance and must be dealt with at levels higher than that of the case manager. Nevertheless, case managers cannot do their job unless they understand domain consensus, financing arrangements, professional ideologies, and the constraints imposed by agency technologies.

Planning has often been described as a rational process that moves from defining a problem to gathering facts, to looking at alternative solutions, to selecting the appropriate one, and then to feeding back the results. This conception of the process tends to obscure the dynamics of planning and the fact that a worker's definition of a problem is often related to his or her theory of causation—for example, alcoholism is a disease; welfare causes dependency.

One's theory of causation will determine one's definition of the particular problem a client presents. The rational theory of planning obscures the values and beliefs that lend support to the selection of some alternatives rather than others by suggesting that all alternatives are weighed on the basis of facts. More likely, the alternatives that one selects for a client result from professional ideology and beliefs, agency dispositions and goals, and certain basic assumptions about human nature that workers and case managers may hold—that aged patients lack sexual desires; that love is more important than any other ingredient in resocializing criminals; that punishment does not deter; and the like.

For case managers, an awareness of their own values and those of others and how they affect the alternatives that are offered clients is crucial. What the case manager defines as help will often end up being precisely the help that is offered. Yet there is a broad range of help that can be offered clients if they are viewed not simply as individuals but as individuals enmeshed in a system of relationships and exchanges with the individuals and groups that make up their environment.

Developing plans and strategies to utilize this system for help is as intricate a process as developing plans for utilizing interorganizational or organizational systems. For example, one source of assistance that is often overlooked by professionals is the natural helping network of the community. This network may consist of churches, civic organizations, friends, neighbors, and various self-help or client groups. These groups also have domain conflicts, ideological biases, concern over status and survival, and the like. Nevertheless, Thomas Powell suggests in the following article that self-help groups may be ideally situated to help clients because of their structure and procedures and their relationship to the client system. To gain this help, professionals must be open to value systems and systems of help different from those upon which clinicians base their own efforts.

The Use of Self-Help Groups
as Supportive Reference Communities*

Thomas J. Powell

While the names of groups such as Parents Anonymous, Smoke Watchers, Alcoholics Anonymous, Synanon, Gamblers Anonymous, Recovery Incorporated, Weight Watchers, and Neurotics Anonymous are familiar to nearly everyone, the organizations themselves have not been widely accepted by or integrated into the professional human service system. Part of the difficulty may be that they are thought to be passing fads, or that they are epiphenomenal with respect to more fundamental events. The point can be made, however, that self-help groups have made a long-standing and substantive contribution to human services in that they meet basic human needs and are instruments fashioned to exploit powerful principles of personal change and reform. This paper will focus on the therapeutic aspects of self-help groups and consider how the professional system of human services might be more effectively related to them.

Self-help groups, supportive communities, and mutual aid societies, or friendly societies as some of their predecessor organizations were known, go back a long time. Of particular note are the mutual aid societies of the Afro-American, which reach as far back as the eighteenth century. These societies, designed as quasi-insurance and burial societies, were among the first organized expressions of black community life. In recent times, a comprehensive but not exhaustive 1960 survey turned up 265 self-help organizations.† Undoubtedly, the number is several times larger now, with a fair amount of the increase attributable to the fantastic growth of locally oriented peer counseling programs. AA alone claims a membership of 500,000, and the membership of Recovery Incorporated is estimated to have now reached a hundred thousand. Even allowing for a good deal of inaccuracy in the individual figures and estimates, the overall number of members perhaps rivals the number of clients served in professional programs.

A separate line of development also points to the significance of self-help groups. During the 1950s and early 1960s, there existed a tremendous faith in the power of the psychotherapeutic process: this process, skillfully employed, could bridge the social distance between client and therapist created by major status differences in social class, race, age, and sex. Subsequently, a similarly exaggerated counterreaction gave rise to claims on behalf of indigenous nonprofessionals, ethnic therapists, peer counselors, and feminist therapists. Another variation of status difference is the distinction between personal familiarity with the

*Excerpted with permission from the *American Journal of Orthopsychiatry* 45 (1975): 756–764. Copyright 1975, the American Orthopsychiatric Association, Inc.

†A. Katz, "Self Help Organizations and Volunteer Participation in Social Welfare," *Social Work* 15 (1970):51–60.

problem and professional interest in it. In this respect, substance abuse programs created a worthwhile innovation in their use of rehabilitated drug users as counselors in formal programs. But even here a shift seems to be under way toward a more balanced service program offered by professionals and ex-addict counselors. Taken together, the point about the self-help movements' roots, magnitude, and connection to contemporary trends indicate that it is a force to be seriously reckoned with by the professional community.

Before taking up the potential points of collaboration between the self-help group and the professional, it may be useful to present a more precise idea of what is intrinsic to a self-help group. This provisional definition is intended to focus attention on the core groups included under the heading, rather than to draw forceful lines at the margins. A self-help group is an organization of individuals who are personally affected by a distressing psychological or social condition. Membership is voluntary and is restricted to those who, either presently or in the past, have suffered the distressing condition. Common activities of the membership include fellowship, crisis assistance, mutual aid, self-development, and social action.

Although the emphasis in this paper is on how the professional and the self-help group can cooperate in offering direct client assistance, there are several somewhat discrete potential uses of the self-help group which should be kept in mind:

1. A professional may use a self-help group as a source of information about the potentially supportive community available to a particular client. In this format, key members of the self-help group operate as consultants to the professional for the purpose of identifying social opportunities and discussing issues of concern to the client.
2. Some clients are either unsuitable for, or do not wish, professional assistance. The reluctant client has an alternative in the self-help group, and it can prove to be a first demonstration of the practical and meaningful assistance a professional can provide.
3. In many situations the preferred means of collaboration will take the form of professional treatment service accompanied by active participation in a self-help group.
4. A final pattern of collaboration between the professional and the self-help group may take the form of consultation and program development assistance offered to the self-help group. This form of assistance has great potential and can be incrementally approached through a series of helpful encounters with particular clients known to the self-help group.

Organizational Dimensions

Whatever the professional's interest in the self-help group, and especially if the referral of a particular client is being contemplated, there are three dimensions of the organized self-help group that should be considered.

The first dimension refers to the self-help group's basic posture with respect to integration with the dominant society and the derivative issue of collaboration with the professional community. A continuum exists that extends from opposition to cooperation with the dominant society and professionals. With a client for whom it is important to remain involved with the dominant community and continue treatment with a professional, it is important to weigh carefully the probable effect of affiliation with groups such as Synanon or various Patient Liberation Groups. Affiliation with a group such as the Gay Liberation Front (depending on the extent of politicization in the local group) may also tip the balance in favor of opposition to participation in larger community activities, including formal human service agencies. Conversely, membership in a group such as Parents Anonymous,* given its built-in feature of a professional sponsor, is likely to strengthen whatever existing inclination there is to participate in treatment. It is important to note, however, that these comments about integration are not to be interpreted as a judgment of the probable positive or negative value of various self-help groups. Instead, the intent is to identify the issue of cooperation with the larger society as a key variable to consider when contemplating the suitability of a self-help group for a particular client; in certain circumstances, withdrawal and opposition to the larger society may be helpful, while in others it may be equally important to maintain existing ties.

A second dimension that must be considered is the nature of the problem, or the way in which a particular problem is defined. For example, clubs such as the Reach to Recovery program in the health field obviously will appeal only to a restricted population. But even in the broader social field, groups such as Weight Watchers, the Mattachine Society, or the Welfare Rights Organization tend to define their interest in somewhat narrow terms. Problems defined more generally are likely to be integrated into the programs of groups such as Neurotics Anonymous or with associations of parents of mentally or emotionally handicapped children, for example.† While it is difficult to make meaningful distinctions about the matter of problem definition, especially when there is so much variability among local chapters, the issue remains an important one to consider in particular circumstances (Parents Without Partners versus Singletarians).

Considerable variation is also associated with the third dimension of organized self-help groups, namely, the actual activities of the program. For example, AA, and Recovery Incorporated to an even greater extent,‡ operate highly structured programs. On the other hand, Parents

*L. Lieber, *Parents Anonymous: A New Direction against Child Abuse* (Inglewood, Cal.: Parents Anonymous, 1974).

†A. Katz, "Application of Self Help Concepts in Current Social Welfare," *Social Work* 10 (1965):68–81.

‡H. Wechsler, *The Self Help Organization in the Mental Health Field* (Ann Arbor, Mich.: Survey Research Center, 1960).

Without Partners is quite flexible about its program, and members may choose to become involved in only selected aspects. For some, a highly structured pattern may be useful in taking the first step to make a connection with the program and allaying anxiety about the nature of demands that may be placed on the individual by the group. This is most evident in a group like Recovery, where some very anxious individuals are enabled to participate by the emphasis on everyday events and by the use of ritualized techniques of spotting and endorsement to comment on these everyday events. The stylized AA program also operates in this direction, although there seems to be more opportunity for extragroup contacts, which add ambiguity to the demands the individual potentially encounters.* Both of these self-help programs contrast with Parents Without Partners,† which places few restrictions on the ways in which individuals might interact. For some this will appeal as a potentially individualized and realistic approach to the problems of single parents, while for others it may seem to spotlight their vulnerability; indeed, for some it seems to invite the possibility of exploitation by other, more dominant members of the group.

Benefits of Self-Help Groups

The benefits of self-help group experience may be compared to those derived from what has been variously called a support group or a supportive community. The group supports a change in the individual's life as it affects the individual's ability to cope with a particular problematic condition. The methods used to achieve the benefits can be conceptualized in terms of the operations that bring about a change in the individual's normative reference group.‡ In place of groups whose ideas, ideals, and modes of conduct support the problematic condition, the objective is to substitute a group frame of reference that will support a more constructive resolution of the problem. The question becomes: what events or operations in the new reference group support more constructive courses of action? In the following discussion six general patterns of operation that benefit the individual will be identified.

1. A person with a problem often experiences a deep sense of alienation and isolation from a group that can support a sense of self-worth,

---

*S. Grob, "Psychiatric Clubs Come of Age," *Mental Hygiene* 54 (1970):129–136; M. Maxwell, "Alcoholics Anonymous: An Interpretation," in D. Pittman and C. Snyder, eds., *Society, Culture and Drinking Patterns* (New York: John Wiley & Sons, 1962).

†G. Pollack, "Sexual Dynamics of Parents Without Partners," *Social Work* 15 (1970): 79–85.

‡H. Kelley, "Two Functions of Reference Groups," in G. Swanson et al., eds., *Readings in Social Psychology*, rev. ed. (New York: Holt, Rinehart and Winston, 1952).

esteem, and respect.* Moreover, there may be a feeling of separation and outright opposition from family, friends, and others in one's social circle.† Through affiliation with a group, the person can share an experience with others who find themselves in a similar struggle and yet are able to maintain a measure of respect for themselves as they pursue the task of finding more satisfying solutions to their problems.

2. Relevant information is furnished by many self-help groups. The single parent, for instance, learns about some of the complexities and some of the potential solutions to the problems of securing financial credit and child care services. The recovering surgical patient may learn about sources and techniques of health care. Gay persons or ex–mental patients may acquire needed information about important civil rights related to housing and employment. Such information has a dual benefit; the information is, of course intrinsically useful, and it also may become the foundation stone of a new source of self respect.

3. In contrast to simplistic assumptions prevailing in the dominant society, the self-help groups are aware of the setbacks that a person may experience before recovery is successful.‡ In short, there is a greater understanding that progress usually does not follow an unbroken pattern of upward movement. This understanding leads many groups to make provision for crisis-related services. The AA sponsor, for example, makes himself available to the alcoholic in danger of relapse. Similar provisions are available to the potential child abuser through Parents Anonymous or to the "nervous" person from Recovery Incorporated.

4. Modification of the individual's problematic life style, or what some have termed resocialization, does not come easily or without cost. The self-help group can function as a realistic antidote to any facile notions that meaningful change can be brought about without commitment and sacrifice on the part of the individual.§ The enviable position of the group stems from the fact that the long-term and successful members have already made the commitment and accommodated to the cost in terms of personal restriction and sacrifice. This feature of the self-help group experience seems inevitable, since the goal is fundamental cognitive and behavioral change. The alcoholic, in accepting the AA creed and following its twelve-step program, commits himself to a radically different set of

*M. Haskell, "Toward a Reference Group Theory of Juvenile Delinquency," *Social Problems* 8 (1960):220–230; A. Vattano, "Power to the People: Self Help Groups," *Social Work* 17 (1972): 7–15.

†B. Rosen, "Conflicting Group Membership: A Study of Parent–Peer Group Cross Pressures," *American Sociological Review* 20 (1955):155–161; R. Volleman and D. Cressy, "Differential Association and the Rehabilitation of Drug Addicts," *American Journal of Sociology* 64 (1963): 129–142.

‡S. Cady, "The Gambler Who Must," *New York Times Magazine*, Jan. 27, 1974.

§N. Hurvitz, "Peer Self-Help Psychotherapy Groups and Their Implications for Psychotherapy," *Psychotherapy: Theory, Research and Practice* 7 (1970): 41–49.

cognitions about alcohol consumption. These, in turn, mandate a radically altered course of conduct with respect to alcohol and all of its associated experiences. Similarly, the person in Recovery Incorporated is furnished with a highly structured set of cognitions about "nervousness," which in turn specify a different course of action to allay anxiety.

5. While a few words may suffice to indicate the value derived from the participation of people who have successfully overcome their problem, a thousand words cannot convey the impact made by the person who is a living demonstration that problems can be overcome. This is not to discount the presence of inevitable distortions and misplaced emphases as the individual encounters a successful member "who has been there before." But perhaps this is what makes it so real and credible. There is little that the successful member doesn't know about, and little that will strike him as surprising—and still there is hope. The individual, with all of his "horrendous" experience and problems, can still aspire to be like the successful member who has largely overcome his problem.

6. A final feature of the self-help group is responsiveness to the changed time economy of the individual. Heretofore the individual spent considerable time with those who supported rather than opposed him in his problematic life style. As efforts are made to disassociate oneself from an earlier life pattern, an inevitable hiatus is experienced. Unstructured time is copiously available; large amounts of it can be the occasion for relapse, not only because the temptation lies in that direction, but because there is nothing else to do and familiar patterns of behavior once again become dominant. By providing a leisure-time and recreational program, the self-help group can deal with this problem. In so doing, the self-help group does much more than fill time; it increases the overall intensity of the program directed toward change in the problematic condition.* . . .

Since case management requires careful analysis of systems, resources, and values, one fruitful way of avoiding roadblocks is to involve other agencies' personnel in the assessment and planning function itself. Various formal and informal means—including information sharing, consultation, case conferences, and interagency teams—are employed by effective case managers both to involve workers at other agencies and to smooth the way for the implementation and monitoring of a coordinated service plan.

*L. Yablonsky, *The Tunnel Back* (New York: Macmillan, 1965).

Coordination and Monitoring: The most difficult aspects of case management are the actual coordinating and monitoring: ensuring that services needed are promised and delivered in a timely fashion. The ability to orchestrate and coordinate an array of services is related to the case manager's implementing and expediting skills. The reader may wish to review Chapter 2, where these issues are discussed.

It is important to note that if one is asking for standard agency service for a client and is willing to take responsibility for coordination, agencies are often willing to comply. On the other hand, the request for extraordinary service, such as the waiving of eligibility requirements, will often be resisted. Nevertheless, it is a common experience to have other agencies, other departments, and other professionals promise to deliver services and not come through, for a variety of reasons: other priorities emerge from their departments and agencies; they do not understand the overall pattern of a particular client's needs and how they fit into it; they are negligent, or in some cases indifferent; or they choose to interpret rules and procedures rigidly.

The problems of monitoring are obvious. How does the case manager gain the authority to order a doctor or nurse to do something? How does a case manager get the authority to ensure that the city housing department provides an apartment? How does a case manager ensure that educational remediation is given when promised?

While it is beyond the scope of this chapter to discuss the variety of new structures and systems of delivery that are being developed to deal with such problems—for example, multiservice centers, nonhierarchically organized agencies—readers may wish to familiarize themselves with some of the readings related to this issue in the Additional Readings at the end of this chapter. The major problem under the present system of service delivery is to ensure coordination without threatening the basic autonomy of the cooperating organizations and professions. Alfred Kahn lists a number of specific obstacles to achieving cooperation, including: (1) the interprofessional status system; (2) differing conceptual orientations to people, needs, and interventions; and (3) the different value systems and cultural substructures of different occupational groups.*

One of the more novel ways of dealing with this problem of cooperation is the development of the client-service contract. This contract has three components: (1) meeting with all the agencies and professionals who will be helping the client; (2) writing the contract specifying who will do what and getting it signed; and (3) overseeing the resulting service. One of the contract's advantages is that it does not threaten the autonomy of the cooperating parties. It gives them the right to sign or to renegotiate or not to sign. Moreover, in one agency, contracts were always developed

---

*Alfred J. Kahn, "Institutional Constraints to Interprofessional Practice," in Helen Rehr, ed., *Medicine and Social Work* (New York: Prodist, 1974), p. 19.

with the clients and signed by them as well. This was done as an aid to monitoring and also as part of the treatment, since it gave some control back to the clients:

> As one worker said: "The contract is a burden to me, but it is also a lifesaver. Clients often complain that I didn't follow through on my commitment. When this occurs, I can always point to the contract. Social workers have a bad habit of always moving ahead of the client. The client never agrees or fully understands the social worker's point of view and concern for him, and vice versa. The contract keeps everyone honest.
>
> "Some agencies' representatives talk about clients as though they weren't at the meeting. In these situations I always turn back to the client. Does she understand? Does she agree? . . . This [must] be done because after the meeting you get, 'How come you let those people say all those things about me?' You're going to have trouble helping a client if this is how she feels after a contract meeting."*

Obviously, contractors' meetings are time-consuming, and contracts are not suitable for every client or situation. Nevertheless, these meetings where the client can see and be seen are potentially very useful in achieving the purposes of the service. It is a lot harder not to provide services when one has met together with other professionals to clarify perspectives on that service.

Other approaches, such as interagency teams, are discussed in detail in Chapter 4, on the colleague role. Such strategies may be effectively used to plan, implement, and monitor coordinated services. Other, less formal approaches include the traditional case conference, in which the case manager calls together all care givers, with or without the client's presence, to share perspectives and goals and, ideally, to come to some basic agreement about the needed services and how they will be provided. Though no interagency contract may be negotiated, the particular service providers come to an interprofessional agreement that is dependent on the goodwill and professional concern that develops out of the group process.

Monitoring the implementation of decisions taken at case conferences is, nevertheless, a significant problem. Ruth Middleman and Gale Goldberg suggest that the case manager must play a number of different roles in the monitoring situation—conferee, broker, mediator, and advocate— depending on the amount and type of influence needed: "If agencies (case managers) and clients are in general agreement about what must be done, the clinical case manager can play the role of conferee, focusing and clarifying decisions. If clients are not able clearly to articulate their needs, the clinician may have to act as broker, stating precisely what is

*Harold H. Weissman, *Integrating Services for Troubled Families* (San Francisco: Jossey-Bass, 1978), p. 102–103.

needed."* When there are real conflicts between goals, the worker may have to be a mediator, and when there is no possibility of agreement, there may have to be confrontation and conflict. Middleman and Goldberg suggest that the case manager use the principle of least contest: if you can persuade someone, then why mediate? If you can mediate, then why fight with them?

Often staff members from various agencies are relieved and pleased to know whom to call if problems develop with a particular client. One of the benefits of contracts, teams, and case conferences is that they can state quite clearly how the plan will be monitored, who will give feedback to whom, when, and at what intervals. Monitoring will be facilitated when there is a clear statement of what is to be done and what objective everyone is working toward.

To manage cases effectively, one must convince the staffs of cooperating agencies or departments of the value of coordinating, including setting joint goals and having some form of client participation. Contract users will also need extensive training in employing contracts as helping mechanisms, as each provider agency actually has a subcontract with each client. Since systematic feedback about what happens to clients is an impetus to organizational change, this latent function of monitoring may ultimately be as important as its manifest function. As one case manager said, "You have to change the agencies and the client at the same time, and that is difficult."

Case managers will rarely have formal contracts to work with. Nevertheless, they can use formal and informal means to ensure that service is delivered; they can operate on the principle of least contest, as articulated above; they can constantly provide feedback on the status of each case—what is improving as well as what is not happening—to the various providers; and they can keep their own agency informed of the various problems that they encounter in managing their cases, so that the agency can make structural changes or at least consider them.

Practice Analogues

The clinical case manager, as well as the clinician, has to possess a variety of therapeutic skills: the ability to listen, to make diagnoses, to establish helping relationships, and to incorporate in his or her work such principles as accepting people for what they are and treating them as individuals and not as cases. It is the depth of skill in planning, coordinating, and monitoring that distinguishes the case manager from the ordinary clinician.

*Ruth Middleman and Gale Goldberg, *Social Service Delivery: A Structural Approach to Social Work Practice* (New York: Columbia University Press, 1974), p. 73.

There are, however, similarities in the basic structure of both roles, especially with regard to the process in which worker, client, and system interact over time to achieve the client's ends. Some theorists conceptualize processes as having a beginning phase (assessment), a middle phase (intervention), and an ending phase (termination), each with its discrete problems and purposes. One would expect resistance and testing in the beginning phase, experimentation and trial-and-error learning in the middle phase, and anxiety in the termination phase. This is certainly true of case management.

The case manager cannot become so involved with trying to get agencies to provide the needed services that he or she forgets the clients. They are not representations on a flowchart that are moved easily from one service to another. They can become confused, discouraged, angry, overwhelmed, and oppositional as well as happy, cooperative, encouraged, and hopeful. The case manager therefore has to possess a clinical understanding of the effects of feelings.

Clients often want their situations—including such significant people as spouses, children, and parents—to change. When they do not change, clients may become not only angry at them but resentful of a worker who does not agree that this is the totality of the problem. Such clients may want change in others to take place quickly, and when it does not their resistance mounts. Problems presented by uncooperative agencies will increase the clients' frustrations. The case manager needs to know how to handle delay and resistance. The more delay, the less able the case manager is to integrate services for the client's benefit.

Unless the case manager has a plan to deal with delay, it is highly unlikely that services will be delivered. To put it another way: the clinician expects resistance. The case manager must also expect it and become adept at anticipating it by noting patterns that emerge repeatedly. Probably the best predictor of bureaucratic behavior is what the bureaucracy has done before in similar situations. If the nursing department has dragged its feet in the past, that is probably what the nursing department will do now.

Resistance and delay can result from misunderstandings about the nature of the service, individual cognitive or psychological factors, and systems patterning.* Analyzing the resistance can be of help to both clients and agencies: engaging others in clarifying its nature, recognizing one's own anger and frustration at lack of progress, asking what one could do differently, and allowing one's anger about the resistance to surface.

Another problem shared by case managers and clinicians is related to the development of the influence they need to do their jobs. The clini-

*Judith Nelsen, "Dealing With Resistance in Social Work Practice," *Social Casework* 55 (1975): 588.

cian's influence derives from his or her competence and concern. Clients listen, are willing to trust, are willing to be supported, because they feel that they and the worker are together and that their interests are going to be maintained in this relationship. Convincing clients of this takes time and effort and skill. It also takes the knowledge of how to increase the clients' influence so that they develop their own sense of mastery and competence.

Similarly, case managers are constantly trying to increase their repertoire of influence, without which they cannot function. They do this by being prepared with relevant information, following through, assisting other departments and other professionals with tangential activities that build up trust, being available when needed, borrowing and pyramiding rewards when the opportunity arises, and so on. The successful case manager is one who has a large reservoir of influence techniques that can be drawn upon as the situation demands.

Attitudes, Values, and Skills

The case management process is very strongly affected by the attitudes of various service providers toward clients and toward each other. The effective case manager will have to employ "conscious use of self" as much as any clinician. The hallmark of clinical professionalism is self-control—one does not let one's feelings interfere with one's commitment to do what is best for the client. The case manager must be absolutely aware of his or her attitudes toward other organizations and professions. An observer of a neighborhood health center funded by the Office of Economic Opportunity noted:

> Nurses felt that physicians tended to take charge, to give orders, despite the official emphasis on collegial team relationships.
> Social workers insisted on the confidential nature of their records, even though the team pattern was premised on full sharing.
> Nurses felt that they were willing to do the dirty work, to touch people; social workers offered nothing tangible and stirred up feelings. Social workers felt nurses sought quick, heroic solutions and did not deal with their own feelings.
> Nurses, social workers, and doctors had different social class backgrounds, different educational status, different personal aspirations . . . and different social distance from the clientele . . . with a variety of resulting conflicts and perceptions in relationships.*

It will take considerable effort in such circumstances for case managers to maintain an awareness of the impact of their professional background,

*Alfred J. Kahn, "Institutional Constraints," p. 19

ideologies, perceptions about clients, and theories of causality on their practice.

The ability to separate one's professional judgment from one's personal belief system is exceptionally important to the case manager. For example, in Alcoholics Anonymous patients admit that they are powerless over alcohol and that their lives have become unmanageable and believe that a power greater than themselves can restore them to sanity. This view generally conflicts with the clinical view that powerlessness must be overcome and that the only person who can overcome it is the client himself or herself. Certainly, most clinical treatment does not begin with having the client admit powerlessness. Yet as Gregory Bateson suggests about this organization:

> Implicit in the combination of these steps is the extraordinary—and I believe correct—idea: the experience of defeat not only serves to convince the alcoholic that change is necessary; it is the first step in that change. To be defeated by the bottle and know it, is the first "spiritual experience." The myth of self-power is thereby broken by the demonstration of a greater power. . . . Philosophically viewed, the first step is not a surrender; it is simply a change in epistemology, a change in how to know about a personality in the world.*

The case manager whose mind is closed to the difference between Alcoholics Anonymous and his clinical persuasion will be unable to make use of such groups. And there are equally substantive differences between recognized professions and professionals, like lawyers, doctors, teachers, and nurses.

Similarly, implicit in every service package and in every plan that a case manager makes is a view of what the client wants and how the client will behave. Many case management plans rest on a view of clients as sophisticated managers, not only of their time, but of their emotions, commitments, and interests, people anxious to actualize themselves and eager to empower themselves and others. Such assumptions often actualize workers more than they do clients. They may be wrong as often as they are right, for they derive from professional ideology, technology, and values, and not from an assessment of clients.

Rather than take the stance of an expert planner, who can foresee all contingencies, the case manager might be better served by the ideas of Karl Weick, who notes that although discrediting the hard-won lessons of experience may seem silly, it may at times be necessary. The key factor in a case management system is the current distribution of information and its dissemination to all parts of the organization so that adaptations may

---

*Quoted in Barbara King, Le Clair Bissell, and Peter O'Brien, "Alcoholics Anonymous, Alcoholism Counseling and Social Work Treatment," *Health and Social Work* 4 (Nov. 1979): 190.

take place. Weick suggests that the real skill of the case manager lies in keeping the delivery system aware of what is happening with the client and creating the conditions that enable the system to make adaptations.*

Perhaps the most important quality that the case manager can possess is a sense of excitement in generating new ideas and new knowledge. How does one orchestrate services? Would a particular client benefit from receiving an array of services all at one time, or would giving him or her first counseling, then job training, be more useful? Or should the job training come first, providing a sense of competence and capacity before one gets involved in providing emotional insight? Interest and excitement about the intellectual and conceptual problems related to case management can go a long way toward helping a case manager deal with the difficulties of the such decisions.

Additional Readings

Austin, Michael, *Supervisory Management in the Human Services* Englewood Cliffs, N.J.: Prentice-Hall, 1981.

Kahn, Alfred J. "Institutional Constraints and Interprofessional Practice," in Helen Rehr, ed., *Medicine in Social Work* (New York: Prodist, 1974).

King, Barbara, Le Clair Bissell, and Peter O'Brien. "Alchoholics Anonymous, Alchoholism Counseling and Social Work Treatment." *Health and Social Work* 4 (Nov. 1979): 181–198.

Ryan, Robert. "Case Manager Function in the Delivery of Social Services." In Bernard Ross and S.K. Khinduka, eds., *Social Work Practice*, pp. 229–239. Washington, D.C.: National Association of Social Workers, 1976.

Weissman, Harold H. *Integrating Services for Troubled Families*. San Francisco: Jossey-Bass, 1978.

*Karl Weick, "Organizational Design: Organizations as Self-Designing Systems," *Organizational Dynamics* 6 (Autumn 1977): 31–46.

CHAPTER 4

COLLEAGUE

In our society the role of colleague is one that resonates with good vibrations. The word conveys cooperation and fellowship; the relationship is the ultimate mark of professionalism. Colleagues provide each other with practical assistance and support.

Yet don't colleagues compete for promotion? Don't colleagues in different professions compete for status and authority within an agency? Isn't the social service department in conflict with the nursing department and the psychiatry department for resources? Which department's budget will get an increase for hiring more staff?

The colleague role has conflicts built into it. Nevertheless, agencies cannot function without a spirit of collegiality. Clients cannot be served adequately if they are viewed as one's personal property; they cannot get what they need if the services of other departments are devalued because one's own department is competing with them for turf. Clients' problems may have to be partialized, but the clients themselves must be seen as whole people, larger than any set of problems that any one person or professional group identifies.

Agencies have both formal and informal techniques for supporting cooperative action among colleagues: staff meetings, case conferences, committees, team approaches, and the like. On an informal level, mutual assistance and aid often serve as a mechanism for collegiality.

If these formal and informal mechanisms worked perfectly, there probably would be little need to write this chapter. But these mechanisms are actually dependent on individuals' knowledge of collegial behavior, and learning this behavior is not an easy matter. Being an effective colleague means limiting competition with others and minimizing one-upmanship in favor of maximizing problem-solving. It sometimes requires one to relinquish power and control and share them with colleagues. It often requires that one devote considerable effort to understanding someone else's point of view and seeing the value in it.

Overview

This chapter describes the knowledge and skills that one must possess to be a colleague. It suggests that one must assertively play the colleague role. One must take the next step when others do not because they lack either knowledge or understanding of the requirements of the colleague role. One does not passively develop into a colleague; one must act like one. To do so, one must possess a very specific set of attitudes, skills, and knowledge.

Knowledge: Collegiality implies cooperation. In social service agencies, the basic assumption often is that people cooperate because it is in the best interest of the clients. This is probably true when it is absolutely clear that cooperation will in fact result in some benefit for a client. Unfortunately, this is not always clear, and in such situations cooperation can be defined by various parties as an attempt by some other group or person to control their actions. In these cases appeals based on proposed benefits to clients seldom hold sway. One should keep in mind that although cooperation on any one client's behalf may in fact help him or her, such an expenditure of resources may not bring about better service for the mass of clients. Colleagues' resistance may be based on this belief and in such cases it will again be hard to persuade them to cooperate.

To gain cooperation, one must buttress the potential rewards of helping clients with a set of other rewards. To be a good colleague, one must have a keen sense of the reward system that exists in an agency.

There are two primary types of rewards, material and psychic, each of which can be further subdivided and subclassified. Material rewards include such things as salary, "perks" and benefits, parking spaces, large offices, and opportunities to promote oneself and be promoted. Psychic rewards include the ability to exercise initiative, assignments that allow for personal growth and development, friendship, the opportunity to act out one's ideology, and recognition by colleagues of one's competence.

These material and psychic rewards can also be considered from the vantage point of cost. One may incur material and psychic costs in organizational life: termination, no increases in salary, poor working facilities, having to work with people one dislikes, burnout, and having one's professional contribution devalued. If the rewards of cooperation do not exceed the potential or perceived cost of a cooperative act, it is highly unlikely that one will get cooperation. A simple request—for example, a social worker's asking a nurse to get something for a client— raises the issue of what other tasks the nurse might have to do, how she feels about social workers and their goals for clients, what she feels about the person who is making the request and the request itself. What values or beliefs give this request a rewarding or costly coloration?

To be a good colleague, one must understand and be sensitive to the values and skills of other professions as well as the demands of their roles and tasks. There is nothing more destructive to collegiality than a suggestion by one profession, such as social work, that its mission is to humanize other professions. What can doctors or nurses or police officers think of themselves if they accept such a statement? It cannot be positive. Yet the social worker may have intended nothing more than to suggest that clients are affected by social and emotional factors that can be overlooked when one has a technical or custodial outlook.

Although it is true that clients should be viewed in their entirety—as wholes, not as parts—it is also true that at times the parts must be dealt with. The police officer has to be concerned with the protection of society as well as the rehabilitation of the criminal. He or she will be less impressed with elaborate diagnoses than with what the social worker can do for a client. To gain cooperation, it is necessary to do something that he or she values for someone. While one profession may see its diagnosis as very valuable in the long run for the treatment of a client, other professionals may not see it this way if it does not help them to do their job as they define it and at that time with that particular client.

Understanding the goals and strains and rewards of the jobs of other professionals is probably the key to gaining their cooperation. Rhoda Michaels and Harvey Treger, in the article that follows, illustrate this point clearly.

Social Work in Police Departments*

RHODA A. MICHAELS AND HARVEY TREGER

. . . It is important to know that the police officer is interested in what the social worker can do that will be useful to him and the client. As he observes the social worker's attitude and prompt willingness to be of service and sees the results of treatment, he becomes increasingly convinced of the value of social work. When the police know that social workers can handle the people and their problems, then referrals from the police will increase. It would be a mistake for the social worker to try, by words alone, to convince the police of the value of what social work can accomplish. The police are action-oriented; talk is not as convincing as action—and may even be counterproductive.

*Excerpted with permission from *Social Work* 18 (Sept. 1973): 67–75. Copyright 1973, National Association of Social Workers Inc.

Setting for Service

A cooperative team relationship between the two disciplines can be more easily created when the police make social services available within the police department itself. This can eliminate communication gaps between social workers and police and thus help expand protection and service to the community. Such a relationship can have a positive effect on the image of both law enforcement and social work, as the community sees a new and vital function being carried out and thus develops an increased appreciation of the police department and the social workers within it.

The client can obtain important benefits by having immediate social services available in the police department. At the time of initial police contact, the offender may be more emotionally accessible than he will be later, since he is in trouble and may welcome some help. When a helping relationship is established at this time, the offender and his family have a stronger desire to continue this relationship than if the referral process has necessitated a break in continuity of service.

The client is more likely to benefit from counseling before he becomes a repeater and becomes more deeply involved in the criminal justice system. A study of federal prisoners who were released in 1956 indicates that the younger the prisoner when first arrested, the more likely he is to return to prison.*

The prognosis for rehabilitation through counseling at a later point in the correctional process, when problems are compounded by stigmatization and labeling, is generally poor. Once the youthful offender has been apprehended by police and referred to juvenile court, the most skilled subsequent rehabilitation services have far less potential for success than they would have had if they had been applied before the youth became involved in the formal criminal justice system.†

It is with young people that efforts toward prevention are most needed and most likely to be effective. The handiest place and earliest opportunity to provide such services are within the police setting when the offender first comes to the attention of the law enforcement officers. . . .

Objectives

. . . The police officer's contribution to the treatment process begins at his first contact with the offender and his family. Besides making a

*President's Commission on Law Enforcement and Administration of Justice, *Task Force Report: Juvenile Delinquency and Youth Crime* (Washington, D.C.: Government Printing Office, 1967), p. 122.
†Ibid., p. 41.

decision regarding disposition of the case, the officer appraises the possible need for social services.

A number of factors may influence this decision and appraisal: prior knowledge of the persons involved, the nature of the offense, initial attitudes of the offender and the family, and the officer's personal attitudes toward the value of counseling. It is important for him to understand in general how counseling is done and who can benefit from it. The officer's personality, his attitude toward the potential client as he deals with the offense, and the way he introduces the idea that the client should participate in counseling with a social worker set the tone for the social worker's initial involvement.

When the officer does his task well, he can make it much easier for the social service section. He may tie in information obtained from a youth or his family to indicate areas in which they appear to need help. Often the officer shows his kindly concern for the individual in trouble, as in the following case:

> Uniformed patrol picked up Penny, a sixteen-year-old girl reported by her parents as a runaway, and brought her to the youth officer at the station. He was able to break through her sullen silence to the point that she cried and expressed apprehension about her father's reaction. The officer called in the parents and encouraged them to talk about the quarrels over Penny's late hours and defiant attitude, also their anger and disappointment over how she seemed to be "turning out."
>
> He observed hostility and lack of communication. However, he recognized that positive feelings were still evident on both sides and recommended that Penny and her parents make appointments with a social worker who could help them talk things over and find ways to get along better together. A temporary truce was declared until they could meet with the social worker to go more deeply into their conflict.

Counseling Urged

An officer usually explains briefly what the social service section can do to help and what both the client and the family might expect. He will probably mention that the social worker may want to work with the entire family, if he has observed that there is serious discord between the client and the family. He may indicate too that committing the offense warrants a precautionary assessment by a social worker of how deep the problem is—even though it may be a first offense and the client may wish to put it behind him and forget it. (At the Niles Police Department all runaways, for instance, are referred to the social service section.)

The officer explains confidentiality between police, social worker, and client and points out that feedback from the social worker to the officer will be about the client's continued participation and response to the service, not about personal matters shared with the social worker. In short, the police officer does a selling job on what the social worker can do for the client and why social services should be tried.

In a majority of instances, part of the officer's contract with a prospective client includes an agreement that the client will take the responsibility of contacting the social service section for an appointment. If the offender does not follow through on the officer's recommendation, the social worker reaches out. The worker tries to tie into something the client is anxious and concerned about. When it is a serious or repeated offense or when the client resists accepting service, the officer reluctantly may have to offer the choice of such acceptance or referral to juvenile court—if not for the current offense, the next time the youth gets into trouble. Clients have the option to go elsewhere rather than use the social service section, but experience indicates that those who refuse service associated with the police department are unlikely to use service elsewhere. The reluctant families have probably resisted referrals by police and schools before. The authors have observed that the parents are more often at the core of such resistance than are the young offenders.

Crisis Intervention

It is preferable, when possible, for the social worker to become involved at the point of crisis. For example, in the situation of a shoplifter picked up and brought to the station, the officer and social worker meet together with the prospective client. The officer carries out his function of investigating the offense, explains the client's legal rights and responsibilities, and discusses alternatives for potential disposition of the case.

After introducing the social worker and making a brief statement about social services in the police department, the officer turns the client over to the worker and removes himself from the rest of the interview. The social worker is then free to use his own interviewing techniques to establish rapport. Immediately after the interview, officer and social worker confer to exchange information and impressions and discuss the disposition plan. The officer may also be helpful in attaining parental cooperation.

Mike, aged fourteen, was caught with another youth in burglary of autos. Known previously to police and referred to the social service after vandalism of a house, the boy had dropped out of treatment at the insistence of parents who were unwilling to participate themselves. The youth officer and a new student social worker met with the boy and his parents. The officer laid it on the line that a second serious offense coupled with lack of cooperation in a counseling program made it necessary to refer the case to juvenile court.

The parents declared their willingness to cooperate in counseling if they could be given another chance. The social worker then talked with them alone and concluded that they had changed their attitude and were willing to agree to participate in treatment, along with their son. The youth officer and the social worker talked over the case and agreed to defer petition to juvenile court until they could see whether client and parents would fulfill the agreement.

Exchange of Information

A police officer finds it valuable to have immediate feedback—to know whether the client accepted appointments, what his attitude was, and what the social worker's initial impressions and recommendations were. After one to three sessions, the workers talk with the officer about how they assess the dynamics of the problem and the treatment plan. Workers obtain the client's signed consent to share information that the officer needs to make a disposition. The officer shares with the social worker his background knowledge of the client, the family, and their initial responses to him. Such sharing can speed and strengthen the social worker's assessment. Police officers often get significant data or impressions that usually cannot be obtained in social welfare agencies without having several interviews.

> In the E family, the officer observed that the mother had been drinking at home alone and that her initial response to news of her son's offense was first to deny and then minimize his behavior. In the G family, he knew that the parents frequently quarreled and that neighbors had called the police because of their disturbances.

Following the discussion of the assessment with the referring officer, the social workers may tell the officer about progress, or lack of it, from time to time. They may report, for example, that the client is coming for appointments and doing well; or they may warn of factors that could precipitate another crisis, possibly one again involving the police with the client. Adding this information to his own, the officer will have a broader base on which to decide how he handles the client. Even though the client may no longer be in treatment, the social service section may have recommended an approach and disposition that the officer will find useful if the client gets in trouble again.

Once in a while, at the time of the first offense, parents do not accept the significance of the behavior and avoid counseling, but the second time around they can "hear" what the officer and social worker are telling them. Experience soon teaches officers and social workers how to work effectively together as a team and respond accurately to what is causative, relevant, and most likely to reach the client.

Effects of Authority

The majority of referrals result in ongoing treatment, and social workers use the modality that seems most appropriate—individual casework, group therapy, marital counseling, or family therapy. At the start, most clients feel that an explicit or implicit pressure of authority is expecting and demanding their cooperation. Without this pressure, the majority would not participate in counseling anywhere. However, after the first few diagnostic interviews, client and relatives become involved to the degree that they come because they are getting something out of the counseling, not because they feel they have to come.

The authority of the police does not usually remain an issue that substantially prevents the development of a sound relationship for treatment. The client and the family may differ in their perceptions of the social worker as an agent of authority. The possibility of a summons to court and the relief when this action is not taken can encourage cooperation until the client learns by experience that counseling offers him something in the way of personal understanding and help. . . .

At times the police officer and social worker can consciously plan their roles to complement each other and achieve a treatment goal with a client. The officer's more directive approach of "laying it on the line" can help greatly when tempered with his understanding and his support of action that is appropriate to the client's need. It is possible for him to give such understanding and support because the social workers have shared with him sufficient information so that he is able to tune in to the client's immediate need in relation to long-range treatment goals. When it is time to close a case, social workers share with the referring officer the reasons for termination, the changes that have been effected, continuing needs, and their recommendations for action. The decision to continue with a client after initial assessment, the modalities and methods of treatment, and termination are social work decisions. Nevertheless, the police, from beginning to end, have an investment in the successful outcome of the referral, and appropriate sharing is essential to working together smoothly. . . .

There is another conceptual way of looking at collegial relationships. One may help one's colleagues by actually sharing their work or by giving advice and providing resources. These can be called the instrumental aspects of collegiality. The expressive or supportive aspects of collegiality are of equal importance. These include valuing what others do, sharing their risks and concerns, and taking into consideration the nature of their work and the stresses related to it. Perhaps the greatest reward one can give to a colleague of whatever status is respect for what he or she does. It is easy to take others for granted. As the maintenance man once said, "The only time people talk to me is when things get dirty; nobody ever talks to me when things are clean."

While it is easy to speak about showing respect, it is very hard to get into another person's shoes. It would be ideal if each person took on another person's job for a day or two every year. A social worker who acts as a child care worker and spends eight or ten hours in a row with children has to feel differently about the child care worker's role once he or she has experienced some of its stresses and strains. Short of such actual role exchanges, observation, discussion, concern, and interest can go a long way toward mutual understanding and respect.

Besides the day-by-day interactions of workers with each other, collegiality is generally played out in several formal structures: staff meetings, committee meetings, and work teams. To play the role of colleague adequately, one must have a clear picture of the potentialities and limitations of these structures.

Staff Meetings: Staff meetings are in essence formal meetings. The main limitation of a formal meeting is that one must be able to justify every statement that is made and certain things cannot be said at all. Can one really say that a particular person is incompetent, fails to follow through on commitments, and is self-aggrandizing? Such a statement would violate a number of norms and would be open to misinterpretation by others who are not privy to the experiences on which one based the accusation.

A less dramatic problem is that staff meetings depend on verbal communication. Each profession has its own sets of concepts and expressions—sometimes called "jargon"—that others may not understand. A social worker might mention the need to humanize an agency's service, and other staff members may take this as a negative comment, even though no slight was intended. When there is a long-term lack of understanding between departments, an agency will frequently call a staff meeting at which each department discusses what it does. Such presentations, however, are rarely heard or understood by workers in the other department.

Confidence in the usefulness of formal meetings often rests on the assmption that problems in cooperation and collegiality are at the core problems in communication. In fact, problems in communication are more often symptoms of underlying status, authority, goal, and value conflicts. To focus exclusively on communication is to miss the essence of what is going on in organizational life. If staff meetings are really to eliminate role confusions and conflicts, a great deal of homework, study, and discussion has to take place in advance.

Committees: The staff meeting is one form of committee, and there are a host of others. Some are designed to carry out a particular task; others exist for years. The committee is in a sense the locus of collegiality. Sometimes committees comprise members of a single department or profession; sometimes they comprise members of other departments or professions as well.

Most often the colleague role is played out in a committee structure. The rationale for setting up a committee is often one or both of the following beliefs: that if people are involved in making a decision, they will be more likely to implement it; and that people can improve policy making by contributing their different perspectives on problems and their different decision-making styles.

Yet it is also true that committees can be used to bury issues; that people often have the feeling, after attending committee meetings, that decisions have already been made elsewhere; that some committees have no power; that people are often afraid to make decisions or to speak for their organization or department. Many people have noticed that committees are very slow; that consensual decisions are not necessarily the best ones; and that many things that should be said are not.

This array of problems cannot be treated lightly. Part of the reason for them is that committee meetings, as was noted above, are formal structures in which it is sometimes difficult to convey the kind of data necessary for making the correct decision. It is therefore vitally important to understand the role of informal decision making and informal information gathering. These processes do not subvert the democratic process; they make it work. If people will not formally say what they know and feel, for fear of retaliation or for some other reason, it is a travesty of administration to allow decisions to be taken in such an atmosphere. Likewise, if people are afraid to make decisions, committees are a waste of time. It should be noted that committees are very costly even if they work well.

To ensure that committees are effective, it is important first to be clear about the different types of committees. There are advisory committees, whose express purpose is to give advice and not to make decisions. There are decision-making committees, whose role is to decide policy in some fashion. And, lastly, there are implementing committees, which are brought together to get some job done. These committees cannot achieve their purposes unless they have on them members who have the resources to achieve the committee's ends. A policy-making committee cannot be made up of bright, able people at the lower rungs of the organization, because they do not have the authority to set policy. So to simply say, "We are going to set policy; who would like to volunteer for this committee?" is to guarantee that the committee will bury an issue or talk about it endlessly.

This requirement that members possess needed resources is especially important for the committee whose job it is to expedite something. Do the committee members have the authority to do so? If not, perhaps they should not be on the committee. There is nothing more frustrating than sitting on a committee that has to do something and hearing the members say, "Well, I have to go back and check." The time-consuming nature of this checking and clearing makes it impossible to expedite. If one is going to work through a committee to expedite, the first step is to make sure that the members have the needed resources, whether of authority or knowledge or skill.

Besides different purposes, committees may have different structures. The two basic types are ad hoc and standing. The *ad hoc* committee is set up to achieve a particular purpose, and once it is achieved, the committee is dissolved. The *standing* committee exists over a long period of time. Its job is to deal with an issue that has a variety of dimensions and requires constant attention: health or in-service training, for example.

The advantage of an ad hoc committee is that one recruits at the outset people who have the resources to do the job. In a standing committee, by contrast, as its task and focus change, one is often saddled with people without the needed resources. Standing committees have the advantages of organizational legitimacy, members experienced in working together, and continuity which can be particularly important for long range tasks. One should be careful in choosing between an ad hoc and a standing committee to do a specific job.

A classic problem of committees is that a few members do all the work and the rest are uninvolved. This is a crucial issue: if one or two people can do all the work, fine; but sometimes they cannot. The trap is that when one or two people do all the work, the other members see that they are not really needed, and so they commit less and less of their energy and resources to the committee. Over time, the committee becomes weaker and weaker, and the two people doing all the work become more and more tired.

Perhaps the most important decision a committee makes is who should be the chairperson. The chairperson who cannot lead the group is a disaster. In an expediting group the key leadership responsibility is often not so much to get a decision made as it is to follow it up and hold people accountable. The chairperson must have a sense of the rewards and costs of serving on the committee. To ensure effective committees, one must ensure that there is an effective chairperson. When the task of the committee changes, it is sometimes necessary to change the chairperson because a person who is good at one thing may not be good at another. Committee rules and procedures should therefore be set up to allow flexibility in changing membership and the chairperson when required.

Committees can create a great deal of peer pressure. People may feel constrained not to disagree. They may not wish to be the only ones out on a limb, and so they may give assent, but when it comes to the actual expediting, nothing happens: all forms of resistances come into play. It is just at this point that leadership is required. Leadership must be able to encourage the discussion of disagreements and help resolve the conflicts. If disagreements remain buried, the committee's follow through will suffer.

The leader has to pay attention in these situations, not only to ensure that a kind of "group-think" does not emerge, but to promote a clear division of labor and system of accountability and, most important, support for people in expediting. He or she must be concerned about the group's morale and sense of purpose and commitment. The expressive aspects of committee leadership are as important as the instrumental ones: it must help ease frustration when things do not go well and when conflicts arise, providing support to get over the hurdles.

Teams: The preceding section suggests that to be a good colleague, one must ensure that the structures in which one works support collegiality. Thus, if one sees that a committee is designed to set policy, one must ensure that those with the requisite authority are on it. If one knows that leadership is going to be crucial, one must take the step of ensuring that a committee does not pick a leader too quickly, before it is clear to all members what is really required to accomplish their task. The same point can be made about teams and the team approach. The team structure is designed to support collegiality. Surprisingly, it often does not.

Rosalie Kane suggests that teamwork has three preconditions: (1) a common team purpose; (2) distinct roles for team members; and (3) a communication method. It is always presumed that people either know or agree on exactly what they are to do and how they are to do it.*

There are two basic types of teams, the *coordinative* and the *integrative*. The first type attempts to coordinate the activities of the team members—for example, in assessing what should be done for a client. Generally, team members from various disciplines work independently of each other: "The large rehabilitation team which follows a patient from a period of physical restoration to psychological counseling to vocational placement, involving a dozen disciplines in the course of treatment, is an example of this type of team."†

The coordinative team can be valuable, yet it is time-consuming. At the minimum it requires clarity about the goals around which team

---

*Rosalie Kane, "Multi-disciplinary Teamwork in the United States: Trends, Issues and Implications for the Social Worker," in Susan Lonsdale, Adrian Webb, and Thomas L. Briggs, eds., *Teamwork in the Personal Social Services and Health Care* (Syracuse: Syracuse University School of Social Work, 1980), p. 139.

†Ibid., p. 141.

members coordinate their efforts. The following article gives a clear picture of how a coordinating team was developed and the benefits and difficulties that evolved from it.

Developing a Multidisciplinary Conference*

THOMAS R. CLARKE,
WILLA L. DISTASI, AND
CYNTHIA J. WALLACE

Mrs. Smith is pushed everywhere in a wheelchair, but she gets up and walks during her physical therapy session. Mr. Jones is disruptive during recreational activities; how does he behave in other social situations? The dietitian has seen Mrs. Lennon fighting with her roommate, but has the social service department been made aware of this? If the appropriate departments of a nursing facility do not communicate their observations about the patients to each other, situations such as these may remain unresolved until a crisis occurs. At that point, crisis provokes action—but at what cost?

In the Bronx, New York, at Morningside House, which contains a 239-bed health-related facility and a 147-bed skilled nursing facility, staff members have established an exciting, productive forum called the Multidisciplinary Team Conference, in which they share information on an interdepartmental basis. Each week staff members representing every therapeutic discipline meet at the conference to share their knowledge, observations, experiences, and concerns about the patients. As they communicate this information to each other, those attending the conference formulate team goals to meet the needs of each patient and methodologies to be implemented by various departments to achieve these goals. Specific plans for implementation are then prepared within the departments by the staff involved. The conferences were initiated by the facility's director of nursing service, director of social service, and executive director—the authors of the present article—who integrated suggestions from other staff members regarding procedures and format and supervised the evolution of the conferences into their final form.

Background

Multidisciplinary team conferences at Morningside House are the result of a grim determination to improve inadequate communication among

*Reprinted with permission from *Health and Social Work* 3 (1978): 166–174. Copyright 1978, National Association of Social Workers, Inc.

staff. When the facility opened in 1974, staff members representing the major disciplines met once a month to discuss the patients' progress, needs, and experiences. However, substantive sharing of information did not take place, goals were not set, plans were not formulated, and a team approach was not initiated. Instead, voluminous forms were completed by the various departments and were eventually made part of each patient's chart, and that is where the information remained. On the basis of their philosophy and beliefs as well as their attempts and failures, the authors realized that an actual dialogue had to take place among the major disciplines to create team plans for patient care. In this way, problems would be solved and individual patient care improved through integrated team efforts.

At this point, the director of nursing service and the director of social service acknowledged to each other in a private conversation that they did not know what problems and experiences other departments were having with patients. Specifically, the director of nursing service was concerned that the nursing staff was not following up on training programs conducted for patients in occupational therapy. The director of social service was concerned that social and familial problems that arose for patients at night or on the weekend were not being communicated to her department. Realizing that they shared the same concern, both determined to discuss this issue with the facility's executive director, who wholeheartedly supported their desire for a forum at which in-depth discussions of patients could take place each week among members of all clinical departments.

Early Stages

At the next meeting of the administrative staff, the executive director broached the topic of a multidisciplinary team conference. He received the response he expected: "How can we have more meetings when we're so busy now we don't have time to do our work?" However, after angrily resisting and then ignoring the idea of attending such a conference, members of the clinical departments were finally convinced that this type of meeting would save them time and would result in improved patient care.

The director of nursing service and the director of social service were assigned leadership roles in developing the format for the conferences, which were to be attended by the heads of the clinical departments. They accordingly wrote up a procedure for carrying out a multidisciplinary team conference and circulated it among the departmental heads for their comments and suggestions. After these recommendations were received, a proposed date for the first meeting was circulated, along with an agenda listing the patients to be dicussed. The first meeting was then held.

The authors were enthusiastic about this meeting and generally thought it a success. However, when they reviewed it in retrospect, they concluded that it had failed to meet the needs of the patients and the facility for the following reasons:

- Team goals had not been delineated. Each departmental head had related the goals of his or her staff, but a comprehensive team approach among departments had not been achieved.
- The input of certain administrative services staff had not been elicited, and it now seemed appropriate that they participate.
- The information shared by the departmental heads was anecdotal and interesting, but it was not helpful in the setting of goals.
- The minutes of the meeting were filed in a folder, and nothing further was done with them. Therefore, conclusions and recommendations regarding the patients discussed were never noted on their medical records.

Unsatisfactory as they were, the meetings continued on a biweekly basis, and staff members remained frustrated and unhappy with them. The requirements of state and federal regulatory codes were being met, but the staff's desire to implement a team approach to patient care had not been realized. Everyone decided to sit back and take another look at what he or she was doing.

Revamping the Conferences

The authors adopted certain measures to improve the conferences. A form was designed on which the goals of each department were to be recorded during a conference. The form would then be put directly into a patient's medical record so that the recommendations agreed on during the meeting would not be overlooked. Moreover, to ensure the review of all 386 patients on an annual basis, staff decided to discuss the progress of six patients of the skilled nursing unit and ten patients of the health-related unit on alternate weeks. The goals of each clinical department for the patients discussed were to be written directly on one of the new forms at the time of the meeting and would then be filed in the appropriate medical charts.

After implementing these measures at a conference, the authors decided that they represented improvement but that some problems remained. Team goals had still not been set. Instead, departmental representatives were simply listing their various recommendations, a procedure that hardly met everyone's desire for setting team goals. Furthermore, the recording of goals was done by secretaries who lacked a clinical background and were unfamiliar with the patients and with the processes of goal setting and goal writing. They were therefore unable to follow the drift of the meeting, and time was wasted in instructing them about what to write on the new forms. In addition, although representatives of administrative services had been included in the meeting, space for recommendations that they would have to implement was not provided on the new form introduced. Last, the heads of the departments had not fully prepared themselves to discuss patients and were still resistant to the idea of weekly meetings and the concept of goal-setting. In short, the staff found that although months had passed, they were still not satisfied with the outcome of the conferences.

Further Improvement

The authors once again re-evaluated the form being used to record goals, the procedures that had been developed, and the overall tenor of the conference and decided to move ahead doggedly. A new form was designed that not only included space for input from administrative services staff but, more important, included a section for defining team goals. (See Figure 1.) Secretaries were to serve as recorders no longer. Instead, the director of nursing service and the director of social service alternated between chairing the meeting and recording goals. In addition, the heads of departments were asked to review in advance the patients on the agenda and to be prepared to discuss the patients' participation, experiences, and adjustments. Out of all these changes grew a valuable, comprehensive conference that was held every week at a predetermined time for one and a half hours.

Figure 1. Form for Listing Team Goals (Used in
            Multidisciplinary Team Conferences)

Name _____ Chart No. _____
Admission date _____ Conference date _____
1. Team goals: _____
_____

2. Methodology:
   Medical _____
   Nursing _____
   Social service _____
   Occupational therapy _____
   Physical therapy _____
   Dietary _____
   Recreational therapy _____
   Pharmacy _____
   Personal services _____
   Administration _____

Signature of Recorder   Review of Date   Initial

Team Goals

The director of nursing service and the director of social service now decided that the conferences should be expanded to include staff members who directly provided patient care. In this way, staff could share their observations and help set team goals for each patient. A team goal had been defined by the staff as that end toward which joint effort is directed. Such a goal must specify a particular aim that realistically can be achieved and a time limit for its achievement. It does not include the means by which the aim is to be realized or the reason for its realization. For example, the particular aims for a given patient might be (1) to increase independence in eating and in ambulation with a walker, (2) to increase weight by four pounds per month, and (3) to increase participation in social activities to a total of five activities per month. The time limit in each instance might be three months.

It has already been explained that both team goals and the methods to achieve them are developed for each patient during multidisciplinary team conferences at Morningside House. The methodology developed at the conferences to implement goals for a patient is broadly identified; the individual plans for the patient's care delineate specific methods to be used to reach the goals. One of the hardest lessons that staff members had to learn was that it is not always appropriate—in fact, it is usually inappropriate—for every department to devise a method for meeting a particular team goal. This does not mean that every department should not have its own plan of care for the patient in question. For example, the pharmacist may not have to devise a methodology for meeting a team goal for a patient, but if the patient is on medication, he is responsible for preparing a regimen of care.

Conclusion

The new form used to record goals and the new procedure instituted began to reap desired results. However, the staff realized that a method for following up on the team goals set at conferences had never been developed. Therefore, the conferences were expanded by thirty minutes so that the goals set three months earlier for patients could be reviewed. At the time of the review, the person recording the goals indicates any changes proposed in the methodology and initials and dates the bottom of the form. If the current team goals for a patient are inappropriate or have already been achieved, he or she is placed on the agenda for the next conference so that new team goals can be established.

As the staff of Morningside House learned about conducting multidisciplinary team conferences, writing goals, developing methodologies, and sharing information, the conferences themselves grew longer and longer. At present, they are held for three and a half hours each week at the same time, and all regular participants are expected to attend or to send an appropriate representative. Everyone is prepared and ready to participate.

As staff members attempt to eliminate crises as the motivating factor behind action, they learned that change is often slow in coming, that resistance is a powerful force, and that determination can overcome obstacles. Multidisciplinary conferences are time-consuming and expensive. But at Morningside House they have resulted in improved patient care, team problem solving, and the saving of time because staff members are no longer continually involved in crisis intervention. This has freed staff for planning and for treating and caring for patients. Can any facility therefore afford not to hold such conferences?

———————————————

From the preceding article it is obvious that Morningside House would have been considerably less effective had it not developed its multidisciplinary conferences. Certainly the residents would have received a less integrated and complete service. The regular conference allows the various disciplines to become familiar with each other's concepts and roles; it encourages mutual support and understanding; and it permits staff members to share some of the strains of the work.

The second type of team, the integrative team, attempts to create a participative structure in which individuals no longer exclusively perform distinct roles but may in fact do similar tasks. For example, therapy is done by psychiatrists, social workers, psychologists, and nurses. No one personnel category is designated as the therapist or the family counselor or assigned responsibility for physical rehabilitation: "The integrative team is characterised by deliberate role blurring, an effort at consensual decision-making, high inter-dependence among group members, and much attention to group process."* Leaders are sometimes rotated or elected by the participants. In an integrative team, any team member could be the leader.

Why has the integrative team developed? First, there are in fact overlapping skills shared by members of different professions. Second, and more important, the specialization that characterizes the coordinated team has limitations and dysfunctions. It can lead each specialty to focus only on a narrow aspect of a particular client. It can also, if applied in large settings, create a sense of anonymity, in that specialists may deal with hundreds of clients and never get to know any of them as a person;

*Kane, "Multi-disciplinary Teamwork," p. 141.

nor can the client get to know overspecialized workers in any real personal sense. The essence of coordination is that it makes it possible to handle large numbers of people; yet largeness, with its attendant anonymity, may itself be inimical to helping people with their problems because part of help is the formation of a relationship not only with individuals, but with the institution.

The integrated team is a mini-institution, and yet it is extremely difficult to operate. Experience has shown, first, that it is easy to talk teamwork but hard to operationalize it in a context where there are large differentials in salary. How can a psychiatrist making $40,000 a year and a nurse making $15,000 both be considered equal members of the team and equally responsible for therapy? The same might be said of a social worker and certainly would be said of an attendant who is told that he or she is now a therapist.

Second, there are innumerable opportunities for disagreement about what should be done with patients. Such disagreements call for strong and effective leadership on the team; they are seldom merely symptoms of authority problems. In mental health settings the team leaders tend to be doctors or psychiatrists, primarily because they are legally responsible for the patient and are the only ones who can prescribe medication. Yet often a psychiatrist who is skilled in therapy is unskilled in the techniques of leadership in a work setting.

Third, many teams are set up without the requisite understanding of the amount of retraining people require to function on a team. Team members will need to be trained in understanding their new roles, each other's value perspectives, and jargon, and to be sensitized to process pitfalls to avoid. This can be quite time consuming. Fourth, collaborative decision making is not difficult; what is difficult is to ensure that something does in fact happen after a decision is taken and that what is implemented is what was decided upon. People have trouble holding their peers accountable. The theory of team management is that if one participates in making a decision, one is more likely to follow through on it. While this may be true, experience shows that there is considerable slippage between decision and implementation.

Finally, role blurring can have disadvantages for the client, who loses the benefit of a "social work view" or person-situation perspective on an integrative team when the social worker is attempting to act like the psychiatrist.*

How is one to be a good team member? First, an awareness of the structural pitfalls in a team approach is important. Forewarning the organization about the need for effective leadership, attention to the effects of salary differentials, and advance planning for follow-up and accountability can save a tremendous among of wasted effort.

*Ibid., p. 139.

Second, the team approach is an administrative mechanism and not an organizational imperative dictated by the value system of the helping professions. In other words, it is to be tried, evaluated in particular settings with a particular mission, and altered, discarded, or kept depending on the results achieved. This means that before it is instituted, indices of success and ways of measuring success are to be established. Kane makes the point that while much useful dialogue has been related to team processes, not nearly as much attention has been paid to goal achievement through teamwork. Perhaps because of the influence of humanistic philosophy, the team tends to become, to be seen as, an end rather than a means.*

Third, Kane warns that the emphasis on teamwork threatens to obscure the general need for attention to the whole range of multidisciplinary issues. The norms of teamwork should not be allowed to discourage open and frank discussion of stereotyped ideas about each other's disciplines, lack of information about each other's backgrounds, perfunctory or inappropriate requests for service, ambiguously written or stated messages, bungled telephone communications, impenetrable professional jargon, or failure to obtain feedback on one's suggestions or follow up on referrals. These are all reasons why plans for interdisciplinary cooperation go awry: "The structural arrangements of an organization—the record system, the office space, the work shifts, the protocol—can all either minimize or exacerbate such problems."† The team approach is not a panacea, and if it obscures attention to other issues, it is unlikely that it will work. The resolution of at least some of the problems Kane mentions is a prerequisite to making the team approach work.

Dealing with these problems will, at times, cause conflict. The important thing is to use a style of engaging in conflict that does not make them worse. Gene Hooyman suggests a practical model of conflict in which one takes into account both what one wants to achieve and one's concern for maintaining a relationship.‡ The importance of each dimension then determines the conflict style. In one style, "win-lose," one's concern is to get what one wants, no matter what happens to one's opponent. One has no interest in his or her needs or in maintaining the relationship. Another strategy, which Hooyman calls "yield-lose," places the relationship above any particular goal or issue. One party yields his or her position in the conflict, and loses, hoping that this will allow the relationship to survive. Another style is compromise. Here one person or both have a moderate degree of concern for both goal and relationship. This style requires the ability to win some and lose some: one simply does not argue

---

*For a discussion of role blurring, see ibid., pp. 143–145.
†Ibid., p. 150.
‡Gene Hooyman, "Team Building in the Human Services," in Beulah Roberts Compton and Burt Galloway, eds., *Social Work Processes* (Homewood, Ill.:Dorsey Press, 1973), pp. 465–478.

out every issue, because one realizes that to win would be counterproductive in the long run. A final style is called integrative. There is a high degree of concern for both the issue and the relationship, and so one attempts to bring people together and to define situations so that everyone ends up winning something. Problem solving is emphasized.

Different styles work in different situations, but the good colleague is someone who *chooses* a style or strategy of handling conflict, rather than blindly getting involved in it.

Practice Analogues

The skills that make one a good colleague overlap considerably with those that make one a good practitioner: "Many of the concepts which have had the greatest currency are applicable to all inter-personal relationships, rather than specific to the multi-disciplinary team. Encouragement of self-awareness, self-expression and productive confrontation, among team members is compatible with general humanistic trends in personal therapy and management theory."*

Of key importance to collegiality is the ability to make common cause with co-professionals and paraprofessionals despite role and language barriers and differences in values. Much of the clinician's work in the early engagement phase of treatment has exactly the same interest. Thus, the clinical skills of engagement and use of self should assist a worker in fulfilling his or her role as colleague.

Perhaps the most important overlap between collegiality and clinical practice, however, lies in the worker's handling of doubt. It is not always clear what is best for a particular client, and this doubt, coupled with the responsibility to do the best possible thing for a client, puts an ongoing psychological strain on workers. Collegiality helps professionals to handle doubt by providing support in difficult situations. It makes it more likely that reasonable risks will be taken at the appropriate time for the client; yet it can also support inadequate diagnoses, inappropriate treatment plans, the refusal, despite evidence, to acknowledge that what one is doing is not helpful.

In the article that follows, David Buckholdt and Jaber Gubrium describe how "staffings" deal with the issue of doubt.

---

*Kane, "Multi-disciplinary Teamwork," pp. 138–139.

Doing Staffings*

DAVID R. BUCKHOLDT AND JABER F. GUBRIUM

Negotiating Progress

. . . There are frequent references [at staffings] to improvement or regression in the status of client troubles. Some clients change for the better, while others remain the same or even deteriorate. One of the major functions of staffing is to assess change. For those who are doing well, current programing can be maintained, but some modification in treatment may be required for those who are lagging. What this fails to make clear, however, is that there is considerable practical work involved in construing the meaning of progress or regress in individual clients.

Consider the following three examples of the construction of client progress in staffings. The first one occurs at Cedarview. The social worker opens the staffing by describing the circumstances surrounding a boy's admission to the center. He then portrays what he sees as considerable progress in the child since admission. The kid runs away from the center much less frequently, he is in better control of his aggression, his bedwetting has ceased, he has less anxiety and is in closer touch with reality, he has developed more self-control and trust, he is more patient in difficult situations, and he is better able to express his inner feelings. The consulting psychologist enters the conversation.

Psychologist:	How can you tell if his trust is shallow or deep?
Social worker:	He tells you about some problems now. He used to keep in problems, then explode, and then forget it. He was mute. But now he will give you some indication of a problem.
Psychologist:	Is that good? Of what utility is it to be able to talk about problems?
Social worker:	He's more aware of them.
Psychologist:	OK, as a kind of substitute for exploding. He has learned to pinpoint his problems better. Then others can help him. So it is a progression.
Social worker:	Yes it is!
Psychologist:	One problem may be his language difficulty. He is in the slow learner category in language. It's hard to express yourself if you have these verbal problems. [Elaborates]
Principal:	We haven't seen much improvement in school. He can't express his reasons for being angry. He still explodes and runs. He doesn't always comprehend what you want from him. He explodes, screams, kicks, but then forgets in ten minutes later. He blocks out the whole thing.

*Excerpted by permission of the Society of Applied Anthropology from *Human Organization* 38 (1979): 255–264.

The principal then reports that the boy has been attending a special class in the public schools in the morning. The boy seems to enjoy it and to be doing well. The psychologist asks if that means that the boy can go home soon. The conversation now turns to the mother and her many inadequacies. She is depicted as uncooperative, ineffective, impulsive, seductive, and sexually promiscuous. Several participants now claim that the boy will never make any real progress until the mother cooperates with them:

> Psychologist: Has he really made any significant gains here [Cedarview]?

Negative head-shaking all around.

> Psychologist: Then why are we thinking of sending him home?
> Social Worker: Because we've reached the limits of what we can do.
> Principal: I disagree. The outside class will be good for him, but what
>   about the rest of the day? He'll really regress if he goes
>   home. I'm convinced that the only reason we see any
>   progress now is that he's gone part of the day and we don't
>   see him as much.

An extended discussion follows about how they might help the mother and what they might do for the boy in order to achieve "at least some" improvement.

Has this boy improved or not? Notice how this judgment changes as the conversation shifts in context. At the beginning, he is said to have made considerable progress, but at the end this is said to be illusory, a function of the staff's seeing less of him. Progress or regress takes on its meaning in relation to a shifting background of meanings. As part of both staff's professional and constructive images of their affairs, it is reasonable and obvious that they, of course, attend to the varied contexts of their business together.

The second example is taken from a Murray Manor staffing. In this particular gathering, the patient's progress is construed in the context of at least two different agendas: a physician's assessment of the patient's behavior during examinations and the nurses' concern with the manageability of the patient. Note how varied accounts are used to make reasonable the disparity of views.

The patient is Cora Kilpatrick, who is being staffed specifically to decide whether she should be transferred from residential care to skilled nursing. The usual complement of professional staff members is in attendance. In addition, a concerned nurse's aid and Cora's private physician have been invited to the staffing. The staffing is more or less aimed at the physician, for he will write the order for whatever action is warranted in Cora's further care.

The staffing begins with the medical review of the patient by one of the nurses. A number of comments are made about specific points in the review, questions and answers concerning Cora's current health, her physical complaints, the medications that she takes, their relative effectiveness, and so on. Her behavioral status then becomes the topic of discussion. According to the charge nurse, Cora has had an unusual number of incidents recently such as falling, sudden lack of steadiness, and bursts of combativeness harmful to others. As a result of the incidents and her general behavior of late, the charge nurse concludes, "We just can't handle her on first [the residential floor] anymore. We just don't have the manpower."

Cora's physician asks to see the incident reports. The director of nursing leaves the room to get them. While she is out, the physician states that he finds it strange that Cora is causing the staff so much trouble since it has been his observation that she is quite steady on her feet—in fact, is comparatively nimble—adding that his observation is based on recent contacts with Cora. Several staff members then respectfully respond that he does not really know what Cora is like in matters of day-to-day living. The aide adds, "Yeah. She's just awful . . . impossible to deal with. She's always runnin' and fallin' all over the place, and she really don't know what she's doin' most of the time." The physician listens attentively, accepting the useful information.

Meanwhile, the director of nursing has returned with two incident reports. Taking them, the physician questions in jest, "Only two? From what everyone was saying, I expected to see a stack three feet high." They all laugh, including the director of nursing, who responds, "Oh, there's more. There's more. You better believe it. You can't record everything. You know how it is." The aide confirms this: "We're just too darn busy to fill out one of those forms every time something happens." Cora's physician assures them, "Yeah. I know what you mean."

The physician then reads through the two reports and notes that, in both instances, Cora's "condition before incident" is marked "senile" (rather than "normal," "disoriented," "sedated," or "other"). As before, he asks why she has been diagnosed senile, because his recent observations stand in contrast. Again, several staff members add that Cora is indeed, as they put it, "really confused" and "unrealistic." The aide even suggests that the physician's observations are invalid when she informs him, "I'm not sure if you can count that, doctor, because she really puts on a straight show when someone like you comes around. That's not the real Cora we all know 95 percent of the time." Again, the physician concludes, "Yes, I see." The director of nursing, in turn, suggests, "Those two incident reports, when you think about it, are just a very small sample of all the things that've been happening with Cora."

As the staffing comes to a close, the administrator addresses the physician: "So we recommend, doctor, that Cora be moved to a skilled nursing floor . . . for her own welfare. What is your opinion on the matter?" The physician answers, "Yes. I think we can do that for the good of all concerned."

By accepting the data recorded on the reports simply as *the* data, it is suggested that what little data are available about Cora's mental condition are a small sample representative of a large number of incidents that went unrecorded. The real fact of the matter becomes, as an aide remarked and everyone accepted, Cora is senile "95 percent of the time."

Subsequent references to Cora's mental condition, in talk and in writing, mention the 95 percent figure and the incident report data as representative cases. The 95 percent figure comes to be spoken of as *the* data on Cora and what *the* data show. The general reference takes on a life of its own.

Underpinning the professional perspective on client data is the use, creation, and/or reconstitution of data in practice. The validity of data on clients is subject to considerable negotiation among staffers. For example, staffers may debate the accuracy of a psychological report completed by someone at a consulting clinic. In one case, at Cedarview, a psychological report stated that a boy had normal psychological functioning but that his parents were disturbed. After considerable debate on this report, staffers concluded that the clever boy had fooled the psychologist. His cleverness was then used as evidence for his severe disturbance. In another case, staffers agreed with the conclusion of an intake report that described a client as a borderline psychotic, but they dismissed the evidence used to support this conclusion. The evidence for this diagnosis actually lay elsewhere, according to them.

The validity of data is not self-evident in numbers, charts, graphs, or whatever, but is negotiated and construed in the context of staff discussions. For example, at Cedarview, there is a heavy emphasis on behavior modification. Teachers, social workers, child care workers, and others are constantly taking counts of one behavior or another. The counts serve as so-called baseline or follow-up measures of a problem prior to, during, and after treatment. The measures are taken to assess treatment effectiveness during and after intervention. In principle, they are believed to be objective measures. Yet during staffings, when counts are reported, this objectivity is often questioned, as seen in the following excerpt from a staffing.

The staffers have been discussing recent changes in a child's behavior. The consulting psychologist asks the teacher to report her counts on fighting.

Teacher:	If you look at this [chart], he is doing pretty well. I've only gotten two fighting episodes each of the past three days. His baseline was twelve, twelve, and fifteen.
Psychologist:	He does seem to be doing better.
Assistant	
Teacher:	I don't really see the change. He still seems to be fighting a lot. I think he knows when you're counting and lays off. He's really sneaky, ya' know. He punches kids on his way by and we don't see it.

Child Care
worker: He's still fighting in the cottage. I'm not counting that but I
                know he's still causing a lot of problems with the rest of the
                kids. [Elaborates]
Teacher: Should I change my counts?
Psychologist: Well, if he hasn't changed much, your data should show that.
Teacher: What should I put, twelve or fifteen or so?
Assistant
teacher: I think fifteen would be pretty close for a day.
Teacher: O K. Fifteen. [Changes her measures]
Psychologist: Watch him more closely, when he isn't aware of what you're
                doing. See if fifteen is about right. It may be even higher. The
                actual number isn't so important as long as we have some
                reading on changes or trends.

Of course, staffers view discussions like this as part of the process of
establishing sound data. It makes good sense to compare data on clients
with what staff know from daily experience rather than simply accepting
data blindly. If the data are believed to be flawed, staff renew their efforts
and revise their procedures for getting at the truth. What they do not
routinely recognize is that there are multiple truths or several reasonable
ways to interpret data on the progress of each client. Which of these
truths wins out, at least temporarily, is as much dependent on sound data
as on the dynamics of discussions in staffings. Staffers may literally talk
themselves into or out of the validity of one or another set of conclusions
despite the balance of data available about a client and the progress in
treating his troubles. . . .

━━━━━━━━━━━━━━

A major skill for a clinician is the ability not to panic in the face of
doubt and not to be angry at clients when doubt results in lack of
progress. Collegial relationships should not be used to engage in professional back-biting, one-upsmanship, and power struggles designed to
cover up the anxiety that arises from doubts about organizational actions.
The beginning of all wisdom is uncertainty. The ability to say, "I don't
know" is the hallmark of professionalism. Allowing for the possibility
that one does not know allows one to search for new solutions. Dogma-
tism cuts off this search.

Yet professionalism has as one of its functions the removal of doubt. It
takes great skill to elicit doubt from another person whose professional
status and professional life are tied up with appearing to know. Dealing
with this professional mind-set is no less formidable a task than dealing
with clients' rigidities and defenses, which are likewise designed to maintain psychological stability and equilibrium.

Buckholdt and Gubrium, in the preceding article, point out how client assessments tends to be negotiated almost as if assessment were a political process. The nurses and aides think that they cannot handle Cora any more, and her physician reassesses his diagnosis as an outcome of the dynamics of the discussion itself and the staff's emphasis on the context of her behavior.

A negotiated assessment is not necessarily a correct one. While it may have been necessary to move Cora, everyone should know that it is not being done because of her senility but because of the needs of the hospital and the staff. Clarity about this is needed to prevent real damage from being done to the client, for people defined as profoundly senile tend to act out their label.

Nevertheless, it is not illegitimate to consider organizational needs when making decisions about clients. How much service can one patient command without depriving other patients of care? How many disabled people can be "mainstreamed" into a settlement house club group without changing the nature of the group? The illegitimate act is to mask organizational interests as clinical assessment.

Another connection between collegiality and practice is related to communication skills. Clinicians are adept at hearing unspoken messages, picking up verbal and nonverbal clues, and getting at the facts and feelings that underlie words. Perhaps the great trap of collegiality is dealing exclusively with overt communication about concrete work plans and paying too little attention to underlying messages and emotional needs. Communication between colleagues is infinitely more complex than communication with one's client. Colleagues often resent any hint that one is "caseworking" or analyzing them, even when one is not, and even when one cannot be direct in making requests of them. In addition, face-to-face contact with colleagues is not always possible; there is not often time to clear up confusions; and there is rarely sufficient attention to the message being communicated.

Communication problems between colleagues are often symptons of a lack of trust and of struggles over power, rewards, and authority. Yet, although we have observed above that not all problems are communication problems, communication problems do in fact exist, and a good colleague is skilled in dealing with these.

A good colleague thinks about the channel of communication he or she is going to use. If dozens of memos are sent around every week in an agency, a memo is probably not a good channel of communication for other than the most routine matters. There are other channels besides the formal ones—for example, friendship groups, status groups, and mutual assistance networks. The medium may be the message.

Just as there are communication barriers between clients and therapists, there are barriers among colleagues. Some of these are merely geographical or mechanical (one's colleagues are based in different buildings); others are related to status (a professional does not think that attendants can observe clients objectively); others come from resentments and hurt feelings (one thinks that one should have gotten a promotion); and others are procedural, rooted in the scale and complexity of the formal communication system, which inevitably create distortions and time gaps (three weeks have gone by, and one's memo has not been acknowledged).

The good communicator is one who keeps in mind the problems of the receiver of the communication. The receiver needs to know if the message is reliable, what the intent of the sender was, what importance or priority should be attached to the message, and what the sender actually meant. Obviously, the only way to handle these problems is to provide opportunities for feedback and not simply assume that the message has been received. One sets aside time for feedback in clinical practice; one should do so in collegial relationships as well.

Another skill that is equally important in clinical practice and collegial relationships is the ability to confront. Confrontation does not have to be angry or aggressive. Nor does it have to result in conflict, although it may. In confronting clients the crucial issue is to state the problem in a nonaccusatory fashion—as an observation, not a criticism. The object of the confrontation is to engage the client in looking at a particular issue while at the same time allowing him or her the space to disagree. Similarly, the object of an organizational confrontation is to enlist collegaues in some common problem solving.

A common difficulty in collegial confrontation is that, as we have noted before, different professions, and at times even members of the same profession, tend to use language differently. There is also the problem of timing. Finally, if there is great distrust between professions—for example, if there are conflicts over turf—this is not the time for confrontation. Without trust, a confrontation tends to develop quickly into an accusatory session, rather than a problem-solving one.

Attitudes, Values and Skills

One's attitudes and values may either aid or impede good collegial relationships and communication. Although the discussion in this chapter has focused on interprofessional or intraprofessional relationships, collegial relationships between workers and administrators are equally important—or perhaps even more important—in the running of social agencies. In other chapters we allude to workers' sense that managers do not care—that they are only concerned with monetary issues or with the routine and stable functioning of the organization. An us-them attitude on the part of workers is not conducive to collegial relationships. Such an attitude is frequently based on a conception of the organization as a parliament or congress in which decisions are made democratically, through voting, rather than through a process that relies on authority. This model is known as *participative management*.

In many ways the integrative team embodies the ideals of participative management: full and free communication of ideas and information, regardless of rank or power; a reliance on consensus rather than top down decision-making a belief that influence should be based on technical competence and knowledge rather than power and authority; a confidence that conflict between individuals and the organization can be dealt with on rational or therapeutic grounds. There are clearly a great many advantages to encouraging more participation in organizational life. Diverse viewpoints and experiences are brought to bear on problems; people have different decision-making or analytic skills that can be tapped; it is possible to win commitment by involving people in the decision-making process.

Unfortunately, as we suggested above, there is an attitudinal problem related to participative management. Staff members may see it as an end, rather than a means; they may believe in it ideologically, rather than accepting it as an administrative technique that will work with some people and in some organizations and not with other people and in other organizations. The ideological commitment to participation stems in part from a fear of "elitism" and a belief that participation can be a substitute for expertise. There is in fact a difference between the two. It is likely that for certain people participation involves merely the sharing of ignorance.

Related problems are the widespread lack of appreciation for the time and expense involved in participation and the tendency to underestimate the difficulty of handling conflict and hostility in organizational life and the value of authority in dealing with such problems. People may also fail to recognize that implementation cannot be separated from decision making and that peers have great difficulty regulating peers.

Finally, as Richard Weatherley points out, "to be successful participative management requires considerable skill on the part of both administrators and workers. Not only are such participative skills difficult to acquire, they can be positively dysfunctional in bureaucracies organized along hierarchical lines. Techniques for active listening, paraphrasing, giving and getting feedback, and reaching consensus, must be learned and practiced in a supportive environment . . . not only do new interpersonal techniques have to be learned, but conventional modes of control and subordination must be unlearned or at least suspended."* These developments would require a radical restructuring of agencies.

The colleague role requires that one see participation as a technique of great potential, but one that calls for experimentation to determine the

---

*Richard Weatherley, "Participative Management in Public Welfare: What Are Its Prospects?" *Administration in Social Work (Spring 1983): p. 48.*

extent to which workers and management can be cooperatively involved in making decisions and the point at which participation causes more problems than it is worth. To determine these limits, an attitude of collegiality between management and workers is absolutely essential. The us-them stance dooms in advance all efforts to improve the functioning of agencies.

On the positive side, collegiality is promoted by an organizational focus on what happens to clients—a belief that one's job is to help, rather than to help in a particular way. What the client wants is service. What the client needs is a worker who is dedicated to providing that service. One sets up teams in part to make it less likely that professionals will retreat to their professional theories and ideologies, seeing only those aspects of the client's problems that fall into their province. Because the team deals with a smaller number of clients, teamwork forces staff members to pay more attention to client's experiences and to the results achieved. Without a goal-orientation, there can be no collegiality. Without agreement about what we are working together for, we will inevitably be working at cross purposes.

Additional Readings

Benitez, Rosalind. "Psychiatric Consultation with Clerical Staff: A Systems Approach." *Social Casework* 60 (1979): 75–80.

Briggs, Thomas L. "Obstacles in Implementing the Team Approach in Social Service Agencies." In Susan Lonsdale, Adrian Webb and Thomas L. Briggs, eds., *Team Work in the Personal Social Services and Health Care*, pp. 75–91. Syracuse: Syracuse University School of Social Work, 1980.

Enelow, Alan, and W. Donald Weston. "Cooperation or Conflict: The Mental Health Administrator's Dilemma." *American Journal of Orthopsychiatry* 42 (1972): 603–609.

Hooyman, Gene. "Team Building in the Human Services." In Beulah Roberts Compton and Burt Galloway, eds., *Social Work Processes*, pp. 465–478. Homewood, Ill.: Dorsey Press, 1973.

Kahn, Alfred J. "Institutional Constraints to Interprofessional Practice." In Helen Rehr, ed., *Medicine and Social Work*, pp. 14–25. New York: Prodist, 1974.

Kane, Rosalie, "Multi-Disciplinary Teamwork in the United States: Trends, Issues and Implications for the Social Worker." In Susan Lonsdale, Adrian Webb, and Thomas L. Briggs, eds., *Teamwork in the Personal Social Services and Health Care*, pp. 138–151. Syracuse: Syracuse University School of Social Work, 1980.

Lowe, Jane, and Marjatta Herranen. "Conflict in Teamwork: Understanding Roles and Relationships." *Social Work in Health Care* 3 (1978): 323–330.

CHAPTER 5

ADVOCATE

To advocate is to plead another's cause. Working on behalf of disadvantaged minorities, the poor, and the handicapped, clinicians are often called upon to act as advocates in order to obtain changes in the interpretation of rules, services to which clients are entitled, redress from arbitrary decisions, and reforms in laws and program structures.

Even relatively affluent and politically potent clients occasionally require advocacy with employers, physicians, teachers, and the like. As a result, the social work literature contains periodic exhortations to social workers to engage in advocacy efforts. Indeed, the obligation to practice advocacy is stated in the Code of Ethics of the National Association of Social Workers.

Conversely, clinicians have for a long time been concerned about doing too much for clients and thus making them dependent and unable to take care of themselves. Although this is a danger, often the time required to teach self-advocacy skills to clients is not available, or the situation is so oppressive that failure to advocate would be both unethical and likely to result in harm to the client.

Overview

Advocacy is an essential component of clinical social work practice. It is also an essential component of social work. Since its inception, social work has distinguished itself from other "helping professions" by recognizing that people's problems have both a psychological and a social dimension. Some social workers have concentrated on changing the psyche; others have concentrated on social reforms. In reality, the two are intertwined. Both individual client advocacy and social advocacy— or, to use the more current terms, both case advocacy and class advocacy—are needed.

Case Advocacy and Class Advocacy: Case advocacy involves work on behalf of individual clients or small groups of clients; tenants in relation to a landlord, a student in relation to a teacher, and so on. Class advocacy involves work on behalf of a category or class of clients who share a similar status and set of related needs or problems. A practitioner of class advocacy might petition for changes in public welfare laws, rights of access for the physically disabled, or fair housing codes.

Although case and class advocacy are conceptually distinct, they exist along a practice continuum. Most social work advocates do some of both. A single case advocacy effort may reveal a need for class advocacy; for example, a school social worker may recommend tutorials for a particular child and then discover that no such service exists. As a result, he or she may enlist others in an effort to get the school board to provide such a service for all needy youngsters. Conversely, efforts at class advocacy can uncover a need for case advocacy among individual members of a class of clients. Workers documenting a need for additional temporary housing for the homeless may encounter individuals who need assistance obtaining Medicaid and similar services.

The article by Brenda McGowan that follows details the history of the child advocacy movement in social work and gives a clear description of the continuum between case and class advocacy. McGowan also discusses the techniques and skills required of a case advocate.

The Case Advocacy Function in Child Welfare Practice*

BRENDA G. MCGOWAN

• • •

Child Advocacy as Cause and Function

The social welfare field has long been characterized by a shifting balance between social reform issues and preoccupation with technical concerns. In 1929 Lee first drew attention to this process, describing it as the movement from cause to function: "The development of social work from cause to function was inevitable; it was also indispensable to the permanence of its own great contribution as a cause. Once the objective of a cause is reached, it can be made permanent only by a combination of organization and education."† Conversely, when concern with technical problems begins to overshadow the original purpose, and, as frequently

*Excerpted by special permission of the Child Welfare League of America from *Child Welfare* 57 (1978): 275–284.

†Porter R. Lee, "Social Work as Cause and Function," presidential address to the National Conference of Social Work, 1929 in *Social Work as Cause and Function and Other Papers* (New York: Columbia University Press, 1937), p. 6.

happens, organizational means become ends, it is often necessary to redirect attention to the social cause.

From World War I until the last decade, child welfare workers defined their case responsibilities in increasingly narrow terms. Instead of focusing on the child and his/her family in their total environment, they concentrated on enhancing the child's physical and emotional growth. This was accomplished most frequently by "rescuing" the child from an unfit or unstable family situation and providing a substitute family experience; other times workers tried to enhance the parenting capacities in the natural family. But whether the emphasis was on supportive services to families or substitute care for children, little effort was made to deal with the social and economic forces necessitating placement or to make community agencies more responsive to the needs of children. In other words, instead of maintaining the social goals identified by the early leaders in the children's field,* child welfare workers became preoccupied with technical problems related to providing service to a small population of children at risk.

It is not surprising, therefore, that the child advocacy movement arose in the context of the social reform initiatives of the late 1960s. The child advocacy movement identified an important gap in service provision for children—the need to monitor and strengthen the services and institutions influencing their lives. Three major themes underlined this concept:

1. widespread recognition of the ecological approach to child development—that children develop not only through interaction with their families, but through transactions with institutions such as schools, hospitals, child care facilities, and recreation programs;
2. increased acceptance of the notion that in the same way parents have inherent responsibilities, so society has obligations to its children;
3. commitment to the idea that since services should be provided to children not as a result of charity or governmental largesse, but as a matter of right and entitlement, the institutions providing these services must be accountable to the public at large and to their consumers in particular.†

The key premise was the children have certain rights in relation to the social institutions affecting their lives and essential to their healthy development. However, because of differential opportunities for access, unequal distribution of resources, and defects inherent in bureaucratic organizations, there was a continual need to monitor and enhance the transactions between children and the social institutions impinging on their lives. The core of the child advocacy movement was the effort to address this need.

---

*One thinks, for example, of the efforts of Lillian Wald, Florence Kelley, Julia Lathrop, Grace Abbott, and others to establish the U.S. Children's Bureau, maternal and child health programs, child labor protections, and the juvenile court.

†Brenda G. McGowan, *Case Advocacy: A Study of the Interventive Process in Child Advocacy* (New York: Columbia University School of Social Work, 1973), pp. 11, 12.

Assuming Responsibility

The early federal initiatives were necessary to advance the _cause_ of children's rights, but it is essential for outside groups to continue to pressure for the expansion of children's rights if the social reform thrust is to be sustained. The critical issue for the social welfare profession is its willingness to assume responsibility for ensuring the rights and benefits obtained through social reform efforts as part of its ongoing _function._

Early in the child advocacy movement, attention was focused on establishing independent child advocacy projects free of vested interests, projects that could challenge the inadequate service provisions of established agencies; and it may have been necessary to develop specialized programs in order to create interest in the advocacy function so neglected in child welfare practice. However, [a] national study reported that the advocacy function—at least on a case level—could be implemented either as a specialized role or as a component of another role.* Recent literature on social work practice has highlighted the need for direct service practitioners to develop advocacy skills as part of their interventive repertoire.† It has been suggested that the professional's obligation to engage in advocacy is mandated by the Code of Ethics of the National Association of Social Workers‡ And at least one recent child welfare study has documented the efficacy of advocacy in preventive service programs.§ Therefore, there is strong rationale and precedent for defining the case advocacy function as an integral component of the professional role in child welfare agencies.‖

The rest of this article presents a model for case advocacy practice developed on the basis of an exploratory study of case advocacy on behalf of children.# The primary investigatory procedure for the study was the critical incident technique.** Study findings were based on 195 reports of

---

*Alfred J. Kahn, Sheila B. Kamerman and Brenda G. McGowan, _Child Advocacy: Report of a National Baseline Study_ (New York: Columbia University School of Social Work, 1972), p. 119.

†See, for example: Scott Briar, and Henry Miller, _Problems and Issues in Social Casework_ (New York: Columbia University Press, 1971), Allen Pincus and Anne Minahan, _Social Work Practice: Model and Method_, (Itasca, Ill.: Peacock, 1973); Max Siporin, _Introduction to Social Work Practice_ (New York: Macmillan, 1975).

‡Ad Hoc Committee on Advocacy. "The Social Worker as Advocate: Champion of Victims," _Social Work_ 14 (April 1969): 16–22.

§Mary Ann Jones, Renee Neuman, and Ann W. Shyne, _A Second Chance for Families_ (New York: Child Welfare League of America, 1976).

‖Class advocacy can also be defined as a component of the ongoing professional role. See, for example, Patrick V. Riley, "Family Advocacy: Case to Cause and Back to Case," _Child Welfare_ 50 (1971): 374–383. However, class advocacy may at times pose ethical dilemmas for the direct service practitioner because of potential conflict between individual and group interests.

#McGowan, _Case Advocacy_.

**John C. Flanagan, "The Critical Incident Technique," _Psychological Bulletin_ 51 (1954): 327–359.

advocacy interventions submitted by thirty-nine direct service practitioners in eight child advocacy programs located in different parts of the country. Although the study focused on the interventive process employed in child advocacy programs, advocacy skills are essential for all direct service practitioners, and the interventive techniques used by advocacy specialists should be equally efficacious when employed by child welfare practitioners.* Since the study was completed, this model has been used successfully by students and practitioners in case advocacy in many different fields of practice.

A Model for Case Advocacy Practice†

Case advocacy is a complex, dynamic process in which there are many interrelated variables. The advocacy process may be initiated by the _Change agent_ (advocate) or the _client_ (person expected to benefit from the intervention), who may be an individual, a family, a group, or a class of similar persons with similar interests—for example, parents of retarded children, or youths suspended from school.

Together the advocate and client system must define the problem. This is a critical point in the advocacy process because the definition determines the target system, the way the intervention should be carried out, and what objective will be achieved. For example, a worker investigating a child neglect complaint might discover that the children in a family were not receiving an adequate diet. He might decide that this was a result of parental ignorance or incapacity, and engage in parent education or counseling. Another worker investigating the same complaint might discover that the family had been denied the food stamps to which they were entitled, and file a grievance with the welfare department. Still another worker might decide that the family were receiving all the benefits to which they were entitled, but because of inflation their food budget was no longer adequate; therefore, he might want to initiate a community organizing or lobbying effort aimed at raising the level of welfare payments.

Thus, there is a strong relationship between problem definition and the target system, objective, and sanction for the worker's intervention. The target system may be internal (the worker's own agency) or it may be some outside service system such as a school, welfare department, hospital, or juvenile court.‡ No matter what the target system, the worker

---

*Two agencies participating in the study were traditional child welfare agencies. There were no significant differences between the techniques used by workers in these agencies and those used by workers in specialized advocacy projects.

†This section is adapted from McGowan, _Case Advocacy_, chap. 6–8. The research on which this section is based was supported in part by a grant from the Office of Child Development, U.S. Department of Health, Education and Welfare (OCD-CB-386).

‡The internal target system is not dealt with in this paper.

must decide whether the objective is to obtain a right or benefit to which the client is entitled, to enhance the quantity or quality of existing services or benefits, or to develop a new resource or service.

The sanction is directly related to the objective because if the goal is to secure an existing right or entitlement, the advocate's sanction derives from the law or administrative regulation that has been violated. If the objective is to enhance existing services or to develop new resources, the advocate's sanction is more likely to derive from the target system's stated policies or goals, professional values, or expressed client need. In the former situation, the advocate knows that ultimately he should succeed because he has the right to use whatever means are necessary to redress a violation of client rights; but in the latter situation, the advocate has fewer strategical options and little assurance of success. For example, if a student has been suspended from school without a prior hearing, the advocate can ask that the student be reinstated and, if this request is not granted, demand that the student get a proper hearing. If a student has not been promoted because he failed an exam, the advocate may request that the teacher reconsider the grade, or may try to persuade the school administration that because of the teacher's attitude, the student cannot learn in this classroom and should be promoted despite the failing grade. In the school suspension case, the advocate knows he will ultimately succeed if the school has failed to follow established due-process procedures, but in the student failure case, the advocate's success depends on the goodwill of respondents in the target system.

Two other variables affect the selection of strategy. The first is the receptivity of the target system to the change. If significant members of the target system are likely to favor the advocate's request, often all the worker has to do is bring the problem to their attention and suggest a possible solution; but if significant persons in the target system are opposed to the proposed change, the advocate may have to undertake more intensive and complex interventions to achieve his goal.

The resources of the advocate also affect the selection of strategy. For example, the knowledge, skill, time, and commitment of the advocate will affect his plan for intervention, as will the degree of support and influence he can expect from other persons in his agency, the target system, and/or the larger community. Similarly, the level of client involvement and resources has a major influence on the selection of strategy.

No single variable determines the mode of intervention. Decisions regarding strategy, which involve consideration of the mode, object, and level of intervention, must be made on the basis of an assessment of all the variables.

Three major strategies are available to the advocate: collaborative, in which the worker attempts to elicit the interest or support of the target system, posing the issue as a joint problem; mediatory, in which the worker acknowledges differences and attempts to negotiate an agreement or compromise between the client and target system; and adversarial, in which the worker perceives the target system as an opponent and attempts to win his objective through actual or implied power. Selection of the basic strategy therefore depends primarily on the advocate's analysis of the degree of convergence between the goals of the client and the target system; yet other variables may also affect the worker's approach. For example, although there may be strong goal conflict between the client and target system, the worker may use a collaborative strategy and try to persuade the target system to adopt his position because he does not have the resources for a power struggle.

Once the basic strategy has been selected, the advocate must decide at what level he wants to intervene, with whom, and by what methods. . . .

Generally, the successful advocate uses a blend of interventions, starting with intercession or persuasion at the lowest level with the most readily accessible members of the target system. If it seems necessary, he may decide to negotiate or intervene with different segments of the target system. If these approaches fail and he has a strong enough case (i.e., the problem is serious and the sanction clear), the advocate may move into an adversarial stance, intervening at the top levels and using pressure or coercion if necessary.

Evaluation of the outcome produces feedback that may lead to a shift in the advocate's assessment of the appropriate object, level, or method of intervention; or the feedback may change the worker's definition of the problem, target system, or desired solution. . . .

The Key Questions

Analysis of the advocacy process indicates that the major questions confronting the change agent are:

- What is the source of the problem?
- What is the appropriate target system?
- What is the objective?
- What is the sanction for the proposed intervention?
- What resources are available for the intervention?
- How receptive is the target system?
- With whom should the intervention be carried out?
- At what level should the intervention take place?
- What methods of intervention should be employed?
- What is the outcome? (If the objective has not been achieved, is there another approach that can be employed? If the immediate objective has been achieved, has another problem been identified that requires additional advocacy?)

The answers to these questions should guide the advocate's decision-making process and shape his activities. Effective advocacy does not rely on careful, logical analysis alone. It also demands sensitivity, flexibility, and imagination, qualities that reflect the skill and style of the individual worker. Yet case advocacy is a rational, if complex, process that can be taught, practiced, and evaluated on a systematic basis; as such, it is an appropriate function for the social work profession.

The success of a social cause depends almost entirely on the zeal, charisma, and imagination of its leaders. Therefore, as Steiner suggested, those concerned about federal policy toward children would do well to involve volunteer community activists and social reformers in their change efforts. The stakes are too high and the value choices too complex to leave the children's cause solely to professionals and existing interest groups.* And if the initial victories of the child advocacy movement in expanding children's rights in relation to the social institutions impinging on their lives are to be sustained, there must also be constant, vigilant effort to ensure implementation of these rights on an individual basis. Child welfare workers should be ready to assume this responsibility by defining case advocacy as an integral part of their professional role.

The Hazards of Advocacy: Although some social workers have always been engaged in advocacy, a re-emphasis on it occurred as an outgrowth of social workers' experience in the War on Poverty in the late sixties and early seventies. While it is hard to refute the necessity for advocacy, in the main this role has not been accepted in the field. Advocacy seems usually to evolve out of the ethical stance of social workers in relation to their clients. Yet advocacy can involve agencies in conflicts with other agencies, with members of their boards of directors, with elected political officials, and with other interest groups. If the agency is unwilling to engage in conflict or puts certain types of it off limits, then the advocate is not a free agent. The agency will determine whom and what he or she may engage in advocacy for. There obviously is fertile ground for sharp disagreement between workers and agencies, related to the basic strain between goal-attainment and agency survival.

Another difficulty for the clinician-advocate lies in the risk involved. During the War on Poverty, each worker was to be an advocate, an ombudsman, even at the risk of personal or agency conflict. Clients were organized to bring political pressure on the bureaucracies. Sit-ins, confrontations, boycotts, and marches were the order of the day. The message was that worker-advocates and the client could hold the agency accountable. The problem with this vision of a worker-client alliance is

*Gilbert Y. Steiner, *The Children's Cause* (Washington, D.C.: Brookings Institution, 1976), chap. 10.

that the needs of the two groups are not identical. Many workers were not willing to risk their jobs by becoming "bureaucratic guerrillas;" others were temperamentally unsuited to conflict. All had a vested interest in agency survival. In other words, the potential costs of advocacy were often seen as too high.

And many clients were not interested in helping other clients; they merely wanted to secure services for themselves. Once they had done so, their interest in joining with other clients to press for services waned.

Another problem is that a clinician's work as a case manager or team member requires a great deal of collaboration. One cannot be in continual disagreement and conflict on one set of issues still and expect others to cooperate on others.

Finally, few advocates in the seventies recognized advocacy as a social process that redistributes rewards and costs to all who are affected by any one transaction. It was easy then to overestimate the potential rewards to clients and underestimate the cost to agency functioning. One way to judge the relationship between rewards and costs is to apply George Homans's theory of exchange.*

In prior chapters we have talked about the material and psychic rewards and the variety of costs—risks, obligations, undesired consequences, and lost opportunities—involved in exchanges. The exchanges occur between individuals, groups, or organizations when something is invested in a human relationship in the hopes of some return or reward.

Advocacy involves an exchange: something is to be given to a client in exchange for something else; in other words, those who give something to a client get some reward for doing it. The rewards and costs of advocacy are affected by (1) what one wants; (2) the procedure that one uses to get it; and (3) the structures that one uses. Some workers find it very rewarding or costly to relate to the people who work at certain agencies and have certain statuses. For example, time and time again case aides have tried to act as advocates for their clients, only to fail where professionally trained clinicians have been successful. The problem was that some professionals wish to interact only with their professional peers. In other situations, for similar reasons, the case aides might have been more successful than the trained clinicians.

The concept of exchange illuminates advocacy by reminding an advocate that what may be rewarding for an individual worker may be very costly to his or her agency or department. If advocacy is to be successful, the rewards must outweigh the costs. This algebra must inform the tactics and strategies utilized by advocates.

The article by Mildred Mailick and Ardythe Ashley that follows provides case examples of conflicts between the advocate role and the

*George Homans, "Social Behavior as Exchange," *American Journal of Sociology* 63 (1958): 597–606.

colleague role. In reading it, the reader should consider these conflicts in terms of an exchange process.

Politics of Interprofessional Collaboration: Challenge to Advocacy*

Mildred D. Mailick and Ardythe A. Ashley

• • •

The Culture of the Interprofessional Collaborative Group

Small-group theory suggests that those engaged in collaborative activities are likely to develop a group culture, ideology, authority system, division of labor, and set of norms. Although these groups may vary depending on purpose, size, auspice, and participants, the *sine qua non* of all of them is the development of the value of cooperation and the push toward consensus. Consensus allows for a unified plan to be agreed on and for each participant to carry out his or her own specific function within that plan.

Collaborative groups have been criticized as being vulnerable to intellectual inbreeding.† The need for consensus and the wish to avoid extending long and burdensome controversies may lead to compromise and decision making based on insufficient information. Collaborative groups sometimes develop stereotyped methods of responding to problems. One theoretical formulation may gain ascendancy and be applied to problems for which it is not particularly appropriate. If one member of the group rises to challenge or to express a difference of opinion about the theory, the inquiry sometimes is interpreted as an indication of disloyalty, contentiousness, or an inability to get along. The questioner may be ignored, responded to in a condescending manner, or subtly punished by exclusion for the elite circle. Cohesion as a primary goal displaces service in the best interest of the client. The pressure on the individual worker to fit in and to maintain the goodwill of the collaborative group is very strong.

The pressure for consensus does not fall equally on all of the participants. The relative autonomy of members of the collaborative group is related to their status and power and is usually heavily dependent on the prestige of the profession and its perceived centrality to the goals of the group. Some group members have legally sanctioned functions that increase their power and authority. Others are more peripheral or are dependent on their colleagues' goodwill to perform their tasks. Personality traits as well as age, sex, socioecnomic status, and racial or ethnic

*Excerpted with special permission of the Family Service Association of America from *Social Casework* (1981): 131–137.

†Bernice T. Eiduson, "Intellectual Inbreeding in the Clinic?" *American Journal of Orthopsychiatry* 34 (1964): 714–721.

factors also contribute to the member's position within the group. The resultant status differentials add complexity to the group structure and culture and create a situation in which low-status or aspiring members are likely to adhere more strongly to the group values, while high-status individuals are relatively independent of them.

The participants' adherence to the norms of the interprofessional culture are also affected by their ties to their own professional associations. When these associations are strong and have the sanction to monitor their members' professional behavior and control their rights to practice, they exert considerable power. Members are likely to develop strong professional group identifications that take precedence over loyalty to the norms of the institution or the collaborative culture. The American Medical Association and the American Bar Association are examples of this type of professional organization. Physicians and lawyers are more likely to invoke their professional code of ethics as justification for not acceding to institutional group pressure. However, when the professional association is weaker, it is less likely to influence its members' behavior, primary identification, and loyalty. Its members, having a weaker external professional anchoring, are more vulnerable to the presure of the collaborative culture and less able to take an independent stance.

Because it does not control access to practice, the National Association of Social Workers can monitor the behavior only of those social workers who voluntarily submit to its sanctions. Its Code of Ethnics is general and could possibly be construed to support either conformity to institutional norms or pursuit of a more radical course. One study of its members suggests that a high professional role identification is not a good predictor of orientation to client needs, but rather appears to indicate either that the social worker will hold conservative conformist attitudes or take an independent client-oriented stance* . . .

Advocacy and Collaboration Considered Together

Advocacy and collaboration share in common many methods of achieving their goals. The provision of information, education, clarification, problem solving, the suggestion of alternatives, and persuasion are all techniques that apply to both activities. Advocacy does, however, imply additional tactics, such as the mobilization of organizational pressure, the development of coalitions, and mild coercion. Most important, advocacy requires placing the interest of the client above other considerations, even though this sometimes results in an increased level of discord with colleagues. The culture of many collaborative groups emphasizes coop-

*Irwin Epstein, "Professional Role Orientations and Conflict Strategies, *Social Work* 15 (1970): 87–92

eration. It should, but often does not, allow for a process to occur in which conflicts, differences of opinion, and approaches to problems are thoroughly aired and resolved. Compliance is achieved at the expense of individual contributions and creativity.

The Practice of Advocacy in the Collaborative Group

Social workers in collaborative groups are often in a quandary about if, when, and how they should challenge the norm of cooperation and consensus and take an independent position in advocacy for their client. Of utmost importance in working with a collaborative group is the capacity to listen, to be respectful, to understand the implications of other professional opinions, to be willing to recognize and accept areas in which the expertise of colleagues is unique, and to defer to special knowledge when appropriate. However, the process of deferring should be based on professional judgment and on an active evaluation of what is best for the client, not on acquiescence to group pressure. Social workers must respect their own values, knowledge, and frame of reference when they have an honest difference of opinion or conflicting perceptions of problems.

When the social worker differs from his or her colleagues, natural questions follow. Who is right? Is there, in fact, a right or wrong position in the situation being considered? Or are the differences related to divergent professional perceptions and value systems? How much of the difference can be attributed to a worker's style? Can the social worker set his or her own style, frame of reference, and value system above those held by others in the collaborative group?*

In a mental health setting with a treatment program for drug offenders, for example, a social worker was seen as constantly giving the clients special privileges and undermining the team's efforts to "socialize" the clients. What the social worker was doing was allowing the clients time off from the program's meetings and activities in order to pursue welfare monies and various other concrete social services. The worker felt a responsibility to advocate for the clients' right to these services, although, for the team, the work of the therapeutic program was paramount.

In the absence of unequivocal answer to these vexing questions, will the social worker respond, as [Robert] Merton suggests, to the pressure of the opinion of the dominant profession in the reference group, redefining or reinterpreting the client's need to coincide with it?

Social workers cannot lay special claim to having a higher level of knowledge or devotion to the welfare of the client than other professions.

*Ronda S. Connaway, "Teamwork and Social Worker Advocacy: Conflicts and Possibilities," *Community Mental Health Journal* 11 (1975): 381–388.

Each professional group has a formal or informal code of ethics that espouses the primacy of client need. Each has defensible knowledge base and theoretical framework that directs the selection of relevant data in defining the problems of the client and developing appropriate solutions. However, the interpretation of what is good for the client may differ markedly. The psychosocial orientation and the holistic approach of the social worker often point to different solutions than those of other professionals. It is difficult for social workers to "go against the crowd." Yet they are bound by their Code of Ethics not to remain silent.

In a day treatment facility for chronic alcoholics, for example, a social worker presented the case of an elderly eccentric artist to the team, which included vocational counselors, a nutritionist, psychiatrists, and paraprofessionals. On the basis of the presentation, a psychiatrist diagnosed the man as being a chronic, undifferentiated schizophrenic and prescribed prolixin for him. The client experienced the medication as punitive and complained that it made him sleepy and unable to paint. The social worker advocated for the client's right to remain drug-free, particularly as he was not currently abusing alcohol. This created extreme tension within the team and, eventually, the worker acquiesced.

Perhaps part of the discomfort or burnout experienced by social workers working in collaborative groups is that they must either bear the disapproval of their collaborative peers and take an independent stance or they must suffer ethical dissonance and loss of identity with their own profession by not adhering to their Code of Ethics.

When to Advocate

A second set of questions facing the social worker is *when* to advocate for the client. Should the social worker take a stand in opposition each time he or she is in disagreement with the collaborative group, or is it better to develop a political approach, choosing only the most important occasions to do so? The worker in the collaborative group runs the risk of losing the respect of colleagues by invoking the right to dissent too often and then may be excluded from the group, circumvented, or ignored, thus losing the capacity for any influence at all. However, when the worker begins to make selections about which client to advocate for, it reduces the sense of consistency and security in decision making. Under the pressure of need for acceptance by the group, the worker may select only the most flagrant cases for advocacy, abandoning those whose situations are less pressing or more ambiguous.

Political acumen is an important component of the practice of advocacy. The worker needs to develop a series of principles to draw on in the selection of situations on which he or she will take a stand. These may include setting priorities for those cases in which advocacy would support the client's right to exercise choice or preference, encourage the establishment of a precedent of importance or value to the total client group, point up a gap in service, or call into question a strongly held theory, value, or stereotype of the collaborative group.

In an outpatient clinic for pregnant women in a highly pressured, research-oriented teaching hospital, for example, the basic nutritional education of the clients was being neglected, in spite of the presence of nutritionists on the staff. However, several research studies on the nutritional patterns in poverty populations were in full swing. The social workers could continue to do the basic education case by case or advocate for a shift in emphasis involving another department's activities. This posed many dilemmas at the individual, team, and departmental levels.

The principles guiding the selection of priorities might vary depending on the institution or field of practice but, if made explicit, should serve to strengthen the decision making of the worker.

How to Advocate

The question of *how* to advocate requires the development of a broader theoretical knowledge base and a wider range of skills. These need to be explicitly included in both class and fieldwork education. Many schools of social work, like the profession as a whole, have been ambivalent about teaching advocacy as a component of practice. They neither disavow it nor adequately support it. Although the educational process encourages the development of diagnostic and treatment sophistication and enhances communication skills, it provides few opportunities to learn the dynamics of organizational behavior or to gain experience and expertise in political intervention in the organization and the community. Simon Slavin has pointed out that a lacuna exists in professional education, in that the positive functions of conflict and methods of analyzing different status positions, role sets, power dimensions, constituencies, and coalitions have lagged behind other areas of knowledge in the curriculum.*

In a newborn nursery of an inner-city hospital, for example, many of the young admissions were infants withdrawing from methodone or heroin because of their mothers' dependency. These babies were referred to by the medical staff as "DA's" (drug addicts). The parents were treated with such disrespect that they often reduced their visits to the nursery or refused to come at all. They would then be persecuted by the staff for being inattentive to their infants. Social work students on the interprofessional team attempted to break this cycle through formal or informal confrontations and failed.

*Simon Slavin, "Concepts of Social Conflict: Use in Social Work Curriculum," *Journal of Social Work Education* 5 (Fall 1969): 47–60.

Conclusion

In addition to better educational preparation, the social work profession as a whole has to offer much stronger support for advocacy. The new Code of Ethics adopted by the National Association of Social Workers in 1979 may facilitate this because it is more specific and detailed in its enunciation of the obligations of social workers toward clients. The professional organization must strengthen its power as a reference group, so that social workers can draw on their identification with it in their interactions with the collaborative group. It should provide forums for social workers to share concern for clients, represent those collective concerns in the political arena, and encourage the development of more effective advocacy approaches in each of the the fields of practice.

Social workers might also be supported in their capacity to advocate if their administrators provided appropriate leadership and modeling of advocacy in their own sphere of influence. The social work department should recognize the strains of working in collaborative groups and provide opportunities for the workers to discuss their problems and develop principles for the practice of advocacy.

Finally, social workers must consider their position within the collaborative group. A full appreciation of the complexity of the collaborative culture and a recognition of the role relationships with each member of the group are necessary. The social worker must come close enough to the collaboarative group to promote cooperative and mutual support, but maintain sufficient distance so that the group's norms will not be overwhelming. In the absence of a powerful position within the group, the social worker can build coalitions with others who have similar orientations. A careful exploration of the group's activities may reveal areas of autonomy that are available either because no one else is in contention for them or because conflicting powers neutralize each other and allow for freedom for the social worker to be independent. Above all, the social worker must understand that he or she is not dealing with a private trouble that needs to be handled in a personal way, but a professional problem for which principles of practice can be developed that will help to guide effective professional behavior.

No formula or rule can determine *a priori* whether a clinician should advocate a client's interests in a particular situation. In this sense, the NASW Code of Ethics is in error because it makes a general case for advocacy without considering the cost to agencies or to the advocate's other functions, such as collaboration. What the code should do is prescribe that every social worker think through the merits of advocacy for every case. The code's second flaw is that it applies only to individual social workers and not to social agencies. Yet the social agency is the hidden reality of social work. It is the agency that ultimately will determine what the worker can or cannot, should or should not, do. Although individual workers can be advocates for their clients in agencies that do not define advocacy as their function, their efforts will constantly be undercut and undermined.

What is needed is a code of ethics for social agencies. One facet of the code should relate to the agency's responsibility to incorporate class advocacy as one of its functions. No accrediting body, of course, can mandate that an agency must do particular things in particular situations, but such a requirement would legitimate the advocacy function in social agencies. This is important because the continual strain between the needs of the client and the needs of the agency inevitably works to the detriment of individual clients. Their interest should be bolstered by a code of ethics.

Those who consider the survival and maintenance needs of an agency illegitimate cannot function is social agencies as they are currently structured and funded; at the same time, those who would do anything to ensure the agency's survival are irresponsibile. Without balance between the equally important goals of client service and agency survival, sound judgments cannot be made.

Robert Sunley's article provides a number of suggestions on how agencies might structure class advocacy as part of their function. It also provides some examples of how particular cases lend themselves to the movement from case to cause.

Family Advocacy: From Case to Cause*

Robert Sunley

· · ·

Interventions

In casework, the worker (and other staff at times) selects the methods and modes of treatment for each client, based on the initial case evaluation. In family advocacy, similar steps seem necessary, from the initial interviews, through the study and diagnostic thinking, to the selection of interventions; the necessary participation of the client or client group is, obviously, on a different level in this process.

*Excerpted with special permission of the Family Service Association of America from *Social Casework* 51 (1970): 347–357.

Family agencies have traditionally used only a small number of the many kinds of interventions available for an advocacy program. The selection of which interventions to use in a given issue is a complex one, involving the nature of the problem, the objective, the nature of the adversary, the degree of militancy to which the agency will go, and the effectiveness of the method, generally and in relation to certain kinds of situations. All of these factors suggest the desirability of expert consultation for many agencies in an ongoing advocacy program. More than one method is usually included in an action program, with the result that the staff and the agency as a whole will become involved in various ways.

In advocacy programs it is important for the agency not to get caught in dilatory tactics so common in bureaucratic procedures; an overconcern for the niceties and politeness of "due process" may dishearten staff and cause suffering for the clients. Yet failure to study the situation carefully may result in a quick action's being dismissed because a necessary step was omitted. For example, a case brought against a school system was dismissed after a period of months because the court ruled that the plaintiff had failed to exhaust other remedies first, namely, an appeal to the board of education. By this time, the school year was almost over, the complaint no longer had any validity, and the child had been subjected to adverse conditions.

The following methods of intervention hardly exhaust the possibilities or the many variations used by groups (mainly nonsocial work) but suggest the wide range and the many types suitable for a family advocacy program.

1. *Studies and surveys*. These often form the groundwork for further action, both for the advocacy program itself and for educational and publicity purposes. Whatever the sources of the material, staff and board must be prepared to answer penetrating or hostile questions, and material should in effect be subjected to such an approach before it is used. Otherwise embarrasing loopholes may be exposed and the effort weakened.

2. *Expert testimony*. Social workers may be called upon to testify as professionals or agency representatives, with or without the backing of studies and surveys. While this method may not have great effect upon legislators or public officials, the absence of the social work voice may be noted adversely.

3. *Case conferences with other agencies*. This has traditionally been one important way in which the agency tries to effect change; by presenting the conditions and results of certain practices and regulations in given cases, one hopes to induce the other agency to change. This method may be of value in the early stages of an advocacy effort, especially if it can involve higher officials of the other agency. It also elicits much about the potential adversary organization and may help to clarify just where the crux of the problem lies—at the level of staff practice, supervision,

middle or top administration, board, or beyond the agency. Such conferences held with clients present can have other values as well and may be the first step in developing a client group determined to go further in action on its own behalf.

4. *Interagency committees.* Such committees, which often have proven to be splendid time-wasters, can offer the advantages of case conferences mentioned above. They can also be developed into types of permanent bodies which can represent yet another method of action in a given locality. In large suburban areas encompassing several small communities, various agencies may provide services within each small community but obviously cannot have a local base in each. An interagency committee can be developed involving local community agencies and the wider-based agencies to hand local issues. For example, the Family Service Association of Nassau County along with another agency started such a committee in one community, originally around overlapping case concerns. Over a five-year period, the committee has developed into a kind of local welfare council, though without separate corporate existence. It takes up local issues and is called upon by other organizations to help in certain situations. This type of committee, for example, can be used by a local agency which may have complaints against the school system but hesitates to take action alone. It also provides a vehicle for the interagency sharing of grass-roots problems arising from specific cases, which councils embracing large areas and many agencies cannot do.

5. *Educational methods.* This refers to activities such as informational meetings, panels, exhibits, pamphlets, and press coverage, all aimed at educating segments of the population. These may include also public appeals on specific issues made through the press, radio, and television. Legislators and public officials may be somewhat influenced by these methods.

6. *Position taking.* The agency formally takes a position on an issue, making it known publicly through the press, as well as to officials, legislators, and others directly. This goes beyond an educational effort in an attempt to put the weight of the agency behind a specific position. Generally, the agency's position will be newsworthy only if it is among the first to take the stand or if board members represent an influence with important segments of the community. The taking of a formal position may be often of greatest value internally—that is, in conveying to staff and clientele that the agency is committed and moving.

7. *Administrative redress.* Governmental bodies usually provide for various steps to appeal decisions at the practice level. While such steps may appear to delay action, they may nonetheless be necessary preludes to further action (such as court suits) or desirable in that they will call the attention of higher officials within or without the agency to conditions. Also, where the imperfect working of a system has resulted in an injustice to one client, grievance procedures through an ombudsman often result

in a correction for that one client. Taking such moves may be necessary although the advocacy program need not stop there in fighting a large battle.

8. *Demonstration projects.* Even though focused directly on problems of the poor, demonstration projects are generally long-term methods of advocacy. They may be necessary in order to elicit the specific material needed for advocacy and to help a group or community develop the awareness, leadership, and determination to embark upon a course of action. Further advocacy is usally needed to carry the message of the demonstration project into a larger-scale service or institutional change affecting the total population involved in a problem.

9. *Direct contacts with officials and legislators.* The agency may approach them formally to make positions known, give relevant information, or protest actions carried out or contemplated. Informal meetings, individually or with groups of legislators, may be similarly used and may enable the legislator to reveal ignorance, ask questions, and listen to more specific material. The agency might attempt to set up some type of regular contact, which in time may result in greater impact as agency personnel and views become known.

10. *Coalition groups.* These can be described as ad hoc groupings of organizations around a specific objective. the advantages lie not only in the combination of forces, but in the fact that agencies do not have to bear the burden and risk separately. The coalition concept also points to the involvement of disparate types of organizations and groups, which maintain autonomy while pursuing a common goal. Each organization usually has a circle of adherents who in turn may be more willing to work in concert than alone. Drawbacks involve the danger of setting too general goals and methods and a proliferation of meetings and committees seeking to "clarify" and "cooperate."

11. *Client groups.* The wide-scale development of the potential of client groups has occurred only recently and has revealed that these are a major instrument of social change. By "client group" is meant any local group or grouping of individuals sharing a problem; while they are not the traditional agency "clients," they are so termed in the sense that they are in some way helped through an agency service. This service may be limited to giving some impetus to the forming of the group, but may continue in the form of consultation to the group, supportive efforts in such ways as helping the group obtain information or gain access to certain people, or mounting collaborative efforts with other community groups. At the outset the advocate may assist in helping the group role-play contemplated action, help solve problems within the group, or suggest ways of augmenting the group. Through community contacts the advocate may help in bringing several groups together to develop coalitions; he may also suggest various methods of action for the group's consideration. Some family agencies have already had valuable experi-

ence with such groups in Project ENABLE, which by its very name indicates the primary role of the advocate in relation to such groups.

There is already considerable literature on client groups that covers many aspects of this method of social change. There are, however, two dangers to which the caseworker-advocate should be alert from the start: one, being too verbal, directive, not remaining where the group is, or directly or indirectly using the group as a means to ends other than what the group develops; second, the failure to develop other sources of support toward the same general objectives and to help the group relate to other support in a meaningful but autonomous manner.

12. *Petitions:* While petitions appear to have little direct effect upon officials and legislators, they are valuable in calling attention to an issue. Getting petitions signed is also a valuable activity for a new group in that it mobilizes members around an action and gives them an opportunity to talk to people about the issue, develop their abilities in making public contacts, and formulate points and rebuttals. It may also provide a way of reaching other interested people who might join or support the group.

13. *Persistent demands.* This method in effect means bombardment of officials and legislators, going beyond the usual channels of appeal. Thus, a welfare group protesting welfare cuts directed one effort against the local board of education, in an attempt to get the board to join in action to influence the state legislature. This method represents a kind of escalation of a campaign, and may be directed against figures inaccessible or unwilling to submit to personal contacts. While within lawful limits, it may be the precursor to "harassment" or other extralegal means.

14. *Demonstrations and protests.* These include marches, street dramas, vigils, picketing, sit-ins, and other public demonstrations. The family advocate should become familiar with these methods, although organizing and conducting them may lie beyond his competence and role. To what extent an agency as such will organize and participate in these methods will have to be determined within the agency. An agency will have to consider carefully, however, whether its other forms of action are not being conducted from too far behind the firing line, and whether commitment may not require some such firing line activity at times.

Selecting the Method of Intervention

The objectives of any plan of intervention are closely tied in with the methods selected and the nature of the issue and of the adversary organizations. An effort to challenge a state law usually will require a massive effort, on many levels and with various methods, whereas challenging a practice of local organization may be accomplished through such means as meetings, pressures, client groups, and administrative redress. A demonstration project may represent a fresh and optimistic approach to a problem that has eluded solution for years; it cuts through a problem in a different way and represents a long-term investment toward an objective. For example, the very early childhood experimental programs now in progress in several places in the country, such as one being conducted by Family Service Association of Nassau County, represent a new approach to one goal of reformers and advocates—that of forcing the school systems to provide vast remedial and enrichment programs for the many low-income children who suffer cognitive deficiencies. The objective of these new programs is to foster early development in the child so that the need for later remedial efforts is minimized or even eliminated. The program conducted by Family Service Association of Nassau County has the additional objective of enhancing the role of mothers and fathers in low-income families, an objective pursued in the past through various other methods.

The family advocate and the agency must consider the order of priority of their objectives, leaving room for sharpening or shifting of focus as practice reveals more clearly the nature of the issues involved and points to new approaches, such as those mentioned in relation to demonstration projects. The family advocate should also be alert to the many seemingly minor petty harassments indignities, and omissions he will suffer—these are often the only part of the Establishment iceberg that is visible to the poor. Ultimately, they may become larger issues than the clearcut injustices, which are amenable to lawsuits or other definable actions. Behind the small indignities lie the encrusted attitudes and structures which are far more impervious to change than a given rule or regulation. As William Blacke wrote in 1804, "He who would do good to another, must do it in Minute Particulars/General Good is the plea of the scoundrel hypocrite & flatterer."*

Agency Structure

The commitment of the agency to action on behalf of families is obviously the cornerstone of an advocacy program. But commitment can rather quickly be dissipated unless a workable structure for advocacy is established. The structure must be one which can and does involve the entire agency, including staff, board, and volunteers in an ongoing activity. Commitment must also be represented by a commitment of time; if advocacy is to be the second major function of a family agency, it must receive the time, attention, and thought that has gone into the counseling program. For example, does the staff time committed to advocacy equal that committed to recording interviews? The staff can tell by such allotments what the agency really means to emphasize. The board, with

*Jerusalem, chap. 3, lines 60–61.

overall responsibility for the agency, will probably need to delegate to a committee the charge for advocacy. Such a committee, already existing in a number of agencies under such names as Public Issues or Social Concerns, should probably be separate from a committee focused on legislation per se, as the latter would be dealing primarily with bills introduced into legislative bodies. At times, of course, the two committees may be concerned with the same issue and even the same legislation.

The advocacy committee has several important functions. One is to become and keep informed on local problems and issues in order to make continuous assessments of priorities for action and give guidelines to staff involved in advocacy; staff in turn will inform the committee on the pressing concerns of the people. Also essential to advocacy is the potential for quick action. The committee consequently must establish methods by which the advocacy staff can move quickly and still be assured of its backing. This can be done only through an ongoing process in which the committee learns to set guidelines by considering the methods, successes, and failures of the staff and others involved in advocacy. A close and continuing contact between staff and committee is necessary.

The committee has a key responsibility in thinking through the implications of any course of action, giving particular thought to follow-through so that client groups are not stirred up and then disappointed by an action that is abandoned. It must also consider the risks involved for the agency in taking action and in making alignments with various groups. Finally, the committee itself becomes involved in action. Members may attend public meetings and hearings or call upon officials and legislators. For example, the Public Issues Committee of the Family Service Association of Nassau County took up the transportation problem in the county as it affects the poor. The committee met with the County Planning Commission and with a representative of the bus companies, obtained much background material, and then, with staff, attended public hearings to present the agency position. Usually board members carry more weight in efforts to influence officials and legislators than do social workers; they not only may speak as residents of a community but may also be able to mobilize other local groups unaffiliated with the agency.

Agency staff also needs to be involved, so that advocacy is not an isolated, specialized function. While historically the caseworker has been seen as one who relays case material to administrators and board, it is evident that staff is for the most part not content with this role, which has no follow-through and which may only occasionally involve any given worker. On the other hand, not all caseworkers can be closely involved in every advocacy action, and there are aspects to advocacy which call for the development of expertise and knowledge to be exercised more centrally in an agency.

Different patterns for staff advocacy are possible, depending on agency size, funding, staff interests, and other considerations. The following are four examples.

1. An agency may have a full-time staff position of family advocate, or a department of advocacy headed by the family advocate. This position, as recently established at the Family Service Association of Nassau County through a foundation grant, is initially projected to include two main functions: first, to work with staff, providing consultation on action on behalf of individual clients, or handling certain situations directly and compiling case material on problems for the Public Issues Committee. In addition, the family advocate will be working to involve the staff in further action, such as the formation of client groups concerned with specific problems, and participation in committees and hearings. It should be noted that clerical staff may also be involved in such actions; most clerical staff in social agencies have or develop a commitment to the purposes of social work, and should have opportunity to ally themselves in their capacity as agency personnel as well as private citizens.

The second major responsibility of the family advocate is to act as the staff person to the Public Issues Committee. He helps the members define priority problems through case material and background information and by bringing in officials and others who are involved in the problems; he works with them to set guidelines and steps for action, to think through implications, to review what has been done, and to evaluate methods. The family advocate may act as agency spokesman and as liaison to officials and legislators; he may act as agency representative with coalition groups and community groups and as consultant to client groups; or he may act as advisor to staff or board people who carry out these functions.

One example will illustrate how guidelines and priorities are established and how the family advocate can take action accordingly. The Public Issues Committee defined several priority problem areas before adjourning for the summer; one involved what appeared to be the inequitable distribtion and possible poor use of federal education funds siphoned through the state (Title I funds of the Elementary and Secondary Education Act provide added services for children of low-income families). The committee had no specific cases with which to document this possible problem; it had been suggested by agency staff whose contacts with schools on behalf of clients gave them good reason to believe this was an area to explore further and possibly act upon. Shortly afterward, the family advocate spoke with the superintendent of a school district which was rapidly becoming a ghetto and needed massive governmental funding to cope with educational needs. The superintendent, failing to obtain funds anywhere, was ready to explore this area.

The family advocate, acting as consultant and organizer, helped prepare factual material which documented the inequitable distribution of funds and helped assemble a group of other superintendents in similar situations. State education officials came to meetings, and one school district instituted a court suit to force redistribution. Throughout,the advocate worked cooperatively with the Title I director of the County Economic Opportunity Council. All this activity took place in line with the priorities set down by the Public Issues Committee, which had not anticipated that this particular problem would suddenly come alive—this rested upon the work of the advocate and the decision of the executive director.

2. Variations on the establishment of a full-time family advocate might include creating a part-time position instead. Or an "indigenous" worker might fill the position. This pattern might require the investment of more staff and consultation time but bring about other advantages such as better contact with local poverty groups.

3. A present staff member might be assigned in agencies where the budget does not permit expansion of staff at present. Or a part-time assignment could be made, as an expedient only, since the conflict between the demands of a caseload and of the advocacy function would be frequent and onerous for the worker.

4. A staff committee might be formed, with a chairman bearing responsibility for the advocacy function, but delegating pieces of work to committee members. This method has the advantages of involving more staff directly, keeping the advocacy function related to the casework, and keeping the staff in direct contact with the board committee. Obviously, it could present difficulties in carrying out actions, as well as in the kinds of demands upon the worker's attention and time mentioned above.

It may be possible, in the context of the four patterns that have been described, for the agency to obtain graduate social work students for the program. This would provide needed manpower. Students can, for example, do much of the background work which is time-consuming for the caseworker but essential to the advocacy function. Some schools of social work, in preparing "generic" workers, may find this a highly desirable type of placement, since it can provide the student with selected cases related to advocacy, client groups with which to work, again in connection with advocacy, and community organization and action experience.

In agencies where a separate position of family advocate cannot be established, staff members carrying the functions in one of the patterns suggested should have direct access to the responsible board committee and work with that committee. Otherwise the resulting delays in cross communication and lack of clarity may impede any action. An agency may find it needs the advice of one or more specialists in the area of agency structuring and functioning for advocacy, orientation to clientele, assisting client groups, and defining areas of action and strategies.

Conclusion

Family advocacy offers a way for agencies and staffs to bridge the gap between the many cases of individual grievances against social institutions and the broader-scale actions needed to bring about institutional change. The caseworker's intimate knowledge of individual families provides a grassroots basis for social action, and his concern for families becomes an integral and vital part of the advocacy process.

The defining of the function of family advocacy points to the need for special knowledge and skills to support the caseworker's activity and to promote social change. A meaningful commitment by the agency is essential to carrying out the second major function of the family agency—improving the social environment of families.

Practice Analogues

The knowledge requirements of case advocacy are fourfold: (1) knowledge of the client or the system in which he or she functions; (2) knowledge of one's own agency; (3) knowledge of the workings of other bureaucratic agencies; and (4) knowledge of community resources.

Clinical therapeutic practice and advocacy have a good deal in common. To begin with, the clinician must have a clear understanding of the client and his or her problem as the client sees it. Case advocacy starts in the same place—"where the client is." Good clinical practice and good case advocacy both begin with understanding the client's definition of the problem, rather than imposing a premature professional definition.

Neither the advocate nor the clinician is obliged to act immediately on the client's definition alone. They also have a responsibility to point out to the client other possible ways of looking at the problem. What distinguishes a professional advocate from a lay person who wishes to engage in advocacy for a client is the ability, and the professional responsibility, to point out different ways of dealing with the client's problem and let the client decide among them. This is the essential analogue between the therapist and the advocate in social welfare: in most cases, they do not make decisions for the client.

In many situations the client may well go along with whatever the therapist or the advocate says. Nevertheless, every effort must be made to ensure that the client makes his or her own decisions as far as possible. Such a stance would be ridiculous from the point of view of a "revolutionary" whose actions are motivated by a larger end. He or she can say, with much justification, that you can't make an omelette without breaking eggs. Professional advocates and clinicians, however do not have the luxury of breaking clients' eggs for them.

Just as a clinician may move away from "where the client is," redefining, analyzing, and reinterpreting the client's problem according to clinical theory, knowledge, and experience, the advocate assists the client in redefining the problem in terms of appropriate strategy and tactics for effecting change. Here the temptation in advocacy is similar to that in therapy—to take the ball and run with it, rather than let the client take the ball. The contract between worker and client should always be based on the premise of "informed consent." Through the contract the client can understand and agree to the potential benefits and costs of advocacy actions.

Both the clinician-therapist and the advocate need interviewing skills. The advocate should know how to interview with advocacy in mind. This requires not only establishing rapport, but asking questions that will disclose areas of unmet needs or bureaucratic unresponsiveness. In addition, the advocate must be able to assess client skills and strengths and draw on them. The client should be as involved in the advocacy process as is feasible.

As noted earlier, clients should be able to act as their own advocates. Often they cannot, because they lack knowledge, skills, status, or personal resources, and in these cases the social work advocate should try to transfer knowledge and advocacy skills to the clients. This fosters independence and the client's ability to act on their own behalf in the future. Some call this process "enpowerment."

One of the more effective ways to empower clients is to let them know about community resources—the relevant services provided by other agencies—and the policies and precedures that govern access to these. This can be difficult in large urban areas, since often there are no current and complete directories of such services.

The analogue between therapist and advocate breaks down on the question of tactics. Most therapists depend on collaboration and mediation and seldom use direct pressure or conflict. The advocate, however, is always ready to use pressure and conflict when mediation and collaboration fail with those who control the resources clients need.

Warren Schmidt and Robert Tannenbaum have delineated the skills of a mediator, whose goal is to turn difference and conflict into creative problem solving. These are similar to the therapist's skills as we define them:

1. welcoming the existence of differences as an opportunity;
2. listening with understanding rather than evaluation;
3. clarifying the nature of the conflict;
4. recognizing and accepting the feelings of the individuals involved;
5. suggesting procedures and ground rules for resolving differences;
6. paying attention to maintaining relationships at well as to resolving differences;

7. creating opportunities and appropriate vehicles for communication among disputing parties; and
8. suggesting procedures that facilitate problem solving.*

By contrast, putting pressure on people is an absolute necessity in an advocacy situation. Here there is an unbridgeable gulf between the client's goals and needs and what the targets are willing to provide or allow. Advocates have an impressive array of allies and tools, including citizens' groups, unions, professional organizations, ombudsmen, politicians, the media, staff organizations, clients, and the courts. They can, if they use an adversary strategy, engage in litigation, picket, make previously hidden conditions visible, contrive crises, bring sanctions to bear through external interest groups, encourage noncompliance with regulations, and the like.

Yet the contrast between the advocate and clinician roles should not be drawn too sharply. The use of pressure tactics is not antithetical to the clinical process. As we have noted, both advocacy and therapy start with the client's perception of his or her problems, both attempt to maximize the use of the client's strengths, and both hope to transfer problem-solving skills to the client so that he or she will not remain in a state of dependency. Moreover, advocacy can be valuable to psychotherapeutic efforts. It can often provide the starting point for work with a mistrustful client by demonstrating that one is willing to extend oneself. In this way a trusting connection may be established.

The transfer of knowledge to the client during advocacy may increase his or her self-esteem. A successful experience in advocacy provides the client with a sense of mastery or empowerment that may serve as a building block for other psychosocial interventions. Naturally, with clients who have been caught up in a cycle of personal failure, it is important to choose advocacy strategies that are likely to succeed. For such clients, another failure could be devastating.

Clients are seldom able to face deep-seated personality problems and conflicts when their basic material needs are unmet. Without the services that advocacy can win for them, many clients do not have the time, security, or personal resources to probe into their psychological problems.

Moreover, both the therapist and the advocate use influence to reach their goals. Influence rests on five bases: authority, rewards, punishments, expertise, and referrant power.† The authority the therapist has by virtue of his or her role often has a considerable effect on the client.

*Warren Schmidt and Robert Tannenbaum, "Management of Differences," in Marvin Weisbord, ed. *Organizational Diagnosis* (Reading, Mass.: Addison-Wesley, 1978), pp. 124–135.

†John French, Jr., and Bertram Raven, "The Bases of Social Power," in Darwin Cartwright, ed., *Studies in Social Power* (Ann Arbor: University of Michigan Press, 1959), pp. 150–167.

Persuasion—pointing out the facts—involves pointing out the positive and negative consequences of the client's actions. Rewards and punishments are thus very much a part of the therapeutic process; their role in advocacy, of course, is obvious.

The client is constantly pondering the expertise of his or her therapist, and the therapist must be able to convince the client of his or her ability. Similarly, an effective advocate is one whom others see as knowledgeable, competent, and able. The effective advocate pursues a strategy of becoming expert in his or her work and making that expertise known.

Referrent power, the influence generated through friendship, social standing in the work network, and the values that one stands for, is an important source of influence. The therapist constantly projects to the client not only concern, but also his or her values and goals. In a work situation, what one does is often more important than what one says. If advocates are viewed as consistent, uninterested in self-aggrandizement, concerned about their fellow workers, and able to understand the organization's problems in providing service, others will look up to them and be more willing to accept their leadership. Clinicians can often garner much more influence than one would expect. An analysis of the various sources of influence is an important starting point in this process.

Attitudes, Values, and Skills

There are a number of values and attitudes that social workers need to be effective advocates. First, they must truly accept the idea that personal problems can have environmental causes that call for environmental solutions. Too many case workers disparage environmental intervention and view meaningful change as occurring only within the client and only through psychotherapeutic insight. Second, social workers need to become more interested in service entitlements, bureaucratic procedures, social legislation, and other potential sources of service to clients. This kind of knowledge is a professional responsibility, and it is critical for effectively servicing clients.

Third, social workers need to be comfortable in engaging in conflict strategies on behalf of clients. One cannot be an advocate in a cloak of professional neutrality. Moreover, one must give up the overriding desire to be liked by one's colleagues at all times. Effective advocates know how to clean up the residue of conflict with colleagues, and they are willing to utilize it whenever it serves the best interests of clients. (The reader may wish to review the discussion of conflict management in Chapter 4.)

Finally, an effective advocate recognizes that the interest of any one client is not necessarily the interest of other clients, nor is it necessarily the interest of the agency. He or she can function in a situation where there is tension between equally good goals and recognize that tension has to surface and be shared among various levels of the organization when legitimate agency goals and client needs are in conflict. The advocate's job is to ensure that tension is generated when clients are not getting what they need and that this tension is felt by those in the organizational structure who have the authority to do something about it. (Julie Abramson's article in Chapter 2 gives case examples of how to accomplish this.)

Advocates must learn to value their own contributions through advocacy to their clients' well-being. They must also recognize that, in the long run, it is debilitating to act as an advocate for one client after another when structural solutions to problems cannot be found. Endless conflict with the school system over services for problem children is not a solution. What organizations need are accountability systems that not only bring problems to the surface but provide leads and suggestions on how problems might be resolved. Without such systems, there cannot be effective services.

Advocacy will always be needed: one recalls the warning that the price of liberty is eternal vigilance. In fact, however, this country is founded not on eternal vigilance but on a constitution that, in effect, created an accountability system for it.

Additional Readings

Epstein, Irwin. "Advocates on Advocacy: An Exploratory Study." *Social Work Research and Abstracts* (Summer 1981): 5–12.
Grinell, Richard M., and Nancy S. Kyte. "Environmental Modification: A Study." *Social Work* (1975): 313–318.
Petrella, Tony, and Peter Block. "Diagnosing Conflict between Groups in Organizations." In Marvin Weisbord, ed., *Organizational Diagnosis*, pp. 136–144. Reading, Mass.: Addison-Wesley, 1978.

CHAPTER 6

PROGRAM DEVELOPER

Many years ago Mary Richmond urged social workers not to neglect the use of case-by-case documentation as a way of generating ideas for new programs and social policies. Although the profession has been active in promoting such changes, it seems fair to say that the impetus for such actions has not come directly from documentation. Instead, innovations are more likely to be the product of a "top-down" approach, with new programs being developed and implemented by administrators. Programs rarely grow out of a chorus of need documented by line social workers.

The bottom-up approach to program development that Richmond espoused did not evolve for several reasons. First, line workers' jobs are generally not defined in terms of program development. Consequently, they are not evaluated on the basis of their promotion of new programmatic ideas, nor are they rewarded for them. Second, most line workers have caseloads of sufficient size to preclude any opportunity for standing back and considering new programs and policies. In addition, during a decade of social welfare expansion, the "grant writer" emerged as a new specialist whose function it was to generate fundable proposals that matched the requirements of the funding agencies rather than those of the clientele.

Nevertheless, there are opportunities for clinical social workers to develop new programs based on their assessments of unmet client needs, gaps in service, bureaucratic obstacles, and so on. The article by Julie Abramson that appears below in this chapter shows how line social workers in health settings can develop programs on a short-term basis to meet specific patient needs. These include: (1) helping groups of clients learn the advocacy skills needed to deal with a particular bureaucracy: (2) settings up discharge planning groups for patients in acute or long-term care facilities or their families; (3) organizing groups of women returning to work among the clients of a family agency; and (4) starting groups of patients with similar disability diagnoses in in- or out-patient settings.

Overview

It is important to articulate the skills associated with the program developer role so that it can be implemented and then made part of the clinical social worker's job description.

Promoting the Program Developer Role: Judith Lee and Carol Swenson make the point that the theory on which clinical practice is based ultimately determines the roles workers play. The program developer role is more firmly implanted in some theories—for example, the ecological model—than in others:

> A life model, combined with the ecological perspective, refocuses attention on the way socially competent people live their lives and interact with their social and physical environments. . . . It means that, wherever possible, the social worker should be located in the usual life space of people. The worker will discover and support or catalyze those naturally occurring processes of helping which exist in social networks and will attempt to connect isolated persons to these.
>
> Problems are viewed as arising from a poor fit between the person and his environment. Helping is directed both at the coping capacities of the person and at the qualities of the environment, with the goal of removing obstacles to growth and relatedness. The worker-client relationship is expanded to include the client and persons in his life space as active participants in change, and the worker assumes a more flexible, reciprocal role as catalyst. Service delivery arrangements need to allow for meeting people where they live their lives and for offering a broad range of interventions in a flexible yet integrated fashion.*

A second condition for the acceptance of the program developer role is a greater concern on the part of agencies with what clients say they want in the way of services. There is considerable evidence that there is a disparity between what the agency sees itself as offering the clients and the clients' view of what they need. Thus, the social work admonition to start where the client is, is honored more in the breach than in reality. If the client's wishes were accorded real value, and if the client were really viewed as a collaborator in developing service networks or his or her own treatment plan, the program developer role of the clinical social worker would take on greater significance. Clinicians would have to discuss the client's view of services, and this discussion would legitimate line workers' suggestions concerning the design of new programs. Mary Carroll's article documents the history of client collaboration and predicts a continued need for it.

*Judith A. Lee and Carol R. Swenson, "Theory in Action: A Community Social Service Agency," *Social Casework* (1978): 361–362.

Collaboration with Social Work Clients:
A Review of the Literature*

MARY CARROLL

Are you and I considering the client. . . . Are we alert to his handicaps, sympathetic with his troubles, or are we so tangled up with intake, investigation, new techniques, politics, interpretations, that moving forward into the complexities of casework we lose sight. . . .—Mary Edna McChristie, 1937†

Mary Richmond, the founder of social casework, counseled practitioners to scrutinize their customary sources of information to ensure against omission.‡ An adventuresome undertaking of Richmond's admonition revealed the clients of the social work profession as an underestimated wellspring of knowledge and energy. This observation was abstracted from the author's review of twentieth-century social work literature on collaboration with clients. Collaboration was defined as the process of client and social worker laboring together for mutual benefit. This review seeks models of collaboration, identifies themes, and discusses implications for practice.

The literature review began with the first issue of the *Family* in 1920 and terminated with the human service journals of 1978. The plan was to review only articles in the major social work journals, but detours led elsewhere. The writings were scattered throughout the literature, rather than connected as building blocks of theory and practice. This study brings together the articles on collaboration, as an invigoration of the foundation of social work theory and practice.

In the 1920s

Early in the 1920s, Lee asserted that the role of the social worker must be achieved client by client, rather than ascribed by professional membership.§ Wannamaker illustrated Lee's view by portraying social treatment from the standpoint of a "resistant" client known to twenty-seven social agencies.‖ The "new" opportunity offered was a relationship in

---

*Excerpted by special permission of the Child Welfare League of America from *Child Welfare* 59 (1980): 407–417.

†Mary Edna McChristie, "Considering the Client," *National Council on Crime and Delinquency Yearbook* 37 (1937): 245.

‡Porter R. Lee, "A Study of Social Treatment," *Family* 4 (Dec. 1923): 193.

§Ibid., p. 198.

‖Claudia Wannamaker, "Social Treatment from the Standpoint of a Client," *Family* 6 (Apr. 1925): 31ff.

which the client would feel free to discuss and criticize the worker's plans. The client accepted the offer and said that she objected to the frequency with which her daughter was taken away from the home for recreation. Subsequently, a new intervention was mutually designed. The mother was then able to talk openly about her struggles and begin to develop her many abilities. Next, the agency asked her to discuss her experience with social services, so that others might benefit. The client did so. Unfortunately, neither follow-up nor parallel studies of Wannamaker's approach could be located in the literature of the decade.

In the 1930s

The literature of the 1930s described two experiments in client participation. In 1936 Churchward reported on the formation of a district advisory committee comprising a cross section of clients served by the Seattle Family Society in a working-class neighborhood.* In 1938 Vigran depicted agency involvement with public welfare recipients in the Basin area of Cincinnati.†

The Seattle Family Society, beset by operating and survival decisions, turned to the client committee for assistance. The committee, responding to questions posed by the agency, made these recommendations:

1. The agency should continue to operate, since it met a vital need in the community.
2. Immediate responses should be made to problems presented by clients.
3. Neither relatives nor employers should be contacted in the course of an investigation.
4. The term "patron" should be used, instead of "client."
5. Birth control information should be available to clients.
6. The relationship should be one of privileged communication.

As a result of the collaboration, the agency became a viable force for clients, and the latter developed strong interest in agency programs. The staff felt closer to the clients on the committee because of the opportunity to hear their point of view, and a shift in attitude occurred:

Where before some of us in casework thought there were many things the family should not know about our processes, we now believe that the more we take them [families] into our confidence, the greater progress we shall make.‡

*Helen Prescott Churchward, "An Experiment in Client Participation," *Family* 17 (Apr. 1936): 43ff.

†Constance Vigran, "An Experiment in Client Participation," *Family* 18 (Feb. 1938): 333ff.

‡Churchward, "Experiment in Client Participation," p. 48.

Some of the recommendations of the Seattle client committee found their way into the policies of public and private agencies, some persisted as theory and practice factors, and some were not heard.

Sharing Information

Two years after Churchward, Vigran wrote on "An Experiment in Client Participation." This experiment was initiated to provide information to clients about public welfare policies and processes. Gradually, the focus on welfare lessened and other areas of client interest surfaced. In response, content dealt with areas such as use of leisure time, parenting, health, mental health, etc. The relationship between the clients and social workers shifted from a we-they dichotomy to one of mutuality, described by one observer:

> I was particularly impressed with the naturalness of the discussion—from the information given and the response received, one might have thought he was at a staff meeting. There was the highest quality of participation on the part of the client; he felt he was an integral part of the organization.*

In the 1940s

The work of Churchward and Vigran reposed as islands in the literature, however, as the 1940s were void of studies based on the pioneer collaborative efforts of the 1930s. No experiments emerged.

In the 1950s

The 1950s brought Blenkner's classic articles on obstacles to evaluative research in casework.† Yet even in these works alertness was not directed to the knowledge and energy of clients of the social work profession. Nevertheless, in the 1950s the Social Work Research Department at Wayne State University, Detroit, launched an investigation of clients' expectations of potential helpers. Although this project was not a study of collaboration, it used a collaborative approach. The project was based on the assumption that a client's commitment to a helping relationship results from two perceptions—competency of the helper and willingness to help. The project examined dimensions of first interviews as they were perceived by and influenced clients. Refined research principles and

*Vigran, "Experiment," p. 333.
†Margaret Blenkner, "Obstacles to Evaluative Research in Casework: Part I and Part II," *Social Casework* 31 (1950): 54ff., 97ff.

methodologies replaced those of earlier decades. This review deals with only one section of the Wayne project, the section that drew upon a sample of actual clients.* Subjects were 150 voluntary clients who had just completed an initial interview with either a caseworker, counselor, or physician at six different agencies.

The Wayne study revealed that tension changes could result in a problem-centered and/or a relationship-centered interview. Problem-centered change referred to a perceived change in tension related to the client's problem. Relationship-centered change referred to a perceived change in tension attributed by the client to the social relationship with the helper. Thus emerged a view of change as a shifting process that can be accomplished by both problem-centered and relationship-centered dimensions of the interview or by one or the other. It was also found that the two forms of change have both common and unique components.

The study also sought to identify actions by the helper that led to change. More often than not, however, the clients associated characteristics of the helper with change. Actions, however, were emphasized in the study. The authors reported that no particular action was found to make or break an interview, and that the same action had different results with different clients. The serendipitous finding of the importance of worker attributes was not further developed. Implementation of the collaborative process requires such development.

With the Wayne project a new collaborative model appears in the literature—an attempt to get information from the client that aids the practitioner in providing assistance, rather than calling on the client for participation in program design. Beginning with the Wayne project, the study of client expectations was brought to the forefront. The meaning of the term "expectation," however, tends not to be defined in the studies.

In the 1960s

Overall and Aronson opened the 1960s with a focus on the psychotherapeutic expectation of clients from the lower socioeconomic class.†
[10:421 ff.]. The impetus came from the startling statistic that more than half of the clients in this socioeconomic class did not return for service after an initial interview. Overall and Aronson examined the speculation that the high dropout rate was associated with unfulfilled expectations.

This speculation was validated by the study findings. Thus, the clients expected the therapists to be more active, supportive, and medically oriented than they were during the interview. The authors concluded that

*Norman Polansky and Jacob Kounin, "Clients' Reactions to Initial Interviews: A Field Study," *Human Relations* 9 (1956): 237ff.

†Betty Overall and H. Aronson, "Expectations of Psychotherapy in Patients of Lower Socioeconomic Class," *American Journal of Orthopsychiatry* 33 (1963): 421ff.

the clients whose expectations were most "inaccurate" were least likely to return for treatment. The choice of the term "inaccurate" suggests the "blaming the victim" syndrome. It appears that what was really studied was the hopes of clients of the lower socioeconomic class. The real issues were the response to clients' hopes and an examination of the preconceived ideas of therapists that interfered with constructive responses.

Gottesfeld also uses the term "expectation" but seems to be identifying hopes or wishes. [4:45 ff.]* Gottesfeld asked professionals and youngsters categorized as delinquent to examine professional methods. The young men were primarily of black and Puerto Rican background. The professionals came from a variety of agencies. The research instrument was a professionally developed questionnaire that listed social work methods. Both groups of participants rated the methods according to value.

The youngsters were revealed as a group of adolescents asking for help with the difficulties of growing up. The author described a typical participant as:

seeking a parental surrogate in the professional. He rejects the professional in the role of a pal and instead wants the professional to be a mature adult who is concerned about him, respects him, teaches him to relate better socially, and helps him take his place in the world.†

The youngsters preferred not to discuss painful or embarrassing aspects of their lives.

The methods selected by the professionals were disconnected from the identified needs and requests of the youngsters. The young men were often referred to other agencies for practical services that resulted in their feeling frustrated. The service the professional believed he had to offer was the professional treatment relationship, with an emphasis on neutrality, nonjudgmentalism, nonauthoritarianism, and permissiveness.

Thus, while the youngsters were requesting a relationship with many teaching aspects, they were being offered the "traditional" one. The message is that while social work speaks to the differential use of the relationship, more work must be done to develop a process for identifying how and when one shifts emphasis among different components.

Reid and Shapiro developed a theme that appeared in Gottesfeld's study as well as a few other works‡—the use of advice in work with clients. Advice was defined as "an explicit or implicit suggestion by the caseworker designed to influence the decisions or behavior of the

*Harry Gottesfeld, "Professionals and Delinquents Evaluate Professional Methods with Delinquents," *Social Problems* 13 (1965): 45ff.
†Ibid., p. 58.
‡William J. Reid and Barbara L. Shapiro, "Client Reactions to Advice," *Social Service Review* 43 (1969): 165ff.

client."* The authors assessed client reaction to advice given by the caseworker. The sample, drawn from a larger study at the Community Service Society of New York, consisted of 106 couples, primarily from the lower middle or working class. These clients had sought help for marital or parent-child relationship problems. The findings indicated that although the clients were generally pleased with the service, some noted lack of advice as a serious omission.

In the 1970s

The theme of advice appears again in the work of Mayer and Timms.† Mayer joined Timms in England to study the reactions of clients to casework. The Family Welfare Association sample of sixty-one consisted mostly of women, chosen on the basis of satisfaction or dissatisfaction with service. The groups were further broken down into clients who sought help with interpersonal problems and those who sought help with material problems.

The study revealed that satisfied clients who had sought help with interpersonal problems felt they were helped through understanding, unburdening, emotional support, enlightenment, and guidance. Satisfied clients who had sought help with material problems felt that they were helped when they received material assistance. This group identified emotional support, guidance, and enlightenment as unexpected bonuses. Additional satisfaction was found in the fact that the experience was not unpleasant, as some had anticipated.

Dissatisfied clients who had come for help with interpersonal problems expected the worker to judge quickly the clients' behavior in the problem situation, and then straighten out the "guilty" party. Dissatisfied clients who had sought material assistance did not receive it, and experienced a feeling of being cross-examined, though this was not the case. In contrast, the satisfied clients had

> perceived the worker as someone they could talk to; someone who was interested in them; someone who trusted them; and someone who lessened their feelings of shame. Viewed longitudinally these cases went through a kind of progression: the client's material needs were given early consideration; once [this was] done, the client—not the worker—made the 'next move'; and finally the worker's handling of new material was considered 'meaningful.'‡

The authors stressed the importance of helping the client bring needs out in the open, to clarify what the professional can or cannot do. This

*Ibid., p. 167.
†John E. Mayer and Noel Timms, *The Client Speaks* (New York: Atherton, 1970).
‡Ibid., p. 129.

process relieves many anxieties. Mayer and Timms asserted that clients like those in their study may eventually find insight-oriented therapy helpful. However, this approach must be appropriately timed and the underlying assumptions clarified with the client. Mayer and Timms suggested that clients be resocialized so they will accept services. . . .

Implementation of aspects of the collaborative model in the various agencies resulted in improved services, increased understanding of the helping process, development of new client skills, client participation in decision making, and invigoration of the agency's functioning.

A major theme surfacing from this review of the literature was the ability and willingness of clients to collaborate. They repeatedly told social workers that different kinds of human need call for different responses. Therefore, the relationship and interventions must be shaped accordingly. Accomplishing this requires ongoing research, with client participation in problem identification, design, and interpretation of feelings.

Another major theme of the review was the tendency of agencies to turn to clients when the agency was at a point of desperation, the collaboration seeming an emergency device, rather than a standard operating procedure.

The implications of collaboration with clients for social work practice are clearcut. Collaboration promotes the primary values of social work—respect for the uniqueness and dignity of the individual, and self-determination. Lack of collaboration often undermines these values, and interventions tend to reflect client problems rather than provide viable alternatives. Collaboration with clients should be built into the standard operating procedures of social work agencies.

━━━━━━━━━━━━━━━━

Although many agencies resist client collaboration for a variety of reasons, ranging from a belief that the patient's point of view about treatment is likely to be distorted to fears over loss of professional status and power, Peggy Giardano points out that "whether out of a desire to pacify or co-opt clients or from a sincere interest in improving effectiveness, there has been a recent proliferation of attempts to use the client in the role of agency evaluator."* There are a number of problems and pitfalls associated with such attempts to achieve consumer satisfaction. Some are discussed in the Practice Analogue section in this chapter, and Giardano discusses others.

On a less formal level, the line workers can contribute to the program planning process by assessing their individual caseloads in terms of the

*Peggy Giardano, "The Client's Perspective in Agency Evaluation," *Social Work* 22 (1977): 35.

services clients need to achieve the level of functioning that both clients and workers are aiming at. At times, the clients may be asked directly, and they will often have some rather clear ideas about what they need. It is possible to raise client frustrations by suggesting that they may need some additional kinds of help that might not be forthcoming. Nevertheless, this risk seems worth taking, if for no other reason than that it signals to the client that the worker is concerned. More important, the answers to the questions may serve as a counterweight to the worker's biases, if any, about client need.

No matter how client need is assessed, it is at this point in the program development process that success and failure hang in the balance. The client perspective, crucial as it is, cannot be the sole basis on which programs are designed. If a program is designed simply to meet client need, it is likely to fail, and this is especially true when line workers attempt to develop a program based solely on their understanding of the clients in their own caseload.

Julie Abramson makes the point that although service to patients is the ultimate goal, one must consider as well the institutional context in which the program will be embedded. Her article, which follows, gives examples of failure and success in programs developed by line workers and notes that failure was often related to neglect of staff concerns over status, value differences, and departmental needs.

A Non-Client-Centered Approach to Program Development in a Medical Setting

JULIE ABRAMSON

Program development in a social agency can be viewed as a strategy for making decisions about the deployment of resources to meet identified client needs. Traditionally, program decisions are based on perceptions of client need along with the professional inclinations of social work staff. The argument of this paper is that these do not provide an adequate base on which to build programs in the complex, multidisciplined structure of a hospital or most social agencies.

A more appropriate model for decision making is one that takes into account "systems" issues as the first priority.* Service to patients (or clients) must be the ultimate goal; the starting point, however, is not the service recipient, but rather the hospital's (or agency's) institutional and

*See Hyman Weiner, "The Hospital, the Ward and the Patient as Clients: Use of the Group Method," *Social Work* 4 (1959): 57–64, for a discussion of "systems" work in hospitals.

interdisciplinary concerns. The task then is the identification of the key areas of interest and perceived need of various segments of the institutional "community."

In taking this approach, it must be understood that the resources available are almost universally inadequate to meet the range of client need that exists within most agency populations. Service choices based on organizational rationales are tactically important in terms of a long-range strategy of gaining more resources and a short-term strategy of utilizing existing resources most efficiently.

Formal and Informal Needs Assessment

The needs assessment to be discussed here focuses on the non-social-work staff's perceptions of client needs rather than client perceptions. Information must be gathered from staff members of all disciplines and on all levels in the areas that will interface with a projected program. The social work program developer will need a focused approach and agenda to do this: for example, "The Social Work Department is hoping to make a staff member available soon in this unit. We're trying to get everyone's ideas about what problems the patients have that we might be able to help with." In addition, the program developer should try to obtain information about past efforts, current unit problems, and general patterns of conducting business in the unit. He or she could ask, for example, "Have you ever had social work help here before? How did it go? I notice that things can get real hectic here. Who helps with that?"

It is crucial to express interest in the functions of other units and to identify the commonalities between their role and that of social work. It is possible in such discussions to obtain a great deal of information about program possibilities and to gain an understanding of factors that might prove helpful or obstructive once program decisions are made and implementation begins. Such data serve to identify target problems and populations and to create a bond with the staff members on whom the program will ultimately depend. Once decisions are made and feedback is provided to the staff, their sense of having been part of the process can serve to break down interdisciplinary competition and create a mutual sense of mission.* The following case study of program development in a hospital emergency room describes such a process.

> When S was hired by the social work department of a large, urban teaching hospital, one of her assignments as supervisor for ambulatory care was to develop social work services in the emergency room. The E.R. had previously been served on an on-call basis. She decided to wait two months

*For a negative case study, see Alfred Stanton and Morris Schwartz, *The Mental Hospital* (New York: Basic Books, 1954), pp. 193–243.

before hiring a worker for that area and to spend that time taking referrals from the E.R. herself.

In addition, she systematically contacted all staff members who worked regularly in the area. She made sure to include nonprofessional staff, such as security guards, clerical staff, aides, and orderlies as well as doctors, nurses, and administrators.* She observed them at work briefly and then met with each to get their thoughts about the main patient and staff problems in the E.R.

The general functioning of the area—the organization of work, the hierarchy of authority for patient care decisions, staff relationships and degree of interaction, patterns of patient utilization, and so on—was the focus of her interest. She kept a log summarizing these contacts, noting recurring issues. Several themes emerged.

Staff members almost unanimously expressed enormous frustration about the "E.R. repeater"—the person who, for a variety of reasons, came to the E.R. with a frequency that seemed to have no relationship to staff perceptions of his or her medical needs. Nursing staff were also greatly concerned about the needs of elderly E.R. patients, noting that many had severe social problems in addition to medical ones. Guilt and uncertainty were expressed about inattention to these problems. The nurses also commented that this population often created conflict between doctors and nurses, usually arising from the doctor's reluctance to admit a "disposition problem" to the hospital.

S had anticipated the concern about the elderly in her preliminary thinking, but the intensity of feeling about the E.R. repeater was something of a revelation. In regard to the former, she assigned a social worker to the E.R. on a weekday basis, with the understanding that the problems of the elderly would take first priority. She planned to have the social worker make rounds in a case-finding effort so that work could begin on assessing the social situation of the elderly patient while he or she was being worked up medically.

A much more extensive process had to take place in order to identify an appopriate means of intervention with the E.R. repeater. Key staff members were further interviewed about this problem, including the E.R. psychiatrist, a variety of physicians, the security guards, and nurses. An effort was made to pin down who these patients were, the likely reason for their repeated visits, their particular impact on the staff and the functioning of the E.R., and other issues. Eventually, a system for identifying these patients and recording their visits was developed, as was a review system. An interdisciplinary team met regularly to review the medical chart and pattern of visits for each repeater and then either assign an appropriate staff member to work with the patient or make contact with some other part of the hospital system to modify the situation. The treatment decision was made known to all E.R. staff so that a consistent approach to the patient could be maintained. S made clear to all involved that the goal would be to treat the patient more effectively and to reduce staff frustration and isolation, rather than necessarily to eliminate the repeating. If that happened, it would have to be seen as a bonus.

*See Harold H. Weissman, *Overcoming Mismanagement in the Human Services* (San Francisco: Jossey-Bass Publishers, 1973) pp. 9–24, for a discussion of the need to involve lower-status staff members in the planning process.

It is clear that the process described above involved a significant commitment of time.* However, the ability to provide "on target" programming minimizes future expenditure of time and energy dealing with unanticipated obstacles. Moreover, the intensity of the bonds developed through such a process by the social work program developer and staff in key areas of the system will continue to pay off for years to come.

Decision-Making Premises

A number of factors should be taken into consideration before a commitment is made to develop a particular program. These are enumerated below.†

(1) Staff Attitudes

Once the informal needs assessment has been completed, the program developer should have a good sense of the attitudes and priorities of most of the staff. Some thought then has to be given to identifying the people whose support is most crucial to the program. This may be the medical chief in one system and the head nurse or some other staff member in another. One must understand what sort of cooperation and resources the proposed program will need in order to decide who the significant actors will be. Decisions about where to locate programs follow quite naturally from such assessments. For example, if social work is a scarce resource, it will make sense to cooperate most closely with the medical chief whose perspective on social work service is most consistent with that of the social work department.‡

> H had to decide which outpatient specialty clinic should receive more intensive social work coverage. The cancer clinic had patients with severe social needs, but the clinic chief had expressed strong reservations about having social workers see the families of patients or discuss patients' reactions to their illness with them. At the same time, he was requesting increased social work involvement in order to obtain more concrete services for the patients. The social work department had been considering the development of a group for cancer patients and their families. However, in discussions with this M.D., it became apparent that he would find such a program threatening.

*For another case example describing such a process, see Jack Rothman, "Promoting an Innovation," in Herman Resnick and Rino Patti, eds., *Change from Within* (Philadelphia: Temple University Press, 1980), pp. 241–242.

†For several analytic tools that can be used in the decision-making process, see "Promoting an Innovation."

‡See John Wax, "Developing Social Work Power in a Medical Organization," *Social Work* 13 (1968): 62–71, and Weissman, *Overcoming Mismanagement*, p. 108, for discussions of the uses of power.

The chief of the diabetic clinic, on the other hand, acknowledged the contribution of social work to the treatment of diabetic patients. He and his colleagues had already demonstrated an understanding of teamwork and of the psychosocial factors affecting the course of the illness. The social work department had also been considering the development of an interdisciplinary educational program for diabetic patients.

When a decision had to be made between the two programs, the diabetic clinic program was the clear choice. H let the cancer clinic chief know that she could appreciate his concern for more services for that population and would provide a social work assistant who would take referrals from the clinic. She indicated, however, that a more intensive service would have to wait until there was a greater consensus developed on the role and function of the social worker. She agreed to regular follow-up meetings with him in order to keep the discussion alive but chose to concentrate her resources in a more receptive area.

Questions could be raised about this strategy. What about the responsibility to educate the cancer clinic physician? Should social work run from confrontation? On the other hand, it should remembered that it is difficult to determine objectively whether cancer patients or diabetics are more in need of social services. It can also be argued that H was educating the physician by the very act of withholding a desired service. In presenting social work services as a reward to be earned, she was promoting a positive view of the profession's contribution, often sorely lacking in a doctor-dominated medical setting. She operated on the assumption that rational persuasion is not the only appropriate form of influence in organizational settings.

(2) The Program's Dependence on External Supports

Even in a hospital setting, not all programs depend heavily on interdisciplinary support for success. A case worker developing a group drawn from his or her own caseload or that of immediate colleagues can establish the program with minimal external support. However, the program developer must always think about the extent to which the program's success depends on factors over which he or she has minimal control, such as referral sources, space, and transportation. These issues can make or break a program, and they should be anticipated and resolved as much as possible before implementation.

(3) Staff Consensus about the Program's Function

It is very important to assess the degree of alignment between the social worker's perception of the function of a program and the perceptions of the non-social-work staff and the target population.* If there is a substan-

*For a summary of research on role relationships among collaborating professionals, see Rosalie Kane, *Interprofessional Teamwork* (Syracuse: Syracuse University School of Social Work, 1975).

tive gap, the future of the program may be in jeopardy. Hidden agendas eventually surface, usually creating a major crisis. Sometimes, when there is substantial support for a program, the program developer can head off problems by communicating about differences in perspective.*

> J was asked by the head of the hospital rehabilitation department to develop a group for paraplegic patients. This was a chronically ill, long-term population in an otherwise acute-care hospital, so that intense interactions were already taking place within the patient group and between the patients and the staff.
>
> Dr. G seemed concerned with providing a more appropriate outlet for some of these feelings and clearly hoped that the group could calm things down. It was also well known that he felt that paraplegics should not be told that they were permanently paralyzed. J was concerned that patients in a group would be likely to confront their inability to walk and thus be more likely to confront their physicians with questions. She also anticipated a period of greater turmoil as the group gave the patients strength to act on their concerns.
>
> It could be predicted that both of these developments would be upsetting to Dr. G. J brought these possibilities up in conversation with him and tried to give him a sense of how they could be handled constructively. He seemed not to take in what she was saying and again affirmed his support for the group. She moved on to implement the program, knowing that if her concerns were realized, she had at least somewhat prepared for Dr. G.

(4) The Relevance of Social Work Expertise to Resolution of the Problem

Many disciplines in a hospital setting share overlapping skills and interests. This can often serve to create territorial disputes and obstacles to program development. If one assumes that there are many more opportunities for service to patients than resources can respond to, it would seem prudent and more productive to home in on those areas where competition is minimal. In addition, it is essential to attack problems that can be expected to respond to social work knowledge and expertise.

It is especially helpful if the problem is one that other disciplines do not feel comfortable handling on their own. The obesity program described in the next section provides one such example. Other staff members felt helpless to promote the weight loss that was seen as the essential ingredient in the treatment of their patients. As a result, they were receptive to the development of an obesity program.

(5) The Value Placed on the Resolution of the Problem

A social worker, L, started a program to aid obese patients in a hospital setting. The program was clearly regarded by other staff members,

*See Alfred Kahn, "Institutional Constraints to Interprofessional Practice," in Helen Rehr, ed., *Medicine and Social Work* (New York: Prodist, 1974), for a discussion of obstacles to collaboration.

particularly the treating physician, as meeting an important need. The most useful barometer of a program's success is whether it addresses a problem that "pinches" a key segment of the institution. If it does, then the potential for institutionalization of the program is significantly higher.*

The obesity program met this criterion in two ways. It attempted to help a fairly numerous population deal with a significant health risk, and, more important, it helped the physician feel less impotent and angry in his dealings with these patients. The fact that success was not guaranteed with this group did not diminish the program's popularity, because the potential for help existed and, most of all, the burden of responsibility was removed from the physicians' shoulders. One could anticipate that any small gains made by social work in this area would be highly respected, whereas failure would not really diminish social work's standing, because of the well-known intractability of the problem.

Several other programs started at the same hospital met similar criteria. A special interdisciplinary patient education program for recent heart attack victims and a similar program for diabetic patients were very well received by medical staff and by the nurses and dieticians who were collaborating with social workers in the programs. Again, the secret for success seems to have been the fact that both programs assisted the staff (particularly the physicians) in treating patients with diseases where (1) psychosocial factors had a major impact on the outcome of treatment, and (2) the staff felt some frustration with existing treatment procedures. The physicians involved with these programs generally seemed aware that they were poorly prepared in comparison with social workers to help patients and families deal with the life style and social impacts of their illnesses. In essence, the nature of the illnesses made the case for social work intervention.

(6) The Program's Consistency with Agency Functions

The proposed program must be clearly consistent with the general function of the agency or unit. If it is not, it cannot be considered a valid expenditure of resources, and it will always be exposed to attack by those whom it threatens. A unit is vulnerable to a charge of inconsistent programming when its own sense of mission is vague or when the idiosyncratic interests of the staff are given primary consideration over other concerns. The latter error can be illustrated by the approach taken in developing another obesity program at the same hospital.

A social worker in the psychiatry out-patient clinic who had lost a substantial amount of weight herself felt that her program might work with psychiatric

*For a discussion of the institutionalization phase of program development, see Neal Gross et al., *Implementing Organizational Innovations* (New York: Basic Books, 1971).

patients. She was aware of the program already in existence in the medical clinics, as was her supervisor, but felt that her approach was different.

She made no effort to survey the psychiatric clinic population to establish whether obesity was prevalent in this group, nor did she speak with potential referral sources within the clinic. When implementation began, she found that the psychiatric clinic did not have significant numbers of overweight patients, nor were out-patient staff members particularly responsive to her efforts. She began seeking referrals from other areas of the hospital. As the other program was already well established, she was not successful.

(7) The Degree of Institutional Visibility

The final factor influencing program choices is the programs' institutional and interdisciplinary visibility. A program developed from an individual worker's caseload cannot possibly have the same impact on the institution as one with a broader base. A program that requires significant interaction with other hospital staff members has greater potential to enhance social work's standing in the institution. For this reason it is often important to move a program from one level of institutional existence to another. The successful obesity program mentioned earlier had just such a history. It was originally thought up by a social work student and her supervisor for the not-so-sound reason that the student needed a group experience. The supervisor, after assessing interdepartmental and inter-disciplinary staff reactions, quickly recognized the patients' and the institution's need for such a program and began to "institutionalize" it.

The hospital's metabolic unit was asked for a consultation, and the medical staff there, a behavioral psychologist, and a nutritionist, all of whom were engaged in different aspects of direct patient care, became involved. The reimbursement structure was worked out through the rehabilitation medicine department, which provided the exercise component of the program. Sanction was sought from the hospital administration, and reports were regularly issued about the current status of the program.

An informal planning committee was developed to evaluate program performance and modify structure and content from year to year. This committee included the metabolic unit's medical chief, the chief physical therapist, the behavioral psychologist, the social work staff member, and her supervisor. Others attended when their presence was needed. The social work department called the meetings and continued to assume the organizational responsibility for the development of the program. As a result, the program remained identified with the department despite its interdisciplinary nature. Written and verbal communication with each patient's physician about individual progress further increased awareness of the program.

This process helps to ensure a program's survival through the development of a broad base of support. If the program is on a solid footing professionally, such a process also exposes a large number of other professionals to social work expertise and provides an effective opportunity to communicate the goals and capabilities of social work. This is particularly true of programs where social work shares the direct leadership with another discipline.

Conclusion

It is the contention of this paper that permitting the political realities of a medical setting to dictate program choices does not undermine social workers' service to patients. Rather, it enhances it by dealing directly with potential obstructions to the development of service programs. In addition, this approach permits social workers to maximize scarce departmental resources and promulgate knowledge about the contribution social work can make toward patients' recovery of their health. I do not mean to imply that lower-visibility programs should not be developed as well. But whatever the choices, it must be recognized that the client-centered focus is a necessary but not sufficient basis for program development. A systems-centered focus is also required.

———————

The program development process can be conceptualized as having three phases: initiation, implementation, and institutionalization. Each of these phases has certain subphases, and each has associated with it a unique set of obstacles to a program's success.

Initiation: In initiating a program, the first question is: who has the authority to allow its development? Related questions ask whether a program is aimed at one worker's caseload or many workers', whether it works with clients from other disciplines and departments, and whether the program requires resources from outside the agency. Obviously the latter two alternatives are more complicated than the program involving only the clients in one's own caseload or one's own unit.

Nevertheless, the issue is the same: who has control over the resources that are required? If the worker does not, he or she has to develop a strategy for getting them. Often workers will have to decide whether the goal is to develop a program themselves or simply to get a new program developed, even if someone else takes the lead and perhaps most of the credit. This decision requires considerable forbearance or, to use a better term, "professionalism," by which we mean an ability to place one's clients' service needs before one's own need for recognition.

It may be, for example, that many women clients of a family agency who are returning to work could benefit from a support group. One strategy for getting a group started would be for the worker to suggest to his or her superior, or to the administration, that one is required. Another strategy is to suggest that all the workers scrutinize their caseloads to see if there are client needs that the agency is not meeting. A support group might be legitimated more easily out of such a common endeavor. A similar strategy might be worked out with other professional groups or other departments. Here the worker relinquishes part of the helping role and its rewards to others in the agency. Agency and departmental involvement are important: no program can be initiated without them, because many new programs require a reallocation of resources. Even if there are new resources, their allocation has important ramifications, if only the fact that new resources used for one purpose cannot be used for another.

Perhaps the greatest problem of the initiation phase of program development is the frequent need to compromise certain aspects of the program to gain the sanction of those who control power and resources in the agency. These compromises can threaten the integrity of the program by limiting resources or drastically altering its goals. For example, to gain the agency's support for the work group discussed above, one might have to agree to hold it in the evening, when most women will not be able to attend. Holding it during the day, according to the agency executive, would disrupt the usual scheduling of therapy.

Implementation: The implementation phase begins once legitimation and resources have been secured and one starts to seek clients, organize staff, and deliver services. Program implementation can be relatively easy if one needs no resources other than one's own skill and time, and if the agency supports one's efforts.

When other staff members are involved, however, the problem is one of creating a structure and a reward system that will support their participation. If other staff members do not see the purpose of the new program, if it is low in their priorities, and especially if it does not fit into their picture of how their job should be done, it is likely to flounder and eventually fail. In such situations, program goals are often displaced or totally subverted.

The article that follows describes attendants' perspectives on programming in back wards. It graphically illustrates that even the most needed and best-intended programs are undermined by the failure to provide a correlative reward system for participants.

Let Them Eat Programs: Attendants'
Perspectives and Programming on Wards in
State Schools*

ROBERT BOGDAN, STEVEN TAYLOR, BERNARD DEGRANDPRE, AND SONDRA
HAYNES

Those who attempt to introduce therapeutic programs at "total institutions" often fail to take into account the invariable effects of the ward setting.† That is, new programs are planned and implemented without a sufficient understanding of the context into which they are being introduced. Many of those interested in change, for example, subscribe to systems of definitions and beliefs which they assume are shared by those in the setting they are attempting to change. Those within the setting, however, may act from totally different perspectives. The result is a poor interface between the change agent and the setting—a factor which inevitably circumscribes the potential effectiveness of the change.

The primary purpose of this paper is to present specific aspects of attendants' perspectives on their supervisors, their jobs, and residents and to show how these relate to the implementation of "innovative" programs designed by supervisory and professional staff to serve the needs of the residents on the attendants' wards. Our discussion deals with a specific kind of total institution that is relatively unknown to social scientists: state schools for the "mentally retarded."‡. . .

The three institutions on which this study concentrates are located on the edge of a middle-sized city and in rural communities. One institution houses 400 residents; another 2,500; and the third 3,000. The wards were an infant/children's ward, a ward for adolescent girls of rather high ability, and a ward for the "severely and profoundly retarded aggressive

*Excerpted with permission of the American Sociological Association and the authors from *Journal of Health and Social Behavior* 15 (1974): 142–154. The authors would like to thank Burton Blatt and Douglas Biklen for their contribution to this paper.

†Erving Goffman, *Asylums: Essays on the Social Situation of Mental Patients and Other Inmates* (Garden City, N.Y.: Doubleday, Anchor Books, 1964); Thomas J. Scheff, "Control over Policy by Attendants in a Mental Hospital," *Journal of Health and Human Behavior* 2 (1964): 93–105.

‡Writings can be found in the professional mental retardation literature (see the *American Journal of Mental Deficiency* and *Mental Retardation*.) For studies in the social science literature, see Dorothea Braginsky and Benjamin Braginsky, *Hansels and Gretels* (New York: Holt, Rinehart and Winston, 1971); Pauline Morris, *Put Away* (New York: Atherton, 1969); Robert B. Egerton, *The Cloak of Competence* (Berkeley: University of California Press, 1967); Jack Tizard, "The Role of Social Institutions in the Causation, Prevention, and Alleviation of Mental Retardation," in H. C. Haywood, ed., *Social-Cultural Aspects of Mental Retardation* (New York: Appleton-Century-Crofts, 1970), pp. 281–340; Michael Klaber, "Institutional Programming and Research: A Vital Partnership in Action," in A. A. Baumeister and E. C. Butterfield, eds., *Residential Facilities for the Mentally Retarded* (Chicago: Aldine, 1971), pp. 163–200.

young adult males" (age range fourteen through forty-four)—what we shall refer to as the "back ward." The wards, as one can imagine from their brief introduction, vary as to the kind of residents and the nature of the environment and services provided. What we have attempted to do is to draw from our data the commonalities in attendants' perspectives that are directly related to understanding the implementation of programs. While we do not maintain that the material we present represents the views of all attendants, we do take the position that it characterizes their dominant views.

"They Don't Know What It's Really Like": Perspectives on Superiors

Attendants share the view that their superiors, be they administrators, line professionals, or supervisors, misunderstand the needs of the residents and the nature of life and work on the wards. It is their belief that their own proximity to the residents and time spent on the ward provide them with a knowledge of ward life which is inaccessible to others. As an attendant from the back ward put it:

> They just sit in the office and tell us what to do, but they're not here. They don't know what we know.

An attendant on the infant/children ward expressed a similar point of view in reference to staff meetings at which decisions are made about residents' placements and from which attendants are excluded:

> We're the ones who spend most of the time with the children. We know what they can do and what they can't do. At the last meeting they had a teacher come who doesn't hardly have anything to do with any of the children. Somebody from O.T. [Occupational Therapy]—they have very little to do with the children. And then Dr. Erthardman* who doesn't even know the children. She might make a decision that a child needs another I.Q. test to see what he can do since the last test. I could tell her what they can do and what they can't do. . . .

As this quotation begins to suggest, the perspective that attendants "know best" is also based on a skepticism of professionals and the procedures and approaches they employ. The attendants, many of whom have not completed high school, believe in direct observation and the application of "common sense," and tend to regard with tongue in cheek test scores, esoteric vocabularies and explanations, and the general approach some professionals use in treating "patients" (as the residents are often referred to). For example, attendants on the back ward as well

---

*This, like all proper names in this paper, is a pseudonym.

as those on the adolescent ward hold a very dubious view of the advice of the institution's professionals:

> Let me tell you, those psychiatrists are all crazy. . . . They just don't know what they are doing. They tell you to sit down with 'em and talk to them when they start going at it [fighting]. Christ, if I tried that I'd get my fuckin' brains kicked out. . . .

Another attendant summarized his own and his co-worker's feelings about the state and the institution:

> It's really bad here—no programs, no nothing. We sit here and watch bodies. I've been here twenty-seven years—the state and the doctors— they're something else. The directors get big fat salaries—they've never had experience on the wards—they don't know what's going on. After they pay them there's no money for the people and services here. When I retire I'm gonna tell my friends in the Capitol about the way things are being run.

Perspectives on Work: "A Job is a Job"

While attendants derive some satisfaction from the intrinsic aspects of their work (such as the companionship other attendants offer), they define their jobs primarily in terms of the extrinsic benefits these jobs provide. Thus, they resemble unskilled workers in other settings in their definition of their work.*

> It's a job—nothing more, nothing less.

As one attendant from the back ward related:

> If I didn't need the checks so bad I'd quit.

Attendants on the back ward place an equal importance on monetary rewards and fringe benefits:

> Everyone is here for one reason and one reason only—money. That's right, they're all here for the money. That's why they took this job. That's why I took this job.

In accordance with this perspective, attendants see themselves not as "professionals" who are responsible for engaging the residents in programmed activities, but, rather as custodians who are responsible for keeping the ward clean and maintaining control and order among the

---

*The alternative to insitutional employment for most attendants is lower-level factory or construction work.

residents.* Witness the following remarks offered by an attendant on the back ward:

> We're supposed to feed 'em and keep an eye on 'em and make sure they're OK. They have people in recreation—psychologists and sociologists. They're the ones who are supposed to train 'em and work with 'em—not us.

This emphasis on custodial care is so strong that the well-being of the residents is often ignored or deliberately violated.† One attendant commented:

> We have no time to keep things as they should be, let alone help the residents. We sometimes have to tie people up so that we can carry on with the work.

Another stated:

> By the time you're done with your work, you're too tired to do anything else.

Attendants develop routines to minimize their custodial work and develop methods of control to deal with troublesome residents. Those on the back ward use "brighter" residents (so-called working boys) to do much of the custodial work and to control other residents. Attendants on all wards form work quotas and goldbrick, as do factory workers.‡ Thus, they spend much of their time "screwing off," despite the fact that they complain that they never have enough time. On back wards a resident is asigned to watch out for supervisors while the attendants pitch nickels, read the newspaper, harass residents, drink, or pass the time in idle conversation. On all wards the television, which is turned to stations of the attendants' choosing, provides diversion during the long breaks. On all wards each observer has been left singlehanded to cover for the attendants while they left the wards for breaks. . . .

Perspectives of Residents: "Low Grades," "Rejects," and "Delinquents."

In view of the importance attendants place on the custodial aspects of their work, it is hardly surprising that they define residents in terms of either their disabilities or the amount of trouble or work they cause. Thus, attendants refer to residents with words which emphasize those

---

*Steven Taylor,"Attendants' Perspectives: A View from the Back Ward," paper presented at the 97th annual meeting of the American Association on Mental Deficiency, 1973.

†Ibid.

‡Donald Roy, "Quota Restriction and Goldbricking in a Machine Shop," *American Journal of Sociology* 57 (1952): 427–442.

characteristics: "puker," "regurgitator," "dummy," "biter," "grabber," "soiler," "headbanger," "low grade," "vegetable," "brat," "fighter."

Certain residents are sources of concern to attendants on all wards. "Hyperactive" residents and those who lack basic self-help skills are especially resented. On the infant/children ward, women attendants complain about nonambulatory children who are heavy to lift. These children are transferred from the ward regardless of age, despite the fact that they are supposed to stay on the ward until they reach the age of twelve years.* On the back ward the population is composed of what the attendants call "rejects" from other wards, residents who were placed there because they were too much trouble for other attendants. And on the adolescent ward attendants believe that about one-third of their residents were placed there not because they are "retarded," but, rather, because they are incorrigible.

> This bunch of girls isn't retarded—they are just delinquents. They don't like school and their parents don't make them go. We get them back when the parents can't handle them.

Few attendants believe in the residents' potential to learn or to change. From their point of view, little can be done for the residents beyond what is already being done. One attendant typified this perspective in her response to a question concerning the futures of the children on her ward:

> Eventually they'll go to another building. Most of them will be this way for the rest of their lives. . . .

The focus of formal attendant training at the three institutions is on the etiology of "mental retardation" and the developmental characteristics of the "mentally retarded." Witness the following quotations:

> We learn about medications, how these people are different from you and I, how to care for them, how to treat them, what to expect, things like that.

> They teach you a lot about causes and things, but you can't use that here. . . .

Innovative Programming

It should not be difficult to imagine what happened when supervisory and professional staff attempted to introduce "innovative" programs onto these wards. In this section, we would like to briefly discuss the impact and outcomes of these attempts.

---

*This practice can have dire consequences for nonambulatory children. Those who cannot walk by the time they leave this ward are transferred to wards for nonambulatory adolescents or adults, where they receive no training to walk. Many, therefore, never do walk.

The program that was introduced in the back ward was what attendants and their supervisors referred to as a "motivation training" program. The attendants were never quite certain of the program's intended purpose and, in fact, received their information about the program from fellow workers on other wards and shifts. In the following quotation, one "ward charge" (supervising attendant) described how he learned about the program:

> I was talking to another charge and he told me about it. You see, it's supposed to be from 6 to 8:30 every night. Then each guy will take twelve kids [age range of residents on the ward is fourteen to forty-four] and sit around and teach 'em things—like how to take care of themelves and dress themselves. And then every ward is getting a popcorn popper and we'll give 'em popcorn every night as a reward.

While some attendants were willing to give the program their guarded approval prior to its implementation, most viewed it with skepticism from its beginning. Some argued that they had too little time and too much other work to implement such a program:

> Now how are we supposed to motivate 'em, and clean this place and everything? We don't have enough employees.

Others believed that the intellectual capacities of the residents precluded significant "improvement":

> You see, the patients we have are all rejects and we're supposed to do something with them. You can teach them so much and that's it. They can't learn no more.

Although this ward's supervising attendant postponed the program's implementation for a period of four weeks after it was supposed to have begun, it was finally introduced with the aid of a "trained" attendant from another ward. The actual program consisted of two activities which were offered on alternative evenings: crayoning in coloring books and listening to children's records. The sessions lasted for periods of an hour to an hour and a half for the time the program was in operation.

How did the attendants see the program? Some viewed it as a means of keeping the residents occupied:

> I don't think it's doing any good. It gives them something to do—that's all.

There was some truth to this statement, for this was, for the great majority of the residents, the only "training" or recreation they received at the institution.

Most attendants, however, perceived the crayoning and the music as some type of "training." In spite of the, at best, tenuous connection between these activities and training, the attendants viewed the activities as the initial stage of a more comprehensive program:

> We're supposed to progress from here—start teaching them how to dress and things.

Yet the residents' performance in these most simple activities served to further confirm the attendants' perspectives that training for these residents and on this ward was futile. Their general belief in the inability of the residents to change was supported and specified. One attendant explained:

> I've been trying to teach them how to color, but it doesn't work for most of them. They don't switch colors when they're coloring, and they won't stay in the lines. I've been trying to teach them, but they just scribble.

The program was unofficially terminated six weeks after its start. One attendant related:

> It kinda fizzled out. We're not doin' it anymore.

And another stated:

> All the wards just about stopped doin' it. The whole institution was supposed to have it, but most of them stopped. I don't know—I haven't been here that long but I think that's the way it always goes . . . it's too hard keeping their attention.

Finally, one attendant summed up his own and his peers' fatalism when he remarked:

> I bet you think we're just a bunch of lazy fat asses here. . . . Well, we do sit around a lot doin' nothin'. We read the paper and watch TV. But actually there isn't much we could do with 'em even if we wanted to.

The program on the adolescent ward lasted much longer than the program we have just reviewed and, in fact, was still operating at last knowledge. This program was designed by the chief of children's services, Dr. Warner, who described the program as a "behavior modification program—token economy—designed to teach responsibility to the girls." According to the plan, the girls were to be rewarded for doing assigned ward jobs and for satisfactory schoolwork by receiving points which could be redeemed for merchandise. As Dr. Warner told one of the authors:

This will reward them for good behavior. I really think it will make a difference. We need a lot more behavior modification here. It's the answer.

While skeptical of Dr. Warner, the attendants initially viewed the point system as a potentially effective way for them to control the residents' behavior and to make their work easier. One explained:

The girls are snapping to it and doing what they are supposed to. If you tell them that they are going to lose some points, they pay attention to you now.

As this comment suggests, the program that was designed to reward residents for "appropriate behavior" was used to punish them for annoying behavior. Thus, attendants took away points for insolence or vulgarity. Since residents could not receive points from personnel other than themselves, this was one of the few means by which the attendants could retain control.

In the eyes of the attendants, Dr. Warner was far too permissive and misunderstood the girls. They claimed that the new system and other innovations would only serve to further spoil them. Witness the following comments offered by one of the attendants:

Have you heard Dr. Warner's latest idea? He wants to let volunteers take the boys and girls with the most points out to dinner at some fancy place. These kids would probably beat up the volunteer.

The precise record keeping which the point system entailed soon became "just a lot of trouble" for the attendants. At the end of the observation period, approximately six months after the program's implementation, the attendants were extremely lax in their point recording, and many of the girls had simply forgotten about the points they had accumulated.

A "range of motion" program was introduced onto the infant/children ward by the attending physician and the day shift ward charge, an R.N. It lasted the shortest period of time of the three programs we have reviewed and, in fact, was never implemented for many of the residents.

The goal of this program was to provide children with the physical stimulation necessary to prevent physical regression and the development of spasticity and irreversible contractures. The program was developed in view of the fact that these conditions had already stricken many children and that, without some program, would strike many more.

The institution's lone physical therapist (institutional population: 2,500) visited the ward, evaluated each child, and wrote a prescription describing the therapy that each was to receive. Each child was assigned to an attendant who had been instructed in the range of motion exercises to be employed daily.

Direct observation on the dorms revealed that few attendants ever provided their designated children with the range of motion therapy. At one point, the daytime charge, who was ultimately responsible for the program's implementation, became aware of the problem and mentioned it to her supervisor in the observer's presence:

> "The attendants aren't doing anything," said Mrs. Dey, the R.N. who was the daytime charge.
> "What kinds of things do you think they ought to be doing?" the observer asked.
> "I think they ought to be doing the range of motion," she responded.
> "Aren't they doing it?" asked Mrs. Dumas, the supervising nurse.
> "No," said Mrs. Dey, shaking her head. "I go into the front dorm, and all they're doing is sitting around."

When they were alone with the observer, the attendants articulated the reasons for their failure to pursue the program. They maintained, among other things, that the wrong children had been selected to participate and that they themselves were neither able (trained) nor willing (sufficiently paid) to do what was expected of them.

Conclusion

Our primary position in this study has been that institutional programs must be examined in the context of the ward settings on which they are introduced. We have studied one aspect of that setting, the way attendants defined their supervisors, their jobs, and the residents under their charge.

In reading a paper such as ours, one might conclude that the problem of programming in total institutions lies only in attendants' attitudes and lack of training. While this is a seductive way of defining the problem, walking through these isolated, massive facilities which are filled with unwanted human beings, one must question whether the problem is not the institutional model itself. Perhaps the feeble attempts at programming we have reported here represent the cruelest lies of this dehabilitating system. Perhaps attendants' reactions to programming are realistic adjustments to the truth of these facilities. To offer programming as a remedy to a system that by its very nature isolates, desocializes, and dehumanizes reminds us of Marie Antoinette's remark when informed that her subjects were starving—that they had no bread. Her response was: "Let them eat cake."

The preceding paper presents a "worst case" scenario of a social agency. It is included to sensitize the reader to the importance of considering staff needs and concerns when developing programs. The "range of motion" program illustrates some of the classic problems of implementation.

Innovators should ask, first, whether the resources to carry out the program—in this case the time and skill of the attendants—were available clearly they were not in the institution studied.

Second, one should consider whether one has sufficient authority to get people to do what one wants, whether they want to do it or not. As it turned out, the attendants' informal authority superseded the formal authority of those officially in charge of the program.

Third, it seems that no one attempted to anticipate problems—role confusion, conflicts over priorities, and the like—and so no plan for monitoring the program was in place before it was implemented. Any new program is going to have problems. Not only can these be anticipated to some extent, but mechanisms can be set in place to deal with unexpected problems as they surface.

A fourth issue related to implementation (not illustrated in Bogdan et al.'s paper) is the need to maintain the sanction and support for a new program. People are often excited by anything new, but as organizational problems emerge, they lose their enthusiasm and withdraw their support.

Thus the program dies. Maintenance of program support requires a conscious plan, even if one is carrying out the new program oneself. Opportunities to observe should be sought out, and reports should be made to those in charge so that administrative commitment can be developed and maintained.

Institutionalization: The institutionalization phase is when the program becomes a permanent part of the structure of services. Problems frequently emerge in this phase because little thought was given in earlier stages to the need for additional resources for institutionalizing the program. Hence, there may be no plans for developing the enlarged sanction required at this stage or for dealing with recalcitrant staff members who may, for whatever reason, oppose institutionalization. Often, little thought is given to the amount of retraining that will be required if staff members are to carry out the program. In such a situation, institutionalization of a program is doubtful.

Any new program redistributes resources and disrupts social relationships. Obviously, institutionalization involves the higher organizational levels. The line worker's ability to understand the requisites for institutionalizing a program can help an administration avoid moving either too precipitously or too slowly. (See Julie Abramson's discussion of the institutionalization of a hospital obsesity program above in this chapter.)

The redistribution of internal power and authority and the disruption of social relationships are generally grounds for some sort of reaction or "counterrevolution," like that of the attendants described by Bogdan et al. Effective institutionalization calls for leadership that is sensitive to the staff's need for support and that can create a climate in which social relationships can re-establish themselves around the new program. In addition, leadership must be able to handle the inevitable tension that the redistribution of power engenders.

Practice Analogues

Feedback from clients can be crucial to developing or generating an idea for a program. Feedback from staff, on the other hand, is crucial to implementing and institutionalizing a program. Finally, feedback from the clients who have participated in a program is useful in refining it. The skills and techniques involved in setting up and maintaining feedback mechanisms are thus necessary to a successful program developer. These coincide to a considerable extent with the skills and techniques that a clincial social worker uses in getting feedback on client's progress in coping with their problems.

Some specific techniques for getting this information are discussed in the chapter on the role of the evaluator. More generally, however, the critical task in setting up a feedback system is the development of trust. It is very difficult to get accurate and reliable information from clients if there is no trust between them and the clinician. The same is true of communication between staff members. The need for feedback can present real dilemmas to the clients, the staff, and the agency.

For clients, there is often a fear of reprisal; that is, they worry that if they say something negative, they will be denied service. Some clients fear that anything written down will be used against them. They will tend to tell the worker what they feel the worker wants to hear. Still others feel that there is no point in giving feedback about programs since nothing will happen. Too often they are right. These are potent sources of resistance.

Agencies may also resist utilizing feedback. They acknowledge that feedback about clients' needs is important, but what the clients need and what staff members want to hear are not necessarily the same. Constant negative feedback, about gaps in service, for example, can in fact be corrosive and demoralizing. One way to establish trust is to give and accept feedback about what is right as well as what is wrong. One hopes that in most organizations there is more right than wrong, since focusing on the negative can create morale problems. This is quite similar to what the clinician does with a client: focusing on the weaknesses and not acknowledging strengths can simply exacerbate the client's problems.

Agencies that are enthusiastic about feedback programs when they are initiated sometimes change their tune when the feedback system brings to the surface major conflicts. This can be especially problematic when the agency has no system to deal with conflict and does not seem to be able to devise one. Without a system for conflict resolution, systematic feedback can challenge the status of professionals, erode the authority structure of the agency, and pose a threat to morale.

The clinician doing family therapy has the same problem. Bringing more problems to the surface when the family is unable to deal with conflict can be damaging, not only to the family but to the process of therapy itself. The ultimate question for the program developer and the clinician alike is: "who is the client?" For the program developer, the client is the agency system. For the clinician, on the other hand, the client is the recipient of service, even though the target of action may be significant others in the client's life. Identifying the client is, therefore, a clinical issue as well as a program development one. This point is critical for clinical workers who want to be, or who must be, program developers, in that there is a natural but incorrect tendency to focus on the individual service recipient rather than the agency system as one develops programs. In fact, such a focus will almost always lead to failure.

Attitudes, Values, and Skills

The attitude that perhaps most limits the worker's ability to develop programs is the assumption that agency clients have come to be diagnosed and treated and that the worker has all the skill needed to define and treat the clients' problems. Clients' views about the help offered are considered contaminated and therefore not important. Another destructive attitude, this one at the opposite end of the spectrum, is that all feedback is good. As we indicated earlier, feedback is not necessarily good; it can disrupt the agency to the point that it begins to operate at a lower level than it did before the feedback was provided. How a feedback system is constructed is important. Clinicians generally have little difficulty empathizing with a client's inability to accept negative feedback immediately. They need to have the same understanding of agencies.

Another attitudinal obstacle to program development—and we cannot emphasize this enough—is a total preoccupation with the needs of clients. What is good for clients may not be good for the agency or the staff. How many people want to work four evenings a week and weekends? The inability to take a systems point of view, to see beyond client need, is debilitating to the program developer.

It is our contention that the therapeutic skill of clinicians are only one set of the variables that affect what happens to clients in agencies.

Although the enhancement of these skills is the *raison d'être* of this book in the area of program development, nothing could be more disastrous than to ignore the need for workers to possess managerial, political, and research skills. In fact, the reason many workers feel that they cannot develop programs may be their sense that their therapeutic skills are not enough to equip them for this role. In this they are correct.

One final problem deserves mention. The organizational structure supports the efforts of managers as program developers. They are evaluated on their ability in this area; they have ample opportunity to exploit organizational events to promote their ideas; and they have a personal stake in enlarging their domains. There is no such support for clinicians, and for at least one such group, who were exposed while in school to much of the material in this book, lack of support from colleagues on their first jobs severely limited their efforts at innovation. What they missed was the support of fellow workers that they had enjoyed as students.

Perhaps the first innovation a clinician should attempt is the development of a network of like-minded staff members to provide ideas, contacts, and enthusiasm and to act as a sounding board and correcting device. Such a group can add immensely to the pleasure of the job and the possibility of developing programs.

Additional Readings

Giordano, Peggy. "The Client's Perspective in Agency Evaluation." *Social Work* 22 (1977): 34–39.

Rothman, Jack. "Promoting an Innovation." In Herman Resnick and Rino Patti eds., *Change From Within*, Philadelphia: pp. Temple University, 1980.

Warfel, David J. et al. "Consumer Feedback in Human Service Programs." *Social Work* (1981): 151–156.

Weissman, Harold H. "Toward a Social Psychology of Program Design." *Administration in Social Work* 2 (1978): 3–14.

CHAPTER 7

ORGANIZATIONAL REFORMER

"Plus ça change, plus c'est la même chose." this rather pessimistic French saying—the more things change, the more they remain the same—can serve as an apology for inaction. From another point of view, however, it can be taken as a warning to consider carefully where one is going to direct change efforts, how one is going to bring about change, what one expects the change to produce, and how to ensure that after this costly process has taken place, things are better than before.

For example, a unit of social workers may be frustrated about their supervisor's general ineptitude and reluctance to let them try innovative approaches to treatment. They define the problem as supervisor incompetence and set about trying to have this person replaced. This is a painful and risky effort, and after they succeed, they discover that their new supervisor is equally opposed to treatment innovation.

What went wrong? Perhaps the initial mistake was assuming individual incompetence rather than considering the supervisor's resistance to change as a symptom of the agency's resistance. Perhaps it was the failure to see that the "supervisor's supervisor" the agency administrator—had a strong ideological commitment to traditional treatment. Perhaps it was the belief that the former supervisor was so bad that *anyone* would be better. Possibly it was all of these and more. In any case, by now their energy has been drained. Unable to initiate another change effort, they are likely to succumb to despair and dull compliance.

Overview

This chapter will concern itself with reforms within the agency: changes in policy, procedures, goals, personnel, and other areas. The content differs from that of the chapter on program development, however, in that the last chapter focuses on starting new programs, whereas this one focuses on changing what exists. Nevertheless, the processes involved are the same: initiation, implementation, and institutionalization. Consequently, the reader may wish to refer again to the earlier discussion of these processes as well as to the discussion of change strategies and influence in Chapters 5 and 8.

The name we give to the role that we are discussing here is "organizational reformer." It may seem a bit grandiose, considering that some of the changes that we will be talking about are relatively small and lack the moral significance usually associated with the word "reform." Yet in organizational life, small changes can have large results.

Organizational Change: Often workers wonder why they should have to be concerned with organizational change. Isn't that the job of management? It is. But there are times when management's perspective is different from that of clinicians because their daily concerns, their interests, and their priorities are different. One may not be able to do one's job well unless one can get the organization to change a policy or procedure. At other times one may have a good idea, but, for a variety of reasons, one's immediate superior will not consider it. And at other times one may simply be demoralized because one lacks the power to get people and departments to cooperate with each other. Ignoring the agency context is a luxury that clinicians who care about their clients cannot afford.

Most clinicians who have worked in social agencies have had fantasies about how changes should take place. The typical fantasy is something like this: one points out the problem and its ramifications at the weekly staff meeting. One's director brings the problem and suggested solutions to the attention of the executive director, and the next week a memo appears informing everyone about the new procedure, which will be immediately implemented. The time elapsed between one's identification of the problem and its solution—one week, two days.

The actual process is much more complex.* The first step is deciding whether one is going to try to do something oneself or whether one is immediately going to involve others. One may not have the knowledge, the power, or the skill to change anything in the organization. To have any chance of success in such a situation, one has to involve others.

One also has to be prepared to answer the challenge "Do you have any idea what you're talking about?" One wants the agency to develop a new outreach program to improve the access to the agency of the poorest clients. Doing that, however, will require retraining staff members to enable them to develop new services; changing working relationships; and altering the skills the agency accords the highest status to. Any substantive change is also related to changes in the agency's reward system: some will lose and some will gain power, status, opportunities for promotion, and the like. A change in one part of the agency will affect other parts. Change the outreach, and one affects intake, service deliv-

*Rino J. Patti, "Organizational Resistance and Change: The View from Below," *Social Service Review* 48 (1974): 370.

ery, and outcome. What if taking in a new set of clients results in an increased number of dropouts from the program, which can affect the agency's funding? When one proposes what seems to be a small organizational change, one is often setting the stage for a lot of complications. This is why organizations tend to pay more attention to suggestions from staff members who are defined as competent.

Once the dimensions of a problem are gauged, the reformer has to decide on a strategy and tactics that are likely to lead to success. Part of this analysis must be concerned with the specific types of resources that will be required: specialized knowledge, time, informal contacts, power, commitment, and so on. Some strategies and tactics require more power to carry out than others. David Mechanic suggests that the source of power of lower level staff is closely related to making others in the organization dependent on them by controlling 1) access to information, or knowledge about people, norms, procedures and techniques; 2) persons within or outside of the organization upon whom the organization is dependent; and 3) instrumentalities, such as parts of the organization's physical plant, or resources, such as money, equipment, and the like.* Generally the longer the staff remains on the job, the greater is its access to people, information, and instrumentalities upon which power is based.

Thomas Peters, in an interesting article subtitled "An Optimistic Case for Getting Things Done," suggests that organizational change is inextricably bound up with the everyday routines of organizational life and requires a long-term perspective. He sees such ordinary events as staff meetings as presenting opportunities to present a point of view. Beliefs and expectations can be affected by frequent, consistent, and positive reinforcement, and one can learn a great deal about how systems respond to small nudges by asking good questions.†

He further argues that such mundane matters as the presence or absence of top managers at organizational events, the location of groups and meetings, the style of presentations, questioning approaches, and follow-up mechanisms can influence change. The important thing is to change an organization's ways of thinking and, ultimately, of doing. A minority can shape expectations if their opinions and actions are consistently fair, honest, and realistic.‡

Edward Pawlak's article, which follows, examines both the mundane and the extraordinary as levers for clinicians to utilize in influencing their employers.

---

*David Mechanic, "Sources of Power of Lower Participants in Complex Organizations," in *Readings in Managerial Psychology*, 3rd edition, Harold Leavitt, Louis Pondy and David Boje, eds. (Chicago: University of Chicago Press, 1980), p. 398.

†Thomas J. Peters, "Symbols, Patterns and Settings: An Optimistic Case for Getting Things Done," in Leavitt et al., eds., *Readings in Managerial Psychology* (Chicago: University of Chicago Press, 1980), pp. 646–665.

‡Ibid., p. 655.

Organizational Tinkering*

Edward J. Pawlak

To tinker means to work at something in an experimental or makeshift way. Although the clinician's position and role in many social welfare organizations preclude him from pursuing ambitious organizational change, he still may be able to work at change in modest, makeshift ways. And despite the fact that clinical social work is usually practiced in an organizational and policy context, many clinicians are uninterested in acquiring the knowledge and skills that might facilitate intraorganizational tinkering on behalf of their practice or their clients. Others are overwhelmed, cynical, or disillusioned by their dealings with bureaucracy.† Some front line practitioners, however, have learned to tinker effectively.‡

To help clinicians improve their talent in dealing with organizations, this article identifies tactics they can use to tinker with organizational structure, modes of operation, rules, conventions, policy, and programs. The specific tactics discussed are tinkering with bureaucratic succession and rules, the white paper or position paper, demonstration projects, modification of board composition, bypassing, influencing grant reviews, leaking information, and protest by resignation.

Although the author takes a partisan stand on behalf of clinicians, it does not follow that managers are necessarily the villains. However, some of the tactics identified here are directed toward those administrators who cause clinicians to harbor severe misgivings about the organization.

This article stems not only from the author's observation of and experience with organizational tinkering, but also from the contributions of others who have addressed similar themes.§ It warns clinicians to bear in

*Reprinted, Copyright 1976, National Association of Social Workers, Inc. with permission, from *Social Work* 21 (1976): 376–380.

†See Scott Briar, "The Casework Predicament"; Irving Piliavin, "Restructuring the Provision of Social Services"; and Harry Specht, "Casework Practice and Social Policy Formulation," all in *Social Work*, 13 (1968): 9–10, 34–36, and 42–43; Archie Hanlan, "Casework beyond Bureaucracy," *Social Casework* 52 (1971): 195–198; Lawrence Podell and Ronald Miller, *Professionalism in Public Social Services*, Study Series, vol. 1, no. 2 (New York: Human Resources Administration, 1974); and Naomi Gottlieb, *The Welfare Bind* (New York: Columbia University Press, 1974), p. 34.

‡See Thomas F. Maher, "Freedom of Speech in Public Agencies," *Social Work* 19 (1974): 698–703; Joseph J. Senna, "Changes in Due Process of Law," *Social Work* 19 (1974): 319–324; and Irwin Hyman and Karen Schreiber, "The School Psychologist as Child Advocate," *Children Today* 3 (Mar.–Apr. 1974): 21–33, 36.

§Rino J. Patti and Herman Resnick, "Changing the Agency from Within," *Social Work* 17, (1972): 48–57; *Social Work* 17 (1972): 48–57; Specht, "Casework Practice," pp. 42–52; George Brager, "Advocacy and Political Behavior," *Social Work* 13 (1968): 5–15; Carl Martin, "Beyond Bureaucracy," *Child Welfare* 1 (1971): 384–388; Warren G. Bennis,

mind the pitfalls and dilemmas of organizational tinkering—that it takes place in a political climate and in a structure of authority, norms, and sanctions.*

Bureaucratic Succession

Bureaucratic succession usually refers to a change in leadership at the highest levels of an organization. Here, however, the author uses the broader concept that includes changes in leadership at all levels in the hierarchy.† Bureaucratic succession must be called to the attention of clinicians because it is an opportunity to influence intraorganizational change. For the clinician to exert influence during this phase of organizational transition, it is essential that he understand certain features of organizational life that frequently accompany succession.

Prior to an administrator's departure, organizations usually go into a period of inaction. Most staff members are aware of the lame-duck character of this phase of organizational life, when any major change is avoided until the new administrator takes office. There are, however, ways in which clinicians take advantage of this period. They can, for example, (1) suggest criteria for the selection of a successor, (2) seek membership on the search committee, (3) prepare a position paper for a new administrator, (4) propose a revision in the governance structure to enhance participatory management, (5) organize fellow subordinates to propose changes that had been unacceptable to the outgoing administrator, or (6) propose the formulation of a task force to facilitate transition.

The "first one hundred days" is another critical phase of bureaucratic succession that should be examined for the opportunities it offers. Although new administrators tend to be conservative about implementing changes until they are more familiar with the organization, they still are interested in development and in making their own mark.

"Post-Bureaucratic Leadership," *Trans-Action* 6 (July–Aug. 1969): 44–52; and Harold H. Weissman, *Overcoming Mismanagement in the Human Service Professions* (San Francisco: Jossey-Bass, 1973).

*See Rino J. Patti, "Organizational Resistance and Change: The View from Below," *Social Service Review* 48 (1974): 367–383; Edward Weisband and Thomas M. Franck, *Resignation in Protest* (New York: Grossman, 1975); Ralph Nader, Peter J. Petkas, and Kate Blackwell, *Whistle-Blowing* (New York: Grossman, 1972); Irwin Epstein, "Social Workers and Social Action," *Social Work* 13 (1968): 101–108, and "Professional Role Orientations and Conflict Strategies," *Social Work* 15 (1970): 87–92; and A. D. Green, "The Professional Social Worker in the Bureaucracy," *Social Service Review* 40 (1966): 71–83.

†For a more detailed discussion of bureaucratic succession, see Bernard Levenson, "Bureaucratic Succession," in Amitai Etzioni, ed., *Complex Organizations* (New York: Holt, Rinehart & Winston, 1961), pp. 362–365; and Alvin Gouldner, *Patterns of Industrial Bureaucracy* (Glencoe, Ill.: Free Press, 1954), pp. 59–104.

This three-month period, therefore, provides opportunities to orient and shape the perceptions of the new administrator, who, until he acquires his own intelligence about the organization, is both vulnerable and receptive to influence.

The following case illustrates how practitioners can tinker with organizational hierarchy by taking advantage of a resignation.

> The resignation of a clinician who had served as director of staff development in a child welfare agency provided the staff with an opportunity to influence the transformation of the position into that of administrative assistant. The agency had recently undergone rapid growth in staff size, resources, and diversity, without an accompanying increase in the administrative staff. Thus, the clinician's resignation became the occasion for examining whether the position should be modified to serve such administrative staff functions as program development and grant management.

Bureaucratic succession, therefore, provides an opportunity for an organization to take pause; to examine its mission, structure, policies, practices, accomplishments, and problems; and to decide what it wants to become. It is incumbent upon practitioners to participate in these processes and to take advantage of the structure of influence during that vulnerable phase.

Rules

Rules are features of organizations that, by their nature, invite tinkering. They act as mechanisms of social control and standardization, provide guidelines for decision making, limit discretion, and structure relationships between persons and units within the organizational structure and between separate organizations.* There are two types of rules—formal and informal. Formal rules are derived from law or are determined administratively or collectively. Informal rules—which may be as binding as formal ones—are practices that have been routinized so that they have become organizational conventions or traditions. Rules vary in specificity, in their inherent demand for compliance, in the manner in which compliance is monitored, and in their sanctions for a lack of compliance.

Clinicians can tinker with rules either by the kind of interpretations they apply to them or by using their discretion, as is permitted with an ambiguous or general rule. Rules do not necessarily eliminate discretion, but they may eliminate alternatives that might otherwise be considered.† Gottlieb describes them as follows:

---

*For a detailed discussion, see Charles Perrow, *Complex Organizations: A Critical Essay* (Glenview, Ill.: Scott, Foresman), pp. 23–32.

†James D. Thompson, *Organizations in Action* (New York: McGraw-Hill, 1967), p. 120.

Rules are not necessarily static. They appear to be a controlling force working impersonally and equally, but they vary both in adherence and enforceability and are used variously by staff in their adaptation to the "welfare bind."*

Hanlan suggests that "in public welfare there exists an informal system that operates without invoking the formal administrative machinery of rules."† The author overheard the director of a community action program encourage new workers "to err on the side of generosity in determining eligibility for programs." A vocational rehabilitation counselor reported that he had had many teeth fixed by liberally interpreting a rule that provided dental care for only those clients whose appearance and dental problems would otherwise have prevented them from being considered for employment involving public contact. This shows that one can tinker with the manner in which rules are interpreted and enforced.

Another way of tinkering with rules is to avoid what Gottlieb calls "rule interpretations by agents of the system alone."‡ She goes on to report that welfare workers encouraged clients to seek help in interpreting rules enforced by the National Welfare Rights Organization (NWRO). It is generally known that legal aid clinics have been called on to give a legal interpretation of welfare rules and rules governing commitment to mental hospitals.

A supervisor for public assistance eligibility once reported that a thorough knowledge of all the rules enables the welfare worker to invoke one rule over another in order to help clients get what they need. This observation is supported by Gottlieb, who points out that rules allow for exceptions and that many NWRO members know the rules better than the workers and thus can challenge their interpretations.§ In his study of regulatory agencies, Nader suggests that rules not only are opportunities for action but are potential obstacles as well and that major effort is frequently required to persuade the agency to follow its own rules.‖

Another way of dealing with rules is to avoid asking for an interpretation. One agency administrator has suggested that personnel should not routinely ask for rulings and urges them to use their own discretion. He commented: "If you invoke authority, you put me in a position where I must exercise it. If I make a decision around here, it becomes a rule."

These ways of tinkering with rules suggest that clinicians should examine the function of rules, discern the latitude they are allowed in interpreting them, and exercise discretion. Although the foregoing exam-

*Gottlieb, *The Welfare Bind*, p. 8.
†Archie Hanlan, "Counteracting Problems of Bureaucracy in Public Welfare," *Social Work* 12 (1967): 93.
‡Gottlieb, *The Welfare Bind*, p. 8.
§Ibid., p. 32.
‖Nader, Petkas, and Blackwell, *Whistle-Blowing*.

ples are primarily taken from welfare settings, the principles outlined can be applied to traditional clinical settings.

Indirect Influence

Too often, clinicians rely on the anecdotal or case approach to influence change in an organization. Such an approach is too easily countered by the rejoinder that exceptional cases do not require a change in policy but should be handled as exceptions. The white paper, or position paper, is a much ignored means of tinkering with organizations.

A white paper is a report on a specific subject that emanates from a recent investigation. A position paper is a statement that sets forth a policy or a perspective. The first is usually more carefully reasoned and documented; the second may be argued instead of reasoned. Both white papers and position papers provide opportunities for social documentation and for formulating a compelling case. Such statements strive for logic and are characterized by their use of both quantitative and qualitative data. As the following example shows, by virtue of their character and quality, both position papers and white papers demand a specific response.

> A student social worker wrote a position paper identifying the number of teenage pregnancies, the number of associated medical problems, and the high rate of venereal disease among adolescents. She argued for the redirection of the original planned parenthood proposal from the main office to satellite clinics in public housing developments and schools. The paper was well received and spurred the executive to obtain funding from the housing authority.

Lindblom has characterized decision making in organizations as "disjointed incrementalism."* Simon indicates that organizations "satisfice"—that is, they make decisions that are good enough. Uncertainties in the environment, the inability to scan all alternatives, and the unknown utility of a solution or decision all preclude optimal decision making. If organizations were to try to comprehend all the information and contingencies necessary before making a rational decision, the complexity would be overwhelming.† Thus, organizations are reluctant to make changes on a large scale because this could lead to large-scale and unpredictable consequences. Resistance to change, therefore, may often be attributed to structure rather than to a malevolent or unsympathetic administrator. This calls attention to organizational structure and pro-

*Charles E. Lindblom, "The Science of Muddling Through," in Fred Cox et al., eds., *Strategies of Community Organization* (Itasca, Ill.: Peacock, 1970).
†Herbert A. Simon, *Administrative Behavior*, 2d ed. (New York: Macmillan, 1957), and *Models of Man, Social and Rational* (New York: John Wiley & Sons, 1957).

cesses, but does not mean that the values and roles of administrators are to be ignored.*

Given this perspective on organizational behavior, clinicians may consider approaching innovation incrementally and on a small scale by first gaining authorization for a demonstration project.† A demonstration project may be bounded by the duration of time or the proportion of the budget or staff time that is devoted to it. The problem with demonstration projects is that the people for whom the demonstration is being carried out are not always specified, nor are they always kept abreast of developments. Often there is a failure to articulate the ramifications and consequences of a successful or unsuccessful demonstration. Practitioners must develop a strategy of demonstration—a means of diffusing innovation throughout the organization or into other organizations and of obtaining commitments from the administration when the demonstration is complete. The following is an example of the commitment one social worker obtained.

> A social worker met with a group of suspended or expelled junior high school students after class to discuss their problems. Realizing that she needed to have a chance to intervene directly in their school behavior, she persuaded the agency supervisor, the principal, and the classroom teacher to develop a pilot project—"the opportunity class"—to be used as a last resort before expulsion. When the project was organized, the social worker remained in the classroom for several periods at least two days each week. She handled the acting-out behavior problems while the teacher continued classroom instruction. Eventually the teacher acquired skill in handling students who were acting out. The class continued without the social worker's presence, and some students returned to a regular classroom, while others were expelled.

Agency board committees are typically composed of elected members and the executive director of the agency. In addition, in some agencies, one or two staff members may also serve on the committee or occasionally attend meetings to make reports. One strategy of tinkering with the composition of the committee and the kind of information and influence it receives is to promote the idea that nonboard and nonstaff members with certain expertise be included on the committee. For example, a psychiatrist and a local expert on group treatment with children might be recruited to join a case services committee in order to provide legitimation to innovations that board members were grudgingly resisting.

Bypassing refers to a process whereby a practitioner avoids taking a proposal for change or a grievance to his immediate superior but seeks

---

*For a useful discussion on organizational resistance to change, see Rino J. Patti, "Organizational Resistance and Change."

†For a negative view of demonstration grants, see George E. Pratt, "The Demonstration Grant is Probably Counterproductive," *Social Work* 19 (July 1974): 486–489.

instead a hearing or decision from a higher level in the hierarchy. In an enlightened organization, this form of bypassing is acceptable and even encouraged; government workers, in fact, are entitled to it as part of "due process." Bypassing is risky, however, in that it can discredit the judgment of the complainant if the matter is trivial or if it appears that it could have been resolved at a lower level in the hierarchy. Bypassing also places the administration in a vulnerable situation because if the tactic is justified, it reflects poorly on the judgment of the superior and the administrators who hired him. This may lead to questions of nonretention or spur a desired resignation. A successful instance of bypassing is described in the following example:

> When a clinician's complaints concerning the physical plant and security of a youth home went unheeded by the director, he demanded to meet with the executive committee of the board. The director admitted that his own sense of urgency differed from that of his staff, but arranged for the meeting. The executive committee approved some of the recommendations for change and authorized that they be implemented as soon as possible.

Agencies often write grant applications for funds to support their programs. A critical phase of the application process occurs at a public review of the grant application, when the funding agency invites comment or a letter of support from the agency or from interested parties. If a clinician is dissatisfied with a particular program, and if it is an important matter, he can provide the agency issuing the grant with dissenting information, testify at the review of the grant application, or respond from the standpoint of an "expert witness." In any event, the grant-review process may be an opportunity to voice concern about an agency's program and to influence the advisory group to give conditional approval or disapproval. As is shown in the following example, clinicians may attempt to influence the review process indirectly—by encouraging an expert third party to raise questions about the grant application—or directly.

> A social worker was asked to serve as a technical reviewer for a volunteer program for young offenders in a regional planning advisory group. The program was modeled after an existing program in another part of the state. The documents supporting the application contained a manual that described the role of the volunteer. It suggested that a volunteer should report any violations of parole to the corrections authority but should not reveal this action to the offender. In seeming contradiction, it emphasized that the volunteer should be a "friend" of the offender. The social worker informed the advisory group of this provision and of his strenuous objection to it. The director of the program had failed to read the manual thoroughly and was unaware of the statement. The advisory group approved the program on the condition that the volunteer not serve as an informer and demanded that the staff codify the conditions under which it may be morally imperative for the volunteer to reveal the offender's behavior.

Social workers are often asked to and frequently do endorse a program or a grant application perfunctorily, without having read the proposal. In other instances, programs and grants are endorsed in spite of strong reservations. Notwithstanding the pressures toward reciprocity that exist among agencies, such exchanges of professional courtesy are questionable.

Social workers should take advantage of requests for endorsement or participation in the grant-review process, particularly if they believe that certain aspects of a proposal or program are questionable. The desire for professional endorsement also underlies agency efforts to recruit clinicians for board membership or as paid consultants. Refusal of such offers is a way of "making a statement" about a program.

Radical Tactics

Leaking information, or the covert release of information about an organization, is a tactic that should be used only in grave matters after all other remedies within the organization have been exhausted. The third party to whom the informant gives the information has to verify it and the credibility of the informant, since he is not willing to put his own character and job on the line. However, until "blowing the whistle" becomes an accepted institutionalized value, and until protections are legislated, it is likely that members of organizations will continue to act like "guerrillas in a bureaucracy."*

Clinicians who anticipate the need to leak information would be well advised to seek counsel, for discovery could result in liability damages. They are obliged to have a thorough, accurate, and verifiable account of the objectionable situation. As the ethics of leaking information have not been well formulated, clinicians need to consider carefully the professional, moral, and legal standards that support such action.† One way in which the clinician may choose to attack the problem is shown as follows.

> The clinician in a foregoing example who was concerned about the physical plant and security of a youth home notified the state monitor about the condition of the home. At the next site visit, the monitor raised questions about the residents' access to balconies and the roof and about the staff-client ratio on weekends.

Resignation in protest, or public defection, is another tactic that should be used only when a clinician experiences unbearable misgivings and

---

*Nader, Petkas, and Blackwell, *Whistle-Blowing*, pp. 15, 25–33; and Martin L. Needleman and Carolyn Emerson Needleman, *Guerrillas in the Bureaucracy* (New York: John Wiley & Sons, 1974).

†For some guidelines on this matter, see Nader, Petkas, and Blackwell, *Whistle-Blowing*, pp. vii, 1–8, 29–30, 225–230.

finds it both morally and professionally imperative to reveal them publicly. The major problem is that the organization has the financial and operational resources to counter the protest, but the employee has none. Also, with few exceptions, resignation in protest has a history of aversive consequences for the protester.*

A resignation in protest may also discredit the agency. Therefore, prospective protesters must be prepared to have their observations and conclusions verified and their judgment subjected to public review and scrutiny. In addition, the protester must realize that future employers will wonder whether such history of protestation will continue. An example follows.

When his concerns went unheeded by the board, a clinician resigned in protest. Moreover, he informed the board and the director that he would discourage any professional worker from accepting employment at the agency. He was effective in discouraging local professionals from accepting employment at the agency unless firm commitments were made to modify policies and practices that were detrimental to clients.

The theory of escalation urges the protester to begin by using conventional and formal means to express grievances and influence change. Only after these have been exhausted, and traditional means have encountered failure and resistance, should he engage in a series of escalations to such unconventional or radical forms of protest as boycotting, "palace revolts," picketing, leaking information, and the like. The essential point of this strategy is that the protester should not begin by engaging in the most radical and abrasive strategy. To document the intransigence of the bureaucracy, change must be approached incrementally. If this is not done, the bureaucracy may point to the failure to follow administrative due process. The protester's etiquette and failure to go through channels then become the bone of contention, and the protester becomes the object of protest.†

As a condition of employment and as a professional right and responsibility, clinicians should have the opportunity to bring their insights into the plans and programs of the organization they work for. Such participation requires that clinicians acquire skill in dealing with organizations. It is hoped that the participation of clinicians in organizational activity will promote responsive service delivery systems and satisfactory work climates.

At the risk of appearing to be a "double agent," the author plans to write a second article to advise administrators on how to cope with the tinkering of clinicians. After all, organizational power—whether in the

*See Weisband and Franck, *Resignation in Protest.*
†Ibid., pp. 55–94; Needleman and Needleman, *Guerrillas in the Bureaucracy*, pp. 285–289, 335–339; and Nader, Petkas, and Blackwell, *Whistle-Blowing*, pp. 16–25.

hands of clinicians or administrators—"must be insecure to some degree if it is to be more responsible."*

━━━━━━━━━━━━━━━━━━━

Gene Dalton conceptualizes the process of personal change as starting with some sort of movement toward specific objectives. A person makes small behavioral commitments in a certain direction and justifies and rationalizes these acts by accepting values and explanations that reduce dissonance between the acts and his or her self-image. Next, old relationships are altered, and new social ties begin to be developed. New relationships buttress new ideas. With heightened self-esteem, the person finds himself or herself capable of making changes and adjustments. Finally comes internalization, when he or she comes to own the rationale for the change. A self-rewarding mechanism is set up; opportunities for application and improvisation with the new ideas are sought out; and clarification occurs through experience.†

Looking at the process of change from an organizational point of view, one can see that the first step identified, movement toward specific objectives, suggests the importance of developing on overall plan and a step-by-step approach to instituting reforms. Objections must be dealt with; value conflicts must be considered; and the sources of stress and tension in the organization have to be analyzed and accommodated in the plan.

The second phase—altering old relationships—certainly occurs in the organization as reforms are implemented. Any reform threatens disruption of existing social relationships, status patterns, power alignments and differentials, and personal senses of competence and self-esteem. Resistance is to be expected, and a plan for dealing with it has to be developed.

The third phase requires that participants develop a sense of the value of the reform. The task of the clinician is to support the client in his or her efforts to change. A reformer inside an organization has to think about who can provide psychological support for reform. A feedback system is required, and supporters must be reassured that all the effort is worthwhile. A reformer in a relatively low position in the organization is not well situated to provide this support, which is why many such reforms falter.

*Nader, Petkas, and Blackwell, *Whistle-Blowing*, p. 15.
†Gene Dalton, "Influence and Organizational Change," in Gene Dalton et al., eds., *Organizational Change and Development* (Homewood, Ill.: Irwin & Dorsey, 1978), pp. 234–237.

The fourth phase is internalization. How is the organization to make the change or the reform its own? How will it be institutionalized? Just as a clinician usually does not simply tell a patient what to do, but rather allows the patient some opportunity to internalize his or her treatment, an organization needs an opportunity to improvise, to try things out, and perhaps even to suggest compromises. It has to readjust status patterns, power differentials, reward systems, and cognitive rationales.

All of the above information suggests that the reformer must be part planner, part tactician, part social psychologist, and part hero or heroine—a tower of strength, a bulwark against the forces of reaction. The reformer may have to be all that, but the process of reform also affects the reformer. He or she not only acts but is acted upon, as Rino Patti's article indicates.

Limitations and Prospects of Internal Advocacy*

RINO J. PATTI

• • •

Impediments to Internal Advocacy

Even a brief look at the parameters of internal advocacy suggests that there are rather significant disincentives to engaging in this activity. Beyond these difficulties, however, there are several professional and organizational factors that serve to impede or retard internal advocacy efforts.

Fear of dismissal

It is perhaps belaboring the obvious to state that the most immediate and practical impediment to internal advocacy is the fear of job loss. To the extent that advocacy involves, as it sometimes does, dissent from organizational policies, the violation of group norms, or open conflict with the executive or board, job loss is, of course, a possibility. While dismissal is not often employed to neutralize advocacy efforts, virtually everyone has heard of such instances, and in a tight job market the exceptional case has a way of appearing to be a statistically significant trend.

On the face of it, dismissal from a job can involve such undesirable consequences as inconvenience, possible embarrassment with friends and family, income loss, forced geographical mobility, and the burden of

*Excerpted with special permission of the Family Service Association of America, from *Social Casework* 55, no. 9 (1974): 537–545.

explaining negative job references. Perhaps just as significant is the loss of professional identity that can occur when one is dismissed from an agency. In the absence of strong societal approval, the social worker's status is defined at least as much by his place of employment as by his professional qualifications. The phrase "I am a social worker" takes on shape and substance for even the relatively informed laymen, when it is followed by an explanation of where one works, one's duties, the clients with whom one works, and so forth. The fact has long been observed in professional circles that a social worker's status in the eyes of the community, and among his colleagues as well, tends to be associated with where he is employed. Under these circumstances, dismissal takes on important implications for the social worker's public identity.

Among those who would promote internal advocacy, there seem to be three general approaches to dealing with the threat of job loss. The first is to treat it as a red herring, a false specter that need not be a real constraint if the social worker will only exercise the rights and utilize the discretion that are available to him as an employee. The implication here is that the problem is really the practitioner's lack of commitment to client welfare and his timidity in the face of authority. A second reaction is to argue that job loss is the price a professional should be prepared to pay in the interest of keeping the welfare bureaucracy responsive to client needs. Indeed, in this view, the advocate is probably being most successful when his job is being threatened. Finally, there is a position which holds that although the practitioner must be prepared to take some risk associated with advocacy, he should not be expected to assume this burden alone. The argument here is that if internal advocacy is to be widely practiced it must be buttressed with institutionalized supports that can be called upon when the agency utilizes punitive measures to curtail ethically sound advocacy efforts. This position promises the most realistic long-range solution to the promotion of advocacy in the profession.

Chance for Advancement

The prospects for internal advocacy would seem also to be centrally related to the nature of upward mobility in social work. To begin with, there is no widely recognized status in the field that might be referred to as "distinguished practitioner." Here and there agencies have attempted to develop a career path and a reward structure for those who wish to remain in clinical practice, but, generally, long years in a direct practice position are more likely to be interpreted as an indication of mediocrity than of professional virtuosity. This attitude applies less to women than to men, a reflection more on the sexist bias of society and the profession than on the value attached to advanced clinical ability.

Therefore, the practitioner who desires more money, status, and recognition must usually seek advancement through the administrative hierarchy, although private practice is an increasingly possible alternate path to upward mobility. This fact alone creates powerful disincentives to internal advocacy, because promotion is very likely to be contingent upon behavioral evidence of loyalty to the organization. This is not to say that intellect and skill are irrelevant to the selection process, because clearly an agency's administrative hierarchy is usually seeking to bolster its capability. Still, a central task of administration is to maintain organizational stability and continuity, and one of the most important ways to do this is to ensure that people brought into positions of leadership are committed to the agency's normative structure.

These preconditions for advancement are not likely to escape the notice of practitioners. The young worker may not feel overly constrained, since lateral mobility is still a viable option for him. However, when career aspirations start to crystallize and considerations of security and status become salient motivators, the potential costs associated with internal advocacy begin to rise dramatically. At this juncture, administrative approval becomes an important occupational asset. . . .

Limits of Participatory Management

Given the difficulty and uncertainty associated with internal advocacy, it is not surprising that most practitioners seek to influence agency practices through the less hazardous but far more convenient and acceptable mechanisms of participatory management. Indeed, on the face of it, this avenue for effecting change would seem to provide the practitioner with ample opportunity to represent the interests of his clients and to do so in a context that is administratively sanctioned. However, although participatory management is necessary and desirable, it tends to be inherently limited as a vehicle for the exercise of practitioner influence and may serve to divert worker-initiated change efforts. For a number of reasons, participatory management should be seen as a complement to, not a substitute for, internal advocacy.

External Pressures

Executives are not as free to act on matters involving policy and program change as is commonly assumed by subordinates. In addition to the needs and interests of those persons who provide and receive the services of his organization, the administrator must also be sensitive and responsive to the expectations of groups and organizations external to the agency.*

*Herman Stein, "Administrative Leadership in Complex Organizations," in Harry Schatz, ed., *Social Work Administration* (New York: Council on Social Work Education, 1970), pp. 290–291.

These external constituencies, which are frequently in a position to affect the flow of inputs (for example, money, legitimacy, and influence) upon which the agency relies for maintenance and survival, can and often do constrain the decision-making discretion that can be exercised by an administrator. What is perhaps more important is the fact that recommendations emanating from the staff in the context of a participatory process, no matter how rational or persuasive from an internal organization perspective, are often difficult to reconcile with expectations being imposed on the agency from without. Clearly, when such things as program support, job security, or agency reputation are at stake, the executive will often find it necessary to give first priority to the interests of external groups. If this situation occurs with any regularity, the administrator is likely to narrow the range of issues in which staff participation is solicited to those which are not likely to pose the conflicts mentioned above. In practice, the result is usually an avoidance of those issues that concern substantive policy or program changes.

Selective Involvement

Staff participation almost inevitably means selective involvement. In an organization of any size or complexity, the administrator must make judgments about which practitioners can meaningfully contribute to the resolution of which issues.* The definition of what constitutes a meaningful contribution rests not only on assessments of competence but, in the last analysis, on value biases and vested interests. In addition, those in positions of power are more likely to respond to inputs by subordinates that reinforce the policy-program direction of the agency than to those that imply criticism or suggest change.† Thus, certain practitioners whose views are unpopular, or potentially disruptive, may be excluded from the participatory process. Where this situation occurs, it is clear that a full range of perspectives and alternatives to a problem will not be considered.

Co-optation

Just as participatory management can result in the exclusion of practitioners whose views conflict with those of management, so too can it be used as a means of co-opting such workers. Indeed, the involvement of dissident subordinates often covers an implicit administrative strategy to contain and neutralize the thrust of their independent initiatives. Although the process of co-optation can involve exchange and compro-

*Ibid., p. 291.
†Joseph Monane, *The Sociology of Human Systems* (New York: Appleton-Century-Crofts, 1967), pp. 137–143.

mise, beneficial to both parties, the skillful use of rewards, punishments, and group pressure often results in an uneven exchange for practitioners who become involved.*

Size and Complexity of Agency

The size and complexity of an organization also have a bearing on the effectiveness of participatory management as a vehicle for practitioner influence. Aside from the sheer logistical problems of staff involvement in a large agency, there are inherent limitations that these conditions impose on participants' effectiveness. For example, no matter how sound a worker's recommendations might be, they can become lost or distorted in the process of being communicated across several administrative levels. This loss can be mitigated if the decision-maker interacts directly with the staff, but there are obvious limitations to how often this interaction can take place. Specialization also takes its toll on the participatory process because practitioners frequently find it difficult to make informed contributions on matters that fall outside their narrow areas of responsibility.†

These, then, are some of the factors that may limit the effectiveness of participatory management as a means through which workers can influence the decision-making processes of their organizations. The intention here is not to suggest the abandonment of this administrative model, but rather to point out that it must be supplemented with other strategies like internal advocacy that will facilitate the inclusion of practitioners' perspectives in the development of policies and programs.

Sustaining Internal Advocacy

The preceding analysis suggests that there are significant professional and organizational factors that impede the widespread commitment to internal advocacy by social work practitioners. The surge of interest in this aspect of social work practice that accompanied the unrest of the 1960s helped to create a normative anlage and precipitate a sorely needed reappraisal of the relationship between social workers and the agencies which employ them. Nevertheless, at this writing, Mary J. McCormick's analysis of the prospects for advocacy still seem accurate. In her view, the anxiety and fear associated with advocacy is likely to continue

---

*This point has also been argued by Charles S. Levy, "Power Through Participation: The Royal Road to Social Change," *Social Work* 15 (1970): 105–108. Although he speaks primarily of clients, similar dynamics are operative in staff participation.

†Harry Schatz, "Staff Involvement in Agency Administration," in Schatz, *Social Work Administration*, pp. 284–285.

until such time as *advocacy in the abstract* (in its conceptual meaning) is internalized, that is, until it becomes an integral part of the structure and function of social work and of the basic convictions of social workers— administrators, educators, and practitioners alike. . . . It is in this process of legitimation, when personal ideas and ideals become absorbed into the social system . . . that advocacy . . . will find justification and support within the structure of social work at the professional level.*

But the history of social work suggests that the absorption of new practice modalities into the professional system occurs slowly. One need only look to the emergence of group work and community organization as evidence. We have no reason to suspect that the road to gaining a full-fledged professional acceptance of advocacy in general, and internal advocacy in particular, will be any less difficult to traverse. Of especially critical importance here is the role that professional schools and the national social work associations must play in altering patterns of professional socialization, modifying curricula to incorporate knowledge about organizational analysis and intervention, and developing mechanisms to enforce ethical prescripts and to protect the rights and interests of practitioners who engage in advocacy.† It seems fair to say that without concerted efforts at these institutional levels, advocacy will continue to be more honored in rhetoric than in practice.

In the meantime, the social work practitioner who is daily confronted with organizational practices inimical to clients must decide whether to invest himself in internal advocacy. This decision will inevitably be influenced by the urgency and magnitude of the problem he faces, his personal inclination, and agency climate. In addition, it should be grounded in an assessment of whether the conditions necessary to sustain an advocacy effort are present. Three conditions which seem particularly important here are: organizational legitimacy, professional credibility, and colleague support.

Organizational Legitimacy

The basic source of legitimacy for the internal advocate, as has been noted, is his ethical obligation to the primacy of client welfare. Where this obligation conflicts with loyalty to the employing organization's policies and procedures, the professional practitioner is committed to give prece-

---

*Mary J. McCormick, "Social Advocacy: A New Dimension in Social Work," *Social Casework* 51 (1970): 4.

†See, for example, the more detailed suggestions contained in the following sources: Ad Hoc Committee on Advocacy, "The Social Worker as Advocate"; David Wineman and Adrienne James, "The Advocacy Challenge to Schools of Social Work," *Social Work* 14 (1969): 23–32; and Willard C. Richan and Allan R. Mendelsohn, *Social Work: The Unloved Profession* (New York: Franklin Watts, 1973), pp. 126–162.

dence to client interests. This ethical prescript is the cornerstone of internal advocacy and provides the practitioner with an essential rationale for assuming this role. As important as this rule is, however, it will probably not be sufficient to justify the worker's advocacy efforts in the eyes of his administrative superiors because he has not been vested with formal authority to perform the advocate's role. In this situation, the worker who is acting in accordance with a professionally prescribed code of conduct may find that his behavior is defined as organizationally irresponsible. To establish organizational legitimacy for the advocacy role, then, the practitioner must seek to justify his efforts in terms that have some relevance to the social economy of the agency that employs him. Generally, there appears to be four ways in which this step can be undertaken.

1. The advocate can claim legitimacy on the basis of substantive knowledge about the problem at hand. That is to say, the practitioner can argue that by virtue of some special knowledge or skill, he can assist the organization in coming to a more rational and effective solution than has heretofore been available to deal with the issue in question. Such an assertion cannot be made in the abstract, but must be buttressed with some visible evidence of competence—for example, a thorough knowledge of the problem, an understanding of those factors that condition the organization's response, a well-documented plan for action, and so forth.

2. The advocate can seek to justify his role as a preserver of organizational values. Here he argues that internal advocacy is a way of keeping the organization's performance consonant with its own formally stated objectives of ensuring that client rights and entitlements are honored and that organizational convenience does not replace client welfare as the criterion for action. His particular contribution is to help the organization avoid the danger of consensually validating itself. To do this, the advocate must be able to transcend the daily struggle for maintenance and assess whether the agency is actually accomplishing the goals that it has set for itself.

3. The practitioner can also seek to legitimate his role on the grounds that internal advocacy is a necessary supplement to the communication processes in an organization. The normal process of communication up through an administrative hierarchy often results in information loss or distortion and can, over time, deprive administrators of the data they need to assess accurately the effects of the agency's programs and procedures. The practitioner can argue that internal advocacy provides unfiltered, timely information to organizational decision-makers regarding matters of crucial importance—a supplement to the usual feedback mechanisms.

4. Finally, the internal advocate can attempt to justify his action on the basis of political self-interest. This approach is more likely to be effective when employed by a group or formal unit of the organization that has

some ability to withhold needed services or otherwise disrupt the organization's normal operations. In this instance, the advocacy system seeks to establish the right to have its interests formally represented in the decision-making process on the grounds that its values and needs will not otherwise be adequately reflected.

Any of these bases for establishing organizational legitimacy may be rejected by administrative superiors as an insufficient rationale for deviating from official role prescriptions. Nevertheless, it seems almost certain that unless the practitioner has a clear conception in which to anchor his claim to legitimacy and the ability to give substance to that conception in his dealings with agency leadership, his advocacy efforts will be difficult to sustain.

Professional Credibility

The practitioner who confronts a potential advocacy situation is inevitably faced with making some assessment of the personal risks that are involved. To a large extent, this assessment involves a consideration of such contextual factors as the quality of his relationships with superiors, the degree of autonomy and role flexibility permitted professional employees, and so on. In addition, however, the risks associated with internal advocacy seem to be very much related to whether the practitioner possesses certain attributes that decrease his vulnerability to administrative reprisals. Three such attributes, which constitute important sources of professional credibility and influence that can be drawn upon in an advocacy effort, are membership in the system, technical competence, and special expertise.

Membership in the system refers not simply to the criterion of employment, but to whether the practitioner is perceived as being an integral part of the group life of the institution. Tenure is an important precondition to achieving membership status, but it is hardly sufficient. Membership in the system is more crucially dependent upon an incumbent's understanding of the organization's normative structure, both formal and informal, its ideology, and its vested interests. It is rooted in having experienced and struggled with problems growing out of limited resources, community pressures, interdepartmental rivalries, idiosyncratic personalities, and the like. It becomes established as one identifies with the frustrations and accomplishments of one's colleagues and superiors and comes to compassionately understand the magnitude of their investment in the existing order of things. Perhaps most important, membership is achieved when one becomes sensitive to the personal costs entailed in organizational change. Until the internal advocate has acquired this perspective, he is likely to be seen as something of an organizational transient, with all the vulnerability that this normally implies.

Technical competence in one's primary role assignment is also an important risk-reducing attribute for the internal advocate. Essentially, technical competence means being thorough and technically proficient in the performance of those duties the agency has hired one to perform. Where these standards of performance have not been met, it becomes all too easy for the organization to discredit the cause being advocated by attacking the credibility of the advocate. The worker whose performance has been shoddy or irresponsible makes an excellent target for those who are threatened or inconvenienced by the changes he is proposing.

Beyond the competent performance of one's organizationally defined role, it is also useful for the practitioner-advocate to possess some *special expertise* that contributes to agency maintenance or development. This expertise can take many forms, including, for example, substantive knowledge of a problem area that is of concern to the agency, "grantsmanship," or relationships with an ethnic community. Whatever the nature of this expertise, it is important that one's administrative superiors recognize it as a special contribution above and beyond that which is normally expected of someone in the practitioner role.

In sum, the risks associated with advocacy are usually relative to the presence or absence of certain worker attributes. The more a practitioner is perceived by his superiors as having one or more of the attributes discussed above, the less vulnerable he is likely to be to the risks associated with internal advocacy—all of which suggests that one of the advocate's first tasks should be to assess his organizational strengths and weaknesses dispassionately and objectively. In the absence of one or more of the attributes discussed above, the practitioner may find that the risks of internal advocacy are unacceptably high.

Colleague Support

One of the most important requirements of a sustained advocacy effort is the presence of support from colleagues and peers. Notwithstanding the occasional dramatic case in which an advocate singlehandedly challenges an organization's policies, most practitioners find it necessary to seek the help of their fellow workers, not only because there is power in numbers, but, more important, because group support helps to mitigate some of the vulnerability and uncertainty attendant on internal advocacy. Generally, two kinds of colleague support are necessary in a sustained advocacy effort: task and expressive.

The energy, time, and skill required in most kinds of internal advocacy are often more than even the most dedicated individual practitioner can offer. It is not unusual, for example, in situations involving substantive organizational changes, for an intervention to consist of a number of data-gathering interviews with people in several departments; access to and analysis of records and reports; personal contacts with representatives of standard-setting, funding, and community-based groups; proposal writing; lengthy problem-solving or negotiating sessions; and so on.

The advocate who must continue to perform his regular duties can seldom carry this burden alone. But, even if he were able to do so, it would probably not be desirable, because the individual practitioner is unlikely to have the range of knowledge and skills required by these diverse activities. A skillful handling of these tasks is usually better achieved by drawing upon the various talents and aptitudes available among fellow workers.

Just as important, the internal advocate also requires expressive support from colleagues or peers in order to maintain his morale and perspective. Because the advocate is operating in largely uncharted waters— usually without clear precedents or previous experience—stress and confusion are not uncommon. In this context, it becomes crucial for the practitioner to have regular access to one or more peers who, in the context of a trusting relationship, can challenge the advocate's assumptions, question his choice of tactics, and help him gain perspective on the motivtions of administrative superiors. Such supportive relationships can also provide the advocate with an opportunity to express feelings of anger, frustration, fear, and self-doubt, which often occur but are not acceptable in public interaction.

Without the kinds of support discussed above, the difficulties normally associated with internal advocacy become compounded. The practitioner who attempts to function without these supports runs a high risk of failure or exhaustion, with cynicism and alienation often the unfortunate after-math.

Conclusion

Despite the increasingly recognized importance of internal advocacy as a means of improving the delivery of social services or removing organizational conditions that are harmful to clients, it is clear that significant barriers continue to impede the development of this kind of practice—job risks, patterns of job mobility, uncertain legitimacy, and underdeveloped knowledge base. Until institutional supports are provided, it is unlikely that internal advocacy will become an integral part of social work practice.

In the meantime, many practitioners are confronted with organizational conditions and practices they would like to change on behalf of their clients. The practitioner's ability to sustain an advocacy effort is vitally dependent upon three conditions: establishing a basis for legitimacy in terms that are organizationally relevant; acquiring certain professional attributes that will serve to buffer the risks of advocacy; and mobilizing the support of colleagues for both task accomplishment and psychological maintenance.

Change and Accountability: Most of the social work literature on organizational change suggests that with sufficient skill and knowledge, lower-level staff members can effectively change organizations, and that the more skilled workers are as change-agents, the more effective their organizations will be.

This view implies that all change has positive results for client service. It ignores the fact that change can become a substitute for effectiveness (some organizations are constantly reorganizing), and that some reformers are more interested in their reforms than in assessing whether these reforms do any good once implemented.

There is an alternative point of view. It contends that Bottom-up change tends to be too concerned with strategy and tactics and not concerned enough with agency structures such as feed back mechanisms that would promote change.* In this view one cannot implement change unless one has some idea 'a priori' of what a change-oriented agency requires in the way of procedures and structures. Weissman contends that line staff would be better served in the long run if they concerned themselves with promoting changes related to their agency's accountability system.† Without accountability, reform can merely result in the substitution of one bad procedure for another and further demoralize the staff.

In private enterprise, profit serves to guarantee a form of accountability: sooner or later Ford must respond to the organizational tension caused by a slump in sales. Nonprofit organizations need an alarm system that does for them what lower profits do for private industry: expose problems and move them toward resolution. While organizations or facilities will always be changed through the actions of individuals, and may often need to be, these individuals will be freer and more able to act responsibly within systems that are designed to accommodate change. Such systems can be best characterized as open systems.

R. G. S. Brown contends that open systems are based on many factors. Organizational reformers play a part in opening up systems, and so do accountability mechanisms. Brown notes that "the operationally important form of accountability is the mixture of formal devices and conventions, rooted in our political culture, for publicizing the workings of a system, so that those who are interested can spot errors and imbalances and appeal to constitutional rules and cultural norms to have them put right. The touchstone is perhaps neither formal accountability nor participation, but openness."‡

Unfortunately, most accountability systems are set up not to help

---

*Harold H. Weissman, "Fantasy and Reality of Staff Involvement in Organizational Change," *Administration in Social Work* 6 (1982): 38–99.

†Ibid., p. 44.

‡R. G. S. Brown, *The Management of Welfare* (London: Martin Robertson, 1975), p. 278.

workers do a better job, but simply to see whether they are doing a job. This is not what Brown has in mind. Accountability, as he uses the term, is not simply a control mechanism to insure that standards are met. For example, not only do agency administrators need information about standards of quality, quantity, and cost of services, but they should be aware of the tension generated in clients by the discrepancy between what they expect and what they receive and the tensions generated in the staff by the discrepancy between what they are asked to do and what they think they should do. If workers and administrators are to utilize this information to bring about changes in the agency, accountability systems must be supported by formal and informal systems of communication that enable them to communicate about the tensions and pressures both groups operate under.

What can clinical social workers do to bring about such a situation? First, they can ensure that accountability systems are not used solely for control and that they do in fact provide feed back of ideas, insights, and leads for program improvements. Second, they can use their "reformer" skills to urge that boards of directors have access to line workers' perspectives and clients' views of the agency. These boards will be less likely to rubber-stamp an administration's decisions when they have access to unfiltered information from other sources. Third, they can urge that the agency attempt to evaluate its programs. While it may not be possible to develop scientific standards of success, it is possible to make better-informed judgments of the results achieved. Fourth, through membership in professional organizations, workers can urge such bodies as state departments of health and the Council on Accrediting Family and Children's Services to require agencies to set up accountability mechanisms whereby they can judge their results.

Parodoxically, overaccountability can create as many difficulties as underaccountability. Overmeasurement can cause goal displacement; that is, programs will be offered simply because they can be measured precisely, rather than because they are most needed. So much time and effort can be put into ensuring accountability that there will not be enough resources available to offer services. Under these circumstances, innovation can be stifled and flexibility lost. Accountability systems must be designed to insure that this doesn't take place.*

Nevertheless, the focus on accountability is crucial because reforms will have little effect if the situation that caused the problem initially has not been dealt with. Are we saying that reformers face a Catch-22 situation: reforms won't work when there is no effective accountability system, yet accountability can cause goal displacement? Not exactly. We want to stress that one must see both the forest and the trees. It is

*Harold H. Weissman, "Accountability and Pseudo-Accountability: A Non-linear Approach." *Social Service Review* 57 (June, 1983):323–326.

certainly necessary at times to reform flawed service systems and deal with incompetent supervisors and confused procedures; yet it is also important to establish an effective accountability system and to create an agency capable of changing itself. Emphasis on one to the exclusion of the other is a serious error. Clients and the agency itself cannot wait for better service until a new accountability system is created. On the other hand, piecemeal reforms will not bring about permanent improvements unless they are continually assessed.

Practice Analogues

In an earlier era social welfare was called moral reform. Although this antiquated term has disappeared from usage, social workers as clinicians are basically involved in "re-forming" their clients in some fashion. No longer couched in terms of morality, our efforts are still focused on change.

There are similarities and differences between the process of changing organizations and that of changing individuals. The therapist or the counselor must consciously use himself or herself, must be nonjudgmental, and must be able to partialize problems, plan, and show concern.

George Brager and Stephen Holloway offer the following example of "partializing" a reform:

> Partializing a goal is an often effective means of minimizing its threat potential. A goal may be partialized by reducing its scope, thus reducing the number of people involved in or affected by its adoption. For example, an innovative idea may be proposed for only one department—the most receptive to the idea—before an attempt is made to diffuse it throughout the organization. Or the content of the goal may be partialized by dividing it into developmental components. Thus, a sequence of steps may be planned. Point A must be effected before moving to Point B, and completing Point B is a requirement of C. Not only does careful sequencing reduce the threat potentials of change, but actions taken in the early stages of a process (e.g., step A) can subsequently be invested with meaning that was not explicit in the initial action. A first step can thus be defined retrospectively as a commitment to fuller action—in this case, a commitment to B and C.*

Although reforms may relate to technology or to various structures in an agency, all change is human change. We have already noted above in this chapter some of the similarities between individual and organizational change. Yet there are considerable differences between changing an individual engaged in therapy or counseling and changing individuals in organizations. A person in therapy is affected by the significant others

*Stephen Holloway and George Brager, "Some Considerations in Planning Organizational Change," *Administration in Social Work* (1977): 356.

in his or her life, and part of the role of a therapist is to help the person to see just how they are affected by others. The organizational reformer will have considerable difficulty in getting colleagues and superiors to see how they are affected by other people in the organization. If the reformer is at the lower level of the organization, he or she is simply not in a position to bring about this level of understanding on the part of others.

The therapist can help guide the client or enable him or her to explore a variety of options for change. In the short run, it is difficult for a reformer to set the stage for an organization to do the same. R. M. Cyert and J. G. March claim that organizations are simple-minded.* They do not search for solutions to problems, but rather propose solutions that seemed to work in the past, and they prefer simple ones. It will not be easy for reformers to get an organization to invest time and resources in thinking creatively about reforms. That is why structures and procedures which orient an agency towards change are so crucial.

Similarly one of the functions of the therapist is to help clients overcome the resistance to change that is born out of fear. The reformer will have a difficult time ensuring that the negatives—the costs related to a reform—are not brought out so soon that the organization does not adequately consider the reform. There are considerable pressures on agencies—time, money, goals, commitments—and the organizational reformer is at a distinct disadvantage in trying to control their influence.

In addition, the organizational reformer is at a disadvantage when confronting group-think. This phenomenon is characterized by a quick and superficial consensus, designed primarily to support the approach to a particular problem that is least disruptive to existing agency patterns and existing commitments of organizational resources. This type of thinking does not lead to solutions, much less creative solutions, to problems. The therapist or clinician is ideally situated in his or her relationship with a client to guard against the resistance that emerges from the group-think that clients often bring to therapy from discussion with friends or their unconscious tabulation of the least dangerous action to take in dealing with their problems.

Harvey Gochros and Joel Fischer, discussing ways of overcoming resistance to change in organizations, make the point that "administrators, supervisors, and line workers all operate according to the same laws of learning which influence our clients' and our own behavior. They tend to engage in behaviors which are reinforced and avoid those which are aversive."† They suggest a number of actions that workers can take to

---

*Richard Cyert and James March, "The Behavioral Theory of the Firm" (Englewood Cliffs, N.J.: Prentice Hall, 1963), pp. 116–118.

†Harvey Gochros and Joel Fischer, "Introducing New Approaches into Social Agencies: The Case of Behavior Modification," *Journal of Sociology and Social Welfare* 4 (1977): 1074–1085.

minimize resistance in organizations, and these would probably work equally well with clients.

A thoughtful reformer can, with effort, often overcome many of the problems noted above. There is another side to resistance, however. Much of the writing in the clinical and organizational literature depicts resistance as a purely negative phenomenon—one that blocks the attainment of therapeutic or organizational objectives and is therefore to be overcome. Donald Klein suggests that this is an erroneous and dangerous view for reformers to hold because the mobilization of opposing forces may be a necessary prerequisite for successful change: "Just as individuals have their defenses to ward off threat, maintain integrity, and protect themselves against the unwarranted intrusions of others' demands, so do social systems seek ways in which to defend themselves against ill-conceived and overly precipitous innovations."*

Klein believes that the resistors are usually saying something important about the nature of the system that the reformer is trying to influence. Reformers should try to understand what such defenders are trying to protect. By so doing, they can modify the reform, change their strategy, and avoid hitherto unforeseen consequences, including defeat. They should, in a sense, see resistance as necessary.

What Klein is suggesting is that reformers utilize both instrumental and expressive rationality. Not only must they plan their campaign instrumentally in terms of what is to be done first, second, and third. They must also plan for the attitudes, feelings, and expectations that will emerge during the course of the campaign. How are these feeling to be handled? Will their emergence affect the timing of what has been planned? Reformers as well as clinicians must be concerned with the dynamic interplay of actions and feelings.

Attitudes, Values, and Skills

Many attitudes and values inhibit clinicians from actively pursuing a reform role in their agencies. Before looking at these negative attitudes and values, however, it is important to understand those that facilitate a reform role. These include a strong commitment to client service. If one is not going to abandon one's clients, one cannot abandon the desire to make organizations function more effectively.

An important attitude is the sense that change is possible. If clinicians did not feel that clients could change, probably few would. The same is true of organizations. In fact, agencies change all the time. The question is, in what direction and toward what end? Most important, clinicians

---

*Donald Klein, "Some Notes On the Dynamics of Resistance to Change: The Defender Role," in Herman Resnick and Rino J. Patti, eds., *Change from Within* (Philadelphia: Temple University Press, 1980), p. 152.

have to feel that they have the capacity to bring about change. No habit is harder to deal with in a client than the hopeless-helpless syndrome; similarly, nothing is more conducive to stagnation in agencies than hopelessness on the part of the staff.

Perhaps the most dysfunctional attitude is the belief that effective organizations are those without conflict. Similarly anything less than perfection is viewed as a sign of inadequate and incompetent administration. These unrealistic attitudes breed flawed reforms and ultimately hopelessness.

There are innumerable conflicts in organizational life that can be managed but never solved. As we noted in Chapter 1, the tensions between survival and goal attainment, authority and communication, quantity and quality, control and consent, are part of organizational life. A worker who does not understand this will be constantly critical of his or her agency without being able to engage effectively in organizational change.

Thus, the issue is how an organization deals with its strains, and not the fact that strains exist. Sweeping it under the rug is one way of handling strain; facing it and trying to deal with it, given an agency's particular constraints, is another. Confrontation and conflict can be functional in terms of the delivery of service.

Many clinicians take the point of view that all agency decisions should be ideal or optimal. Yet there are limits to what agencies can do. Any one decision has many effects, and sometimes a decision that partly meets a program need may be the best that one can hope for. There is nothing more detrimental to effective reform than the inability to compromise and be content with changes that improve service delivery even if they are not ideal.

Another disabling notion on the part of the clinician who would be a reformer is the assumption that the people in administration do not care about clients—that only lower-level workers care. More likely the administration is caught in a set of constraints and is unable to extricate itself or to think creatively about them. The more staff members accuse such an administration of not caring, the more likely it is to dig in its heels and act defensively, further limiting its ability to seek creative solutions.

One reason reform is necessary is that those who are dissatisfied with the organization tend to move on while those who are less committed to change stay and make their peace with the organization. Over time an organization tends to become more rigid in its thinking and approach. The reformer, if he or she is serious, must stick with a problem and struggle toward a solution. Above all, he or she must make a commitment not to abandon the ship until it is absolutely clear that the chances of satisfactory solutions to agency problems are nil.

There is no question that it is difficult to be a reformer. When conflict and confrontation are chosen as tactics, one may lose friends. When inaction seems wisest, rasher colleagues may question one's commitment and values.

The cautious emphasis in this chapter is not meant to dissuade reform; rather it is intended to preserve reformers. Many an agency reactionary began as an agency reformer.

Additional Readings

Brager, George, and Stephen Holloway. *Changing Human Service Organizations*. New York: Free Press, 1978.

Finch, Wilbur A. "Social Work vs. Bureaucracy." *Social Work* 21 (1976): 370–375.

Donald Klein. "Some Notes on the Dynamics of Resistance to Change: The Defender Role." Herman Resnick and Rino J. Patti, eds., *Change from Within* pp. 148–158. Philadelphia: Temple University Press, 1980.

Patti, Rino J. "Organizational Resistance and Change: The View from Below." *Social Service Review* 48 (1974): 367–383.

Weissman, Harold H. "Fantasy and Reality of Staff Involvement in Organizational Change." *Administration in Social Work* 6 (1982): 38–99.

Weissman, Harold H. *Overcoming Mismanagement in the Human Service Professions*. San Francisco: Jossey-Bass, 1973.

CHAPTER 8

SUPERVISOR

Although some theoreticians would do away with it and many social workers complain about it, supervision is one of the hallmarks of social work education and service giving.* At its best, supervision enhances and reinforces high-quality service while promoting the professional development of those who are supervised. At its worst, it prevents quality performance and is stultifying to those who must suffer under it.

The relationship between a supervisor and a supervisee is complex and crucial to both individual professional achievement and agency goal attainment. Given the costs of supervision—the supervisor's salary, the time involved, the span of control that the supervisor has, and the like—any flaw in the functioning of the supervisory system represents a major organizational problem.

Social workers are likely to be involved in supervision at each stage of their agency careers. As students they are generally supervised by an agency-based field instructor. As line workers they may function as supervisors to paraprofessionals or volunteers, and they are very likely to have over them a supervisor who monitors and evaluates their own work. As they move up the agency hierarchy, they may take on the role of supervisor to other line workers or social work students. Finally, as agency administrators they will find themselves supervising the supervisors.

Overview

The foregoing discussion suggests the great importance of the role of supervisor and the process of supervision to clinical social work practice. In this chapter, we discuss the managerial and educational aspects of supervision. We describe two types of supervision—individual and

*See Alex Gitterman, "Comparison of Educational Models and Their Influences on Supervision," in Florence Kaslow, ed., *Issues in Human Services* (San Francisco: Jossey-Bass, 1972), pp. 18–38.

group—each with its own advantages and disadvantages. Both are potentially valuable tools for promoting effective clinical practice.

Managerial Functions: Much confusion about the supervisor's role in social agencies begins when a clinician first enters a school of social work and encounters his or her first supervisor, the field instructor. In this context the supervisor's role is basically educational: his or her responsibility is to teach the new clinician to use the tools of the trade. Generally, the student clinician has a limited and selected caseload and is insulated from many of the problems of agency functioning that line workers experience.

On the job, however, the supervisor is more of a manager than a teacher. The working supervisor's job is to delegate responsibility, provide information to staff, coordinate work with the staffs of other departments, adjust conflicts, handle clients' complaints, and implement change. The main task is to secure the resources that workers need to do their job well. These resources cover much more than therapeutic knowledge and skill; clinical social workers need cooperation from other departments, authority to carry out their tasks, positive working conditions, and the assurance that their ideas are given consideration by the agency's administration. In addition, they need to feel that they are a valued part of the organization. The supervisor who cannot handle these managerial functions is probably going to have considerable difficulty helping workers to improve their clinical skills.

Clinical supervisors sometimes make the mistake of conceptualizing their job solely as overseeing their unit of supervisees and not as concerned with the agency context. This is a critical error because these supervisors will not have sufficient authority to get the resources that their workers need. Control over such resources as policy and procedural changes is generally vested in those above them. By remaining in their offices and limiting themselves to discussions of the therapeutic process, supervisors forfeit the opportunity to gain influence with their superiors. All a supervisor's knowledge about human behavior and all his or her ability to teach will often lead nowhere if the office typewriters and lights are not repaired. In colloquial terms, the supervisor has to be able and willing to "go to bat" for the workers. This involves a repertoire of influence that goes beyond skills in rational persuasion. (The reader may wish to reread the section in Chapter 5 on the "repertoire of influence.")

To secure these resources a supervisor must ensure that her superiors have confidence in her. First, she should make sure that they are aware of her ability. In our society it is often thought to be inappropriate to be "pushy." What is suggested here is not self-aggrandizement. Nevertheless, it is essential that one's real competence is perceived. The more one is viewed as competent, the more influence one enjoys.

In organizational life it is not always clear why people are valued. Yet in social work agencies as in many other organizations, management traditionally evaluates supervisors in terms of their ability to increase or maintain the productivity of their workers. (Productivity in social agencies is defined in both qualitative and quantitative terms.) Numerous scholarly articles have been written on the subject of improving worker productivity and morale. Many of these articles rest on the assumption that if morale is improved, productivity will be improved as well. In other words, the happy worker is the more productive worker.

While there is certainly a connection between high morale and high productivity, recent evidence suggests that high productivity comes first.* Thus, the most important supervisory task is to make it possible for workers to be productive, to achieve something, to have a sense of competence and mastery. High morale will follow, provided that they also have a sense that their clients are actually being helped and that their efforts are part of a meaningful system. Without this, an individualized sense of mastery will in the long run lead to innumerable organizational conflicts and poor morale.

Marvin Weisbord contends that professionals, at least in the health area, learn a rigorous scientific discipline as part of their training. This inculcates the value of autonomous decision making, professional growth and development, and the importance of improving one's own performance rather than that of the institution. For most professionals, Weisbord believes, self-esteem does not accrue from organizational effectiveness but from personal achievement.† If Weisbord in correct, the autonomous professional and the agency may be at odds with one another. If it is not possible to get a sense of success and mastery from what the agency achieves, it is understandable that workers retreat to "doing their own thing" and gain their sense of mastery and competence from their individual achievements.

The supervisor who does not realize that the ability to supervise is affected by the total agency system will undoubtedly run into problems. He or she will fall victim to the age-old assumption that all problems are reduceable to workers' lack of skills, even though workers' skills are only one of the factors that affect the agency's ability to provide adequate service to clients. Often a supervisor who focuses narrowly on his or her supervisees began by conceptualizing the supervisor's role strictly according to a human relations model. This approach, emphasizing participation and openness about feelings, is exemplified by the following statements: "My door is always open. I want to share everything. We are all

*George Strauss and Leonard Sayles, *Personnel* (Englewood Cliffs, N.J.: Prentice-Hall, 1980), pp. 2–26.

†Marvin R. Weisbord, "Why Organizational Development Hasn't Worked (So Far) in Medical Centers," *Health Care Management Review* 1 (Spring 1976), p. 19.

professionals." This supervisor often ends up as an authoritarian, autocratic leader, disillusioned and angry if the agency itself won't tolerate disagreement. There is no avoiding conflicts and differences in authority and power in organizations. If there is no mechanism for workers or supervisors to express discontent, anger is the inevitable result. The agency can become a real *Catch 22* for supervisors and students.

One administrator has stated that he is not interested in hiring clinically trained social workers for administrative positions, no matter how much experience they have, simply because they are not skilled in making organizational decisions. Unfortunately, the social work literature offers evidence that supervisors of social work students tend to interpret directness and assertiveness as symptoms of a student's desire to control clients or to fend off criticism from a supervisor.* In such cases, students learn to play the game, give supervisors what they want, and not be assertive. The power relationship that permits a supervisor to determine a student's career discourages assertiveness. Yet in organizational life it is often important to be assertive and to make decisions for others, and the ability to make good decisions is one of the factors that affect management's view of a supervisor's competence.

Sometimes there is not sufficient time available for full discussion; or it is too costly to bring everyone together to make a decision; or there is no consensus after a lengthy discussion; or, even when there is concensus, the majority is wrong (consensus is not a substitute for expertise); or fear and uncertainty paralyze some and therefore a decision must be made by others.

Traditionally, clincians have been taught a rational problem-solving process: define the problem, gather the facts, search for a variety of alternative solutions, anticipate consequences, make a choice, and get feedback. The implication is that when information is shared among all parties and thinking is clear, good decisions will result. This highly individual model denies the effect of a series of constraints, both from the organization and in the process itself, that make it unlikely that the process can be carried out in sequential, logical fashion. A number of factors must be considered:

1. *Problem definition*: Our values, attitudes, and assumptions affect our definition of a problem. Are workers being unreasonable, or is their conflict a symptom of a lack of communication between two departments in the agency? One can define a worker's complaint as based on an inability to accept authority or as based on a real flaw in the agency's structure. "Has the problem been adequately defined" is the crucial question.

*John Mayer and Aaron Rosenblatt, "Objectionable Supervisory Styles: Students' Views," *Social Work* 20 (May 1975): 184–189.

2. *Time*: Most supervisors are faced by workers who want immediate decisions. Lack of time limits one's opportunity to think about alternatives and consequences; it is one of the major constraints causing poor decisions.

3. *Search*: Will the organization spend time looking for alternatives or will it accept the solution that worked that last time the problem came up? One of the commonest problems in decision making is that differing points of view are not allowed to surface. The supervisor may not like disagreement; he or she may even view it as disloyalty. Workers seldom disagree in such a situation. The supervisor's role in fostering divergent ideas is extremely important. A related issue is the failure to allow all the ideas that surface to receive full consideration. Often new ideas are shot down because their disadvantages are brought out before their advantages are fully explicated.

4. *Participants*: Everyone does not have to be involved in every decision. Who should make decisions or be involved in them depends on (a) who will have to live with these decisions; (b) who can contribute knowledge and expertise to the deliberations; and (c) who must enforce the decision. If these parties are not involved, chances are that the decision, even if good, will not be carried out effectively. This judgment is not based on a participatory ideology, but on organizational necessity. If all interested parties are not involved, they will nevertheless make their interests felt in one way or another.

5. *Implementation estimate*: One of the major pitfalls for supervisors is making a decision and not implementing it. Before any decision is made, the logistics of carrying it out should be considered. If a decision cannot be implemented, there is no point in making it.

6. *Feedback*: The only way to tell if a decision is a good one is by the results. Before a decision is made, some mechanism should be set up for determining whether it was correct or not. It will be particularly helpful if this can be determined quickly, when there is still time to change.

7. The principle of *optimize versus satisfice*: It is the professional responsibility of clinicians to provide the maximum service and benefits to their individual clients. In making organizational decisions, supervisors are often faced with constraints and concerns that go beyond the interests of individual clients. They must see the total picture. The supervisor cannot look only for the optimal decision for any particular unit but must find the alternative that best satisfies a number of constraints.

   Rino Patti and Michael Austin summarize the difference between the supervisor's and the clinician's approaches as follows: "The decision mode for the manager is one of satisficing, rather than optimizing, and while this may be considered unfortunate, in given instances, the managerial culture recognizes this both as a necessary and an ethical approach to decision-making."*

8. *Leadership*: Often there is a certain amount of risk and uncertainty involved in the decisions supervisors must make. One cannot gather all the facts, one cannot be sure of the outcome, and particular outcomes could have unfortunate consequences. In such a situations the supervisor

---

*Rino J. Patti and Michael J. Austin, "Socializing the Direct Service Practitioner in the Ways of Supervisory Management," *Administration in Social Work* 1 (Fall, 1977): 270–271.

has to become more than simply a routine manager; he or she must be a leader. One of the advantages of participative decision making is that a group provides support in the face of risk and uncertainty. Yet it may be precisely in such circumstances that the desire for security may impel a bad decision that temporarily lets everyone feel better.

Supervisors must be capable of leadership. While there are many theories of leadership, the simplest analysis identifies two facets: the instrumental and the expressive. The leader not only has to help those making decisions to spell out the steps that will be taken, but must also be able to provide the emotional support that people require in making decisions and carrying them out. One person described this role as both laying out the steps—a, b, c, d, e—and putting a carpet on them.

Supervisors routinely carry out numerous managerial tasks—delegating work, handling personnel conflicts, dealing with clients' complaints, implementing policy changes, and the like. While a full discussion of these tasks is beyond the scope of this chapter, they are all concerned in some fashion with the supervisor's ability to utilize authority. (The reader may wish to review the discussion of this concept in Chapter 2.)

Teaching Functions: If one cannot make good decisions and go to bat for workers, it is unlikely that one will be viewed as a good supervisor and a good teacher. One may know a great deal about psychodynamics, about insight, and about therapeutic techniques, but this expertise cannot insulate one's clients from the rest of the agency or from other agencies in the system.

Supervisors do not simply teach as lecturers do, nor do clinicians learn like passive members of an audience. Workers learn not only by thinking, but also by doing, modeling and observing. What the supervisor does is as important as what he or she says.

In organizational jargon, we speak of formal authority and functional authority. *Formal authority* given to a supervisor by the agency, implies the right to tell subordinates what to do and to impose certain rewards and punishments. *Functional authority* is granted by subordinates as a result of their perception of the supervisor's abilities and positive qualities. If the supervisor is to be an effective teacher, he or she will rely more on functional than on formal authority.

Some have argued that the teaching function and the managerial function should be separated, since each is so complex as to require specialization. In a similar vein others argue that the monitoring function of a supervisor inhibits the teaching process.* Our opinion is that this is an artificial distinction. One may, for example, garner functional authority through one's managerial expertise and then use it in one's teaching function.

*For a discussion of a variety of such issues, see Gitterman, 'Comparison of Educational Models," pp. 28–38.

The two roles are related in subtler ways as well. Workers have to develop defenses against stresses and strains on the job. Taking a longer lunch hour should not automatically be viewed by a supervisor as an idiosyncratic authority problem being acted out by a worker; it may in fact be an adaptive mechanism. The supervisor's task is to understand the stresses of dealing with hostile clients on a constant basis and to structure ways of relieving these stresses into the system.

The teaching aspect of supervision are intertwined with the job's control or performance aspects. Basically, each clinician is held accountable by his or her supervisor for both performance standards and personal development objectives. The performance standards measure productivity, consistency in following procedures, and the like; personal development includes the ability to learn new skills and techniques, generally related to working with clients. It is usually advisable before supervision begins to agree on objectives in both categories and on some method of evaluating progress toward them at the end of a period of time. This agreement can take the form of a written contract in which role and performance expectations are explicitly stated. "Where, when and for how long will supervision take place? . . . How many and what kinds of cases will be assigned? . . . What is the [worker] to be evaluated on, and what is the process by which the evaluation take place? . . . How do supervisors wish [workers] to help structure the supervision over time?"* The virtue of written contacts is not only that they dispel confusion, but that in the process of developing them workers have an opportunity to state their preferences and therefore are more likely to assume the major responsibility for their own professional development.

To carry out his or her supervisory role, the supervisor needs an understanding of the social and psychological needs of clinical workers. Usually the supervisees want (1) a sense of confidence; (2) recognition for their work; (3) assurance that they are going to be treated fairly; and (4) respect for what they have done and not done. Respect is partly determined by our culture (for example, screaming publicly at workers is considered disrespectful) and partly determined situationally (for example, inviting all the workers but one to a meeting is a sign of disrespect for the excluded worker). A supervisor must create the conditions that satisfy the foregoing needs.

Another misconception about supervision, sometimes derived from socialization in schools of social work, is the idea that the individual supervisor-supervisee conference is the major locus of learning. There is abundant evidence that this is not the case. First, people learn in different

*Marion H. Wijnberg and Mary Schwartz, "Models of Student Supervision: The Apprentice, Growth and Role Systems Models," *Journal of Education for Social Work* 13 (Fall 1977): 110–112. This article provides numerous examples of issues that might be incorporated into formal contracts.

ways. These have been categorized as the thinking, the doing, and the feeling, or head, hands, and heart, though few people fall completely into one category. While the thinker is most likely to learn directly in the supervisory conference, a supervisee who learns by doing, through trial and error or observation, would be wasting a good deal of the supervisor's time and his or her own in such meetings. This person will learn much more by observing the supervisor and then discussing his or her observations.

The empathic learner, the "feeler," also requires a different kind of experience. One can, for example, suggest techniques for and readings about dealing with nonverbal clients. One can discuss their feelings and probe their motivations. Yet empathic learners learn best when they are confronted with an actual situation. Thus, a worker who asks for advice about a silent client can receive silence back from the supervisor. Then his or her feelings about the supervisor's silence, and the client's can be probed.

In order to adapt to individual learning styles, a supervisor must make an educational assessment of each worker. What does the person need to learn? The supervisor can discuss this question with workers, read their records, and observe their performance. Where does the person learn best? There are innumerable opportunities and places for learning: the supervisory conference, group supervision, controlled observation, classes, controlled experiences with certain clients, controlled caseloads, and so on. Is his or her primary learning pattern thinking, feeling, or doing? What motivates him or her to learn? The adult learner learns because he or she wishes to grow and develop and become more competent; yet we are not adults at all times. Some of us learn because of competitiveness, a desire to be loved, or fear of not learning. The following article, by Raymond Fant and Andrew Ross, while it focuses on child care workers, provides a clear discussion of a variety of effective techniques and procedures that can be employed in supervision.

Supervision of Child Care Staff*

RAYMOND S. FANT AND ANDREW L. ROSS

Supervision is the backbone of residential treatment programs and other forms of residential care† for children. There are three reasons for this: (1) few universities provide a formal curriculum in child care practice; (2)

*Reprinted by special permission of the Child Welfare League of America from *Child Welfare* 58 (1979): 627–641.

†Residential care facility is defined here as an institution, group home, or hospital whose program serves emotionally disturbed, neglected, dependent, delinquent, and/or intellectually impaired children in the seven- to eighteen-year-old age range.

residential care facilities are complex organizations; and (3) the children served by the facilities have experienced a great deal of trauma and psychological damage. However, experience indicates that supervisors in residential care facilities often assume that role without sufficient training. This paper identifies the basic concepts and techniques of supervisory practice as they relate particularly to child care staff.

Objectives

The main objectives of supervision in residential care facilities are to: (1) provide effective service to the client; (2) aid the staff in dealing with the emotional stress of the work; (3) ensure integration of the service; (4) aid the organization in meeting its needs; and (5) help the supervised workers maintain a high level of practice competence.

Supervision can have an impact on the quality of service by helping the child care worker develop the necessary attitudes and understanding to be a helping person and teaching the worker specific skills needed to cope with the many demands and challenges children present in everyday life. Child care work makes heavy emotional and physical demands, and supervision provides an important support system in aiding the worker to cope with these demands.

Child care work is practiced within organizational settings that use a variety of disciplines—child care work, education, social work, psychiatry, psychology, medicine, and all the support services (i.e., food service, maintenance, etc.). Therefore, supervision must be regular and consistent, to ensure that the various disciplines are integrated and coordinated for each child.

Supervision is the primary mechanism sustaining an organization. Accreditation standards must be upheld, board and administrtive policies must be carried out, and agencies must account for public and private dollars.

The psychodynamics of troubled children, the ever-changing relationship between the child care worker and the group, and the complex organizational structures of institutional settings are reasons even the most experienced child care worker needs consistent stimulation by a supervisor to maintain proficiency. The challenge to the supervisor is to help the child care worker sharpen skills so that the worker is able to intervene in a pro-active, rather than a re-active, way and eventually to achieve more independent functioning.

On-Line and Formal Supervision

There are two main types of supervision—on-line and formal.

On-Line Supervision

On-Line supervision is based on the belief that the skills and practice of child care work are best taught by demonstration. It is essentially an inductive approach to learning. The techniques of formal supervision are discussed later in this paper; however, it is pertinent here to focus briefly on modeling, evaluating, anticipating, directing, and providing a tone for learning, as each pertains to on-line supervision.

Modeling refers to the supervisor's practicing child care and problem-solving skills within the view of the worker. Whenever time permits,the supervisor solicits from the worker the particulars (e.g., timing, tone of voice, wording, etc.) of what was observed about the supervisor's practice, and the concepts behind intervention.

Evaluation refers to discussing with the worker the intervention that has or should have taken place. The discussion is either at the time of the intervention, or later as part of a formal supervisory session.

Anticipation refers to the supervisor's helping the worker think through the consequences of an intervention, program, or plan prior to its inception.

Directing refers to the supervisor's carrying through with the worker an instance of practice—for example, co-leading a group meeting, a parent interview, a confrontation with a child, etc.

The fifth component, providing a tone for learning, involves the supervisor's inviting the worker to criticize the supervisor's interventions with children and soliciting the worker's suggestions as to how the situation could have been handled more effectively.

Formal Supervision

The vehicle for formal supervision is the supervisory conference. An essential aspect is the agreement between the worker and the supervisor establishing: (1) the mechanics; (2) the content; and (3) the process.

The mechanics of the supervisory conferences must be made clear to the worker, who needs to know that supervision will take place on a regular basis as to time, length, and noninterruption, and in a comfortable, private place.

The major content of the conference should consist of joint solving of practice problems. Time should also be allocated for information sharing, program planning, checking on the basic needs of children, such as food, clothing,and medical care, and dealing with the worker's personal concerns as they may affect the job. The content should also include ongoing evaluation of the worker's performance.

The process element refers to how the supervisor and the worker work together toward long-range goals, as well as the specific objectives for the week. Process involves style, method, and technique.

Three Components of Supervision

Both formal and on-line supervision have three main components—administrative, supportive, and educational.

Administrative Component

Although administrative tasks and expectations for supervisors vary with individual agencies, many aspects are common. Administratively, supervisors assign work, deploy staff, clarify and interpret policies for line staff, assess needs, analyze and plan client contacts, and evaluate staff. In essence, the administrative aspect deals with coordinating, integrating, and monitoring every aspect of service to the client. Supervisors facilitate work, check on quality of services, serve as advocate for the worker, and act as a communication link between administration and worker. They also represent the institution's point of view, act as buffer between administration and clients, and help formulate policy, as well as communicate with other agencies in the community.

Supportive Component

Supervisors should keep in mind that the child care worker is expected to model ethics, mores, values, personal well-being, and *joie de vivre*. However, the unpredictable nature of the work and the general frustration in dealing with severely troubled children can sap the worker's emotional energy and decrease the capacity to be an effective model. Therefore, the supevisor must support the worker both in the supervisory hour and throughout the week. For example, the supervisor may call upon the worker following a difficult incident the worker had to manage. The supervisor may give the worker a chance to feel important (i.e., report on a successful group meeting at the staff meeting, present his/her practice at an in-service training session, or explain the cottage program to a board committee, etc.). The basic idea is to find ways to reassure the worker that she/he is a vital team member worthy of consistent support.

Educational Component

The educational component of supervision focuses on teaching the worker what is necessary to know in providing specific services to the children and families. Child care supervisors need a strong conceptual base of child care practice and specific teaching techniques to be effective in helping child care workers provide specific services. Since a discussion of the conceptual base is beyond the scope of this paper (and Kadushin has written a great deal about the educational component of supervision),* the focus here is on techniques available to the supervisor in educating child care staff.

Techniques

Modeling

How the supervisor handles the many facets of supervision is in itself a technical aspect of the educative component. Child care workers learn from the experience in the supervisory process and from identifying with the supervisor's technique in their work together. The supervisor's ways of being empathetic, listening, understanding, reaching for feelings (particularly negative), setting an emotional tone, freeing up, accepting the expression of intense feelings, etc., are effective teaching devices. The worker tends to act in a similar way with clients.

> An example of supervisor modeling occurred when a well-liked child care worker in the Bellefaire day treatment facility was terminating her employment to enter graduate school in social work. The worker defended against her sadness and guilt by becoming very busy and precise about bringing evaluations and other written material up to date. Her supervisor expressed his sadness in regard to her departure and asked how she was feeling. The tone of this session, along with the supervisor's ability to share his own emotion, freed the worker to talk about her sadness, feelings of unfinished business, worry about the children, and difficulty in showing her feelings in front of the children and her colleagues. This gave her supervisor an opening to support an appropriate display of emotion, something that children feel they must defend against. Up to this point, the children were not expressing their feelings about this staff person's leaving, though there were several episodes of acting out directed at her.
>
> After a follow-up session with her supervisor, the worker held a group meeting and, with tears in her eyes, shared with the children her sadness at having to leave them. Several children then spoke about how hard it is to have people leave and to adjust to new staff. They talked about how sad it was to lose someone who really cares. Other children appropriately verbalized anger about the agency, stating that their favorite persons are the ones that always seem to leave.

Use of the Agenda

Each supervisory conference should have an agenda, preferably submitted to the supervisor a day in advance. When the supervisor requires the worker to prepare for the conference in advance, it sets the expectation that to practice effectively one must plan. There are other reasons why an

*Alfred Kadushin, *Supervision in Social Work* (New York: Columbia University Press, 1976).

agenda is a useful tool in supervision: (1) it maintains a focus on the work; (2) it actively involves the worker in the learning process; and (3) it is a useful diagnostic tool; that is, the supervisor gets a sense of the worker's priorities, worries, clarity about the task, level of dependence, etc. It is also imperative for the supervisor to be prepared for what the worker will bring up at the conference. The supervisor may need time to enlist the aid of other staff members to answer questions of policy or procedure, to plan strategies, or to get suggestions on dealing with specific concerns.

Concept Identification

Specific interventions related to general concepts and theoretical formulations help child care workers to generalize those interventions to a variety of situations. For example, a supervisor points out to the worker that at snack time the food should be arranged tastefully on platters on the table before the children return from school. The worker will carry out this expectation if she/he understands the concepts behind this request, such as demonstrating caring, giving a sense of order and predictability, showing respect for the children, and so forth. This kind of knowledge helps the worker to become creative, use his or her own ideas to demonstrate these principles, and generalize the learning to dinner time, cookouts, etc. Bruner noted: "Perhaps the most basic thing that can be said about human memory after a century of intensive research is that unless detail is placed into a structured pattern, it is rapidly forgotten. Organizing facts in terms of principles and ideas from which they may be inferred is the only known way to reducing the quick rate of loss of human memory. The principal problem of human memory is not storage but retrieval, and the key to retrieval is organization."*

Directing

If a supervisor is specific and directive, it helps inexperienced workers and workers carrying out an unfamiliar assignment. Workers learn specific interventions from supervisors. Once they have had experience with the intervention, they find ways to revamp the intervention to fit their styles and personalities. The following example illustrates the technique.

A new child care worker has the task of preparing the group for a new child and making the child feel welcome. The supervisor directs the worker to: (1) see that the bedroom is clean; (2) make sure the bed is properly made; and (3) call a cottage meeting to: (a) remind the children when the new child will arrive; (b) answer any questions the group may have; (c) help them to recall what they felt like on coming to the agency, to sensitize them to the new

*Jerome Bruner, *The Process of Education* (New York: Random House, Vintage, 1963), pp. 24, 31.

youngster's anxieties; (d) help the group make or purchase a welcoming gift; (e) engage the group in planning an activity consistent with known interests of the new child; and (f) elicit volunteers to show the new girl around, help her unpack, and so on.

Process Recording

Process recording refers to writing down from memory a specific occurrence between a child care worker and the child and/or group. For example—Steve: "I'm not letting you search my room!" Worker: "Why not! You have given me reason to believe you were smoking dope in here." Steve (angrily): "So what! This is *my* room! I don't search your room, you don't search mine. Now get out!" Worker (firmly): "I'm not going to battle with you."

Process recording is an essential tool in the supervisory process. Careful recording helps convey the worker's objectives, conceptual skills, diagnostic ability, and understanding of the interaction with the client.

Here are some of the questions a supervisor should consider in analyzing an item of process recording:

- Does the worker have specific reasons for presenting this process or make specific requests for help?
- What are the tone and setting of the incident?
- What is the problem as the worker sees it?
- What interventions flow from the worker's definition of the problem? Are the interventions in accord with the worker's understanding of the problem?
- What is the affect during the worker's intervention?
- How much are the worker's feelings and interventions recorded in the process?
- What themes permeate a specific process or series of processes from the same worker?
- What messages are being given by the client, and is the worker responding to these messages?
- Is the worker aware of how his interventions are affecting the client?
- Were the worker's responses appropriate and helpful?

Committing to Paper

Written material other than process recording can also be analyzed by the supervisor and used for training purposes. For example, a worker may be asked to submit a summer camp program for a latency-age group in advance of a trip. The supervisor then is able to learn whether there is a theme to the trip, the goals reflect the group's needs, the program is designed to achieve these goals, the worker understands the need for transition times, the activities are sequenced, appropriate for the group and its skill level, etc.

Forecasting

This technique helps the worker compile and use existing relevant data to ensure productive outcomes. The supervisor—more experienced and knowledgeable than the worker—should be able to help the worker think ahead, predict, and therefore be ready for what is to come. Forecasting involves helping the worker read subtle as well as obvious clues, understanding and interpreting individual and group surface behaviors. New workers need assistance in accumulating data to aid in planning.

Another specific way the supervisor can assist a worker in forecasting is to inquire about various facets of an event. This may help the worker think through counteractions to various situations. For example, planning a trip to the ice cream store may seem uncomplicated to the new worker. Therefore, the supervisor helps the worker be prepared for possible problems: it may be a humid day; there is a financial limit; the lines at the ice cream parlor may be long; the radio in the van may break; one boy may be allergic to chocolate; Johnny's body tics may be more pronounced when he's anxious. After going through this, the worker should recognize that the trip may not be simple after all.

Showing Curiosity

A show of curiosity by a supervisor often helps the worker slow down and become more aware of the details in the work. It helps the worker to discover how patterns in thinking may be productive or impeding. This technique often takes the form of "Why do you . . ." or "Are you aware that . . .?" Wondering out loud pushes responsibility back onto the worker to examine her/his thought process, as well as actual responses to various situations.

Breaking It Down

Daily practice problems often seem complex, overwhelming, and unmanageable to child care workers. When frustrated by a complex problem, workers tend to present the problem in a distorted fashion, losing perspective on a situation as it relates to other experiences. Shulman, reflecting on the group in supervision, suggests, "By translating the problem into a more manageable form we help the members overcome the immobilization which accompanies an overwhelming task."*

*Lawrence Shulman, "Social Work Skill: The Anatomy of a Helping Act," in *Social Work Practice* (New York: Columbia University Press, 1969).

A supervisor's task at these times is to help the worker break down the problem, and see it in a more manageable light. If a worker walks in and announces "I've had it! I'm not helping these kids; nothing seems to work!" the supervisor should permit a reasonable time for ventilation, then help the worker sort out what is going on by asking pertinent questions. The supervisor gets the worker to grasp the reality of the situation, and this may free her/him to continue in the work.

Structured Observation

Structured observation is used primarily when the worker lacks awareness and/or sensitivity or does not have a mental picture of the goal and how to achieve it, or when the supervisor wants to demonstrate how to carry out an intervention. The following vignette illustrates the technique.

> Cottage 1's staff was new and inexperienced. The cottage lacked structure in general, and mealtimes were disastrous. The supervisor sent one of the least experienced staff members to another cottage to observe its mealtimes, providing an image of a successful mealtime. The supervisor heightened the worker's awareness by outlining what to look for (i.e., how the meal started, how the table was set, the tone of the conversation, the values communicated at the meal, how disruptive behavior was handled, how the meal ended, and so forth). The worker was asked to report back to the total group at a staff meeting.

The crux of this intervention was the supervisor's giving the worker an outline of what to look for, not leaving this to chance.

Role Play

Role playing is a training technique in which the worker plays out the kinds of problem encountered in day-to-day work. The technique is used to stimulate discussion, acquire insight, gain awareness, and reveal the worker's thinking process and mode of interacting with a child. A necessary condition for effective role play is that the supervisor have enough expertise to provide alternative ways of intervening to the worker involved in the role play. The following are simple ways of role playing:

- *Simple role play:* The supervisor provides a short explanation of the situation and the role the worker is to play.
- *Role reversal:* The supervisor plays the worker and the worker assumes the child's or parent's role. The purpose is to permit the worker to experience how her/his message is coming across, and also to perceive the client's point of view.

• *Mirror role play:* This technique is used to exaggerate weaknesses and errors. By the supervisor's "mirroring" back in an exaggerated way the worker's interventions, the worker becomes aware of himself as perceived by others. Morris (Fritz) Mayer* gave the example that follows:

A child care worker was working with a provocative twelve-year-old boy. The boy poked the worker with his finger practically every time she was on duty. She came to supervision almost in tears over frustration in attempting to deal with this behavior. The supervisor ask the worker what she did when Johnny poked her. She said she told him to stop, but added that it didn't seem to help. The supervisor played this out with the worker, pretending to poke her. The worker said quietly and sweetly, "Now, Johnny, you must stop that." The supervisor, playing Johnny, grinned, only to poke with more intensity. The supervisor then stepped out of the role play and asked the worker, "Is that really how you tell Johnny to stop?" She naively said, "Why, yes."

The supervisor then played back the scenario, taking both roles and in an exaggerated fashion mimicked the worker's pathetic limit-setting response, "Now Johnny, you must stop that." The worker blushed as she picked up on the mixed message she had been given Johnny. In no way did her facial expression, voice inflection and total affect match her words.

After the mirroring back, the supervisor and the worker rehearsed this scene several times. The supervisor demonstrated his anger at being poked by looking the worker straight in the eye, grabbing her wrist and stating, "Stop it. I don't like being poked!" Continuing to hold her wrists firmly, he asked convincingly, "Do you understand, John, what I'm telling you?" "John" meekly said yes, and the supervisor let go.

Simulation

In role play, the supervisor is attempting to get a point across. In simulation, the supervisor is experimenting with a new idea to see if it will work or to gather data to improve the idea. For example:

A group of child care workers decided that the best way to conduct a weekly review in the two-hour cottage staff meeting was to allocate four minutes for each of the fourteen children (fifty-six minutes) and use the remaining time to discuss the children who had particular difficulty that week. Any child who needed more than 4 minutes would be referred to the second hour. The staff members hypothesized that in this way they would be able to touch base with every child in the cottage, yet still have time to focus on children who needed more discussion. The supervisor pointed out several problems with the system, but the staff wasn't convinced. The supervisor then suggested a simulation to test the idea. What the staff learned was that this format did not allow for staff participation and discussion, and that staff could not end discussion with one child and move on to another child at the end of a four-minute period.

*Past executive director of Bellefaire and the Jewish Children's Bureau, Cleveland.

Problem Solving

A main goal of supervision is to teach a worker to solve problems. A problem-solving approach assumes that once the problem is clearly identified, the worker can be helped to think through various productive responses. This approach points out to the worker that problems in child care do not have stock answers, but rather there is a continuum ranging from ineffective responses on the one end to productive responses on the other. The supervisor helps the worker: (1) to state the goal; (2) to identify the problem; (3) to break down the problem and define the parts; (4) to develop a plan of action for each part of the problem; (5) to anticipate pros and cons of each plan of action; (6) to develop a system of feedback to monitor the intervention; and (7) to evaluate outcomes and make adjustments.

> The cottage staff in an adolescent boys' cottage locked up the silverware as a response to an increase in the disappearance of knives, spoons, and forks. Staff members viewed the problem as carelessness on the part of the children and themselves, and therefore thought a better policing system would solve the problem. It didn't.
>
> The supervisor pointed out that the staff members had jumped to a conclusion, and wondered if they should not think about other aspects of the phenomenon. Pushed to think, the workers observed that the boys seemed to have a poor sense of "group," let alone a positive group image. They didn't seem to acknowledge the value of other material things in the cottage, not just silverware. Their low image as a group was reflected in how they dressed, ate, and generally interacted. As the pieces evolved, the supervisor helped them see this problem as symptomatic of a larger problem of self-image, deprivation, anger, and a lack of power projected back to staff as a battle of wills.
>
> The staff took the locks off the silverware drawer and through a series of meetings with the total cottage developed several creative activity programs.
>
> In a few weeks, the child care staff decided to push the problem back to the group. In one of several cottage meetings the staff established an activity fund to help the group carry out popular programs such as athletic events and off-campus trips. In addition, the staff gave up paper drinking cups and plastic dishware and bought a set of inexpensive but attractive dishware, along with stainless steel silverware the boys selected themselves. Part of the group's agreement was to use the activities money for replacement of any lost or damaged dishware or silverware. The cottage group, in addition, wanted to fine the total cottage from their weekly allowances to help pay for replacements. The staff suggested they give their new program a decent chance to succeed, without establishing a fine system.
>
> The child care staff evaluated this process two months after the locks were removed from the silveware drawers. No silverware had been reported missing. No dishes were lost or even accidentally broken. And staff members themselves were making further efforts to beautify the dinner tables with centerpieces, colorful serving bowls, and novelty water glasses.

Reconstruction

In supervision, as in almost everything else, there is much Monday morning quarterbacking. Reconstruction is based on the assumption that people learn from mistakes and generalize this learning. The reconstruction process helps the child care worker look back over what happened to see if there was any way to alter the outcome, to be more effective at reading cues, to become more aware of the variables to be manipulated in any given incident, and to develop insights. Process recording is an excellent tool for assisting the worker in this. Reconstruction is accomplished by getting the worker to state in detail all the steps leading up to the incident and by asking pertinent questions to get the child care worker to look at alternatives in handling the situation.

Summarization

Each supervisory session must have some time at the end for summarization. The supervisor uses this time to get feedback from the child care worker as to what was learned from the session, what was lacking, how they worked together, etc. This time is also used to gain direction for the next conference.

Conclusion

High turnover of child care workers has plagued residential care centers for many years. This also is true for group and foster homes and other group residence facilities. Recent papers on stress and burnout have attempted to pinpoint some of the causes of such turnover.*

A committee studying child care turnover at Bellefaire recently indicated several contributing factors. Job stress and compensation were not, in many cases, the reasons given for leaving the job. A lack of sufficient nurturing was a major factor.

A total nurturing of all child care staff obviously cannot be achieved just through supervisors. This paper's purpose is to heighten professional awareness of those ingredients of a structure for supervision of child care staff that is supportive, produces growth, promotes a feeling of personal and professional self-worth, and enables child care staff to feel gratification and a sense of significance in their role in the agency team. The supervisor and the organizational system exert their impact upon this nurturance.

---

*Christina Maslach, "Burned Out," *Human Behavior* (Sept. 1976); Martha A. Mattingly, "Sources of Stress and Burn-out in Professional Child Care Work," *Child Care Quarterly* 6 (1977); Stanley Seiderman, "Combating Staff Burnout," *Day Care and Early Education* (1978).

For many years the predominant pattern of supervision in clinical practice was a one-to-one private relationship. Increasingly, however, the value of group supervision is being considered. It helps workers to accept the fact that they are not alone in having particular problems and perhaps to gain support from each other in dealing with the particularly stressful aspects of their work, and it is more efficient than individual supervision. Unfortunately, not all people can benefit equally from group supervision. Paul Abels describes the dynamics and the structure of groups as mediums for supervision. Kenneth Watson's article, noted in this chapter's bibliography, gives examples of other supervisory modalities, such as a case consultation, peer group supervision, team supervision, and the like.

On the Nature of Supervision: The Medium Is the Group*

PAUL A. ABELS

• • •

The System with Supervisor

In addition to provision of educational resources, the major tasks for the instructor in the learning group are: (1) to help create the conditions under which learning can take place; (2) to help the worker to focus and integrate some of the learning experiences that are vital to the professional role; and (3) to help the staff make the best use of the group learning situation.

As with all groups and learning processes, certain obstacles to learning are likely to appear, and it becomes the function of the supervisor to help staff discern the nature of these obstacles and find ways to deal with them. These obstacles may include: (1) the inability to look at one's own or a fellow student's practice in an objective manner; (2) the manner in which one presents or interprets material; or (3) inability to work on a problem that has a "loaded" meaning to the learner.† The supervisor must be able to help the group deal with blocks to its learning.

It is the supervisor's responsibility to keep the group focused on the material to be learned. The responsibility for working on the learning problems, however, lies primarily with the group members, just as in a one-to-one supervisory conference the responsibility to work at learning is the student's.

*Excerpted by special permission of the Child Welfare League of America from *Child Welfare* 49 (1970): 304–311.

†See Bernard Bandler, "Ego-Centered Teaching," *Smith College Studies in Social Work* 30, no. 2 (1960): 125–136; and the discussion by Jerome Bruner, "Perceptive Metaphors," in *Toward a Theory of Instruction*, pp. 134–138.

The learner-teacher transaction, whether "one to one" or in group, calls for a commitment by both parties and a sharing of responsibilities. The roles of each actor must be explicated as clearly as possible and the working agreement or contract clearly stated,* connoting that each has something important to contribute.

The decision-making procedures in this give-and-take relationship between members and teachers and among members will depend to a great extent on the manner in which the supervisor-teacher wishes to exercise his authority. The relationship creates problems for the student and the supervisor as well. Jenkins, in discussing the leadership conflict in the classroom, suggests ways of minimizing it, and points up some required teacher actions.

(1) The teacher accepts his power and authority. (2) He develops a working understanding with the class about areas of authority—which ones he retains and which he gives the class—and behaves consistently. (3) He sets behavioral limits. (4) He permits class members to suffer the consequences of their decisions. On rare occasions, he will interfere and explain why he does so. (5) He works in a context of stated educational goals. (6) He respects the aspirations, wishes, and needs of students and expects the same consideration in return. (7) He is willing to be influenced by students in the same manner he expects them to be influenced by him.†

Phases in the Teacher-Learner Transaction

Practitioners and researchers concerned with small groups have noted that there appears to be a natural progression in the development of a group's life. This progression is generally marked by the following phases: (1) initial group formation; (2) a period of testing of the group and its limits; (3) a period of productive accomplishments by the group; and (4) a phase generally seen as the termination, or change in the purpose or activity of the group.

The stages in the supervisory transaction can also be perceived in this manner. They call for different action patterns on the part of the group members and discrete action responses from the supervisor.

1. *The Encounter:* At this stage in the life or prelife of the group, the nature of the supervisory relationship is brought to the attention of the group members. This may be through: (a) a brochure that describes the nature of the agency or supervision; (b) contact with social workers or discussions with other staff; and (c) contact in some way with the agency.

*See Leland P. Bradford, "The Teaching-Learning Transaction," in Warren G. Bennis, Kenneth D. Benne, and Robert Chin, eds., *The Planning of Change* (New York: Holt and Rinehart, 1961), p. 493.

†David H. Jenkins, "Characteristics and Functions of Leadership in Instructional Groups," in *The Dynamics of Instructional Groups*, p. 183.

In essence, this exposure is an advance signal that something unusual may transpire in this learning situation.

Contacts with agency staff prior to the arrival of new staff may be required.

2. *Contracting:* The initial contact between learner and supervisor is the beginning of a relationship in which the initial goals of the transaction are worked out and the means of achieving them are discussed. Reasons for using the group method of teaching in the field should be pointed out and the value of the participation of the members emphasized. The building of trust to enhance learning must start immediately; the nature of the early relationship has an important bearing on the subsequent frame of reference of both learner and teacher.

The supervisor interprets and clarifies the nature of the group. He helps define the goals, sets forth the expectations of both members and supervisor, and discusses the individual learning assignments and the responsibilities inherent in a supervisor-learner situation. The supervisor may also discuss the teaching techniques to be used. Guidelines for admissible types of concerns are discussed.

With new staff, the supervisor points out common learning needs and sketches the type of cases that the staff are likely to have, as well as anticipated problem areas. Discussion should follow on the role of the supervisor in group and individual conferences. The matter of confidentiality of material also should be discussed; the supervisor should point out his responsibility to use the material brought up in the group with both the agency and the school.

The expectations and responsibilities of each group member should be discussed. The initial contract is the first in a series that establishes rules of the game with the group, but also seeks to gain "credit" from the group while members learn to trust both the group and the supervisor.

3. *The reconnaissance:* This refers to the "scouting" period in which group members get to know each other and the supervisor, and the supervisor gets to know them. There is a general testing of members, limits, and the supervisor.

The group member is uncertain of what is expected of him in the agency and the group and often is dependent on the supervisor and other members for direction. This is "normal," but efforts to utilize the supervisor as expert and to negate the value of the group should be discouraged.

At first there may be few attempts at risking of self, but as the group starts to be helpful and supportive of the member, the risk of self increases.

The supervisor must assume some initial responsibility for bringing to the group material of immediate and common concern, such as intake, recording of material, discussion of agency policies and clientele, and so forth. He immediately begins to make demands on the group to work on these problem areas, using the contributions of group members in the problem-solving process. The nature of the material required to make an adequate assessment of client need is a subject that lends itself to this type of discussion.

The supervisor helps the group members bring out learning needs that they, as beginners, feel are urgent in order to start working with a client; these concerns become significant parts of the group's agenda. He permits differences of opinion, even with him, and helps the group see that it can handle differences and still function productively. Toward the end of this phase group members are able freely to bring in practice for discussion in front of the group.

4. *Autonomous learning:* As the trust in both the group and the supervisor develops, the ability of the group members to risk themselves increases. They are able to deal with more significant material. The supervisor encourages this, acting as a mediator if the material gets too threatening to any one individual, scapegoating occurs, and the group is not able to work. The supervisor begins to demand increased work from the students and often brings in material from a student record. This should be discussed with the student beforehand if it is material he might not want to share in public.

As the material is fed into the group, the supervisor and the members share in the solving of the problem. The supervisor points out implications of action that might have been overlooked, helping the group to focus on the practice being discussed, although at times the group might help with a problem that is not necessarily a common one to the group but is related to a particular member's learning experience.

Individual Conferences

Although the group is the medium that the supervisor has selected for teaching, there are times when individual conferences are in order.

1. *Initial encounters with the agency and supervisor:* In addition to the group orientation sessions, individual sessions may be held at which the worker can discuss at his own pace some of his concerns with the experience that he is about to enter.

2. *Evaluations:* The periodic evaluations aimed at assessing staff's growth and problems should be done individually. This becomes a private matter in which the individual's strengths and weaknesses, his performance with the client, and his total learning experiences are discussed. Needless to say, the group as a group must also have periodic assessments of its own development and ability to work on problems.

3. *Requests for individual conferences:* When the worker makes a specific request of the supervisor for a discussion of material that he feels cannot be discussed in the group, an individual conference should be

arranged. Afterward, the supervisor may ask the worker to bring the matter up in the group. If this type of request from the worker is repeated too often, the reasons for this have to be examined.

4. *At supervisor's discretion:* At times the supervisor may feel that individual conferences are needed because the student is not making progress in the group or is not able to use the group as the medium. The supervisor can then help the worker on an individual conference basis. He should still be expected to work and learn in the group.

The Contract with the Group

The basis contract is that the group is a work unit, and that both the supervisor and staff are there to work. The goal of the group is to increase skills as professional social workers. In this agreement, the supervisor is expected to bring his advanced knowledge, educational skills, and understanding of behavior; the worker brings his time, interest, knowledge, and the desire to participate in the work of the group. This goal is achieved not only through work with the clients in the field, but through work in the supervisory group, and by contributing examples, questions, concerns, insights, and differing views.

Just as in individual supervision, the ability to give of oneself in group supervision develops as one feels he can trust the experience and the people he is involved with. [Gisella] Konopka, in discussing the role of the worker, points out, "Nothing significant can happen until the members have learned to trust him." Just as the supervisor in individual sessions cannot expect trust to develop on initial contact, this does not happen immediately in group sessions.

There is a possibility, however, that the involvement of a worker in a situation with his peers, with common goals and concerns, helps create a climate of trust. The members gain strength to share their concerns, from the group and from the knowledge that this is a group expectation. There is less concern with authority and control as the group shares with the teacher the authority for teaching and control. The control rests in the problem to be solved and in the combined efforts of the members. The members become dependent on each other, not only on the teacher. The group will demand that members carry a fair share of the work. They, as well as the supervisor, will confront the student who is not able to share his experiences or contribute to the analysis of the material under discussion. They will point out the overdependence of a novice on the group or teacher and wrestle with similar concerns within themselves.

Conclusion

Staff workers bring different backgrounds and abilities to the group. Some have more social welfare experience than others. New workers may add their own brand of inquisitiveness. If they have come directly from a school or inner-city community, they can contribute the latest theoretical concepts or neighborhood views. The supervisor's task here is to help them find a common ground, so that they recognize the contributions and responsibilities of each that are necessary in the group experience.

If one goal of the teacher-learner transaction is to help develop an autonomous professional, the supervisor, too, must be autonomous. He must be ready to attempt new ideas, and experiment with teaching techniques. As a professional he should be able to influence the agency and the profession.

When not certain of an answer, he can say, "We will explore and find the way together." The group has a way of maintaining honesty; the supervisor shares power with the group members, and they add their power to his. One result can be a lessening of the threat of the conference held behind closed doors. The teaching and the learning, the risk and the rewards, are in the open, and all must come to terms with the situation. This is the power of the group—it helps determine the function of the leader; it can give or withhold, and these dynamics are of grave importance to the teacher. The group will demand honesty, work, and risk from the supervisor, just as he demands them from the group.

This give and take makes group supervision a complex process requiring a high degree of understanding of both individual and group behavior. It calls for teaching skills that enable members to make use of each other as well as the supervisor. It requires supervisors who can create the climate in which learning can take place and in which the concerns with control and authority are minimized. Although the demands on the supervisor and the members are high, the rewards can be well worth the effort. There are an excitement and a sense of urgency in the work group that perceives the fruits of the struggle. As the members experience self-learning and teaching and their goals come into sight, there is a thrust to inquire more, to learn more, to accomplish more, to be more. This is the human quest that education really is.

John Wax has summarized the positive and negative aspects of group supervision. On the positive side are increased communication among workers, increased access to the knowledge and experience of others, reduced dependence on supervisors, and a reduction in worker defensiveness. On the negative side are a tendency to shift the discussion from one topic to another too quickly; the hesitancy of less secure workers to discuss their cases; a tendency to strive for consensus and support and to submerge conflict; and a tendency to move more slowly than gifted workers would like.*

Whether group or individual supervision is the chosen modality, in general supervisors should proceeed through the following steps:

1. secure their relationships with the administration so that they can serve as an effective advocate for their supervisees' needs;
2. discuss with the supervisee his or her professional goals as well as agency expectations;
3. formulate an educational assessment with the supervisee during the probationary period, covering content, learning style, motivation, and structural arrangements;
4. have supervisees prepare agendas for supervisory conferences;
5. use recording as an educational tool: focused recording on particular aspects of a supervisee's work can be effective and less time-consuming and costly than process recording (see the article by Rosalie Kane in Chapter 9); and
6. set performance, productivity, and personal development objectives before supervision begins and develop indices for the evaluation of progress toward these objectives.

Patti and Austin make the point that the supervisor-supervisee relationship is influenced by organizational issues (such as funding patterns), the interpersonal dynamics of the relationship, motivation, trust, attitudes toward productivity and professional growth, such attributes of the supervisor and supervisee as age, sex, race, values, attitudes toward work, and theories of human nature.† All these factors determine the atmosphere or character of the supervisor-supervisee relationship, which must be conducive to trial-and-error learning. This type of learning can only take place where there is an element of trust.

The beginning supervisor will recognize that he or she is not seen simply as an individual. The agency has a history of supervisory relationships, and this history influences peoples' attitudes. For example, if a patient commits suicide and the agency immediately looks around for someone to blame, this will affect the learning atmosphere in that agency. If mistakes are treated as ammunition to be used against workers, this too will have a negative effect. How crises are handled also affects the atmosphere. How does the agency handle firings? What does it tell other staff members, and how does it deal with the staff's reactions to events?

This is an important reason why a supervisor cannot think of his or her job as just arranging for workers' education.‡ The whole agency is a learning system, and the supervisor must take an active part in the agency

*John Wax, "The Pros and Cons of Group Supervision," *Social Casework* 40 (1959): 307–314.

†Patti and Austin, "Socializing the Direct Service Practitioner," pp. 275–276.

‡For a discussion of these issues, see Lois Abramczyk, "The New M.S.W. Supervisor: Problems of Role Transition," *Social Casework* 61 (1980): 83–90.

in order to affect its learning atmosphere; if not, the atmosphere will affect him or her. If there is any axiom in administration, it is that whoever or whatever has an influence over one's ability to do one's job is someone or something that one must develop influence over.

In recent years the social work literature has reflected social workers' frustration over unnecessarily lengthy supervision. Supervision is costly, and holding conferences that are simply meaningless rituals where the supervisor asks the supervisee how he or she feels about something is wasteful and ultimately infantilizing. Many social workers have argued that other professions allow their practitioners to practice autonomously after they have received their degrees or completed an internship. Others suggest that the low status of social workers in interdisciplinary practice is related to a supervisory structure that casts doubt on workers' professional judgment, and competence.

Laura Epstein has argued that agencies should move toward autonomous practice and abandon the supervision of skilled workers.* Others counter that this is not completely possible because of the strains between the needs of professional workers and the needs of organizations. The need for authority relationships and accountability cannot be ignored.

Wax has taken the middle ground in recommending time-limited supervision.† An agency's administration should determine how many years a worker needs to be supervised after receiving his or her master's degree in order to reach a level of competence to perform adequately the services that the agency offers. In his hospital the period of supervision lasted two years. If workers did not meet the required level of competence after two years, they were let go. If they did meet it, they were no longer systematically "trained" but were offered consultation, although they remained accountable to an administrative superior, who served as their communication link with the rest of the agency.

Wax argues that agencies should decide the length of supervision on administrative grounds—that is, on a cost-effectiveness basis—and not on educational grounds. For him, the issue is not whether workers can and should increase their skills through supervision, but rather what level of skill the agency deems necessary to do the job acceptably. Supervision costs money that, once competence is achieved could be better utilized for client service.

Perhaps the central question is whether an agency has a responsibility to educate workers beyond the level required for them to do their jobs. From the vantage point of any one agency, the answer would probably be no. From the vantage point of individual workers with a desire for mobility and professional growth, the answer is probably yes, and yet

*Laura Epstein, "Is Autonomous Practice Possible?" *Social Work* 24 (1979): 5–19.
†John Wax, "Time-Limited Supervision," *Social Work* 8 (1963): 37–43.

these self-same workers do not want supervision ad infinitum. An internship program might be one way out of the dilemma.

Nevertheless, as we have noted, there is more of a strain between the autonomous professional and the effective agency than the literature suggests. The desire for personal achievement cannot be completely meshed with organizational needs. If social workers cannot derive satisfaction from what agencies achieve, they will be disappointed, no matter how much skill and competence they develop on the job. A salaried profession is different from an entrepreneurial one. (The effect on clinicians of different management styles and organizational structures is discussed in Chapter 10.)

Practice Analogues

There are numerous analogues between supervisory and clinical practice. Most clincians begin work with the point of view expressed by one beginning worker: "I expected the supervisor to be to the worker as the worker is to the client." This view permeates what is called the growth model of supervision: "Professional education in social work was concerned not only with the knowledge imparted to students, but also with their personality growth. To believe in the possibility of growth of the client, one must have known the release of growth in the self, through help consciously sought and professionally controlled.* This model of supervision depicts it as akin to therapy.

A number of objections to this view may be raised: (1) its basic assumption—one cannot help clients if one has not been helped in the same manner oneself—is certainly open to question; (2) what may be therapeutically called for in the worker's supervision may in fact be quite dysfunctional for the agency and the client; (3) the time required to deal with growth issue would be better offered to clients; and (4) clinicians have a right not to deal with their personal problems at work if they choose not to.

The therapeutic view of supervision rests on the idea that the more psychologically healthy the worker is, the more effective the agency. The danger of this view is that it may make self-awareness a final objective rather than a means to learning the helping techniques and skills to perform the job. Although agencies need stable and insightful workers, the workers' psychological state is only one factor in the agency's ability to deliver services. Treating supervision as therapy encourages agencies to define their problems in attaining their goals in terms of the personal problems of individual workers, and not in terms of funding rela-

*Jessie Taft, quoted by Wijnberg and Schwartz, "Models of Student Supervision," p. 108.

tionships, community relationships, the agency's structure, communication patterns, social policies, and the like.

On the other hand, the conscious use of self is a basic skill of clinicians and supervisors. Feelings and attitudes are appropriate subjects for supervision, but they should be discussed only in relation to their effects on a particular client, not in relation to the clinician's well-being.

Certain other aspects of the conscious use of self are equally crucial to the supervisory relationship. How does the supervisor deal with his or her own lack of knowledge? How does the supervisor deal with the fact that he or she likes some supervisees more than others? How does the supervisor deal with hostility, deserved and undeserved, from supervisees? How does the supervisor deal with supervisees who do not follow instructions? How comfortable is the supervisor about telling supervisees what to do? How important is the supervisee's performance to the supevisor?

Perhaps the critical practice analogue between supervisory and therapeutic relationships lies in the absolute necessity of establishing trust. Without it, nothing of any permanence will be accomplished. It is more important for the supervisor to establish trust than it is to point out a problem a worker is having and turn immediately to his or her defenses and limitations. In clinical practice one would never begin by attempting to knock down the defenses of clients or by focusing solely on their problems. Partialization is an important process in both clincal practice and in supervision.

Workers, like clients, sometimes resist help. A worker's helplessness may be related to flawed organizational procedures or arrangements, or it may be psychological in origin. Some classic expressions of psychological resistance take the form of dependency—automatically believing whatever the supervisor says; passive aggressiveness—for example, slowness, lateness; distancing, sometimes in the form of pointing out mistakes before the supervisor does; and negativism.

Some forms of workers resistance can be handled as one would handle client resistance. The difference is that in supervision the resistance is related to the job and the object of getting through it is to get the job done. The dependent worker does not have to resolve his or her basic dependency needs, but only to take more initiative on the job. The supervisor can provide support and opportunities for this. It is quite possible to help a worker become less dependent on the job, with or without a carryover into his or her personal life.

Certain judgments have to be exercised in supervision that are not part of the clinician's role. If a particular problem affects a clinician's work 5 percent, or even 2 percent, of the time, is it worthwhile to devote 100 percent of the supervisory conference to it? We think not. Perhaps the problem is not something that the person can deal with or wants to deal with; if so, it is perfectly appropriate to ignore it. The problems of clinicians have to be put into proper perspective by their supervisors. A clinician is paid to do a job, not to achieve psychological well-being.

Supervisors should determine who can best handle a supervisory problem and where. Perhaps it would be best handled through group supervision, through structured experiences, through providing workers with techniques to help them get past certain obstacles, or through intervention by another staff member. This is seldom the case in a clinical practice.

Perhaps the major difference between supervision and clinical practice lies in the fact that although clients are forever telling their therapists what the therapists should do or how they should act, supervisees seldom take that liberty with supervisors. On the other hand, it is very helpful for the supervisor occasionally to ask what he or she does that helps or hinders the supervisee's progress. If trust is present, the answer to this question can be very useful.

Finally, supervision and clinical practice share the goal of developing autonomous human beings. Thus, the structure and process of supervision must be designed to help workers take the major responsibility for their own professional growth and development—beginning with student placements and continuing through internship, time-limited supervision, and ultimately some form of self-directed practice.

Attitudes, Values, and Skills

If a supervisor believes that people are basically lazy and need to be watched and controlled, his or her supervisory style will certainly be different from that of a supervisor who believes that people basically want to do a good job. A variety of attitudes influence a supervisor's conduct.

Another important supervisory skill is the ability to live with tension. Some supervisors take the view that their job is to solve all problems. It should be clear by now that we believe that there are many organizational problems that are only manageable, not solvable: the problems of control and compliance, the need for routine and the need for initiative. (These continuing organizational dilemmas are discussed in Chapter 1.)

A supervisor who feels that all tension and disagreement must be resolved will ultimately err in his or her job performance. Supervisors should allow themselves to make mistakes; they do not have to be perfect. If supervisors can allow clinical supervisees to see their mistakes, it will be a lot easier for supervisees to admit their own. Most workers do not expect their supervisors to know everything. They do expect their supevisors to try to help them with their particular difficulties, and, if the supervisors do not know about a particular issue, to find out about it. Concern and willingness to work on a problem are the crucial elements.

President Johnson once said that he could disagree without being disagreeable. The ability to correct someone without criticizing him or her requires cultivation and understanding.

Perhaps the trait most desired by supervisees is consistency on the part of the supervisor. There is nothing more frustrating than to work for someone who is totally unpredictable. Supervisors who begin by telling supervisees that "we are all equal" and end up being authoritarian give their workers the message that they cannot be trusted, that they are not stable, and ultimately that they do not know what they are doing. As a consequence, an authoritarian supervisor may be more desirable than an inconsistant participative one. The authoritarian at least presents a consistent approach that people can adjust to or work around. The inconsistent supervisor, applying one standard now and another one later, confuses everyone.

Still, it must be remembered that a supervisor is never a free agent in handling relationships with supervisees. In a highly centralized, authoritarian organization, it would be difficult for a supervisor to be completely open and participative. It is in fact dysfunctional to involve people, give them a sense of participation, and go along with their ideas if the administration is not really interested in considering them. When workers are led down the garden path—told that they are participating when they are being manipulated—they will respond with rebellion and resentment.

The supervisor is in effect a middleman, paid to meet the demands of those beneath and those above him or her. This is an uncomfortable role, one with strain built into it. Those who cannot handle tension will not be effective supervisors. They will either pander to those above or those below or retreat into neurotic frustration. The demands of both groups are important and valid, and because they express different interests and different concerns, the conflict between them can never be resolved. One set of demands will receive priority at one time and another set at another time. This is not expediency; it is reality.

Additional Readings

Austin, Michael J. *Supervisory Management for the Human Services*. Englewood Cliffs, N.J.: Prentice-Hall, 1981.

Getzel, George, Jack Goldberg and Robert Salmon. "Supervising in Groups as a Model for Today." *Social Casework* 52 (1971): 154–163.

Patti, Rino J. and Michael J. Austin. "Socializing the Direct Service Practitioner in the Ways of Supervisory Management." *Administration in Social Work* 1 (1977): 267–280.

Shulman, Lawrence. *Skills of Supervision and Staff Management*. Itasca, Ill.: Peacock, 1982.

Watson, Kenneth. "Differential Supervision." *Social Work* 18 (1973): 80–88.

Wax, John. "Time-Limited Supervision." *Social Work* 8 (1963): 37–43.

CHAPTER 9

PRACTICE RESEARCHER

Most clinicians have taken one or more courses in research during their training. Unfortunately, in the main these courses have a very narrow focus, emphasizing classical experimental research designs and requiring control groups, random sampling, and the like. They have attempted to inculcate the prescriptive value that professional clinicians should engage in research and that research is crucial to their practice.

While it is hard to find fault with this sentiment, it is also true that clinicians are seldom in a position to carry out experimental research. Besides the ethical problems surrounding the denial of services to control groups, agencies rarely define clinicians' jobs in ways that enable them to carry out this form of research. It is generally the agency and its funding sources that determine what research will take place, when it will take place, where it will take place, and whether it will take place at all. As a result, the research skills imparted in traditional research courses are not utilized, and the skills and attitudes that promote individual research by clinicians are likely to atrophy.

In this chapter we take a much broader view of research and the techniques in its armament. Rather than viewing every clinician as having a responsibility to engage in research per se, we suggest that every clinician is involved in knowledge development, whether he or she recognizes it or not. The range of knowledge that clinicians require is considerable: they need to judge why a particular client does not come to clinical sessions, to describe clients' progress, to develop working hypotheses about the effects on clients' behavior and feelings of particular types of treatment, and to determine whether programs do any good in the long run.

Suzanne Osterbush makes the point that information is the energy of practice.* The important thing for practitioners is not to prove something but to discover something. Discovery requires a systematic, organized focus in their work. It involves quantitative and qualitative research

---

*Suzanne Osterbush, quoted in Harold H. Weissman, "Teaching Qualitative Research Methods," in Scott Briar, Harold H. Weissman, and Allen Rubin, eds., *Research Utilization in Social Work Education* (New York: Council on Social Work Education, 1981), p. 65.

methods, skills of observation, of interviewing, and of analysis. These are all part and parcel of the training of clinicians. In research terms, clinicians need both quantitative and qualitative methods.

Knowledge development is not an abstract exercise. For clinicians it almost always takes place in the context of the agency in which they are employed. The knowledge developed may be generalizable to many clients, in many different agencies, in many different settings, or it may be specific to a particular set of clients at a particular agency at a particular time.

In either case, knowledge development is part of the accountability process. For the last decade or so, social service agencies have been under increasing pressure to be accountable for the resources that they expend, the work that they do, and the clients that they serve. These pressures come from funding sources, the social work profession itself, and potential or actual consumers of agency services. In a climate of scarcity, we can expect these pressures to increase.

It is not uncommon for line social workers routinely to have to collect and compile information about their clients and the services they receive for purposes of program monitoring and evaluation. This activity is often considered bureaucratic drudge work without relevance to clinical practice. On the contrary, it is our contention that accountability is as relevant to the clinical social worker as to the social work administrator, for a number of reasons. First, clinical social workers make decisions all the time about eligibility for service, the types of service clients are to receive, when service should begin, how frequently it should be received, when it should end, and so on. Such decisions involve considerable administrative discretion, and it is our view that workers should be answerable for them.

More positively, the worker who actively engages in monitoring and evaluation of his or her own work is in a position to use accumulated clinical experience systematically to build his or her own practice knowledge and skill. The key word here, however, is "systematically." Only through the systematic evaluation that accountability should require can workers transcend the biases that are likely to enter into less systematic, more "intuitive" approaches to knowledge building.

Such knowledge building is certainly valuable in itself. In addition, it is a preventive against worker burnout, a concept that will be discussed in greater detail in Chapter 10. We will note here only that clinical social workers often fall prey to a sense that their work is meaningless, repetitive, and unappreciated by clients or by the community at large. Systematic evaluation of one's own clinical practice helps workers to recognize their successes and make positive use of their failures. It provides a built-in reward for a job well done and ensures that even the occasions on which the social worker is not able to help will contribute to future improvement of clients' experiences.

Evaluation is too important to be left solely to professional researchers or administrators. The clinical social worker's responsibility for ongoing evaluation is implicit in Briar's notion that all line social workers should be "clinical scientists."* By this he means a practitioner who:

- uses with his or her clients the practice methods and techniques that are known empirically to be most effective;
- continuously and rigorously evaluates her or his own practice;
- participates in the discovery, testing, and reporting of more effective ways of helping clients;
- uses untested, unvalidated practice methods and techniques cautiously and only with adequate control, evaluation, and attention to client rights; and
- communicates the results of her or his evaluations of practice to others.

Briar's model is probably more research-oriented than most clinical social workers are now able to be; it assumes a higher level of agency support for its implementation than is likely to be available; and it has been generally linked to a particular kind of clinical methodology—that is, behavioral techniques—that many clinical social workers do not use in their practice. Nevertheless, it is important because it encourages clinical social workers to make critical use of the research literature in selecting practice interventions, and it stresses the need for both the systematic evaluation of one's own work and sharing of practice knowledge.

Overview

In this chapter, we discuss the contribution that clinicians can make to three different aspects of clinical social work practice: (1) diagnostic assessment and treatment formulation; (2) worker and client monitoring; and (3) practice knowledge.†

Diagnostic Assessment: Diagnostic assessment and treatment formulation is the first step in clinical practice. It requires the systematic gathering of relevant information from the client and significant others concerning the nature and extent of the client's problem, eligibility for agency service, motivation, and so on. Once this information is gathered, it is sorted and

*Scott Briar, "Incorporating Research into Education for Clinical Practice in Social Work: Toward a Clinical Science in Social Work," in Allen Rubin and Aaron Rosenblatt, eds., *Sourcebook on Research Utilization* (New York: Council on Social Work Education, 1979), pp. 132–133.

†For a more complete discussion of the application of research concepts and techniques to these clinical functions, see Tony Tripodi and Irwin Epstein, *Research Techniques for Clinical Social Workers* (New York: Columbia University Press, 1980).

sifted until the social worker arrives at a "psychosocial assessment" describing the client's problem, major contributants, and available resources as a basis for selecting the most appropriate strategies of intervention. The more specific and accurate the diagnosis, the greater the likelihood of success. Nevertheless, as Alfred Kadushin points out, many clinical social workers rely on "Aunt Fanny" diagnostic statements that have neither the precision nor the specificity required for effective practice: "The professionally trained counselor is prone to an approach somewhat similar to the 'Barnum effect' in writing diagnostic reports. This has been identified as the 'Aunt Fanny description.' The statement is diagnostically valid for the client but would be equally true of his—or anybody's—'Aunt Fanny '"*

In his study of this phenomenon, Kadushin provided sixty social work supervisors with one of three case summaries. The first described a five-year-old boy (Larry) referred to a child guidance clinic. The second described a fifteen-year-old girl (Sylvia) referred to a family service agency by a recreational agency. The third described a woman in her late thirties (Mrs. L) referred to a family service agency by a psychiatric facility. The reported cases showed markedly different problems, symptomatology, and background characteristics.

Each of the supervisors was then asked to rate a "universal" diagnostic summary, written by a student, appended to each of the case descriptions. The diagnostic summary read as follows:

> Larry (or Sylvia or Mrs. L.) is reacting to a difficult life situation. The situational problem is, however, superimposed on the trauma of emotional deprivation during earlier, crucial periods in the client's developmental history. There is ambivalence toward parental figures and while the client shows some capacity to develop healthy object relationships, potentialities in this regard show some impairment. There is tendency to convert emotional difficulties into physical symptoms as a mechanism of defense. The client's tendency toward anxiety is evident in relation to dependency needs and in the area of sexual identification. Agressive drives are turned away from the more significant figures in the client's environment and directed toward self either through self-punishment or in masochistic instigations of punishment by others.
>
> There is limited capacity to control unacceptable impulses and reactivation of guilt when such impulses break through the barrier of superego control. A considerable amount of emotional energy is being absorbed in internal conflicts so that limited energy is available to deal constructively with environmental difficulties.
>
> The client is basically insecure, having experienced some rejection by parents and peers.
>
> The fact that the client seems disturbed about the situation would indicate that there is reasonably good motivation toward acceptance of treatment at

*Alfred Kadushin, "Diagnosis and Evaluation for (Almost) All Occasions," *Social Work* 8 (1963): 12.

this time. A supportive relationship with a warm accepting worker would be of therapeutic value. In such a permissive atmosphere that would permit the expression of negative feelings without condemnation, the client can be helped to gain some understanding of the problems faced. Resolution of the marital problem, implied in the material, would likewise be helpful in reducing stress on the client's ego.*

Not surprisingly, Kadushin found that most superivors rated the foregoing Aunt Fanny statement average or slightly above average, irrespective of which of the three cases they received. In other words, the same statement was seen as equally applicable to all of the present cases and presumably many others as well.†

In a critique of the Kadushin article, Lynn Kaplan observes that diagnosis does not take place in a vacuum:

The extensive occurrence of the "Aunt Fanny description"makes one wonder *why* this is so common in practice; unfortunately Kadushin fails to address this question in his article. Specifically, Kadushin does not explain under what conditions is the practice of overgeneralized assessments allowed and/or encouraged.

Is its occurence a reflection of lack of training in accurate assessment or lack of time for accurately recording assessments? While differential diagnosis is emphasized in school, in practice the emphasis may be on deciding on that diagnosis which conforms most to a Department of Mental Hygiene reimbursement classification. Or following the medical model, which involves the use of labeling, the focus of assessment may be on the similarities between disease classifications rather than highlighting unique characteristics that may make diagnosis more difficult.

The pressure to fit symptoms into diagnostic classifications may subtly reinforce the tendency to employ universal statements to justify a diagnosis and treatment strategy. In addition, time pressures may limit the ability to elaborate on details in recording-keeping. Also, the need for more individualized reporting may not have been made clear by agency superiors. These are important factors to take into consideration when determining how to begin to change the state of affairs and encourage more individualized and, hence, more useful assessments.‡

Organizational and professional pressures affect the way diagnoses are written and construed, and probably what is done to clients as well. It is clear, therefore that the solution to the problems Kadushin and Kaplan note is not simply more specificity and rigor on the part of clinicians. While these are obviously important, part of the solution must come from an organizational structure that facilitates systematic and focused diagnoses and provides appropriate service responses. This issue highlights the inextricable interconnection of clinical practice and the agency en-

*Ibid., p. 17.
†Ibid., p. 18.
‡Lynn Kaplan, unpublished student log, Hunter College School of Social Work, 1982.

vironment in which it takes place. It also shows clearly that a social work clinician cannot conceptualize his or her work as a form of private practice taking place in an office provided by the agency. There is no such thing as totally autonomous practice. One's practice can be relatively autonomous, in the sense of providing a great deal of room for initiative and creativity, but it cannot be autonomous in the sense of totally lacking organizational constraint. Because of this, it is necessary for clinicians to participate in agency policy setting and decision making. This participation does not imply that clinicians must have the final say on all policy issues, but must include possibility of clinicians making their ideas and views felt. If clinicians do not do this or are not permitted to do this, their work will be affected nonetheless.

Every diagnostic assessment rests upon some theory of causation that explains the connection between observable facts. Some have suggested that clinicians are not in a position to study their own practice. They base their case on the assumption that the role of the clinician is to help people in need, and not to study them or the helping process. To study practice requires disinterestedness and iconoclasm: one must be one's own harshest critic and question all authority. Yet, as Edward Shoben has stated: "When the chips are down, as they generally are in professional practice, skepticism . . . is a luxury that few can afford."* Roseblatt notes that "the inevitable temptation of clinicians is for them to view their work in terms of their hopes and to avoid gathering information that produces dissonance. This is especially so when clinicians are expected to be accountable for the defects in their practice."† In these circumstances, when they perform well as researchers and identify flaws in their practice, they cause trouble for themselves as clinicians.

Whether Rosenblatt is correct or not, it is clear that the agency affects clinicians' ability to be systematic and thoughtful about their work. The agency must be open to consideration of its theories and practice principles, and this openness should certainly be an object of clinicians' reform activities in the agency.

There is no question that it is threatening to have one's practice confidence threatened. If one has been acting on certain principles for fifteen or twenty years, opening these to questions may seem to open one's professional life to question. An attack on an idea is often taken in such a situation as an attack on a person.

It is striking that clinicians who have strong empathic feelings toward their clients act in a most nonempathic way toward their colleagues when issues of practice theory are involved. It is as if their conscious use of self is put into abeyance whenever theoretical disagreements occur. The same clinician who scrupulously partializes problems will engage in global

---

*Quoted in Aaron Rosenblatt, "Research Models for Social Work Education," in Briar, Weissman, and Rubin, *Research Utilization in Social Work Education*, p. 24.
†Ibid.

thinking in an argument over Freudianism or behaviorism or systems theory.

What clinicians need to do is to gather, on a case-by-case basis, evidence that adds to the common knowledge about the utility of particular techniques. Harvey Johnson and others, for example, use a technique of individual goal planning to monitor the performance of clients in treatment. An outline for monitoring a client's participation in treatment group activities allows the clinician to define the compliance goal for the client, its rationale, different possible levels of attainment, treatment techniques, and so on. Although this approach does not measure ultimate treatment outcomes, the practitioner can learn a great deal about the potential for treatment success by monitoring the extent to which the client is engaged in the treatment process:

Goal Plan

Name of Girl: Joan Smith

Goal for Girl: That Joan participate in group activities. (Group activity is an activity that requires Joan to interact with other girls.)

Necessity of Goal (How will achievement of this goal help this girl?): Joan has poor relationships with her peers. In participating in group activities where she is required to "risk" herself, Joan will develop skills in the area of relating to her peers.

Levels of Predicted Attainment:

   Level 1: Most unfavorable outcome thought likely: Joan participates in an average of one group activity per week.

   Level 2: Less than expected success: Joan participates in an average of two group activities per week.

   Level 3: Expected level of success: Joan participates in an average of three group activities per week.

   Level 4: More than expected success: Joan participates in an average of four group activities per week.

   Level 5: Most favorable outcome thought likely: Joan participates in an average of five group activities per week.

Target Outcome: Three months or time of next case conference.

Measure: Living unit staff will keep a weekly record of the number of group activities Joan participates in. They will report the average per week at next conference.

Service Technique: Life space counseling from child care staff regarding how to relate to peers.

Completed by: _____ *

This goal plan depends on the staff's keeping track of the number of times the client participates in group activities. Goal attainment scaling does not have to be based on numerical measurement; it only has to be

*Harvey L. Johnson, Carolyn Nutter, Lyne Callan, and Richard Ramsey, "Program Evaluation in Residential Treatment: Some Practical Issues," *Child Welfare* 55 (1976): 283. Reprinted with special permission of the Child Welfare League of America.

empirical, which means that it is subject to verification through observable events. So, for example, a behaviorist social worker may assess a client's depression quantitatively by counting the number of times during a treatment session that the client begins to cry and timing the duration of the crying episodes. A nonbehaviorist clinician might make a similar diagnostic judgment based on the client's body language, self-reports about affect and activity, and so on. While the nonbehaviorist does not translate these observations into numerical indices, the judgment that the client is depressed is nonetheless empirical; in other words, it is based on observable client behavior.

An empirical but nonquantitative approach to diagnostic assessment and treatment planning and evaluation is the Problem-Oriented Record (POR). This technique involves the restructuring and reorganization of client process records so that they satisfy both agency accountability requirements and the knowledge development needs of the practitioner. This approach is particularly helpful in that it encourages the social worker to be explicit about client problems, treatment goals, and progress without requiring him or her to translate them into numerical indicators. As a consequence, psychodynamically oriented social workers often find it more compatible with their treatment orientations and ideologies than the more quantitative practice-research techniques.

In the following article, Rosalie Kane describes in detail the use of POR and its potential for knowledge building and social work education.

Look to the Record*

ROSALIE A. KANE

• • •

The Problem-Oriented Record

The Problem-Oriented Record (POR) was developed by Weed for the purpose of reforming the unwieldy and impractical medical record.† It provides a framework of organization that permits even long records to become coherent, usable, and goal-oriented. With a few adaptations, Weed's recording system could be applied to all methods and fields of social work practice. Since the goal was to correct many of the same flaws in the medical record that have been noted in the social work record, familiarity with POR could be useful to professional social work. The

*Excerpted with permission from *Social Work* 19 (1974): 412–419. Copyright 1974, National Association of Social Workers, Inc.

†Lawrence L. Weed, *Medical Records, Medical Education, and Patient Care* (Cleveland: Case Western Reserve University Press, 1969).

plea here is not for social work to adopt the Weed system wholesale, but for the profession to develop methods of record keeping that can be utilized on all fronts in the struggle for accountability.

Before describing POR, it might be well to address the issue of the appropriateness of any model for social work recording. In Hamilton's classic monograph on the subject, she suggests that a model form would be inimical to social work practice:

> There is no such thing as a model record, or, if there were, one's first duty would be to destroy it because people and situations and agencies differ each from the other and the record should reflect these variations and particulars. The record should be a flexible instrument responsive to the kind of case, to agency functions, to realistic conditions of practice, to what group uses the record, and what clerical help is available.*

Despite this caution, however, Hamilton insists that a record is to be used and, therefore, "within a well-organized framework workers must be able to find the significant facts easily."† POR reconciles the need for flexibility and usability. The reader does not have to make heroic efforts to decide or guess which facts are "significant," because all entries are linked to previously defined problems. Such a framework neither dictates nor stifles content but allows it to emerge in a meaningful form.

POR consists of four components that correspond to four tasks in problem solving: (1) acquisition of an adequate data base, (2) identification of problems derived from the data base, (3) development of a plan for each problem identified, and (4) implementation of the plan.

Data Base

The data base comprises the initial information that is collected when a case is opened. Such material is traditionally included on face sheets or in a social history. The essential data from which problems are identified vary according to the nature of the agency, the type of presenting problem, and the demographic characteristics of the population served. For example, a suicide prevention center would, in all likelihood, decide on a different kind and amount of baseline data than would a child guidance clinic. The crucial issue is that the data base should be defined in advance.

Once an appropriate data base is defined, the information must be gathered consistently. Too frequently, within a single agency, and even within the work of a single practitioner, there is variation in the amount of background material that is recorded. Such material may range from long

---

*Gordon Hamilton, *Principles of Social Case Recording* (New York: Columbia University Press, 1945), pp. 8–9.
†Ibid.

and detailed to short and skimpy and seems to be dictated solely by mood and convenience. But if records are to be reviewed in terms of prognosis or effectiveness of intervention, the initial data must be uniformly collected and transcribed. According to Weed:

> Failure to define the initial data base is like playing football with a different number of men each time on a field of no definite length. Individual plays can be perfected but their value is unclear because their context is not constant and complete.*

If the worker's customary level of intervention is with the group or the community, the principle of establishing baseline data still applies. The group worker must decide in advance what data are needed for each prospective client. The worker in a youth recreation program might collect different material than the worker in a group psychotherapy setting, and the group worker who acts as a consultant to a residential agency with a constantly shifting population might decide to collect different data still.

Similarly, the community worker requires minimum data before identifying the problems around which he will structure his activities. Such data should not be collected haphazardly or, as sometimes happens, on the basis of what reports happen to exist, but should be the result of preliminary decisions about the information necessary to begin treatment. Fund raising for a community chest, conference planning for a state agency, or legislative lobbying for a community action program are all activities that call for a specialized data base as a starting point. In each instance the minimum necessary information should be predetermined.

The Problem List

A number of problems emerge after the baseline data are collected. As soon as possible, these problems are listed by number on a sheet at the front of the record. For convenience, many hospitals have devised forms that allow current problems and problems that have been resolved or are dormant to be entered into an active or inactive column.

The problem list is exactly what its name implies—a list of problems but not necessarily a list of diagnoses. A problem may be any matter that concerns the worker, the client, or both. People require help with problems, not with diagnoses. The problem is listed at the level of sophistication possible at that time. "Loss of sleep" is a clear statement of a problem. Later it might be realized that the problem of insomnia is caused by illness, a noisy neighborhood, or even by a constellation of

*Weed, *Medical Records*, p. 16.

factors grouped together as "depression." Similarly, "fear of close relationships" is a problem that may or may not be part of the diagnosis "schizophrenia." Listing the problem as it is manifested avoids premature or unnecessary labeling.*

A label peculiar to social work is the "multiproblem family"—a designation that carries a world of innuendo but little specific meaning. The problem list of the POR forces the recorder to avoid jargon or sweeping categories and to indicate problems at the highest level of understanding supported by the available data.

A problem may be listed by a diagnosis if the recorder has sufficient information and the ability to synthesize the components to draw a valid conclusion. In such a case "depression" becomes a cue that conveys real information to the reader. But it is equally respectable for a problem to be listed without being placed in a pattern or using technical terminology.

Physicians using POR are encouraged to list such social problems as unemployment or inadequate housing. They may not be able to be precise about the social problem or even plan to deal with it directly, but the list should convey at a glance an overview of the problems as they are currently identified. Similarly, the worker in a social agency would list medical problems or legal problems.

The problem list, then, serves as an index of the entire record. Problems are eliminated from the record as soon as they are resolved, and the data of resolution is noted. Occasionally a problem is removed from the list by redefinition—for example, "school failure" might later be redefined as "retardation" or "poor hearing." Even after the problem is resolved, its identifying number is not reassigned; each number is used to trace the course of a single problem through the record.

In Table 1 the first four problems were delineated on the basis of data acquired at the intake interview, whereas Problems 5 and 6 were added later. Problem 4 was considered to be resolved in June, presumably after the client had found and been able to hold an appropriate job. The particulars of the client's employment would be entered in the body of the record under the date shown on the problem list. Problem 6, although not a social problem, has obvious implications for the client's behavior.

The problem list is a convenient device for improving and focusing social worker intervention. It is a concise summary of the problems and their state of resolution and serves as an index of dated entries in the body of the record. It also provides a checklist of all items needing attention to prevent the social worker from focusing exclusively on a single problem. In social casework such a format could be an antidote to the rambling, chronological style of recording in which original problems can be lost or forgotten. In group work the list would include not only the problems of

---

*See D. L. Rosenham, "On Being Sane in Insane Places," *Science* 179 (1973): 250–258, for a chilling article on the "stickiness" of the label of schizophrenia. He points out that the subsequent behavior of persons so diagnosed is likely to be interpreted to fit.

Table 1. Problem List for a Client Interviewed by
a Probation Department

Active Problem	Date	Inactive Problem	Date
1. Probation for auto theft	4/10/73		
2. Uncontrollable at home	4/10/72		
3. No male figure	4/10/72		
4. No spending money or job	4/10/72	Resolved	6/5/72
5. Failing school	1/6/73		
6. Mother develops cancer	3/8/73		

individual members but the worker's problems in managing the group. Again, such a list would prevent the worker from neglecting the problems of any one member.

The Plan

Once the baseline material is recorded, two rules govern all subsequent entries. Each note in POR must refer to a specific problem, and the basis for all decisions and information must be recorded. The following format for the note evolves: (1) subjective information, obtained from a client or a customer group; (2) objective information, gleaned from clinical observation, tests, referral information, census data, and so forth; (3) assessments or conclusions drawn from the data; and (4) the plan. (The acronym SOAP has proved a useful reminder of the four components of the note.) The plan generates more data, both subjective and objective, which call for reassessment and a new plan. Thus, the process is a continuous cycle.

An early progress note listed in the problem list as Problem 2—"uncontrollable at home"—might read as follows:

Subjective: Mrs. X is very upset and worried about John's behavior; she claims he is out all night and openly defies her. She fears she will lose her grip on the younger children as well.

Objective: The juvenile court record indicates that the disturbed relationship between Mrs. X and John did not begin until he entered his teens. Although the worker has observed affection between John and his mother, Mrs. X's interactions with her son have usually been in terms of demands. The school record reports no discipline problems with John.

Assessment: The worker feels that Mrs. X has no conceptual tools for working with her children and that her sense of helplessness and lack of knowledge are contributing to her ineffectual management.

Plan: (1) Refer Mrs. X to an effectiveness training group for parents; (2) arrange for baby-sitting services for the younger children during group meetings; (3) evaluate after two months.

The time dimension included in the plan has obvious importance for monitoring the effectiveness of interventions.

If a system such as POR is used, a long social study followed by a curt and vague prescription for treatment, such as "family therapy" or "supportive treatment to enhance self-esteem," would no longer be possible. Just as POR forces all physicians to relate all orders for drugs and tests to a specific problem, so would social workers be expected to associate plans, referrals, or requests for consultation to a numbered problem. In institutional settings or agencies where other personnel help to carry out plans, POR has the effect of helping each participant understand why he is acting in a certain manner.

The organization of notes in POR will permit the social worker, his supervisor, or an outside consultant to review the way in which a particular problem is handled simply by scanning the entries under the identifying number. Similarly, an administrator or a researcher can extract from a volume of records all entries pertaining to a particular problem and trace both the nature of the problem and the way the agency has handled it.

Action

[Scott Briar has] asserted that this age of accountability takes nothing for granted.* Social work records, unfortunately, have taken for granted that action invariably follows planning. POR takes note of the results of any actions taken. In essence, three kinds of plans are available to the worker in approaching a problem. He may get more information, intervene, or do nothing and observe the problem. In each instance the plan should be put in a time frame to ensure that the next progress note will indicate whether the plan was in fact implemented. Returning to the case example given above, a note under Problem 2 written two months later might read:

> *Subjective:* Mrs. X states that she feels more relaxed about John, and John reports less quarreling at home. He claims he does not feel as "uptight."
> *Objective:* Mrs. X has been attending a parents' group at the Q Agency since May 1. Her attendance has been perfect, and the group leader reports that she has been actively involved. The worker has observed her using the new precepts she has learned in discussing a problem with John.
> *Assessment:* The problem seems much diminished.

*Scott Briar, "The Age of Accountability," editorial, *Social Work* 18 (Jan. 1973): 2.

Plan: (1) No further direct intervention after the group ends in two weeks; (2) review in a month to determine if the summer vacation brings new stress; (3) evaluate at that time for removal to inactive list.

The point-form enumeration of the plan is a helpful device to facilitate its implementation, especially if another worker has to handle the case.

The closing summary should also be problem-oriented. For each numbered problem, an entry should indicate the status of that problem, the prognosis, and the recommendations. This affords a succinct picture of the progress and status of the problem at its close. . . .

Implications for Social Work

Social work practice invariably involves complex, interrelated problems. Weed writes that "multiple problems may interact and sophisticated understanding and management of any one of them requires at least an awareness of all of them."* The Problem-Oriented Record would help social work practitioners keep these complexities in the foreground.

POR could help make social work plans explicit and provide a technique for determining whether goals have been met. At present social work is called to account by outsiders to prove its effectiveness in terms of such measurable indicators as a decline in delinquency, decrease in divorce, or even reduction of welfare rolls. Although social workers point out that such measurements are not always appropriate to their goals and that the profession's process is so individualized as to defy a single indicator of success, they are often helpless in providing alternative ways to evaluate their activities. POR would facilitate the definition of problems and goals in terms of professional values. Practitioners would need to define problems at the outset, and these would not disappear until solved or consciously reformulated. Thus, the practice would be exposed to risk. If social workers fail to define problems, they may never be able to report success, but neither do they have to report failure. The realization that the client had ten problems at the outset and had the same ten problems one year later would be sobering information for both the worker and the agency.

Those who object to the notion of holding social workers to stricter account often argue that social work is an intuitive process that eludes description. Such a rationalization would probably not convince hard-headed disbursers of funds. Nor would it convince Weed. A similar objection to POR was voiced by physicians who claimed that its confining rules would detract from the "art of medicine." Using analogies from art and music, Weed suggests that such criticism shows a misunderstanding of the form and discipline that make art possible:

*Weed, *Medical Records*, p. 105.

Art is in relationships and combinations of objects and acts as well as in the single objects and acts themselves, and the degree to which the quality or lack of quality of our art can be discerned. . . . The question is whether the unstructured, undisciplined form we have had is a vehicle adequate to the full expression of medicine as a science and an art.*

The Concept of Audit

The Weed system has greatly facilitated the audit of medical records by the physician's peers. POR may be reviewed by asking four seemingly simple questions: (1) Is the data base complete and appropriate? (2) Have the problems been fully identified? (3) Is there an appropriate plan of action for each problem? (4) Is there any indication that the plan has been carried out?

Physicians as a group are no more eager to expose themselves to peer review than are social workers. Yet reports of routine auditing programs have shown that it is possible to institute an audit of POR by a random review of active records so that any remedial action can be taken immediately.† At first such auditing may be threatening, but once the participants realize the practical implications of the procedure, it will also be exciting.

For social work, the notion of peer audit has not been widely developed, but it could evolve into an attractive idea. The time-honored techniques of supervision in social work—a combination of teaching, counseling, and administrative control—are producing discontent among practitioners. A survey indicates that social workers most resent those aspects of the supervisory process that they perceive as not directly related to professional concerns.‡ At present some workers are striving for "autonomous practice" that would be contingent on professional sanctions, legal licensure, and professional surveillance by peers.§ The last requires a form of record keeping that lends itself to peer review.

Leaving aside the question of autonomous practice, the Problem-Oriented Record could lead supervision away from issues of personality to focus on the substance of practice itself. One reason why social work supervision, especially in casework, has tended to concentrate on the adjustment of the worker is because the interaction between the worker

*Lawrence L. Weed, "Questions Often Asked about the Problem-Oriented Record," in J. Willis Hurst and H. Kenneth Walker, eds., *The Problem-Oriented System* (New York: Medcom Press, 1972), pp. 53–54.

†Robert W. Putsch, III, John Humphrey, and J. S. Schuster, "Quality Care, Problem Orientation, and the Medical Audit," in Hurst and Walker, *Problem-Oriented System*, pp. 173–182.

‡Nina Toren, *Social Work: The Case of a Semi-Profession* (Beverly Hills, Cal.: Sage Publications, 1972), pp. 77–79.

§Laura Epstein, "Is Autonomous Practice Possible?" *Social Work* 18 (Mar. 1973): 5–13.

and client has been unobserved and unobservable. POR could give content and substance to the supervisory process.

Social Work Education

All the advantages that POR would have for practice also apply to the teaching of social work students. By reviewing the records, the instructor would be able to discern the proficiency of the student in gathering and organizing information, the accuracy of assessment, and the appropriateness and resourcefulness of planning. POR gives the instructor the advantage of precisely identifying any weakness in diagnostic skill—for example, a lack of sophistication in identifying problems—and of noting any improvement.

Another compelling advantage of POR as an educational tool is its ability to highlight the recorder's actions and responses. Professional education may be defined as a process of planning behavioral change; its goal is to produce practitioners who perform in the desired way. POR exposes the learner's behavior so it may be reinforced or corrected. Student-teacher interactions can focus specifically on what the student has done and why.

POR cannot be used as a substitute for direct observation of the student. It will not indicate whether the student's information is accurate or whether he conducted himself during an interview in such a way as to win the trust of a client. Neither is POR an adequate instrument for measuring interview and relationship skills. But to pinpoint strengths and weaknesses in problem solving, the Weed system is superb. More important perhaps, use of POR will inculcate in the student the notion that he has a responsibility for acting purposefully in solving identified problems and in evaluating his plans to see whether he is achieving the desired results. Once the student realizes that good intentions and a flair for building a relationship are not enough, he is on the way to becoming an "accountable" practitioner.

In a discussion of process recording for students, Dwyer and Urbanowski make a plea for greater structure.* They point out that the student needs a format to clarify his thoughts concerning the purpose of an interview and practice in organizing concepts in relation to contacts. To this end they devised a plan to give form to process recording. POR would answer their requirement that the student be provided with "an operational framework that can be adapted to his own particular needs and his own rate of growth and development."†

---

*Margaret Dwyer and Martha Urbanowski, "Student Process Recording: A Plea for Structure," *Social Casework* 46 (1965): 283–286.
    †Ibid.

Summary

It has been shown that POR is a format that could be adapted to recording all aspects of social work practice. Its four components follow logical steps of problem solving. POR makes it possible to keep the entire group of problems and their interrelationship in mind and prohibits the record from focusing on diagnosis rather than on intervention.

A system such as POR allows a review of social work practice in terms of whether it achieves its own objectives. For this reason, POR could be a useful tool for supervision, administration, and teaching, as well as a means for the practitioner to address the total situation.

———————————

Monitoring and Evaluation: Behaviorist and nonbehaviorist practitioners alike have to concern themselves with the validity or accurancy, of their judgments and observations. In other words, are the observable events consistent with the labels one is attaching to them? Judgments about validity apply to diagnosis assessments as well as to the evaluation of treatment outcomes. Thus, one might raise questions about whether a diagnosis of "borderline personality" has been correctly applied, asking whether the diagnosis is consistent with observable events in the client-worker interaction and whether those events fall into a pattern consistent with the diagnosis.

Likewise, when we assert that a client has "improved" during the course of treatment, the judgment should be made on the basis of observable events. Is the client's affect more cheerful? Do the client's verbalizations include more positive statements about his or her own situation? Is the client more actively engaged in work, family, community, and so on? One need not count these phenomena to make judgments based upon them.

Sometimes observable events are not so easy to interpret, and more subtle clinical skills are called for. For example, a client may demonstrate a remarkably cheerful disposition even though something disastrous has just happened. In such circumstances, the clinician must make a judgment of the client's psychological status that considers both affect and the circumstances within which it is displayed. This judgment, however, is not less empirical than simpler ones—in fact, it includes more empirical information about observable events, including the appropriateness of the client's affect to what is known about his or her situation.

In practice, all clinicians make these judgments all the time. Workers who systematically evaluate and monitor their practice, however, give a great deal of attention to the validity of their judgments. Monitoring refers to the empirical assessment of the extent to which clients are receiving the prescribed intervention in quality and quantity consistent with agency and professional standards. In addition, it can focus on the extent to which the client complies with the implied or explicit contractual agreement with the worker. Self-monitoring can even go beyond performance on an individual case or with a single group. Clinical social workers may set peformance objectives for themselves involving the quality or quantity of services they provide.* So, for example, an adoption caseworker may try to locate 10 percent more potential adoptive homes in the next year.

Effective monitoring requires setting qualitative or quantitative standards, gathering and analyzing data on the attainment of these standards, assessing discrepancies between desired and actual performance on the part of the clinic or the client, and making decisions to continue, stop, or modify the implementation strategy depending on the foregoing assessment.

Monitoring should be based upon valid and reliable information. Research concepts and techniques can facilitate the systematic collection, analysis, and interpretation of this information. To do this, however, one need not be a highly sophisticated researcher. In the following article we see how much can be learned about a community mental health program simply by looking at attendance data.

Using Attendance as a Means of Evaluating Community Mental Health Programs*

RICHARD KREBS

It seems that one of the reasons that some mental health professionals do not do research is that they feel that research must involve control groups, complex statistical analyses, and elaborate measures. In the following paper, it will be suggested that the evaluation of programs can be done rather simply, with a minimum of data collection and a research design that can be handled by a clerical person.

The research technique involves noting whether or not a person is present and then relating presence or absence to other variables.

---

*For a discussion of the selection of performance objectives, see Donald K. Granvold, "Supervision by Objectives," *Administration in Social Work* 2 (1978): 199–210.

*Excerpted with permission of the Human Sciences Press, 72 Fifth Ave., N.Y., N.Y., 10011, from *Community Mental Health Journal* 7 (1971): 72–77. Copyright 1971.

Outside of the professional world, attendance is continually used as an indicator of success or failure. "He stood me up. I guess he wasn't really interested after all." "There were 68,000 fans at the baseball game. It was one of the biggest games of the year." Clinicians also use attendance as an indicator of motivation. "He failed to show up for his first appointment. I wonder if he really wants to be in therapy?"

Admittedly, attendance is a global measure. There are many reasons why people do or do not attend something. They may come because they feel that what they are going to is worthwhile. They may come because someone they fear or respect tells them they should. They may come because there's nothing else to do. They may stay away for a wide variety of reasons: illness, bad weather, other commitments, lack of interest.

While the measure of attendance undoubtedly harbors many variables that do not really interest the program evaluator, it seems reasonable to assume that basically a person attends a program because it is seen by him as worth the effort involved to attend. Most program directors are probably already using attendance as a basic indicator of the success of their program. If no one comes, the program has obviously failed; if people come, the possibility exists that they have been helped.

Obviously, this technique does not give conclusive results. It does, however, make it possible for a program director to begin to systematically study what is going on in his program.

The remainder of the paper will be concerned with two examples of research or program evaluations that utilize attendance as the basic measure of success or failure.

The Effectiveness of a Community Worker in the Follow-Up Care of Psychiatric Patients

Sinai Hospital's Community Mental Health Center used community workers to help to get patients to keep their appointments for follow-up care after they were discharged from Springfield State Hospital. How the community liaison workers did their job is described elsewhere.* Patients' attendance at their initial follow-up visit was used as an index of how effectively the workers were accomplishing their task.

Figure 1 suggests that the community liaison workers did indeed have a positive influence. More patients kept their appointments after the liaison had been established than had before the liaison existed. It is interesting to note the downward trend in the percentage of patients keeping their appointments that occurred after December 1966. Between January and June of 1966, the first worker reported that she feeling overwhelmed by the enormity of her task and started to withdraw from regular contacts on the wards. The big drop in attendance that occurred

*Richard Krebs, *Report for Fiscal Year 1969*, mimeograph, Department of Mental Hygiene, Maryland.

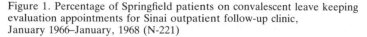

Figure 1. Percentage of Springfield patients on convalescent leave keeping evaluation appointments for Sinai outpatient follow-up clinic, January 1966–January, 1968 (N-221)

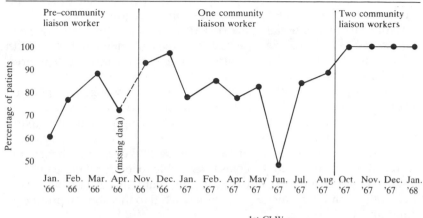

in June was at the time of her vacation. It is clear that her absence had a detrimental effect. In July, she learned that a second worker would be joining her shortly and this boost enabled her to again begin visiting the wards on a regular basis. The dramatic shift came when the second worker actually started at Springfield in October of 1967; from that point on attendance ranged between 95 and 100 percent. . . .

An Attempt to Shift a Group of People Away from Their Role of Patients

The Therapeutic Social Club was developed by the community mental health center staff in the fall of 1968 as a transition program for chronic psychiatric patients. For many chronic patients the visit to the center for medication and counseling had been one of the few activities that brought them outside of their homes. The program was designed to help move this group of patients out of the regular out-patient department therapies, out of their patient status, back into the community. This transition had to be made with a minimal degree of threat so that it would not be necessary for these patients to return to a psychiatric hospital.

Two means of attaining the goal of a patient's functioning socially in the community were considered: (1) helping the individual patients find suitable social groups in the community; or (2) moving a total group of patients out into the community as a social club. The second alternative was decided on for several reasons that will be discussed later.

Initially two groups of ten patients each were set up. Each group was run by a community liaison worker with consultation from a senior social worker and a staff psychiatrist. Assisting the community liaison worker were a psychiatric technician and several volunteers.

After several weeks the two groups merged because one of the community liaison workers left Sinai to take another job.

Within an organizational framework of a rotating chairman and permanent secretary and treasurer selected from the club membership and with the assistance of the staff, the group was able to plan and execute a series of social functions which were financially supported by Sinai.

The group went to the movies, race track, bowling, and planned several parties which were held in the center's dayroom. It is interesting to note that whenever the group began planning an outside activity, attendance dropped off (Figure 2). Actual attendance at these activities also tended to be quite poor. On the other hand, the activities held at the center were well attended. It seems reasonable to interpret these findings as indicating that any move into the outside community arouses anxiety in this group of chronic patients, and they reacted to this anxiety-producing situation by withdrawing.

The club members showed this same withdrawal pattern for the activity planned for June, a money-raising luncheon to be held at Sinai. This luncheon was to be open to the department staff as well as to friends and relatives of the club members. Again their was a decline in attendance as the plans were made. However, the activity itself was much better attended than those activities outside of the clinic (twelve for the lunch as compared to the four-to-eight range for the outside activities). While the increased pressure of having outsiders come into the group and trying to raise money rather than merely spending it did arouse anxiety in the group, they were able to continue functioning.

Because the club members had such difficulty moving out into the community even when they made this move with the support of the staff and other group members, the staff decided not to encourage the group members to individually join already existing community groups. Rather, an additional intermediate step was planned. The club moved out into the community as a group, staffed by the volunteers who had been working with the program. These volunteers were in turn supported by the professional staff who had been working with the club.

These two studies demonstrate how attendance can be used as simple evaluation technique in community mental health programming. It can be used both as an outcome measure, as it was in the first program, or as a means of studying the process or development of a program as it was in the second study. . . . Attendance can and should be used as a measure for evaluating programs for several reasons. (1) It has face validity. People generally come to things that have meaning for them and stay away from things that do not. (2) Attendance is an easily available piece of data that is usually reliable. Most centers already have procedures for keeping attendance. If they do not, the procedures are easily implemented, and attendance is one of the most reliable pieces of data available in a clinical setting. A person is either present or absent. The judgment is an easy one. (3) Given a measure that is reliable and has obvious face validity, it becomes possible to relate attendance to a wide range of variables.

Figure 2. Attendance at therapeutic social club

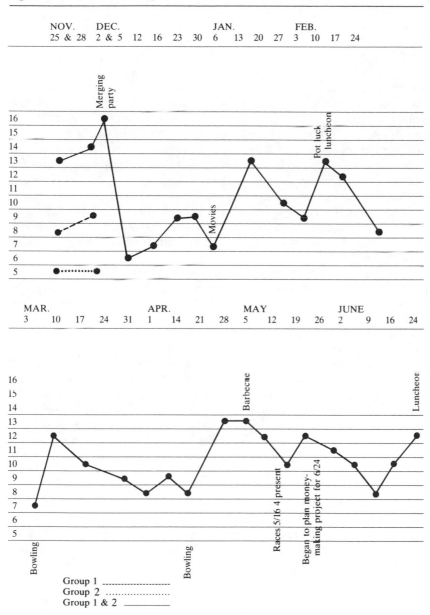

The program evaluator has in his hands a useful tool: attendance. The ways of using it are limited only by the imagination of the evaluator and the conceptual boundaries of the measure.

━━━━━━━━━━━━━━━━━━

Treatment evaluation is one of the two major types of evaluation that take place in social agencies. Whereas *program evaluation* focuses on the effectiveness and efficiency of whole programs, *treatment evaluation* attempts to evaluate the success of a single social worker with a single client or client group. Probably the most significant recent contribution to treatment evaluation methodology has been the development of *single-subject* (or *single-case* or *N = 1* or *practitioner*) *research*. Whatever the label used, this research attempts to generate information about the efficacy of treatment through a case-by-case approach using data collected during the course of treatment by the practitioner. This research method does not require the clinical social worker to accumulate large numbers of comparable cases to learn from his or her practice efforts. Every caseworker with a caseload of one or more can potentially employ this approach.

Single-case research may involve any number of research designs. Although they vary, each attempts to establish a causal connection between intervention and outcome on the basis of strategic comparisons. Thus, in the simplest single-case research design, the *AB design*, comparisons are made between the client's condition or circumstances before and after intervention.

In implementing the AB design, a series of measures of the client's problem are taken prior to intervention. This record is commonly referred to as a *baseline*. After treatment begins, the client is again assessed during each treatment session, using the same measures as were employed during the baseline period. The results are then graphed in a manner very similar to that used by Richard Krebs for the research described in his article. Comparisons are made between the client's pre- and post-intervention scores. To the extent that other possible explanations can be ruled out, the differences that emerge can be attributed to the worker's intervention.

Another important aspect of single-subject and program research is *data collection*. This process involves the systematic gathering of valid and reliable information about the individual client, the client's circumstances, and the client-worker interaction. These data may be gathered in a number of ways. Clients may fill out self-administered *questionnaires* concerning their problems; workers may *interview* them; and workers may employ *observational methods* that do not rely on the client's perceptions of his or her own problems. These observations may be recorded directly, or they may be culled from case records. The latter approach is referred to as *content analysis*. These are but a few of the methods employed to gather information for single-case research purposes. All are intended to produce valid and reliable data free from the individual biases of the worker.

Data analysis is the final stage of clinical evaluation. In its simplest form, it involves a logical interpretation of the facts collected and an inference about the impact of intervention. Or, as we indicate earlier,the worker might graph a client's progress and examine the results to see whether the client has improved over time. Although there are many more complicated approaches to data analysis, they all try to do the same things: to determine whether the client has benefited from social work intervention, to determine the extent of this benefit, to rule out other possible explanations for the improvement, and, finally, to determine whether the results of the research are generalizable.

In the following article, Neal Broxmeyer applies a relatively simple form of single-case methodology to his treatment of an eleven-year-old boy diagnosed as "borderline psychotic." The study describes not only the achievement of treatment goals for the youngster but also the relationship between achieving these goals and the worker's interventions. Thus, it contains elements of treatment monitoring as well as evaluation.

Practitioner Research in Treating a Borderline Child*

NEAL BROXMEYER

The present article seeks to illustrate the value of a relatively new form of social work called "practitioner research." It is hoped that one means of reducing the historical gap between researchers and practitioners will be demonstrated through an examination of a study undertaken by the author regarding his relationship with an eleven-year-old borderline psychotic client.† . . .

*Excerpted with permission from *Social Work Research and Abstracts* 14 (Winter, 1978): 5–11. Copyright 1978, National Association of Social Workers, Inc.
†For a discussion of this gap, see Aaron Rosenblatt, "The Practitioner's Use and Evaluation of Research," *Social Work* 13 (Jan. 1968): 53–59.

Phases 1 and 2

The study to be described took place at the Hawthorne Cedar Knolls School, a residential treatment center for emotionally disturbed children. An eleven-year-old boy, who will be called Robert in this article, was seen by the author in individual treatment twice a week from October 1976 through May 1977. The presenting problems that required Robert's placement were severe truancy from school and inadequate parental supervision. Other difficulties experienced by the boy and noted in the summer of 1976 at the time of intake were severe depression, poor peer relationships, basic mistrust, occasional losses of reality, and poor impulse control and tolerance of frustration. The study encompassed the first twelve interviews that took place with Robert over a period of approximately six weeks.

In Phase 1 of the study, which will now be summarized, the author examined data from the first interview with Robert, in which he tried to determine effective interventive techniques for dealing with the boy's agressive physical and verbal behaviors. In Phase 2 of the study, he examined data taken from the third interview through the twelfth interview. Data were not collected during the second interview. During Phase 1, the practice problem was formulated in two parts as follows: (1) how can Robert's destructive behavior be effectively controlled? and (2) how can Robert be helped to transform destructive behavior into socially appropriate behavior?

As might be expected, interventive techniques that satisfied both parts of the problem were not immediately discovered by the author. He spent most of Phase 1 trying out different techniques for controlling Robert's behavior, which was the more immediate aspect of the problem. The search for effective interventive techniques was complicated by the author's initial belief that firm limit-setting behavior would be incompatible with the resolution of the second part of the problem, namely, transforming Robert's destructive behavior into behavior that was socially appropriate. He felt that by serving in an authoritative, restrictive role he would make it virtually impossible for the boy to form a trusting relationship with him. However, by the end of the first session no other choice presented itself, and limit-setting behavior was implemented and found to be somewhat effective in modifying Robert's behavior. Socially appropriate behavior was not observable. At the end of the first session, the author was searching for interventive techniques that would modify Robert's aggressive and destructive behavior and increase his appropriate behavior. Specifically, it was hoped that Robert would be helped to engage in discussions about the meaning of his behavior.

At this point, the author consulted the work of Masterson in an attempt to discover effective interventive techniques. Masterson has stated that the borderline child's acting-out behavior should be seen as primarily defensive and symptomatic in nature.* He postulates that such behavior is used by children as a defense to protect themselves against underlying feelings of what he terms "abandonment depression" and to test whether the therapist cares and is competent enough to control them. In addition, such behavior protects children against their fears and anxieties about being abandoned by the therapist as they were in earlier relationships.

Masterson has identified three stages in the treatment process: testing, working through, and separation. In the testing phase, children continually employ their acting-out defense, and consequently, a therapeutic alliance (defined as the worker and the client working toward the same goal) cannot be established at this time. In the working-through phase, a child's defensive acting out diminishes significantly, and he or she begins to experience and work through underlying feelings of abandonment depression with the therapist. A therapeutic alliance can be established only at this time. The separation stage is marked by the child's significant working through of the abandonment depression feelings and by his or her ability to begin to function in an acceptable autonomous manner.†

Using Masterson's conception, the practice problem studied can be redefined in the following terms: how can Robert be helped to move from the acting-out, testing phase, in which a treatment alliance is not in effect, to the working-through phase of the treatment process, in which such an alliance is established? In the following statement, Masterson himself answers this question by indicating that such movement may be accomplished through limit setting:

> Not only is it impossible to wait for a relationship to be established before setting limits, but the setting of limits as early as possible is the unique means of establishing the therapeutic alliance.‡

Moreover, he has described the acting out phase as follows:

> The goal is the control of acting out (through limit-setting) and the establishment in the eyes of the patient of the therapist's competence and trustworthiness. . . . The control of acting out which brings affect to awareness and memory into consciousness enable the patient to begin the painful work of mourning involved in separation.§

These statements partially support the author's findings that limit-setting behavior was necessary to control Robert's acting out. At the same time, Masterson's comments are enlightening because he claims that, far from being prevented by limit setting, the treatment alliance is

*James Masterson, *Treatment of the Borderline Adolescent* (New York: John Wiley & Sons, 1972), pp. 42 and 114.
†Ibid., pp. 109–112.
‡Ibid., p. 238.
§Ibid., p. 110.

actually achieved only through the setting of limits. The author's initial findings after working with Robert neither reject nor confirm this hypothesis. This may be attributable to the following reasons: (1) Masterson's postulation is incorrect; (2) the proper limit-setting behaviors were not used by the author; or (3) the author's expectations for Phase 1 were too high.

Masterson's premise was tested in Phase 2 of the study. Acting-out behavior was defined as any behavior, verbal or physical, in which the client (that is, Robert) attempted to abuse himself, the author, or the surrounding environment. Limit-setting behavior was defined as any behavior with which the author tried to control the behavior of the client by saying "no," either physically or verbally. The author then set out to determine the validity of the following premise in his work with Robert: if the worker controls the client's defensive acting-out behavior through limit-setting behavior, the worker will be able to influence the client's behavior significantly and help him or her begin to experience, talk about, and understand underlying feelings that are present.

The author used an exploratory-formulative design in his investigation because such a design is flexible and helps the investigator prepare for systematic research in relatively undeveloped areas. As Finestone and Kahn have pointed out, this kind of design is concerned with the following:

> the conceptual definition of variables and ways to measure them, the search for useful hypotheses, the development of methodological approaches, and the investigation of the feasibility of research.*

In addition, the study was set up with a single-subject, criterion-oriented design and was organized accordingly around four elements: (1) the specification of the target behavior in measurable terms; (2) the measurement of the target behavior before, during, and after interventions; (3) the specification of the interventions in empirical terms, and (4) the specification of a criterion of success regarding the effectiveness of the interventions.

Finally, the study used an AX design in which A represented the baseline of data derived from the author's first meeting with Robert (Phase 1), and X represented the set of interventions practiced during the third through the twelfth meetings (Phase 2), or after planned intervention was derived from Masterson. The design is described as AX rather than AB because it involved the use of several interventions rather than one intervention only.† The data presented are taken from the author's written process recordings.

---

*Samuel Finestone and Alfred J. Kahn, "The Design of Research," in Norman Polansky, ed., *Social Work Research* (Chicago: University of Chicago Press, 1973), p. 61.

†Edwin Thomas, "Uses of Research Methods in Interpersonal Practice," in Polansky, *Social Work Research*, p. 269.

In Phase 1 of the study, the sequence consisting of Robert's specified aggressive and destructive behaviors in the first interview, the author's responses to the particular behaviors, and Robert's responses in turn were examined. Phase 2 of the study began with the premise that Robert's aggressive and destructive behaviors were not unique and could be substituted for one another because their aims were the same; that is, they all helped Robert defend himself against his feelings of having been abandoned. This premise suggests that a particular response on the part of the worker need not be limited to a specific behavior of the client but instead could be used with all forms of acting-out behavior. Masterson's support for this idea may be seen in the following observations, in which he expresses a belief that there are specific ways of working with all forms of acting-out behavior in the first stage of the treatment process:

> The therapist sets limits to control the acting out, defining it as self-destructive. Repeatedly, he points out the relationship of affect to behavior. . . . Tentative preliminary investigtions are made as to why someone would want to be so self-destructive. . . . [The suggestion that] a more constructive way of dealing with the feelings might be to check the impulse to act out and verbalize the feelings in the interview [is made].*

Accordingly, Phase 2 of the author's study examined the relationship between his behavior and Robert's response when all forms of the client's acting-out behavior were classified under one general category.

Phase 1 Findings

Tables 1 and 2 present critical findings and baseline data from Phase 1 of the study. Table 1 focuses on Robert's verbal acting-out behavior, which was defined as his vocalized expression of profane or nonprofane insults to the author. An example of the latter type of insult would be "You're an idiot!" Table 2 focuses on Robert's physical acting-out behavior, which was defined as any behavior in which he attempted to do bodily harm to the author or himself or to damage the surrounding environment. Examples of such behavior would be Robert's physically attacking the author, Robert's attempting to drop a filing cabinet on his own foot, and Robert's throwing marbles against the wall.

For purposes of the study, empathic behavior was defined as behavior in which the worker responded to the client with concern, acceptance, and understanding on both a feeling and an intellectual level. Talk about feelings was defined as the client's vocalization of an affective state. An example of such behavior would be Robert's saying, "I'm mad at you" to the author. It may be seen from Table 1 that the author responded to Robert's verbal acting-out behavior with empathic behavior alone a total

*Masterson, *Treatment of the Borderline Adolescent*, pp. 110–115.

Table 1. Worker's Behavior Regarding Client's Verbal Acting-out
Behavior, and Client's Response, Baseline, Phase 1

Worker's Behavior	Frequency of Worker's Behavior		Client's Response					
			Continues Acting Out		Discontinues Acting Out		Discontinues Acting Out with Talk about Feelings	
	Number	Percent	Number	Percent	Number	Percent	Number	Percent
Empathic behavior alone	8	100	2	25	4	50	2	25

of eight times. Robert discontinued his behavior four times and on two occasions discontinued his behavior with talk about his feelings. Thus, the author's response was effective in inducing Robert to discontinue his behavior 75 percent of the time.

Data presented in Table 2 indicate that limit-setting behavior by the author in response to Robert's physical acting-out behavior was much more effective than other responses in helping the boy discontinue his behavior. None of the author's responses were helpful in inducing Robert to talk about his feelings. In response to a total of twenty behaviors on the part of the author, Robert continued his behavior 70 percent of the time and discontinued his behavior 30 percent of the time.

In summary, data from Phase 1 that are shown in Tables 1 and 2 suggest that empathic behavior helped Robert discontinue his verbal acting out in 75 percent of the instances in which such behavior was used by the author. As already indicated, limit-setting behavior was the most effective of all responses in helping Robert discontinue his physical acting-out behavior; such behavior was effective in 45 percent of the intances in which it was used. Discontinuation of behavior with talk about feelings tended to be rare. It occurred in 25 percent of the instances in which empathic behavior was used in response to verbal acting out, and it did not occur at all with any intervention used in response to physical acting out. These findings suggest that some combination of empathic and limit-setting behaviors should be used to deal with all forms of acting-out behavior by the client. The author's behavior as represented in Table 3 moved toward this goal.

Phase 2 Findings

Table 3 describes that author's behavior in response to Robert's acting-out behavior, considered as one general category, and the boy's responses in turn after planned intervention was begun in the third inter-

Table 2. Worker's Behavior Regarding Client's Physical Acting-out Behavior, and Client's Response, Baseline, Phase 1

Worker's Behavior	Frequency of Worker's Behavior		Client's Response					
			Continues Acting Out		Discontinues Acting Out		Discontinues Acting Out with Talk about Feelings	
	Number	Percent	Number	Percent	Number	Percent	Number	Percent
No response	4	20	3	75	1	25	0	0
Empathic behavior alone	5	25	5	100	0	0	0	0
Limit-setting behavior:	11	55	6	55	5	45	0	0
Verbally says "no" to the client's behavior	2	10	0	0	2	100	0	0
Addresses the client's feelings, verbally says "no" to the client's behavior	3	15	3	100	0	0	0	0
Addresses the client's feelings, ignores the client's behavior	5	25	2	40	3	60	0	0
Physically restrains the client	1	5	1	100	0	0	0	0
Total	20	100	14	70[a]	6	30[a]	0	0[a]

[a]Number represents percentage of client's overall behavior.

view. Interventions 1 through 4 were interventive behaviors used by the author throughout the course of treatment in response to Robert's acting-out behavior. They were introduced successively until the desired outcome, which was, first, discontinuation of acting-out behavior, and, second, talk about feelings, was achieved. Thus the author's primary goal was to use Intervention 1 exclusively whenever possible, that is, whenever it was successful in achieving the desired outcome.

Intervention 1 consisted of the following behavior: the author pointed out to Robert the relationship of affect to behavior and then defined the boy's behavior as self-destructive. He then asked Robert questions about his underlying feelings. When Intervention 1 was not successful, Intervention 2 was introduced. Intervention 2 consisted of the following: the author pointed out to Robert the relationship of affect to behavior and then defined the boy's behavior as self-destructive. He then interpreted the boy's underlying feelings aloud to him.

Table 3. Worker's Behavior Regarding Client's Acting-out Behavior, and Client's Response after Planned Intervention, Phase 2[a]

Worker's Behavior	Frequency of Worker's Behavior		Client's Response					
			Continues Acting Out		Discontinues Acting Out		Discontinues Acting Out with Talk about Feelings	
	Number	Percent	Number	Percent	Number	Percent	Number	Percent
Intervention 1	29	42	10	34	10	34	9	31
Intervention 2	20	29	5	25	8	40	7	35
Subtotal	49	71	15	31	18	36	16	33
Intervention 3	12	17	2	17	6	50	4	33
Intervention 4	5	7	0	0	5	100	0	0
Subtotal	17	24	2	12	11	65	4	23
Intervention 5	3	4	3	100	0	0	0	0
Total	69	100	20	29[b]	29	42[b]	20	29[b]

[a]Percentages may not total to 100 because of rounding.
[b]Number represents percentage of client's overall behavior.

When Intervention 2 was not successful in at least inducing Robert to discontinue his behavior, Intervention 3 was introduced. Intervention 3 consisted of the following: the author threatened to stop the session and then defined Robert's behavior as self-destructive. He then proceeded to interpret the boy's underlying feelings. Intervention 4 was only introduced when Robert was rampantly out of control. In Intervention 4, the author asked a child care counselor to intervene physically. Although under most circumstances Intervention 4 was not introduced until the other interventions were carried out first, it was used immediately in some situations because of the severity of Robert's acting-out behavior. This is in accordance with the author's being criterion-oriented and interested in using the intervention most effective in changing the client's behavior. Intervention 5, which consisted of physical intervention by the author, was introduced under similar circumstances. It was soon discarded, however, because it was found to be completely ineffective.

It should be noted that Interventions 1 and 2 have an empathic, interpretive quality to them as well as a limit-setting quality. This is because they are concerned with both discontinuation of the acting-out behavior and talk about feelings connected to the behavior. Intervention 1 was used most frequently because it did not involve the author's use of educated guesswork to interpret Robert's behavior. In addition, it encouraged Robert to begin to connect his underlying feelings with his behavior, thereby fostering the development of an observing ego. Intervention 2 was used second most frequently because it also encouraged Robert to connect his underlying feelings with his behavior. The main drawback of this intervention was that it required the author to interpret Robert's feelings.

Intervention 3 and 4 were primarily concerned with the discontinuation of the acting-out behavior. Although a fairly severe limit-setting measure, Intervention 3 also allowed for the connection of underlying feelings to behavior, but this was not its primary goal. Intervention 4 was a strict limit-setting measure used only when absolutely necessary for the reasons already described. It was not concerned with inducing Robert to connect his underlying feelings to his behavior. In reviewing these interventions as a whole, it should be noted that they involve a move from empathic, interpretive measures by the author to more severe limit-setting measures.

An examination of the the data in Table 3 reveals that the desired outcome, the discontinuation of acting-out behavior followed by talk about feelings, occurred 29 percent of the time. Discontinuation of behavior without talk about feelings occurred 42 percent of the time. Overall, then, discontinuation of behavior occurred 71 percent of the time.

Interventions 1 and 2 accomplished their primary goal, namely, discontinuation of behavior with talk about feelings, in 33 percent of the instances in which they were used. Discontinuation of behavior alone occurred in 36 percent of the instances in which these interventions were used. Overall, discontinuation of behavior occurred 69 percent of the time when Interventions 1 and 2 were introduced. Interventions 3 and 4 accomplished their primary goal, namely, discontinuation of behavior alone, in 65 percent of the instances in which they were used. Discontinuation of behavior with talk about feelings occurred in 23 percent of the instances in which these interventions were used. Overall, discontinuation of behavior occurred 88 percent of the time when Interventions 3 and 4 were introduced.

These data suggest two interpretations. First, the author's combined use of mild limit-setting behavior with empathic, interpretive behavior was usually effective in inducing the discontinuation of acting-out behavior by the client. Subsequent talk about the client's underlying feelings often took place. Second, more severe limit-setting measures with less emphasis on empathic, interpretive behavior was effective in inducing discontinuation of acting-out behavior when previous interventions were unsuccessful. Less talk about underlying feelings took place when stricter limit-setting measures were used. Some combination of empathic and limit-setting measures is therefore seen as the most effective means of achieving the primary goal: discontinuation of behavior with talk about underlying feelings. . . .

Implications

It may be inferred from the study that limit-setting measures undertaken by the author were effective in helping the client discontinue his acting-out behavior. It can also be tentatively postulated that combining empathic, interpretative measures with limit-setting measures may be relatively effective in helping clients discontinue their acting-out behavior and connect the reasons for their behavior to their underlying feelings. These outcomes are primary goals for workers. In addition, it may tentatively be concluded that clients begin to use the relationship with the worker differently when limit-setting measures are introduced. Further research is needed to confirm whether this use of the relationship is in fact movement toward the establishment of a therapeutic alliance with the worker, perhaps indicating the beginning stages of what Masterson called working through.

These implications should not be viewed without reservations at this point because of the study's failure to control other possible factors adequately, such as the maturation of the client and the influences of elements external to the worker-client interaction. Nevertheless, the author considers it reasonable to state that the findings of the study provide better evidence of the effectiveness of intervention than would overall clinical impressions. . . .

Neal Broxmeyer's article demonstrates one approach to empirically based treatment. Earlier, in discussing Scott Briar's concept of the "clinical scientist," we noted the importance given to the selection of the practice methods and techniques known empirically to be the most effective ones. Treatment formulation should be as empirically based as diagnostic assessment. This requires a review not only of one's own practice experience in working with a given problem, but of the experiences of professional colleagues within and outside the agency in which one works. Consulting with a supervisor or co-worker is a good place to start. In addition, the clinical social worker should consult the professional literature to locate studies related to the problem.

The second process may require one to read some of the purely theoretical literature concerning diagnostic entities and their etiologies, case histories in the form of descriptive qualitative studies, and rigorous quantitative studies of specific intervention strategies. As these works are read and assessed for their applicability to the problem at hand, the criteria of validity, reliability, and representativeness should be kept in mind.

Validity—the correctness of clinical judgments—broken down by clinical researchers into three types. Some are more rigorous than others. The least rigorous, *face validity*, is based on the purely logical relationship between a judgment and the empirical events that serve as the basis for it. Hence, in assessing the face validity of a diagnostic label applied to a client, one would look at the logical relationship between the label and the evidence observed. In the context of the Broxmeyer study, for example, one would ask to what extent is Robert's behavior logically connected to the concept of "acting out."

Internal validity refers to the certainty with which one can say that a clinical intervention or set of interventions has actually helped the client. Here the concern is with the causal relationship between service to the client and the client's subsequent condition. In other words, if Robert has improved, how certain are we that his improvement is attributable to the treatment? Might it be the result of other events in Robert's life?

External validity concerns the extent to which findings based on a single case can be applied to other, comparable cases or are so idiosyncratic that they cannot be generalized. Researchers sometimes refer to this quality as *representativeness*. How typical a "borderline child" was Robert? Can we generalize from his response to treatment to the probable response of similar clients?

Reliability depends on the internal consistency of clinical judgments. There are two kinds of reliability. *Intra-judge reliability* refers to the consistency of the same clinician, over time, in applying clinical judgments. How consistent was Broxmeyer in categorizing Robert's different forms of acting-out behavior? If presented again with the same actions, would he categorize them the same way?

Inter-judge reliability concerns the consistency of one clinician's judgments with those of other qualified clinicians. Would other clinical social workers categorize Robert's behavior in the same way that Broxmeyer did?

Knowledge Development: Every clinician has an opportunity to participate in the development of practice knowledge by utilizing single-subject designs, by setting goals with clients and then comparing his or her results with those of other clinicians, and by keeping up with the literature. Every clinician should at least be a competent consumer of knowledge and research in the field. Intelligent consumers should have a frame of reference to guide their reading, asking first, what theories and assumptions about people an article is based on; and second, what practice principles are being articulated; and, finally what indices of success are taken as proof of the efficacy of those principles.

Although it is possible to criticize many articles and research studies on the basis of methodology and design, a clinician has a simpler option: comparing what is said in one article with what is said in another. Aaron

Rosenblatt was quoted above in this chapter as saying that skepticism and the ability to suspend judgment are difficult for practitioners; yet he overlooks the fact that clinicians have a strong desire to see their clients improve—not only for the clients' benefit, but also for their own self-esteem. It is difficult to work continually in settings where people have extreme difficulties if one cannot feel that one is succeeding in helping them. No amount of professional rationalizations about "resistances" or labels such as "hard to reach" will overcome the sense of frustration that clinicians must feel when they are unable to detect progress in their work.

Even though a clinician may not feel qualified to decide whether ideal standards of reliability and validity have been reached in a particular study, this does not discount the value of reading the article and thinking about the issues discussed. The clinician can derive practice principles and then try to apply them in single-case studies or consider their utility in relation to clients for whom he or she has set particular goals. In this sense even seriously flawed research can serve a practice purpose.

To be an effective consumer of research and to participate in the development of professional knowledge requires a certain amount of skepticism. It also requires a focus on outcomes, a concern for what actually happens to people, and a desire to collect these data. This attitude is not antithetical to clinical practice; rather, it enhances clinical effectiveness and efficiency.

Practice Analogues

Although many clinical social workers consider evaluation and clinical practice to be quite different, the two have a good deal in common. Both are problem-solving efforts that proceed in a logical fashion. Both are ultimately concerned with promoting clients' well-being through knowledge development. Both require the systematic and comprehensive collection of valid and reliable information. Both require a logical interpretation of empirical events. Both are concerned with issues of generalization to other clients. Both are concerned with the sharing of knowledge with other social workers.

Nevertheless, there are some important differences between the two. Most significantly, evaluation efforts are inherently cautious, emphasizing knowledge-based action. Often, however, social workers cannot wait for certainty to be achieved before they act: their first obligation is to help clients, whether or not there is complete knowledge about what kind of intervention would be most effective in the particular instance.

Related to this conflict is the ever-present concern of the evaluator with establishing causality—the cause-and-effect relationship between intervention and outcome. The evaluator's need to compare intervention and nonintervention when all other factors remain constant is the reason control groups are used in experimental studies. In single-case studies, the desire to validate cause-and-effect relationships is expressed in ABAB designs, withdrawal designs, and the like, which strategically eliminate or decrease service in order to determine whether positive effects diminish. Faced with the choice between the development of knowledge in this way and the maximum provision of service, however, the clinical social worker may opt for the latter.

On the whole, nevertheless, the therapeutic role of the clinical practice researcher and the role of evaluator have more in common than is generally assumed.

Attitudes, Values, and Skills

Probably more has been written about clinical social workers' antipathy toward research than any single topic discussed in this book. This rejection of research stems from several assumptions: (1) the research orientation is cold and antihumanistic; (2) clinical social work is an art that cannot and should not be subjected to scientific inquiry; (3) attempting to be more scientific will destroy the more creative, intuitive aspects of clinical practice; (4) research necessarily involves complicated statistical procedures and the use of control groups.

All these assumptions are invalid. We view research concepts and methods as adjuncts to quality service. Research-oriented practice does however, require that practioners be systematic in their work and willing to confront their failures as well as their successes and to build knowledge on both kinds of experience. As a matter of fact, the research-oriented practitioner probably learns more from failures than from successes.

Social workers should view research as not only an aid, but part of the challenge of the profession. Treated as simply another bureaucratic task, it is unlikely to provide information that will help in serving clients. Instead, it will probably be performed in a cynical, perfunctory manner that may satisfy accountability requirements but will do little to improve the quality of service.

The research-oriented clinical social worker places a high value on his or her own knowledge building as well as the accumulative knowledge building of the profession as a whole. This value recognizes an obligation to make a contribution to others besides one's present clients—those who will follow and those who will be served by one's colleagues. Professional values and ethical principles strongly endorse this position.

The most basic research skill is the ability to conceptualize one's own practice—to break it down into understandable, identifiable parts and to subject these parts to close scrutiny. The clinical social worker has to be able to ask whether the client is truly benefiting from service and on what basis this judgment is made. Would other competent observers make the same judgment? Would the client? To what extent can changes in the client's condition or behavior be explained by factors extraneous to the client-caseworker relationship? The clinical social worker who takes the role of researcher seriously must be scrupulously honest about the value of his or her practice. Only in this manner can the best possible service be offered to clients.

On occasion, and hopefully with increasing frequency, clinicians will find themselves acting as participants in formal research projects, as agencies hire professionally trained researchers in order to carry out some experimentally controlled study. In such situations clinicians have an important role to play. They should not automatically assume that because the researchers are skilled at designing experiments and analyzing and interpreting data the research will in fact be useful. Even for the relatively few research projects that have been carried out in agencies, experience has shown that the results are often less helpful when professional staff members do not participate in the formulation of the research design.

Clinicians can play an important part in social work research if they keep the following rules in mind.

1. They should urge administrators and researchers to consult with them on the purposes and potential consequences of the research prior to its initiation. There is nothing more devastating to a research project than an administration that wants to use it for fund-raising purposes, a clinical staff that feels that clients are being denied service, and a research staff that feels that clinicians and administration have no understanding of research.
2. The should recognize that research cannot begin until indices of success have been adequately described. It is demoralizing for researchers and agency staff alike to learn that clients are neither better nor worse off for having been involved in a program. Sometimes this may be true. At other times, though, inadequate attention to the validity of the indices results in an erroneous view of program effectiveness. Clinicians have an important part to play in setting indices of success.
3. They should urge that the impact model, the interconnection of programs and program parts, be completely explicated. For example, if a counseling program, an education program, and a work-training program are intended to help an adolescent prepare for a return to his or her natural parents, exactly how is this supposed to come about? Are the programs offered simultaneously or in sequence? What are the connection between changes in attitude and behavior and the program? Clinicians must impress upon researchers that they need to know not only the connections, but also where breakdowns occur, if there is to be improvement.
4. They should accept the idea that research is concerned both with the verification of facts and theories and with the development of knowledge. Evaluation must provide operating staff not only with information on how well or poorly they are doing their work, but, more significantly, with information on how they can improve it. Staff should insist that researchers keep this distinction in mind when formulating the focii of research.

Additional Readings

Grinnell, Richard M., Jr. *Social Work Research and Evaluation*. Itasca, Ill.: Peacock, 1981.

Jayaratne, Srinika, and Rona L. Levy. *Empirical Clinical Practice*. New York: Columbia University Press, 1979.

Reid, William and Audrey Smith. *Research in Social Work*. New York: Columbia University Press, 1981.

Tripodi, Tony, and Irwin Epstein. *Research Techniques for Clinical Social Workers*. New York: Columbia University Press, 1980.

Weissman, Harold H. "Clients, Staff and Researchers: Their Role in Management Information Systems." *Administration in Social Work* 1 (1977):43–52.

CHAPTER 10

EMPLOYEE

In the preceding chapters we have noted some of the tensions in the structure of agencies that affect how workers do their jobs—the conflict between the need for routine and the need for initiative; the need for goal attainment and the need for organizational survival; the need for clear lines of authority and the need for open communication. In this chapter we shall introduce another—the tension between the needs of clinicians as workers and the needs of clients.

Student-clinicians seldom anticipate any conflict between what they will want for themselves as worker-clinicians and what clients need. Although they may be aware of conflicts between their own learning needs and the needs of clients and agencies, their student status allows them to align themselves with the client. Once one the job, clinicians find that they are interested in salaries, working hours, working conditions, and job security and promotion. To suggest that there is no conflict between these interests and what might be best for clients is to obscure reality. How many clinicians are willing to work five evenings a week and on weekends? How many are willing to work for low wages, even though it can be shown that social work is a labor-intensive service and, to some extent, more money for workers means less money for services. No amount of apologetics concerning society's allocation of funds for defense or police or other services will obscure this fact.

If social work were a religious vocation, there would be les3 tension between the needs of clients and the needs of workers. Since it is not, this area presents a serious problem for clinicians. They will have to balance their concern for clients with their own personal concerns without sacrificing either of these legitimate interests.

To manage this tension realistically, clinicians must understand what rewards they seek from their work. They must also be aware of the stresses generated by the differing expectations and perceptions of agency clients, staff, and administrators. Burnout is the result of a clinician's inability to manage stress and the employing agency's inability to structure itself so as to mitigate stressful situations.

We believe that the major responsibility for avoiding staff burnout rests with the administration: this is what administrators are paid to deal with. Yet this book is focused on clinicians, and this chapter aims to provide clinicians with the tools and skills they need to maximize their personal rewards, even if the managers for whom they work are not as adequate as might be hoped. The chapter rests on the assumption that unless clinicians can attain some modicum of satisfaction in their work, in the long run they will be less effective and less able to help clients.

Overview

Most social workers desire job security, opportunities for professional development, adequate salary and opportunity for advancement, pleasant and stimulating colleagues, opportunities for autonomy and the exercise of initiative, and success with clients. In trying to attain these rewards, they meet a series of constraints from a variety of sources, including the clients themselves. The clients may not perceive the service as adequate or the worker as helpful. Often social workers deal with involuntary clients in welfare departments, probation departments, or mental hospitals.

Stress and Client Relationships: Although clients themselves may not be a source of satisfaction for the worker, a major index of professionalism is the ability to gain satisfaction from one's work with clients. Peter Blau has documented how eager and motivated new workers change when confronted with clients who lie to them or do not want their help.* These workers, in modern parlance, were "on an ego trip."

The article by Stuart Copans and associates that follows shows very clearly the stresses on workers and their need for support groups to help them deal with job strains and obtain the satisfactions that they need to work effectively, when such satisfactions are not immediately available from clients.

The Stresses of
Treating Child Abuse*

Stuart Copans, Helen Krell, John H. Gundy,
Janet Rogan, and Frances Field

. . . Work with high-risk families is difficult, and often it does not help the family's problem. In some cases this is because resources are too limited or intervention begins too late, but in many cases it is the lack of adequate

*Peter Blau, "Orientations towards Clients in a Public Welfare Agency," in Peter Blau, ed., *On The Nature of Organizations* (New York: John Wiley & Sons, 1974), pp. 170–186.
*Excerpted with permission from *Children Today* 8 (Jan.–Feb. 1979): 22–35.

training and support for workers that hampers the delivery of care. Work with high-risk families is particularly difficult because of the highly charged feelings aroused by such work. These feelings often prevent workers from making proper decisions and mitigate against good management of cases, even when the cases are adequately understood. A crucial part of a worker's training involves learning to recognize, examine, and work with these feelings. However, the process does not stop with training, and ongoing support for such self-examination should accompany any job involving work with high-risk families.

In this article we will describe an experimental child abuse training program developed for a wide range of community workers involved in the care of high risk basic knowledge about child abuse and continued with 1½-hour group meetings once a week for six months. The task of the group was to examine the feelings aroused in workers by their work and to discuss how these feelings aided or interfered with effective delivery of care.

Factors That Interfere With Delivery of Care

It is clear that knowledge about child abuse does not always lead to effective management of cases. What makes it so difficult for workers with adequate knowledge to function as competent professionals when dealing with high-risk families?

Through group discussions, eleven major sets of feelings and processes that frequently interfere with effective delivery of care by workers were identified. These were:

- anxiety about the effects of a decision;
- need for emotional gratification from clients;
- lack of professional support;
- denial and inhibition of anger;
- feelings of incompetence;
- denial and projection of responsibility;
- difficulty in separating personal from professional responsibility;
- feelings of being victimized;
- ambivalent feelings toward clients and about one's professional role; and
- the need to be in control.

Each of these sets of feelings warrants more detailed discussion. . . .

Anxiety about the Effects of a Decision

An example of this form of anxiety was given by a nurse who had been working with an alcoholic mother for over a year. It had become clear that the children were being mistreated; yet the mother kept promising to do better and threatened to kill herself if the children were taken away. The nurse was reluctant to report the case because of the mother's threat. After the group discussed the case, the nurse filed a report, the children were removed from the home, and the mother sought help from a local Alcoholics Anonymous group for the first time. The nurse was able to see that her fear that she would be responsible for the mother's suicide had led her to act inappropriately, exposing the children to unnecessary risk.

Need for Emotional Gratification from Clients

Most workers wanted to be liked by their clients and to feel professionally competent. High-risk families typically do not gratify these needs, causing much frustration for the worker. One worker from an outreach project recognized her need for gratification through discussion of the following case.

The worker had been seeing a family at home several times a week. Each time she had visited the family, she had been asked to do a favor for one of the members. Soon the favors occupied the whole visiting period and longer, as she was asked to do such things as drive the mother to an art show and borrow money for the family from a local priest. The worker began to feel that she was being "used" but hated herself for having that feeling. The family liked her, but she was becoming angry with them, and she also recognized that the family was not making any progress. As she discussed this case in the group, it became obvious to her that she did these favors for the family because she needed them to like her and to be grateful to her. By satisfying her own need to be liked, she was fostering excessive dependency. Once the group helped her to identify her need to be gratified by her clients, she was able to set limits on their demands on her, and they began to solve their own problems more effectively.

This same worker began to question her motives relating to other aspects of her behavior on this case. Through introspection in the group and through insights obtained from other members, she realized that she had been avoiding the mother's boyfriend and knowledge of his continued bruising of the child because she was afraid of him. As a result of working through her feelings in the group, she was able to approach the boyfriend's behavior therapeutically. She found him to be sad, lonely, and jealous of the attention the mother had gotten from her and very responsive to help. Subsequently, complaints from the neighbors that the boyfriend was beating the child ceased. Other group members also discovered that they acted inapproriately at times out of fear or to make their clients like them. Almost every group member also said that one of the most difficult things about his or her work was the clients' lack of appreciation.

Lack of Professional Support

Lack of support from their professional "family" of co-workers seemed a common problem among group members. This lack of ability to support one another was closely linked to the need for support mentioned earlier. As one worker put it, "I've got so much to deal with, I don't feel like having anybody else unload their problems on me."

One worker offered an example from her own agency. A new worker was having severe emotional difficulties. The other agency workers refused to recognize the man's symptoms, and he was allowed to continue to work. The group member who was attempting to deal with the situation alone had become so angry and agitated that she was unable to do her own work effectively. Finally, she came to the group in tears, asking for support. She had held back such a request earlier out of fear of "breaking down" in front of the group. Apparent in this case was a reluctance to admit "weakness" in self or others. Such reluctance is common and leads to difficulty in asking for, or giving, professional support.

After group discussion of this difficult problem, the worker returned to her agency and, by dealing directly with the head of the program, was able to obtain professional help for the disturbed worker and to have him temporarily relieved of his clinical reponsibilities.

Workers frequently came to the group with difficult cases they had not been able to discuss with their fellow workers or supervisors. Prior to the formation of the group, they had rarely discussed the uncomfortable feelings aroused in their work. As the group progressed, members were able to bring their feelings and conflicts into open discussion and, later, to resolution in their own agencies.

Denial and Inhibition of Anger

One worker described an instance when she had waited outside a house in the rain for hours knowing that the mother whom she had come to visit was inside, although no one answered when she rang the doorbell. When asked how she had felt about the situation, the worker said, "Oh no, I wasn't angry with her." After further discussion in the group, however, she discovered that she did have angry feelings toward that family. Other members of the group said that they usually avoided this kind of child abuse case and had become aware that their avoidance was one way of expressing anger that they did not consciously recognize. As one worker put it, "The nice thing about having a large caseload is that when a case gets too difficult or frustrating, you can ignore it for a while because you always have too much else to do."

Feelings of Incompetence

Feelings of incompetence seemed universal among our group members. These feelings are hardly surprising given the difficulties inherent in their work and their inability to support one another.

One very competent worker said that she felt professionally inadequate most of the time. Since she rarely received comments on her work, she assumed it was not good. It was a great relief to her to discover that others shared these feelings of failure. As a result of recognizing this problem in the group, many workers returned to their agencies and asked for critical feedback on their work. Most of them also felt much less incompetent, as they could see from case discussions that there is generally no "best way" or "right answer" in such work.

Denial and Projection of Responsibility

An outreach worker in the group told how she had been working with a family for several months and suspected that one of the children had been abused. She reported this and discussed the case briefly with the protective services worker, who agreed to see the family very soon. The outreach worker ceased to work with the family, assuming that the other worker had taken over. Two months later she checked on the family and discovered that they had never been seen by the protective services worker. The outreach worker was furious. After "stewing" about it for several days, she called the worker and "gave him hell" for not seeing the family. He became defensive and angry. He said that since he had such an overwhelming caseload, he attended first to cases in which no other agency was involved, and that the outreach worker should have been following the family. In this case, each worker had denied his or her own responsibility and assigned it to the other. Meanwhile, the family had been attended by no one. In the group these two people were able to resolve their differences and to devise a treatment plan by which the family obtained necessary services. . . .

Difficulty in Separating Personal from Professional Responsibility

One worker in the group explained that she had been a public health nurse in her native small town for several years. She had been hardworking, diligent, and competent, and had worked with many high-risk families. One family began calling her at any hour of the night for minor complaints, and she had responded by going out to the home each time. She had become exhausted and was unable to carry out her duties and care for her own family. However, she considered it wrong to refuse to come when called; she felt it was her personal, professional responsibility to meet a client's need at any time. After much discussion in the group, she was able to set limits on clients' excessive demands. Furthermore, she was able to decide to take a day off to celebrate her daughter's birthday—something she would never have done before.

A second manifestation of the difficulty in separating personal emotional involvement from professional responsibilities was illustrated when a group member was asked to testify as an expert witness in a case of child abuse in which the state petitioned the court for termination of parental rights. After a thorough investigation, the worker had considered it best to terminate parental rights and had so testified in court. The mother was in the courtroom at the time. During the hearing the worker began to feel guilty about her testimony. She avoided looking at the mother and had to keep telling herself to remember that she had been asked to make a recommendation regarding the children, not the mother. Nevertheless, the worker felt remorseful afterward. She considered herself a failure as a professional and a "bad" person for having recommended that a mother be deprived of her children. It was only after discussing her feelings and frustrations in detail that she was able to see that she had acted properly.

Feelings of Being Victimized

Repeatedly, the workers in the group blamed case failures and frustrations on families who "just weren't motivated," on "other agencies which weren't cooperating," or on the state government which was "full of bureaucrats who wanted to glorify themselves." This enabled the workers to avoid facing their own limitations and failures, as well as the disturbing fact that for certain families there is nothing one can do.

Often a hopeless attitude towards the system kept workers from advocating change within it. A worker from one protective services office explained, "We'll never get any more workers in our office, so why try?" Nevertheless, shortly after they had discussed this in the group, a new director was able to hire two more workers for the same office.

Other participants observed that members from the office were unrealistically pessimistic. This engendered group discussion about how expecting too much from families can leave workers feeling depressed and demoralized. Case discussions among group members enabled each of them to be more realistic about their families, and, as a result, members felt less "burnt out."

Ambivalent Feelings toward Clients

Ambivalent feelings frequently interfered with effective client care. For example, one worker had been visiting a home for months. One day she gently suggested that the mother might dress her children in warmer clothes for the winter. The mother became extremely angry and shouted at the worker for over twenty minutes. The worker felt great concern for the mother and children, but she also disliked the mother for becoming so angry. At first she handled this by denying both her feelings and the problem. She avoided visiting the home for weeks, using the rationale that the family's problem "wasn't that bad" and that she would do more harm going where she was not wanted. Her gnawing conscience had led her to bring the problem to the group, and, as a result of the discussions about it, she became more aware of her own feelings and conflicts and was able to become involved in home visits again. Initially the mother was cool toward her, but the worker persisted and slowly re-established their trusting relationship.

Other members in the group also discovered that they had acted inappropriately at times out of ambivalent feeling toward their clients.

Ambivalent Feelings about One's Professional Role

One worker talked about quitting his job because of his ambivalent feelings about it. He often worked twelve-hour days, seven days a week, but then complained bitterly about the long hours. He was unable to reach a balance between feeling responsible and liking his job and feeling overworked and hating it. Sometimes when a case truly demanded after-hours care he would become resentful of that particular family. Many other group members admitted feeling the same way. Partly as a result of the group discussions, the first worker resigned from his agency, to work as a cabinetmaker for over a year. Later, he again sought work in the area of child abuse, and he now sets limits on what he can do and feels much more satisfied and less ambivalent about his professional responsibilities.

The Need to be in Control

Most workers mentioned that they had at some time felt a need to control their situation with clients or to control the clients themselves. Some had insisted on a certain degree of motivation in the parents before they would work with a family, despite their knowledge that abusing parents are difficult to work with because of their poor motivation and that it is necessary to reach out to them to establish a working relationship . . .

Agencies must recognize the stresses that clinicians are under. As Copans and his colleagues make clear, practitioners have to be concerned about the policies and practices of the agency: protective service work demonstrates very well the difference between private practice and agency-based practice. No amount of personal therapeutic skill or insight on the part of clinicians is sufficient to handle the risks, stresses, and complexity of such jobs.

Although some of these difficulties could be dealt with through individual supervision, support groups among workers are better able to help workers to cope with them. If agencies do not recognize the necessity for such structures, then clinicians should advocate for them. (The strategies and tactics noted in Chapters 5, 6, and 7 will be useful in this effort.) This advocacy need not be defensive; rather, it should be assertive in pointing out that there are inevitable stresses on the job, and the agency has a responsibility to help workers deal with them. Simply to say that problems like those noted in the Copans article stem from workers' inadequacy is to miss the complexity of the work.

A considerable body of literature deals with the strain on professionals of working in a bureaucratic organization. Much of this book is oriented to providing professionals with tools to enable them to work more effectively in bureaucratic settings. Yet the Copans article illustrates the fact that some professional services—child protective services, for example—could not occur outside an organizational setting. The organization, if properly structured, can be a positive force supportive of workers.

Wilbur Finch makes the point that continued concern with the issue of professional autonomy versus bureaucratic control may offer little help to future social workers. This view encourages the idea that the way to improve services to clients is to increase the autonomy of workers rather than to recognize the effects of the structure of organizations on service delivery and search for alternative structures.* Nevertheless, no matter what the structure, our contention is that the strain between staff needs and organizational needs cannot be completely eliminated. The challenge for the clinician is not to avoid, but to manage, the strain between the organization's desire for productivity, survival, and adherence to rules and procedures and his or her professional desires for autonomy, initiative, and commitment to client service.

Going through Channels: In the struggle between clinicians and organization, most of the power lies on the side of the agency. Workers have attempted through a variety of means to alter this power imbalance. One strategy focuses on going through channels and using the agency's formal procedures and structures for the redress of grievances. These include board personnel committees, staff committees that regularly meet with

*Wilbur Finch, "Social Workers versus Bureaucracy," *Social Work* 21 (1976): 370–375.

management, and personal conferences with agency directors or their representatives. Certainly these channels should be tried before any other approaches are utilized. (The reader may wish to refer to prior chapters where the tactics of collaboration, bargaining, and pressure strategies are discussed.)

The problem with "going through channels" is that it involves formal procedures that make it difficult to do or say certain things. Can one tell the director that the supervisor or assistant supervisor of a unit other than one's own is incompetent? How is this to be proved? If the accusation is stated publicly, how can the parties continue to work together?

Generally formal channels work best when used in concert with other mechanisms. The way to get an incompetent supervisor fired is to let his or her mistakes be seen and felt in the agency. Surprisingly, however, workers often cover up for incompetent superiors, just as students sometimes cover up for incompetent teachers by acting animated, asking pertinent questions, and generally participating at a higher level than usual when a faculty member is being observed.

As a rule, the time for the staff to complain formally is after clients and community representatives have written to the agency's executive about the supervisor and his or her work. The same is true of complaints about bad policies and procedures.

Unions: Existing formal channels will not always work, and therefore many workers look to unions for help with their work frustrations. Howard Hush describes some of the dynamics of collective bargaining in the article that follows.

Collective Bargaining in
Voluntary Agencies*

HOWARD HUSH

The move toward trade unionism and collective bargaining by the professional employees of voluntary agencies in the social welfare field poses some harsh questions: Will unions destroy, or save, the voluntary agency? Will the contributors to united community funds support hard bargaining by professional employees, or will they withdraw their support in protest? Who is "management" in the collective bargaining process of a legally autonomous agency supported by a united fund?

For the uninitiated in such matters, the response to these questions

*Reprinted with special permission of the Family Service Association of America from *Social Casework* 50 (1969): 210–213.

may be explosive, violently prejudiced or partisan, or heavily flavored with the so-called puritan ethic—and perhaps only remotely related to reality. For many of us involved in the administration of large voluntary agencies in the Detroit area, where collective bargaining is in its third year, the response to these questions is likely to be one of studied restraint and evasion.*

Why are such questions, once they become a part of everyday reality, almost beyond approach? The fact that they are virtually unapproachable is, in itself, part of the problem. There is a communication blockage that is difficult to remove or circumvent. I should like to suggest some of the factors contributing to the difficulty of meaningful exchange.

1. Most professionals in the field of community and social service are sympathetic to organized labor and collective bargaining on philosophical grounds. Moreover, the profession of social work has been so throughout its history. Problems arise, however, when a philosophical, humanitarian view of workers' rights, which evolved from the needs of employees paid by the hour in an industrial, profit-making enterprise, is applied to the collective bargaining process involving salaried personnel in a nonprofit community service enterprise in which "management" and "labor" are of the same educational and professional background and, presumably, have the same goals.

2. A collective bargaining relationship is by definition a conflict relationship between employer and employee. The conflict is out in the open; it is legally recognized; most of the ground rules for dealing with the issues are set by federal or state law or regulation. By legal definition, certain elements of an organization are "management" and certain other elements are "labor." Furthermore, the adversary relationship is not restricted to the bargaining table at a given season of the year. In varying degrees it pervades the whole organization. It may be minimal, it may peak at certain times of the year, or it may flare up around certain issues. But it is never completely absent.

3. In a voluntary social welfare agency, there is likely to be lack of sophistication on both sides of the bargaining table. For example, when members of the staff believe, as too many still do, that a collective bargaining relationship is simply an orderly, businesslike way of employing someone to get more salary for them and that all other attitudes, relationships, and conditions of employment remain unchanged, they are naïve. They are overlooking the fact that an outside, third force—the union—is an entity in and of itself; it is part of the Establishment; it has its own thrust and its own political and survival pressures; and it has its well-established techniques for protecting and promoting its own self-interest. Staff members are beginning to learn that a collective bargaining

---

*In this article I am setting forth only my own observations and reflections on the implications of collective bargaining in one metropolitan area.

agreement is a two-way instrument that defines in legal terminology what both administration and staff can and cannot do.

4. Finally, a collective bargaining relationship does not pose new questions so much as it puts into very sharp focus some old and very difficult questions: What are an employee's services worth in dollars? What values determine the worth? Who makes the judgment?

As if these questions were not troublesome enough, the problem of employee compensation is compounded by concepts of "charity," "dedication," and "sacrifice," which are now obsolete. Whether one likes it or not, these concepts are "out" as far as most urban employer-employee relationships are concerned, and one had best not try to use them to avoid paying decent salaries. At the same time, I believe that professional social workers must share with the general community and with boards of directors a substantial responsibility for their own compensation problems. Too many of them enjoy a kind of disengagement from the general community and do not get beyond the sterile complaint, " 'They' should pay 'us' more."

The Dilemmas and the Issues

For the Staff

The dilemma for the professional employee can easily become one of a conflict of loyalties. How much of his loyalty belongs to the union? How much to the agency? How much to the client? How much to the community? To what extent should he be guided by his own hard-nosed, short-term self-interest? Being faced with this dilemma provides a heyday for the person who lives by confusion and enjoys conflict for the sake of conflict. But it is a nightmare for the person who likes a quiet, diligent pursuit of his goals, an orderly arrangement of his loyalties, and a minimum of organizational commotion.

There is, too, a shift in the climate of relationships among staff, administration, and board. Relationships tend to become depersonalized, rigid, and legalistic. There is more sensitivity to the concept of "ultimate authority" in administration—not the particular decision or the basis for it, but who has the authority to make it.

Perhaps the greatest problem for professional employees is that so many of them are inexperienced and naïve about the ramifications of a collective bargaining agreement. For example, one member of an agency staff, who was an officer of the union and an especially active member of the bargaining team, requested a "merit" salary increase for himself after the contract had been signed for the current year. The agency administrator was dumbfounded by the simple innocence of the request and the lack of sensitivity to the broad implications of collective bargaining for the agency and for the financing of the program. The staff member, however, was even more dumbfounded to discover (1) that one purpose (and certainly the effect) of a collective bargaining relationship is to deny to administration discretion in individual salary adjustments based on merit, competence, or superior performance, and (2) that the very contract he had just signed would not permit the agency to give him or anyone else in the bargaining unit the kind of individual salary adjustment he had requested.

For the Executive Director

The dilemma for the agency executive director is no less troublesome than it is for the staff. First, whether he likes it or not, he *is* management, and he cannot avoid this role in relation to his staff and his board; he and the board sit on one side of the bargaining table, and the members of the staff bargaining committee sit on the other side. Fundamentally, his role must be clear. It is true, however, that he also can retreat into isolation, a kind of legal sanctuary, if his survival is at stake.

Second, once a contract is signed, he is responsible for ensuring that it is fulfilled. The terms of the contract affecting salary, fringe benefits, insurance, working conditions, and so on cannot be modified by either the board of directors or the staff bargaining unit. The operating authority is the contract; it is not the board of directors, the personnel committee, or the agency's administrative staff.

Of greatest concern to some executive directors is the development of a kind of legally and morally justified disengagement among staff, administration, and governing board. Each of the three segments of agency operation tends to become legally defensive, more concerned with what it can and cannot do and less concerned with what it should or should not do. Particularly during the actual bargaining process, suspicion and conflict of interest among the segments are intensified. Long-term common interests and goals, if indeed they exist, tend to become obscured by more immediate concern with short-term goals and the struggle for power.

For the Board

The initial response of the governing board to the fact of a collective bargaining procedure may be one of surprising and disappointment. Very quickly, however, the attitude can become one of detached sophistication. Of necessity, the board has to take an official position on the issues; it must follow the rules of the collective bargaining process; it must eventually agree to a settlement.

It should not be surprising to executives (but it has been to many) to find that their boards relax quickly in the presence of a collective bargaining agreement, with some discomfort, to be sure, but almost with relief.

Why? Because a collective bargaining agreement provides an orderly, legalistic resolution of issues involved in employer-employee relationships. The board becomes one step removed, more detached. It relies upon the collective bargaining machinery; it looks to the labor negotiator (usually an attorney, and a "must" for the employing agency) for advice and direction; and it depends upon the executive to administer the final contract. Just as the fact of a collective bargaining agreement influences the operation of the agency at the staff level, so it also has a pervasive effect on the relationship among board, administration, and staff.

Hope for the Future

In this era of the "participation explosion," it is both fashionable and easy to play the game of confusion, of challenge for the sake of challenge, and of simple scapegoating. Nevertheless, with respect to salary issues and the collective bargaining process in voluntary agencies, the situation is not hopeless, unless we want to make it so. What are the sources of hope for the future?

We can hope for greater sophistication on the part of staff members in the adaptation of the collective bargaining process to the social agency setting. Specifically, we can hope that they will have conviction enough to challenge the outside union's "pros," many of whom know only the union contract model of the hourly rated employees in a profit-making enterprise in the industrial community. They must evidence a high degree of sophistication even at the time they first consider the move toward a collective bargaining relationship. What are the issues, both short-term and long-term? What are the implications for staff, for agencies, and for the financial structure of voluntary agencies? What are the alternatives to collective bargaining?

These questions are not easily answered. And the answers are likely to reflect emotions, values, and moods much more than facts or rational judgments. But at least these questions should be asked before, not after, the decision is made to seek a collective bargaining relationship. I am persuaded that it is in part because such questions were never seriously considered that we have a much higher staff turnover rate in the Detroit agencies, particularly among union officers and members of bargaining teams, after contracts have been signed. Also, there are a few bitter souls who now say that neither the professional association *nor* the union seems able to deal with the compensation problem. The staff's problem does not necessarily reflect, however, the failure of unions and collective bargaining. Rather, it reflects the staff's initial lack of understanding, its unrealistic expectations, and the lack of a national model for collective bargaining for public service personnel—social workers, teachers, nurses, policemen, and so on.

We can also hope that once the staff makes the decision to engage in collective bargaining, it will adopt a more critical attitude toward certain concepts very important to the union movement among hourly rated industrial employees. Take, for example, the concept of seniority and the traditional trade union position that seniority should be the primary factor in determining wages, promotions, demotions, dismissals, and so on. When rigidly applied to a professional service, the seniority concept has a disastrous effect; too many of the rewards are reserved for tenure, even though performance may be mediocre. Yet young professional social workers, with a proud disdain for the Establishment and for people over thirty years of age, can sit at the bargaining table and defend the traditional labor concept of seniority when matters of self-interest are at issue, apparently unconcerned with the inconsistency.

On the part of administration and board, we can hope for sharper, more realistic decisions in the over-all management of the agency's program. The decisions must be sharper, often hard-nosed, simply because the pressures of collective bargaining put the issues and the conflicts into sharper focus. I should like to offer three illustrations.

1. The assessment of professional performance during a six-month probationary period assumes critical importance. During this period, the administration may have full discretion in keeping or not keeping a staff member, but it has very little discretion after the staff member's name has been placed on the seniority list. Administration must make a clear decision, one way or another, at the end of the probationary period; no evasion, no wait-and-see attitude, and no sentimental indulgence can be permitted.

2. The salary issue must be faced squarely in a collective bargaining agreement; there is little, if any room for an appeal to "dedication" or "sacrifice" and the like. Each party at the bargaining table has a paid advocate to defend his position. The competitive spirit is dominant. Sentiment, if any, is likely to be rhetorical or theatrical; sheer self-interest takes on a vigor and frankness strange to some of us. It is not my intent to judge or to suggest what is "right" or what is "wrong." I want only to highlight the shift in climate and the compelling pressure to face issues openly and squarely.

3. Inevitably the pressures on the agency's budget will sharpen the issues with respect to program, priorities of service, and effectiveness of performance. We can hope that as operating costs increase because of the improved benefits for the staff, the administration and the board will become increasingly critical of the traditional ways of delivering service— particularly if there has had to be a curtailment of service. In automobile plants, for example, as labor costs went higher, there was a shift to more and more automation. Probing by administration and board will cause discomfort for many practitioners—usually a conservative force in agency operation—but collective bargaining is a two-way street. If used

well, it can bring benefits to clients and to the community, but the benefits cannot be taken for granted.

The Crucial Question

Will the outside union destroy, or save, the voluntary social agency? It will probably do neither. But it will provide a measure of the community's current commitment to the voluntary agency. It may force the community to decide how far it will go beyond token support. In the meantime, if the union is sensitive to the issues, it will have to decide how far it will go in a gamble with the future of the voluntary agency.

━━━━━━━━━━━━━━━━━━━━━━━

To date the experience with unions in social welfare has been mixed. On the one hand, unions have been an effective force for increasing wages and providing job security for clinicians. In addition, unions allow workers to feel more independent and less under the control of management. It can therefore be argued that they promote psychological health: workers no longer need to feel like puppets manipulated by an arbitrary management. Another frequently cited value of unions is that they provide backbone; that is the union makes it more likely that workers will speak out against what they see as ineffective agency practices, since they no longer have to fear arbitrary dismissal.

On the other hand, unions are, as Hush notes, social organizations subject to their own self-maintenance needs. They need their members dues. Their primary activity is to protect the working conditions, salary, and tenure of their members, although some progressive unions struggle to balance their concern over such issues with concern for clients.

While each clinician must make up his or her own mind about the value of unions and the ethics of striking in particular situations, it is clear that as social services increase in size and scope, there will be increasing unionization. As social services compete for funds with police forces, sanitation departments, and highway departments, the inevitable conflicts will be settled only through bargaining among pressure groups with suffiicient power to promote their demands politically. The union is that kind of pressure group.

There is a danger that strikes will unintentionally pit the needs of workers against the rights and service needs of clients, as Hush contends. Unions may take actions in their own organizational interests—prolonged strikes, jurisdictional disputes with other unions, for example—that can have profound effects on clients and individual workers. As unions become an increasingly important fixture in the social welfare field, individual clinicians must pay more attention to what unions do.

Participative Management: Many clinicians have urged that organizations involve them more in decision making, feeling that if they participated more in management, they would be able to mitigate many of the strains of their jobs. And they are correct in this judgment.

Given the professional training and values of social work practitioners, social agencies cannot operate in a strictly hierarchical fashion, allowing decisions to be made by those in formal authority without input from clinical staff. Clinicians have important knowledge that should influence the decision-making process.

On the other hand, some clinicians invest their hopes for participation in a concept of the agency as a democratic assembly where votes are taken and the majority rules. Implied in this view are political parties that press certain policies and procedures. This legislative conception of an agency has as many problems in it as the traditional hierarchical structure: peers have great difficulty in regulating peers; some decisions require experts; the time and money required for real participative management can deflect on organization from its goals; power, rather than more discussion, may be required in certain situations; and participation may engender conflict and hostility, rather than resolve it. (The reader may wish to refer to the discussion of participative management in Chapter 4.)

Some urge that rather than focusing on participation per se, clinicians should put their energy into devising new organizational forms to improve the delivery of services and ameliorate the stresses and strains on workers. Their suggestions have generally revolved around nonhierarchical structures (too often ignoring the problems that emerge with the disappearance of the hierarchy), but there are other possibilities.* The development of such alternative structures is also an important area for program innovation as Miller and Phillip point out.†

The following article, by Carole Joffe, shows both how structure affects service and how staff can and do participate in management in both a formal and an informal way. She suggests that the needs of clinicians are a legitimate concern for those who design social programs.

---

*See Rosabeth Kantor, "The Impact of Hierarchical Structures on the Work Behavior of Men and Woman," *Social Problems* 23 (1976): 415–430, and David Stoesz, "Innovation in Service Delivery: The Family Life Center," *Social Work* 26 (1981): 401–407.

†Henry Miller and Connie Phillip, "The Alternative Service Agency," in A. Rosenblatt and D. Waldfogel, eds., *Handbook of Clinical Social Work* (San Francisco: Jossey-Bass, 1983), pp. 779–791.

Abortion Work:
Strains, Coping Strategies,
Policy Implications*

CAROLE JOFFE

Studies of family policy should not be confined to the impact of such policy on family members. Because more and more family services are delivered in institutional settings, the proper study of family policy has to encompass these institutions and the persons who work in them. Such studies should not only examine the fit between clients' needs and the institutions' offerings; they must also analyze the impact of institutional activity on those offering the services.

Abortion work is a good example of a service with powerful ramifications for both families and social service workers. The profound, sometimes contradictory implications of abortion for families are familiar. They include the possibilities of limiting family size; the avoidance of pregnancies that are unwanted by some family members but desired by others and, hence, the potential for conflict between family members; and the abortion as a "life crisis" that may lead the family to seek further professional help. Less familiar, though, are the effects of legalized abortion and its consequent incorporation into mainstream social agencies for the new occupational category of "abortion counselor." To develop a policy on abortion that meets the complex needs of individuals and families in a sensitive manner, it seems imperative to take into account the strain involved for people delivering abortion services.

Although these workers have been studied relatively little, both a small research literature and popular accounts point to the troubling aspects of this work for the professionals involved.† Nurses, especially those in volved in second-trimester abortions, apparently experience the most difficulty; but some doctors, social workers, and counselors also report discomfort, even while they maintain continuing political support of abortion. This article will explore some of the complexities involved for social service workers doing abortion work and will report on attempts to humanize this work.

*Reprinted with permission from *Social Work* 24 (1979): 485–490. Copyright 1979, National Association of Social Workers, Inc.

†Judith Bourne, "Influence on Health Professionals' Attitudes towards Abortion," *Journal of the American Hospital Association* 46 (July 1972): 80–83; W. F. Char and J. F. McDermott, "Abortion and Acute Identity Crises in Nurses," *American Journal of Psychiatry* 128 (1972): 952–957; F. J. Kane et al., "Emotional Reactions in Abortion Service Personnel," *Archives of General Psychiatry* 28 (1973): 409–411; Howard D. Kibel, "Staff Reactions to Abortion," *Obstetrics and Gynecology* 39 (Jan. 1972): 128–133; and Marianne Such-Baer, "Professional Staff Reaction to Abortion Work," *Social Casework* 55 (1974): 435–441.

The information presented here was drawn primarily from the author's year-long participant observation study of "Urban Clinic" during 1976–77. Urban is a private, nonprofit family-planning clinic in a large north-eastern city. Among its other services, the clinic offers first-trimester abortions on an out-patient basis. About 150 abortions are performed weekly. This article focuses on the eight abortion counselors who work at Urban and three middle managers—the clinic director, the associate director, and the head counselor. The duties of the counselors include giving information and counseling prior to the abortion and accompanying clients through the procedure itself. The duties of the managers are largely administrative and supervisory but also include some direct service in the abortion clinic.

The counselors at Urban range in age from early twenties to late thirties. Seven of them have BA degrees; the eighth was working on hers during the course of the study. Several of the counselors had prior work experience in other social service settings before coming to Urban. Two worked as hospital nurses, and Urban was the first postcollege job for two others. Many of the counselors are seriously contemplating a return to school for a higher degree—typically to a social work or counseling program. For most of these counselors, then, abortion counseling represents one step in a rather fluidly conceived social service career.

Strain of Abortion Work

For counselors, the strain associated with abortion-related work derives from several different sources: the larger social and political climate surrounding abortion, the moral dilemmas raised by their own involvement in the abortion procedure, and the behavior and perceived attitudes of abortion recipients. These factors will be discussed separately, but it should be understood that each reinforces the impact of the others.

The embroiled political climate surrounding abortion creates practical problems for the counselors. For example, Urban, like many other abortion clinics, is regularly picketed by "right-to-life" groups, and staff and clients are frequently subject to verbal harassment. Moreover, staff are always on the watch for "crazies" who might break into the clinic and disrupt its activity. In addition, the continuing uncertainty during the period of this study about the status of federal and state funding for abortions for Medicaid patients made it very difficult for Urban to live up to its policy of providing abortions to all who desire them.

Troublesome as these practical issues are, however, the major problem posed by the larger political context is that it forces workers who give abortion services into a rigid ideological position. The continued and increasing pressure of the antiabortion forces, six years after legalization, compel counselors to cling, at least publicly, to a rhetorical proabortion position. The subtlety of the counselors' response to abortion, in which they attempt to make a crucial distinction between being "proabortion" and "prochoice," is hard to maintain in such an embattled atmosphere.

The counselors' involvement in the abortion procedure inevitably raises a number of moral dilemmas—dilemmas that are hard for them to fully articulate for this reason. As a result of their work, counselors come to have questions about the viability of the fetus, the possible destruction of potential life that may be taking place, and so forth. And although the first-trimester procedure done at Urban is significantly less upsetting than second-trimester procedures done in hospitals, the occasional confrontation with a discernible fetal part magnifies such feelings of discomfort. Several of the Urban counselors, like those elsewhere, reported having "abortion nightmares" early on in their work in the abortion service.

However, the most intense conflicts that counselors experience are not primarily focused on such larger issues as the "destruction" of life but rather on the ease with which they see abortions becoming routinized. To fully understand the counselors' feelings on this issue, one must recall the enormous qualitative difference in abortion services before and after the 1973 Supreme Court decision legalizing abortion.* Before 1973 abortions—illegal or legal—were hard to find, their safety was problematic, and they were often performed in a punitive, intimidating atmosphere. In contrast, in the present situation, elective abortions have a very high safety record, and first-trimester procedures are still relatively accessible for all but low-income women. Many clinics, like Urban, have apparently succeeded in offering abortions in a nonjudgmental and supportive atmosphere.

Ironically, however, some abortion workers are beginning to suspect that perhaps they and their colleagues have been *too* successful in upgrading abortion from its "back-alley" past. Right-to-lifers notwithstanding, it appears to counselors as if some sectors of the population now accept abortion too readily. This is shown most strikingly by the apparent willingness of some women to view abortion itself as an acceptable means of contraception.† In response to this perceived cynicism among clients, some counselors have begun to refer to themselves as "accomplices" engaged in a "conveniencing" process for those who cannot be "hassled" by birth control.

Thus, counselors bring contradictory feelings to the abortion situation. They have a strong belief in a woman's right to choose a safe, legal abortion. However, they also have a growing feeling that in the process of routinizing abortion services, the moral aspects of abortion—which are becoming more and more important to them—are becoming less important to others.

*Doe v. Bolton, 410 U.S. 179 (1973); Roe v. Wade, 410 U.S. 113 (1973).

†See Kristin Luker, Taking Chances: Abortion and the Decision Not to Contracept (Berkeley: University of California Press, 1975).

Clients obviously play a crucial role in determining which side of this contradiction becomes predominant for counselors.* Clients in desperate situations—those who are young, poor, single, or unprepared for child rearing—reinforce the counselors' belief in the necessity for abortions. At the other extreme, better-off, more mature women who undergo repeated abortions but claim to want children someday accentuate the counselors' disaffection.

However, it is not just the objective situation of clients that is important in shaping counselors' reactions but their demeanor as well. Clients who appear sobered by the forthcoming abortion experience, who are open to the counselor's therapeutic skills, and who show a serious interest in discussing future contraceptive plans emphasize for counselors the heroic aspects of their job. Conversely, clients who appear cynical about the forthcoming abortion and who repudiate efforts at counseling and discussion of birth control are demoralizing to counselors. Most upsetting of all in this latter group of clients are the "repeaters"—women returning to the clinic for their second, third, or forth abortion.

Counselors' Strategies

Counselors' responses to the strains of working with abortion can be divided into two categories: "ideological" and "structural." Among the most important ideological devices used by counselors are "professionalism" and "pronatalism." "Professionalism" in this context refers to the attempt to honor the cardinal principle of abortion counseling—that its major purpose is the facilitation of decision making for the client. Any decision concerning a problem pregnancy is considered valid, as long as it is truly the client's and not imposed by another party, such as a counselor or a family member.† For some counselors, the conception of professionalism helps them to accept more philosophically "wrong" decisions on the part of clients, such as the decision by a thirteen-year-old to continue a pregnancy. Similarly, a sense of professionalism, with its implications of impartiality and a certain detachment, is useful in assisting counselors to respond more supportively to potentially upsetting clients such as "repeaters."

Coexisting with these aspects of professionalism is a strong, though not always expressed, culture of "pronatalism" among counselors. This does not mean that counselors either explicitly or implicitly encourage uncer-

*See Carole Joffe, "What Abortion Counselors Want from their Clients," *Social Problems* 26 (Oct. 1978): 112–121.

†See Terry Beresford, *Short-Term Relationship Counseling: A Self-Instruction Manual for Use in Family Planning Clinics* (Baltimore: Planned Parenthood of Maryland, 1977); and Leah Potts, "Counseling Women with Unwanted Pregnancies," in Florence Haselkorn, ed., *Family Planning* (New York: Council on Social Work Education, 1971), pp. 267–280.

tain clients to continue with pregnancies or that counselors have become antiabortion. Rather, this pronatalism refers to the elation counselors feel when they do encounter a wanted pregnancy, either among clients at the clinic, such as those coming for a pregnancy test, or among their own associates. As one staff member remarked after a former colleague had dropped by with a new infant, "It's such an upper for everyone to see a baby around this place!" Counselors' pronatalism also expresses itself in the fantasies they have of future clinic programs. Counselors continually argue for more prenatal services, childbirth education classes, and even obstetric facilities. As one counselor said, "There's no reason we can't do abortions on the third floor and deliver babies on the fifth." Thus, pronatalism at Urban has to be understood as part of the counselors' impulse to see their abortion activity in the context of the broadest possible sphere of human activity.

The "structural" responses of counselors refer to ways in which they manipulate their assigned duties to reduce the strains of their work. Deliberate "slowdowns" and "secret caseloads" are two of the most important of these devices. "Slowdown" here means consciously taking more time than normally allocated for an interview with a prospective abortion recipient. Unlike classical industrial slowdowns, the motive in this instance is not a protest against management, but is simply the counselor's desire for additional time with the client.

"Secret caseloads" are an extension of the slowdowns. Occasionally, when a counselor encounters a client who has too much psychological "material" to deal with even in an extended session, the counselor will urge the client to return without charge for another session. This is an arrangement made strictly between counselor and client, without mediation by the clinic office. The focus of any subsequent session is not usually a decision about the abortion per se, since this is usually decided on at the first session. Rather, the counselor and client consider related issues that have emerged because of the abortion decision.

In sum, the slowdowns and secret caseloads suggest the counselor's tremendous belief in the cathartic possibilities of genuine "therapy" (as opposed to merely sharing information). In their eyes, abortion is not wrong as long as it has not been decided on lightly; abortion counseling is not simply "conveniencing" as long as the opportunity exists for sufficient interaction with the client.

Managerial Strategies

Management's responses to the difficulties imposed by abortion work can also be divided into two categories: practices directly associated with the abortion service itself and those associated with the operation of the clinic as a whole. Of the former, perhaps the most important is the unofficial tolerance of the secret caseloads and slowdowns. Although the clinic's director and associate director make periodic statements at staff meetings about the problem of clients waiting for a long time to be seen, and although the secret caseloads theoretically violate clinic policy, there seems to be no serious attempt to crack down on these practices as long as they do not significantly interfere with the counselors' handling of other responsibilities.

Another response of the managers is to maintain their own involvement in direct service in the abortion clinic. This serves several important functions. From the managers' point of view, it gives them the opportunity to keep in touch, both with their own clinical skills and with what is actually happening in the abortion service. From the counselors' point of view, such administrative involvement is a significant morale booster. As one counselor said of the clinic director, "After an abortion, she'll be in there with her sleeves rolled up, washing out the equipment. She doesn't ask us to do anything she wouldn't do herself."

Another important attempt on the part of the managers to humanize abortion work is limiting the number of abortion clinics a counselor is expected to work at each week. Although Urban usually offers five abortion clinics per week, strenuous attempts are made to limit each individual counselor to no more than three per week. This limitation not only offers a relief from the work itself but provides the opportunity for counselors to engage more fully in other tasks at the clinic. These include training of volunteers, contraceptive counseling of teenagers, and working with special interest groups such as the handicapped. In addition, Urban's program is fluid enough at this point to allow the counselors to initiate new activities. The most notable of these, implemented shortly after the author finished her observations, is a counseling clinic, which is not confined to pregnancy and abortion but extends to such matters as sexuality, sexual dysfunction, personal relationships, and so forth. It appears that the secret caseloads of individual counselors are being legitimated and absorbed into the clinic's regular practices.

As another humanizing measure, the head counselor has instituted "processing" sessions—periodic occasions for counselors to express feelings that are aroused by abortion work. Sometimes these are internal, informal sessions; sometimes they are led by an outside consultant. These sessions allow counselors to express negative feelings about their work without sanctions from their supervisors.

Finally, management's attempts to humanize abortion work cannot be separated from ongoing efforts to upgrade general working conditions at the clinic. Serious attempts are under way to improve the level of in-service training. This involves going beyond discussions pertaining solely to the technical aspects of abortion and contraception to incorporate larger topics, such as the politics of family planning at the national level. The administration at Urban is also taking significant steps toward more democratic forms of management. These steps include sharing of detailed information on the clinic's budget and that of its sponsoring agency, the involvement of staff in hiring decisions and other policy decisions, and the participation of the clinic's staff in various committees that had formerly been confined to management and members of the board of directors.

Costs of Humanization

These various strategies on the part of both counselors and managers to reduce the strains of abortion-related work are, in the author's opinion, fairly successful. The counselors at Urban do not exhibit symptoms of "burnout" to the same degree as counselors elsewhere. Although according to abortion lore counselors typically "burn out" within eighteen months, six of the eight counselors observed at Urban had been at their jobs for two years or more. Also, none of these counselors showed the most extreme forms of emotional exhaustion described by Maslach as characteristic of burnout in the social services, such as turning on clients or weeping on the job.* Although counselors experience their work on the abortion service as difficult, they also acknowledge it to be gratifying. The author was continually struck by the fact that abortion counseling carried the highest status at Urban. Staff who were confined to contraceptive counseling constantly pressured supervisors to transfer them to the abortion service.

From the administrative standpoint, however, these humanization measures are not without their costs. First among these is a higher degree of inefficiency. Toleration of slowdowns, managerial involvement in direct service, blurred and changing job descriptions for staff, and a constant renegotiation of scheduling all lead to increased job satisfaction, but they also contribute to a less tightly run clinic. Similarly, more democratic forms of management also have ambiguous consequences. A greater sharing of information and some participation in policy making does, in one sense, increase staff commitment to the clinic; yet these participatory opportunities arouse considerable anger on the part of staff over what they cannot change, such as their own low salaries and the overall priorities of the agency. During the author's period of observations, for example, the issue that most divided staff and management was the crisis caused by the withdrawal of Medicaid funding for abortions and the resulting question of how many free or reduced-fee abortions the agency could afford to subsidize. Finally, the "processing" sessions, although designed to help cope with the strong emotions brought on by working with abortions, always run the risk of uncovering too much

*Christina Maslach, "Burned Out," *Human Behavior* 5 (Sept. 1976): 16–18.

emotional material, thus rendering individuals incapable of proceeding with their work.

In spite of these costs, however, management at Urban is continuing with these policies. It may be that such measures are not only more humane but are ultimately necessary to keep the abortion clinic functioning effectively. The reasons for this lie in two emerging trends. First, there is in general an increasing incompatibility between social service work and traditional forms of management. This is due to such factors in contemporary service work as a relatively highly educated work force, job descriptions that are quite fluid, and the constant necessity to learn new skills on the job.* Second, abortion work in particular may represent an emerging class of "dirty work" tasks in the human services—services to the dying would be another—that necessitates these types of concessions from administrators to maintain the loyalties of a competent work force.†

Policy Issues

This article has thus far dealt with the strains associated with abortion work, some of the devices used to offset these strains, and some of the costs associated with these humanizing measures. In this final section, the author will briefly indicate some of the implications of these factors for the development of future policy regarding abortion.

Limits of Professionalization

At first glance, students of the human service professions might expect abortion counseling to follow the familiar route of increasing specialization and, hence, move toward increased "professionalization."‡ Abortion counseling does contain a number of characteristics conventionally associated with such a process, including a growing body of technical knowledge, specialized training techniques, stable institutional bases in which to practice and to train new recruits, and a work force that is doing such work full time. Yet the author does not believe that abortion work will—or should—follow this typical sequence toward increased specialization. Her observation at Urban Clinic suggested that most abortion counselors themselves resist assuming an occupational identity built

*For a discussion of the gradual obsolescence of traditional management patterns in general, see Warren Bennis and Philip Slater, *The Temporary Society* (New York: Harper & Row, 1968). For a specific application of the argument to social service settings, see Seymour Sarason, *Work, Aging and Social Change* (New York: Free Press, 1977).

†See Everett Hughes, *The Sociological Eye: Selected Papers*, vol. 2 (Chicago: Aldine, 1971), pp. 343–345.

‡See ibid.; and Harold Wilensky, "The Professionalization of Everyone?" *American Journal of Sociology* 70 (Sept. 1964): 138–156.

solely around abortion work. Furthermore, many of the steps taken by Urban's managers to upgrade this work involve precisely the integration of abortion-related activities with other duties.

Thus, the most intelligent strategy for planners and managers of abortion services to follow may be to develop a new occupation within family-planning clinics of "reproductive counselor." Abortion-related work would be combined with contraceptive and genetic counseling, sex therapy, and a variety of prenatal and postnatal services. The justification for this integration of abortion work with these other activities is not, to repeat, that counselors object to participating in abortion services. Rather, it is the potential for demoralization in a work situation revolving entirely around abortion. For abortion counselors, as with many others in this society, abortion is most acceptable when it can be seen as part of a larger mosaic of human activity.

Needs of Family Members

As suggested earlier, a particular strain the abortion counselor often faces is the necessity to confront the opposing needs of different family members, as in the following common situations:

- A woman feels she is being pressured into an abortion by her husband or male partner.
- A teenager insists on continuing her pregnancy, and her mother vehemently demands that the clinic perform an abortion on the grounds that the daughter is incapable of caring for a baby and the mother is unwilling.
- A young teenager requests an abortion but demands that her parents not be told.

In these kinds of situations, legal rulings in themselves do not provide firm guidelines for clinic policy. For example, at present clinics may legally offer abortion services to teenagers without informing their parents. Yet such guarantees cannot be maintained if the abortion results in complications that necessitate hospitalization. Perhaps, given the unique set of circumstances presented by each woman who seeks an abortion, it may seem unjustifiable to speak of a "policy" for handling family conflicts. Each case, one might argue, should be handled on an individual basis. The author maintains, however, that there are some reasonable policies that clinics can adopt in regard to families.

As one example, clinics could endorse as a formal policy a current informal practice of many counselors: to include in the counseling session whatever family members or relevant others the pregnant woman wishes to introduce into the situation. One role of the counselor would then be to facilitate discussion among family members about the consequences of any decision made regarding the pregnancy. For example, in the case of a conflict between mother and daughter such as the one cited above, the counselor would help each party clarify her expectations of the other in the event of a continued pregnancy. This would then lead to a discussion of the teenager's options in light of the mother's refusal to assume any responsibility for the forthcoming baby. But at the same time that a clinic should be open to working with families, however broadly defined, a commitment to the pregnant woman herself as the primary client must remain central to the clinic's policy. This implies recognition and support of the woman's right to choose, even if such a choice is offensive to other family members or to the counselor herself.

Needs of Abortion Personnel

The argument stated at the outset of this article was that to best meet the needs of individuals and families, abortion policy must also be sensitive to the needs of the personnel delivering abortion services. Yet in a number of instances the needs of these groups conflict. Slowdowns, although undertaken by counselors with the best of motives, mean that other clients are kept waiting for long periods of time. The premium that counselors put on in-depth counseling may be annoying to clients who simply want an abortion and see no need to talk about it. Although a sound abortion policy must take into account the needs of families and of abortion personnel, it is clear that there will not be a perfect fit between the two. The critical point is that social service professionals, including abortion counselors, do neither their clients nor themselves a favor by denying the personal costs entailed in certain work situations.

Thus, the most humane abortion policy—and quite likely the most effective one—would try to meet the needs of both groups to the greatest extent possible while acknowledging the inevitability of certain trade-offs. For example, as mentioned above, counselors must ultimately commit themselves to the principle of the client's right to make her own choice, even if particular choices seem wrong. Similarly, if counseling prior to an abortion is so important to the staff's sense of values, perhaps some form of minimal counseling should be required of all potential abortion recipients. Whatever the eventual resolution of these issues, abortion work is an excellent example of the necessity to make the needs of human service workers a legitimate issue of social policy.

━━━━━━━━━━━━

Accountability: How are clinicians to get an administration to allow them to participate in policy decisions? How are they to get the administration to recognize legitimate job stresses? One answer lies in an effective accountability system. As Thomas Cruithurds puts it, "Management must be accountable too."* This means that some body, such as a board of directors, has to be concerned with the outcomes or the results of agency services. If the services are effective, then there is no strong argument for the involvement of the staff in administration. If they are not effective, then this may be a remedy.

Boards of directors should not tell an administrator how to run an agency, but they should insist that the agency be effective. Clinicians' best chance for having their concerns given due consideration lies in an accountability system that scrutinizes both the results achieved with clients and the reasons for these results.

Accrediting organizations should insist that agencies have such a system before they are accredited. Robert Walker has called social welfare the "land of no consequences,"† meaning that when things do not go well in a social service agency, nothing happens—no one loses his or her job, and there is no decrease in funding. (Conversely, when things go well, there is no increase in funding.) Management can afford to be arbitrary if it is not going to be held accountable. If it is held accountable, it will be interested in what the staff has to say.

Another facet of an agency's accountability system is the method and procedures it uses to evaluate workers. One of the best-kept secrets of organizational life is that agencies feel considerable pressure to evaluate their workers, but much less pressure to evaluate themselves. Weissman contends that agencies avoid consideration of their own efficiency and effectiveness by focusing on the efficiency and effectiveness of their employees.‡ The practice of evaluating workers annually on or about the anniversary of the day they began employment allows agencies to examine the problems of workers individually and not in relation to the problems of the agency. The effects of agency structure, interorganizational relationships, funding arrangements, policies, and a host of other factors are ignored, yet these factors may account more for the results achieved with clients than the particular skills of any one worker.

Ideally, worker evaluation should take place immediately after the agency engages in a process of self-evaluation. This would make the evaluation of clinicians more realistic, as the standards that they are expected to meet would be seen in the context of the agency system as a whole. If the evaluations reveal that the majority of workers have trouble with some particular aspect of the job, then it will be more difficult for the problem to be viewed as the result of a worker's inadequate skill level or personality. Rather, it will be exposed as an organizational issue, that must be dealt with organizationally.

*Thomas Cruithurds, "Management Should Be Accountable Too," *Social Work* 21 (1976): 179–180.

†Robert Walker, "The Ninth Panacea: Program Evaluation," *Evaluation* 1 (1972): 53.

‡Harold H. Weissman, *Overcoming Mismanagement in the Human Service Professions* (San Francisco: Jossey-Bass, 1973), pp. 47–59.

The introduction of bottom-up evaluation—from the clinician to the supervisor to the manager—could also help clinicians force agencies to address their problems. The data from this evaluation, which should be available to the board of directors, would form the basis for a meaningful dialogue between clinicians and administrators.

Instituting bottom-up evaluations will be difficult. Workers' unwillingness to criticize their superiors for fear of reprisal can be mitigated by anonymity and by careful phrasing of questions. For example, the question should not be "Was Ms. X adequate as a supervisor?" but rather "Did you gain new ideas, knowledge, and skills from supervision?"

It is important not to overload the system by attempting to attain too many ends through bottom-up evaluation. The primary purpose should be to bring to the surface broad problems and trends in the agency, not to pinpoint individual incompetence. Attempts to use evaluation to transmit messages about incompetent supervisors to higher-ups will create insecurity among supervisors and administrators and ultimately lead them to sabotage the system itself.

Perhaps the crucial issue for clinicians is what to do if an administrator refuses to consider bottom-up evaluation, support groups, or an accountability system oriented toward problems in agency structure and procedures, as some do.* The techniques and skills discussed in many of the preceding chapters offer a partial answer to this question, and there are other possibilities as well. A common and understandable error is to focus all one's efforts on the agency itself. Another strategic option is to look to the agency's external environment as a lever for internal change. For example, through their membership in the National Association of Social Workers or other professional or community groups, clinicians can play a key role in urging standard-setting and credentialing bodies, public and private, to revise their codes of practice for accrediting agencies.† They can use the media to educate the public and create alliances with a variety of public interest groups to agitate for bottom-up evaluation, support groups and the like. The orchestration of internal and external efforts is the key.

Practice Analogues

We have suggested that clinicians must take an active role in dealing with the problems and strains that they face working in an agency. Many of the skills involved are similar to those they use in working with clients: they have to understand the stresses clients are under; they have to know a

---

†Harold H. Weissman, "Fantasy and Reality of Staff Involvement in Organizational Change," *Administration in Social Work* 6 (1982): 37–38.

†Harold H. Weissman, "Accreditation, Credentialing and Accountability," *Administration in Social Work* 4 (1980): 41–51.

good deal about their own and other organizations; and they have to see not only the particularistic aspects of problems, but their broad social ramifications as well.

Those who work in crisis situations, increasingly engage their clients in a social and political analysis of problems once treated as individual misfortunes. Many incest victims for example, express extreme relief at discovering that they are not the only ones in the world who have been victims of such acts. For years, feminist therapists have been utilizing a political and social analysis of women's status to help women clients.

Such approaches assist clients by relieving them of the burden of their uniqueness. Similarly, by developing analytical skills and engaging their colleagues in broad discussions of agency-worker dilemmas, clinicians can increase their own sense of mastery, with benefits for their self-esteem and their progress at work. Many workers, in their incessant criticism of the agency, seem like the client with the hopeless-helpless syndrome. This client has, at least temporarily, lost the capacity for doing anything about his or her problem. The syndrome has somehow to be reversed if there is to be any possibility of improvement in the client's situation.

The professionally trained clinician has, presumably, many more skills than the ordinary client. What we are suggesting is that rather than continually complaining, that the clinician use these skills—advocacy, analysis, and the like—to get the agency to offer the support workers need to maximize their rewards on the job. We have suggested support groups, more collegiality in the agency's administration, bottom-up evaluation, unions, as well as an accountability system that holds administration accountable as well as employees. These structural supports are, in a sense, analogous to concrete services for clients.

Mary Williams describes these services as "a way in which the social work profession may begin to break into the deprived person's view of us as magical . . . unfeeling . . . preachy. I would define concrete services as any substantive act on the part of the practitioner which is readily discernible to the client, ideally proposed by the client and having about it the result of immediate relief from stress."* Williams subscribes to client supports because they start where the clients are and give the caseworker the opportunity to diagnose their problems and counteract their sense of hopelessness and distrust while relieving stress and demonstrating good-will. An enlightened administration would do well to consider Williams's statement, substituting "worker" for "client," "administration" for "caseworker," and "worker supports" for "concrete services."

Williams goes on, however, to suggest that we can place too much stress on concrete services when their provision is only a beginning for a

---

*Mary Williams, quoted in Hettie Jones and Harold H. Weissman, "Psychological Help for the Poor," in Harold H. Weissman, ed., *Individual and Group Services in the Mobilization for Youth Experience"* (New York: Association Press, 1969), p. 104.

significant proportion of our clients. They can have a "temporary, limited, palliative effect," making people feel good but not clearly suggesting to them the need to analyze and overcome the hopeless-helpless syndrome.*

Following her logic, clinical social workers should be a clear about the part they individually play in their own lack of satisfaction. No matter how well structured the agency, clinicians must be able to function amid continual tension between equally legitimate interests and ends: the agency's, the clients', and their own. They will have to tolerate and manage occasional conflict between what they are willing and able to give clients and what clients might need, and they will have to be aware that there are stresses and strains on the administration as well as on them. They must accept the fact that in a democratic society the public dictates what services should be delivered and that although they may disagree with the public, they are in fact its servants on the job. Under these circumstances, it is not, always possible for clinicians to optimize, either on their own behalf or on clients'; sometimes they will have to satisfise—to make the best possible decision given a set of constraints. Tensions and problems are to be expected in a social agency, but the way they are handled is open to negotiation.

Attitudes, Values, and Skills

In recent years, the concept of burnout has received considerable attention. Definitions vary; sometimes it describes the effects of high-stress work, including low productivity and disengagement from clients, and sometimes the depletion of personal psychic energy faster than it can be restocked. Sometimes the term covers a combination of the two.

There is some question about whether burnout is a new phenomenon. It seems likely that as the seventies progressed and more efforts were put into accountability schemes, less time was available for service to clients and workers had less discretion in organizing their work. This lost discretion may have provided the margin that allowed workers in the past to handle job-related stresses. Moreover, workers may resent time spent in staff meetings instead of seeing clients. Increased routinization of treatment and referral of interesting cases to other agencies or private practitioners may be other sources of frustration. The physical environment of the agency, either inadvertently or by design, may influence not only clients' attitudes (see the Maluccio article Chapter 1), but also workers' ability to support one another.

The literature offers numerous suggestions for overcoming burnout: more support groups, participative management, restructuring of jobs,

*Ibid., p. 54.

staff training, empowerment of workers, stress reduction techniques, more decentralization, and the like. It is clear is that burnout is not simply a psychological problem of individual workers. The problem has psychological, structural, and environmental aspects. As Carole Joffe succintly shows, for example, stress in the abortion clinic was related to the nature of clients' problem, public acceptance or lack of acceptance of abortion clinics, the structure of the clinic, and the personalities and value conflicts of individual workers. This complexity explains why there cannot be any one solution to burnout.

As we have observed, much of the literature on burnout is still committed to the old, and perhaps incorrect, hypothesis that high morale breeds high effectiveness and productivity. Emerging as a theme in the organizational literature is increasing evidence that job satisfaction does not necessarily improve qualitative and quantitative productivity. Rather, the reverse is true: qualitative and quantitative productivity, if adequately valued by the organization, create job satisfaction.* The newer hypothesis suggests that the focus should not be on alleviating burnout or increasing morale, but rather on increasing effectiveness. There is nothing more satisfying to professionals than spending their work lives in an organization that they feel is effective.

A point made by Marvin Weisbord and quoted in an earlier chapter bears repeating here: the socialization of professionals, including clinical social workers, work against cooperation and interdependence—and satisfaction—in organizational life by placing too much importance on improving one's own performance rather than that of any institution.†
Weissman too contends that the social work agency is too infrequently a source of satisfaction for workers.‡ Indices of organizational success are vague, and funding is seldom connected with effectiveness. Thus, self-esteem does not accrue from the agency, but primarily from personal achievement.

Yet in a salaried profession like social work, one must accept the overriding importance of the structure through which one offers one's services. The competence of the agency should be as high a priority to the profession as the competence of individual practitioners. If agencies are not effective, clients suffer, and workers suffer.

A reorientation of the basic attitudes and values of the profession is required. The National Association of Social Workers sees its main function as assuring the public of the competence and skill of individual social workers. It needs to broaden its purview to assure social workers

---

*George Strauss and Leonard Sayles, *Personnel* (Englewood Cliffs, N.J.: Prentice-Hall, 1980), pp. 17–26.

†Marvin Weisbord, "Why Organizational Development Hasn't Worked (So Far) in Medical Centers," *Health Care Management Review* (1976): 19.

‡Harold H. Weissman, "Can Clinicians Manage Social Agencies?" *Social Casework* 63 (1982): 166.

and the public that social agencies are truly professional and to insist that agencies establish effective accountability systems, bottom-up evaluation, and the like. Individual efforts are also relevant. Workers would be well advised, during job interviews, to interview the agency to determine whether it is a fit place in which to work. This means informing themselves not only about their legal rights and protections against various forms of discrimination and harassment based on race, sex, or ethnicity, but also about the structures and procedures the agency has in place to improve its own effectiveness and that of workers.

Additional Readings

Finch, Wilbur. "Social Workers versus Bureaucracy." *Social Work* 21 (1976): 370–375.

Maslach, Christina. "Burned Out." *Human Behavior* 5 (Sept. 1976): 16–18.

Rappaport, Lydia. "In Defense of Social Work: An Examination of Stress in the Profession." *Social Service Review* 34 (1960): 62–74.

Sparrow, Jane. *Diary of a Student Social Worker*. London: Routledge and Kegan Paul, 1978.

Tambor, Milton. "The Social Worker as Worker: A Union Perspective." *Administration in Social Work* 3 (1979): 289–301.

Wasserman, Harry. "The Professional Social Worker in a Bureaucracy." *Social Work* 16 (Jan. 1971): 89–95.

EPILOGUE

When the pioneering schools of social work were developing in the first two or three decades of the century, the names they took reflected their approach to the field and their history.* Those that called themselves schools of applied social sciences usually had been started by people trained in sociology or had actually developed out of sociology departments. Others called themselves schools of social service administration. In their view social workers administered services in the sense of delivering them to clients. This book is very much part of this old tradition in the field. We believe that the function of clinical social work is to deliver a range of services to people in order to help them.

What we have tried to do is to broaden the knowledge of the skills and competencies required to deliver these services, although in no way do we wish to downgrade the importance of psychotherapeutic skills. The nature of practice has changed in response to changes in society and the helping professions. A narrow focus on the client and his or her relationship to the worker is seldom adequate. Instead, the social worker must address many relationships and interrelationships in dealing with a particular case.

When service is given through a social agency, clinicians must be able to draw upon a repertoire of roles if they are to help people. We have attempted in each chapter to show the connection, where it exists, between the insight-oriented and relationship-forming skills of the clinicians and the skills required to fulfill the particular role discussed in the chapter. We have tried to do the same for traditional attitudes and values.

Perhaps the clearest case example of our approach is the documentation in the Practice Research chapter of the vague diagnostic statements written by many clinicians. The traditional response would be to train clinicians to be more precise. Without discounting the importance of this, we also point out that such assessments are affected by the time available for the task, the relationship of diagnostic statements to reimbursement

---

*Harold Lewis, personal communication. For a broader discussion of these issues, see Frank Bruno, *Trends in Social Work* (New York: Columbia University Press, 1957), pp. 138–144.

formulas, assumptions about client behavior, the demands of accountability mechanisms, the agency's desire for stability and predictability, the agency's decision-making process, and the availability of specific resources.

Thus, assessment, screening, and case planning are not simply technical problems related to individual workers' skill and judgment.* They take place in an environment that affects how they are carried out. To help people, as we noted earlier, clinical social workers need to know how to deal not only with the changing nature of practice, but also with the context in which they practice. The role descriptions in each of the chapters are designed to help clinicians achieve these ends.

The conceptual base that we have drawn upon comes from many sources. Social-psychological ideas underpin our discussion of decision making; public administration concepts infuse our analysis of implementation. Our material on advocacy and reform is derived from political science. Dynamic as well as behavioral psychologies help illuminate the problems of employees of social agencies, and overall, we have been influenced by the sociology of organizations.

Our discussion of roles draws heavily on the concept of influence and theories of how to develop and utilize it. Yet we agree with Rosalie Kane that a reversal of power relationships to put social work at the top of the health or any other hierarchy need not in and of itself be better for clients.† We are no less prone than teachers, nurses, doctors, or psychologists to error and self-interested action. Our purpose is not to produce social work Machiavellis, but to enable clinicians to give better service to clients and to demonstrate and test new ways of doing this.

Similarly, we are skeptical of programmatic trendiness.‡ Talking dogmatically about problems in broad humanistic terms is not the same as proposing and testing solutions for them.§ Others are more likely to be impressed with our results than our rhetoric. If there is any value that we espouse in this text, it is the acceptance of the possibility of being proven wrong while at the same time doing what one believes is right. This acceptance marks the difference between an ideologue and a professional clinician.

Throughout the text we have suggested that it is important not only for workers to advocate but for agencies to do so as well, for workers to engage in organizational change and for agencies to be structured for flexibility and adaptability, for workers to do research and for agencies to

*See Carol Austin, "Client Assessment in Context," *Social Work Research and Abstracts*, 17 (Spring, 1981): 4–12.

†Rosalie Kane, "Lessons for Social Work from the Medical World: A Viewpoint for Practice," *Social Work* 27 (1982): 315.

‡For a discussion of this issue, see Maeda Galensky and Janice Schopler, "Warning: Groups May Be Dangerous," *Social Work* (1977): 89–94.

§Kane, "Lessons," p. 4.

concern themselves with knowledge development. In this sense staff development is only one part of the equation. To be successful, it must go hand in hand with agency development.*

We hope that clinical social workers who have arrived at this point in the text have expanded their repertoire of skills for helping people and agencies. Society changes, agencies and professions change, and people change. For this reason, this book will continue to be rewritten. We invite the reader to participate and welcome comments and views.†

*Ruth Middleman and Gale Goldberg, *Social Service Delivery: A Structural Approach to Social Work Practice* (New York: Columbia University Press, 1974) p. 175

†Write in care of the Hunter College School of Social Work, 129 East 79th Street, New York, N.Y., 10021.

INDEX

AB designs, 284. *See also* Practice research, single-subject research designs

Abels, Paul, 250

Abortion clinics: ideology vs. practice, 318–319; management of, 321–323; moral dilemmas, 319; policy dilemmas, 324–326; strain on staff in, 317

Abortion counselors: limits on professionalization of, 324–325; responses to stress of, 320–321; strains on, 318–319

Abramson, Julie, 65–73; 169

Accountability: agency evaluation, 327; change, 224–225; clinical social work, 263; interagency mechanism for, 71; problem-oriented case record, 275–277; workers' tactics for promoting, 328

Action system, 76

Adversarial strategy, 65

Advisory committee, 119

Advocacy, 57–58, 104–105, 141–143; and agency conflict, 167–168; as an agency responsibility, 154–155, 161–162; and agency structure, 160–163; case and class on a continuum, 141, 155, 156–159; in a collaborative context, 150–152; conflict between agency effectiveness and survival, 147–148, 155; definitions, 140; in emergency rooms, 57–58; as an exchange, 148; in family agencies, 155–164; and informed consent, 164–165; and inter-agency conflict, 147; key questions for the advocate, 146, 152–153; links to clinical practice, 140, 164; as mandated by NASW Code of Ethics, 140, 143, 154–155; professional neutrality, 167; and psychotherapy, 166, 167; risks of, 147–148; role of family advocate, 162–163; sanction to engage, 145; skills required, 165–167; strategy selection, 145–146, 159–160; target of intervention, 144–145; types, 156–159; value elements, 167; the War on Poverty, 147–148. *See also* Case

advocacy; Change; Class advocacy; Client needs; Conflict theory; Exchange theory; Informal structure

Agency, effect on practice, 3–4

Ashley, Ardythe A., 148, 149–154

Aronson, H., 174

Assertiveness, and supervision, 234

Attendance rates: as aid in program planning and implementation, 281–284; community organizing, 279–280; as indicator of effectiveness, 280–281; as outcome measure, 282–284

Austin, Carol D., 83–93

Austin, Michael, 4n

Authority, 166–167; competence as a source of, 60; definitions of, 59; delegation of, 60–61; formal, 59–60, 236; functional, 60, 72–73, 236; lines of, 60; relation to responsibility, 60–61; requisite for expediting, 59; role of sanctions, 59

Autonomous professional, 233–257

Bargaining: as collaborative strategy, 65; as exchange, 62; referral as, 68; for resource control, 61

Baselines, 284

Behavioral approaches, and case coordinators, 77

Bergman, Anne S., 54–55

Bertsche, Anne Vandeberg, 76–80

Blenkner, Margaret, 173

Boards of directors, 17–18; and accountability, 225–327; and reviews, 312–313. *See also* Formal structure

Brager, George, 226

Briar, Scott, 264, 294

Broker role, 104–105

Brown, R. G. S., 224

Broxmeyer, Neal, 285–294; 195

Bruckholdt, David R., 130, 131–135, 136

Bureaucracy, positive and negative aspects, 11

337